# HAWTHORNE: CALVIN'S IRONIC STEPCHILD

# HAWTHORNE

## Calvin's Ironic Stepchild

AGNES McNEILL DONOHUE

THE KENT STATE UNIVERSITY PRESS

Copyright © 1985 by The Kent State University Press, Kent, Ohio 44242
All rights reserved
Library of Congress Catalog Card Number 84-12550
ISBN 0-87338-310-9
Manufactured in the United States of America

4 lines from "The Waste Land," in *Collected Poems, 1909–1962:* From "The Waste Land," in *Collected Poems, 1909–1962* by T. S. Eliot, © 1936 by Harcourt Brace Jovanovich, Inc.; © 1963, 1964 by T. S. Eliot. Reprinted by permission of the publisher.

From "East Coker," in *Four Quartets,* © 1943 by T. S. Eliot; renewed 1971 by Esme Valerie Eliot. Reprinted by permission of Harcourt Brace Jovanovich, Inc.

**Library of Congress Cataloging in Publication Data**

Donohue, Agnes McNeill.
   Hawthorne: Calvin's ironic stepchild.

   Bibliography: p.
   Includes index.
   1. Hawthorne, Nathaniel, 1804–1864—Criticism and interpretation. 2. Hawthorne, Nathaniel, 1804–1864—Religion and ethics. 3. Calvinism in literature. 4. Irony in literature. I. Title.
PS1892.C36D66   1985        813'.3        84-12550
ISBN 0-87338-310-9

*For*

Kay and Don T. McNeill and Don P. McNeill, C.S.C.

> *"All other things, to their destruction draw,*
> *Only our love hath no decay;*
> *This, no tomorrow hath, nor yesterday,*
> *Running, it never runs from us away,*
> *But truly keeps his first, last, everlasting day."*

# Contents

# *Preface*

My approach to Hawthorne is a consistent and chronological reading of a Hawthorne betrayed into irony by a damnatory Calvinism that yet provided the healthiest climate for the dramatic tension of his art. In spite of Hawthorne's ambivalence toward the Puritanism of the American past, especially that of his own ancestors, his artistic imagination, creative consciousness, and conscience were conditioned by Calvinism. Particularly, Calvinist dogmas of total depravity and predestination infused themselves throughout his art so that beneath deceptive clarity and lucidity of style there is a brutal dooming underview of man's moral nature. The much debated ambiguity of Hawthorne, particularly in the endings of his novels and tales, can be clarified partly by perceiving the consistent ironic mode. This use of irony ordained by Calvin's damnatory theology is illustrated by chronological, close reading of Hawthorne's literary works illuminated by his prefaces, notebooks, and letters. The irony conditions Hawthorne's use of the narrative voice; the aesthetic distance he establishes or fails to establish between himself, his readers, and his stories and characters; his ordering of ritualistic structure; the development of characters; the atmosphere, setting, and the repetitive antitheses: light-dark, head-heart, prison-grave, forest-clearing, mask-bareface, innocence-shrewdness, garden-labyrinth, journey-return.

Hawthorne seems to feel a necessity to see everywhere a reenactment of the Fall from Eden from his nineteenth-century survival amidst the moldering remnants of the American Dream of New Jerusalem. Hawthorne's seven years abroad in the Old World dispensation of sophistication and insensitivity to moral corruption dissipated his rigorous New England conscience enough so that in his last novel, *The Marble Faun* (written in Italy and England), he permits along with the exigent reenactment of the Fall, the possibility of the fortunate fall—good coming from evil.

However healing to his sense of guilt his seven-year European expatriation was, it destroyed for him his old ironic conviction of fallen man's expulsion from Eden. The dramatic tension in his fiction disappears if there is a way back to Eden garden. Hawthorne's art was emasculated of its primal terror and stress; the heart of his mystery had been plucked out. After his return to America and during the last four years of his life he attempted six romances that aborted—a mute testimony to his impotence.

I will sketch briefly the content and divisions of the chapters. Chapter 1 is introduction, definition of ironic mode, brief biographical account of Hawthorne, and a summary of the theology of Calvin. Chapters 2 (*The Scarlet Letter*), 3 (*The House of the Seven Gables*), 4 (*The Blithedale Romance*), 5 (*Twice-told Tales*), 6 (*Mosses from an Old Manse*), 7 (*The Snow-Image*), and 10 (*The Marble Faun*) have a loose six-part structure: 1) Theme and Intention (the Fall, Hawthorne's tragic view, isolation, and alienation); 2) Voice (aesthetic distance, point of view, setting, tone, diction, alternate explanations of events, rhetorical questions, adumbration, voyeurism); 3) Symbolism (image, type, emblem, witchcraft and the supernatural, death and time, appearance and reality); 4) Structure (plot, set pieces, moral); 5) Character (consistency, probability, development, anomalies); 6) Judgment and Final Interpretation (Calvinism and the ironic mode). Chapters 8 and 9 (*English Notebooks* and *French and Italian Notebooks*) are concerned with Hawthorne's response to life abroad, conflict of emotions and ambivalence to religious beliefs, home and homelessness, marriage and death. Chapter 11 (*The Abortive Romances*) examines the six aborted fragments. Chapter 12 (Epilogue) is a summary statement.

The works of Hawthorne that are excluded from this study are *Fanshawe*, which Hawthorne disavowed; the children's stories; and *Our Old Home*, based upon the *English Notebooks*, studied here in chapter 8.

Chicago, Illinois
February 1984

# *Acknowledgments*

It is a pleasure to be able to express my gratitude without ambivalence or ambiguity.

First of all I wish to thank Loyola University of Chicago for a paid semester's leave, two summer grants, and a book subvention and its officers for their kind and genuine interest in my research and its progress. I can testify personally that the traditional ideal of Jesuit concern with the liberal arts and the humanities is living and well at Loyola University of Chicago.

My obligation to my graduate students who study Hawthorne with me and to those who take the seminar in Puritan literature (in which the basic text is Calvin's *Institutes*) is not a debt that can be repaid—only humbly acknowledged. These students and the five who chose to do dissertations on Hawthorne or Puritan literature helped, by their skeptical questions and refusal to take my or anyone else's interpretations for granted, "to tent me to the quick." For this, much thanks.

I am grateful to L. Neal Smith, textual editor of *The Centenary Edition of the Works of Nathaniel Hawthorne* at the Ohio State University, a true gentleman and scholar who gave me the most generous hospitality and access to the soon to be published Hawthorne letters.

Catherine Kenney, former student and friend, caught my original leviathan of a manuscript "with an hook" and reduced the kraken to a docile fish. Carole Hayes, colleague and friend, with a busy blue pencil, read the manuscript *twice,* an act of supererogation that passes praise.

Brooks Bouson and Charles Van Hof, former students and friends, helped enormously in the early days of the manuscript during a hot and humid summer—Brooks with her raised eyebrows at some of my liberties with mechanics, and Charles in conferences about Calvin.

I am grateful to my friend Henri J. M. Nouwen for his generous interest in my work.

Maurita Willett and Louis Broussard, former colleagues at the University of Illinois, Chicago, read a few chapters and gave me some necessary cautions.

I am grateful to Robert Bireley, S.J., and Carl Burlage, S.J., for help and encouragement.

Thanks to Patty Szott for helpful reading, to Cheryl Sporlein who had to learn to read a new language as she typed from my own handwriting, and to Kimberley Hunt for her proofreading help. Also thanks to Paul H. Rohmann, Jeanne West, and Carol Horner of the Kent State University Press.

Finally, I want to thank my family, friends, and colleagues who still endure patiently my preoccupation with Hawthorne and total depravity!

# Hawthorne's Calvinist-
# Ordained Irony

*"This great power of blackness in him derives its force from its appeals to that Calvinistic sense of innate depravity and original sin, from whose visitations, in some shape or other, no deeply thinking mind is always and wholly free."[1]*

## I

In these days of structuralism, poststructuralism, and deconstructionism, the attempt to discover Hawthorne's intentions and to consider their complicated connection to a body of religious doctrine seems a rather old-fashioned occupation. However, with Frederick Crews[2] I believe that these "isms" will pass like the most recent virus and that the investigation of Hawthorne's elusive and cunning messages to his readers is a valid and valuable endeavor.

Critics have acknowledged a *certain* amount of Calvinism and a *certain* amount of irony in Hawthorne's works, but a reading that reveals irony and especially Calvinist-ordained irony as his pervasive mode has never been attempted. Nor, I would imagine, do many critics think it should be. Yet a chronological reading of the Hawthorne corpus will serve to illuminate much of Hawthorne's infamous ambiguity about man's moral nature. This ambiguity is the greatest challenge and pleasure for his readers.

This study will demonstrate Hawthorne's consistently Calvinistic habit of mind until 1853, when it began to recede with his seven expatriate years in England and Italy. It will reveal that his Calvinism speaks brokenly in his last completed novel, *The Marble Faun,* but that upon his return to America in 1860, it became, by its absence, the pall that effectively deadened his creativity so that he was unable to finish any of the last romances before his death in 1864. What we shall learn, ultimately, is that Hawthorne's repressed Calvinism ordained the profound irony that forced him into ambiguity, conditioned his aesthetic distance and his authorial voice, ordained the alternate choices of endings or interpretations, spawned the rich imagery and symbolism, and dictated the complex structure of his novels and tales. Certainly, Hawthorne was suspicious of all doctrines or sects (he thought of himself as a Christian but never went to church). But, the important point is that his imagination was stimulated by the Calvinist dogma that *man sins necessarily and yet bears full responsibility for his sin.* No one has attempted a consistent reading of Hawthorne to show that through all his works runs a covert and probably subconscious loyalty to the basic tenets of Calvin, which in his best tales and novels demands the ironic mode. The damnatory voice of that terrifying Geneva reformer, declaiming his vision of a vengeful, angry, and jealous God ruthlessly judging pitiful and depraved humanity, penetrated the recesses of this diffident artist's heart and ordered ironic stories and novels of brutality, obsessive guilt, and secret sin.

Calvin's damnatory tenets conditioned Hawthorne's artistic conscience so that his characters sin, like Chillingworth, by "iron necessity" and wander fruitlessly in the labyrinths of their minds, as do Hester and Dimmesdale. Hawthorne's characters are unaided by any mediation between them and God—by the Church, an ordained clergy, the salvific sacraments, or the intercession of the Virgin or the saints. Thus, Hawthorne places his characters in that loneliest and most isolated of spaces—the great chasm between them and the remote God of absolute justice, who will not be mocked. With this Puritanism which Hawthorne could neither accept nor disavow, it is no wonder that he summoned up the most frightening dilemmas of human existence and then *apparently* withdrew into a rather conventional moral statement or an evasion, for he was unwilling to push his tragic vision of man's moral nature to its logical conclusion. A nineteenth-century reluctant Calvinist could lapse into total despair or into the polite, insipid moralities of transcendentalism; or he could use an ironic mode which allows him to suspend judgment, offer alternative explanations, cloak the tragic vision, and sham the innocence and modesty of the author who wants only to write a "series of good little tales." Hawthorne settles for a furtive but coruscating irony that deceives and baffles the casual reader.

This irony discloses a signal ambiguity in Hawthorne—his attitude toward humanity's moral nature. Sometimes he seems to assert the depravity of mankind while at the same time he dreams of an Adamic hero, guileless in his prelapsarian Eden. He demonstrates an apparent, not real, vacillation between trusting the human heart's intuitions as good and advancing his conviction that the heart is a "foul cavern" which must be destroyed in order to be purified.

Hawthorne's ambivalence about innocence and guilt can be seen as a lodestone that draws into its magnetic field all other major problems of human life. He writes of innocence, initiation, and experience; secret sin and isolation; compulsive rituals of atonement and sacrifice; self-righteousness and fanaticism; science against Original Sin; witchcraft and devil worship; carnal knowledge and guiltless love; and of the unending search for a home, a father, a self—in short, of man's dark odyssey in an alien world.[3]

Hawthorne's narrative voice, characteristically weighty and ironic, penetrates his superficially plangent, lucid style with such an undercurrent of primal terror, savagery, and brutality that it roars into the ears of the sensitive reader, forcing him beneath the bland surface of the tales and engulfing him in the tortured deeps of this Salem Jonah. Hawthorne's journey and ours is as prickly and obstacle-ridden as that of Calvin's Everyman, who was always in tension with his sinful yet natural desires. Hawthorne is honest enough not to provide explicit landmarks for the human spirit because he himself is only too sensitively aware of the hidden, unknown perils of the journey. He settles for remarkable evocations of the complexity and mystery of life.

Hawthornean irony is unique and pervasive when he is at his best. At times it is rather easily recognized and traditional, as for example, in the last paragraph of "The Gentle Boy."[4] But in a work such as *The Scarlet Letter,* which compels several readings, the reader gradually becomes aware that a sleek and stealthy irony has mandated the novel's theme and intention; contrived its symbolism and imagery; dictated its structure; decreed the type of character; and consequently enjoined an ironic reading. The ironic voice of the ostensibly distanced third-person omniscient narrator in *The Scarlet Letter* gradually effects a closure of aesthetic distance. The point of view shifts as the voice becomes more directive, the reader is manipulated by the sombre tone, rhetorical questions, and alternate explanations. Thus, the irony, ordained by Hawthorne's covert Calvinism, forces upon the wary reader the tragic conclusion that Hester, Dimmesdale, and Chillingworth must be damned in order to humanize the elf-child Pearl. The irony is only compounded when we realize that Pearl, in her newly acquired human nature can be, just as surely as her mother, father, and stepfather, subject to reprobation. Hawthorne's irony, then, unlike that of the stinging Swift, the acid Austen, or the desolate Hardy, is a delicate but almost undetectably omnipotent scalpel that cuts all the way through to the errant hearts of his characters and readers.

This sorrowing yet ironic voice exposes the corrupted dream of a country that promised Eden but imposed a reenactment of the Fall on its new Adams and Eves. From the burden of this debased dream, the blasted American Eden—the *Mayflower* that spawned the black slave and the white master—came the impulse to expatriation, to become a "citizen of somewhere else," to flee to "Our Old Home," to the comfortable, unembarrassed corruption of the Old World where man may be damning and damned but with no flouting of innocence nor any longed-for utopia-Eden because centuries of sophistication, cynicism, crudity, and contempt for the world have obliterated any hopes of earthly paradise.

Hawthorne inherited this corrupted American Dream. The original, paradoxical dream of the first Puritan settlers was to establish, despite their depravity, a new Eden, a *Civitas Dei*, the New Jerusalem. In spite of the crumbling of their dream with the second generation of Puritans and its total distortion by the time of the Revolution, the dream has so much power over man's imagination that a lingering desire for prelapsarian, primal innocence subverts, for all Americans, the grim fact of its failure. Like Jay Gatsby, we all seek to recapture the past and with it the "incorruptible" dream. Hawthorne well knew that the flowers of this new Eden, trodden on by later Calvinists and rooted out by the deists and pragmatists of the eighteenth century, were black—not the pink roses that grew outside the prison door in *The Scarlet Letter*. This dark knowledge becomes the climate of his art, much as he must have wished it would not.

The consistent irony which undergirds Hawthorne's art—his seemingly harmless prose, his Calvinist conception of character, and the actions which these characters decree—enables us to comprehend a deeper meaning in the tales and novels and a subtler relationship among the works. It especially elucidates the blackness of Hawthorne's tragic vision that Melville uncovered in his early essay, unsurpassed for its intuitive reading of this complex, troubled writer.[5]

I will make no attempt to relate the dilution, compromises, mistaken emphases, heresies, and schisms that the rigid Calvinism of the settlers of Plymouth and Massachusetts Bay underwent between 1620 and Hawthorne's beginning literary efforts about two hundred years later. What mattered to Hawthorne and all of those susceptible creative intelligences who have inherited the Puritan tradition was not the parochial controversies that preoccupied the divines and their flocks, but Calvin's bowel-shattering, awesome vision of depraved mankind, hounded incessantly by an immanent, jealous, and angry God. The eighteenth-century American rationalistic, deistic reaction to this heart-stopping Deity was the invention of zealous, a-religious, pragmatic businessmen, who were absorbed with revolution and constitutional establishment and who could tolerate, even appreciate, a benevolent absentee Architect, undoubtedly now blueprinting new universes, already bored with this one, an abdicated, neo-pagan, benevolent Jupiter who required nothing more than an occasional casual acknowledgment from his off-hand, pleasant creations that they were busy and happy.

Benjamin Franklin had no difficulty creating a god for this universe in his own image and likeness. He was quite certain that there were other superior gods, but it was only prudent for him to acknowledge the being who might have manufactured him and his visible system of planets: "I imagine it great vanity in me to suppose that the Supremely Perfect does in the least regard such an inconsiderable Nothing as MAN. . . . I cannot conceive otherwise than that he the Infinite Father expects or requires no Worship or Praise from us, but that he is infinitely above it." Yet to be on the safe side—"I think it seems required of me, and my Duty as a Man, to pay Divine Regards to SOMETHING. . . . It is that particular Wise and good God, who is the author and owner of our System, THAT I propose for the object of my praise and adoration. . . . He is pleased when he sees Me Happy. And since he has created many Things, which seem purely design'd for the Delight of Man, I believe he is not offended, when he sees his Children solace themselves in any manner of pleasant exercises and Innocent Delights. . . ."[6] This amiable, ungodly deity is known today in the social convention of the community church, the ultimate triumph of ecumenism, of the least common denominator: "I think I believe in God, if He exists. Amen."

But to the sin-haunted, guilt-eroded Hawthorne, it was as if the American eighteenth century had never taken place, nor its sequel, nineteenth-century transcendentalism, with the ever-smiling Emerson giving assurances of man's infinite perfectibility as he beatifically expands into his own divinity, unassailed by an evil which is not. Despite the raptures of Sophia Hawthorne and the transcendental brotherhood and despite the few months Hawthorne spent at Brook Farm, where the "gold mine" or manure pile seemed to him the greatest reality, Hawthorne could not be transported out of his tragic conviction that man's heart is a dirty, squalid cavern; that human motives are corrupt and duplicitous; that family relationships are perilous; that nothing is what it appears to be; that man's best efforts are doomed to failure; and that death, terrifying as it is, is the only consummation devoutly to be wished.

## II

Hawthorne's biographers succumb to as vast a puzzlement as do his readers. There are a great many facts of unassailable authority: we know who his ancestors were on both sides of his family; we *apparently* know the salient facts and dates of his life; we know a great deal about his publishers; we know about him from the hundreds of letters written by and to him, from his notebooks and journals dutifully kept during most of his life, and from the volumes written by his friends, his family, and his acquaintances. Yet the essential Hawthorne eludes us except in his works. Unfortunately, the literary critics can luxuriate in Hawthorne's artistic ambiguities and produce, to our amazement, *their* Hawthorne. Consequently, some critics see Hawthorne as a shrewd, political man; others view him as an active social reformer; and in the 1960s, Hubert Hoeltje's sunny biography, *Inward Sky: The Mind and Heart of Nathaniel Hawthorne,* assures us that Hawthorne was in every way normal—a dubious compliment to be sure—a man who, although shy, reveled in society, was gregarious, hospitable, and neighborly.

Joining the critical fray is dangerous to one's health, but *my* Hawthorne, who does not differ greatly from his elder sister's and his friends' view of him, is a reclusive, driven, almost possessed man, a man of paradoxes and opposites. There is the Hawthorne who hates writing and yet desires above all else to be a great and famous writer; the Hawthorne who fears and dislikes women, especially the pseudo-intellectual, "scribbling" women who surround him, yet tries to present himself as an idyllically happy married man; the Hawthorne who sees man's heart as irredeemably corrupt, yet joins the Brook Farm utopian experiment, temporarily attempting to demonstrate the reality of communal betterment; the Hawthorne who complains in the preface to *The Marble Faun* that America lacks tradition, shadow, and history, and is prospering too much in the sun, yet sets his own greatest stories and tales in the dimly lit, Puritan witch-haunted colonies of the seventeenth century.

Certainly, we have many biographical facts about Hawthorne,[7] yet the facts that we do not have are the provocative ones. Why did his mother, after her widowhood in 1808 when Hawthorne was not quite four years old, choose to return to her family's household, leaving behind her children's paternal grandmother, two maiden aunts, and an uncle? In Salem, she moved next door to the Manning household, which consisted of a grandfather who died within five years, Hawthorne's maternal grandmother, four unmarried aunts, and four unmarried uncles (three of whom, two uncles and one aunt, married later). Into this family of ten came the widow Hawthorne with her three young children—Elizabeth, older than Nathaniel by two years, Nathaniel, and Maria Louisa, born about the time of her sea captain father's death by yellow fever in Surinam. Famous for her beauty, Hawthorne's mother, who was widowed in her late twenties, retired to her room in the Manning household and remained a recluse until her death during the time Hawthorne was writing *The Scarlet Letter*. In an age of New England eccentrics, the Mannings and Hawthornes were stellar planets.

Hawthorne was by all reports spoiled as a child, partly because of his remarkable physical beauty and partly because he injured his foot playing ball when he was nine, after which he seems to have been an invalid for over two years. During this time he read, voraciously and precociously, Scott, Spenser, Bunyan, Shakespeare, and Milton, developing a lifelong habit of study. It must have been during these boyhood years that Hawthorne was dragged unwillingly to the Presbyterian meetinghouse in Salem to hear long, threatening sermons that he recalls with irritation and dislike in *Our Old Home*. After he became an adult, he never again willingly entered a church, except when he was abroad and went sight-seeing. The Mannings were of early American heritage, but were notable in business not history, unlike Hawthorne's paternal ancestors who figured so largely and terribly in colonial history. William Hathorne[8] arrived from England to Massachusetts Bay in 1630, later settled in Salem, became speaker in the House of Delegates, major in the Salem Militia, defied Charles II, and became a bitter persecutor of Quakers. His son, John, is remembered for his infamous role as the unrepentant magistrate of the Salem witch trials. These were the ancestors who fired Hawthorne's imagination, his pride, and his shame, and of whom he writes so eloquently in "The Custom House."

In *Our Old Home* we have Hawthorne's word that as a young boy he attended church and Sunday school in Salem and suffered mightily from the experience: "severe and sunless remembrances of the Sabbaths of child-hood, and pangs of remorse for ill-gotten lessons in the catechism, and for erratic fantasies or hardly suppressed laughter in the middle of long sermons."[9] A letter written to his elder sister, Elizabeth, while he was at Bowdoin, shows his amused contempt for the religious requirements of the college and his resentment of "red hot" Calvinist sermons:

> Some of them [laws of the College] are peculiarly repugnant to my feelings, such as, to get up at sunrise every morning to attend prayers, which law the Students make it a custom to break twice a week. But the worst of all is to be compelled to go to meeting every Sunday, and to hear a red hot Calvin-ist Sermon from the President, or some other dealer in fire and brim-stone. . . . By far the greater proportion of the Members of College are yet in the "bond of bitterness and the gall of iniquity," but there is a consider-able congregation of Saints. The first bell rings and I must . . . attend meeting. Afternoon—Meeting for this day is over. We have had a Minister from the Andover Mill, and he "dealt damnation round" with an unsparing hand, and finished by consigning us all to the Devil. . . . I must close my letter as I have a Bible Lesson to get to recite after prayers. I believe it is not the custom in any other College to recite Lessons from the bible, and I think it a very foolish one.[10]

No evidence indicates that he ever attended church after leaving Bowdoin until, as a tourist, he freely visited churches in England, France, and Italy. Contrary evidence does suggest that he spent Sundays peeping out his window at others going to church and that his wife, Sophia, did not convert her husband into a confused, rhapsodic transcendentalist, à la Emerson and Margaret Fuller. Certainly, then, Hawthorne was not a practicing Calvinist, nor a member of any formal religious group. How-ever, the basic tenets of Calvin, impregnated in his New England soul, were never tried until his seven years in Europe. They were always with him, in his darkest depths, and although never consciously stated, they ordered the black climate and the informing irony of his best writing.

Hawthorne's Bowdoin years began his lifelong friendships with Hora-tio Bridge, Henry Wadsworth Longfellow, and Franklin Pierce. Just before Bowdoin, Hawthorne decided to become an author and he made the announcement in a letter to his mother with sarcasm and a sense of fatality:

> *What do you think of my becoming an author, and relying for support upon my pen?* . . . How proud you would feel to see my works praised by the

reviewers, as equal to the proudest production of the scribbling sons of John Bull. *But authors are always poor devils, and therefore Satan may take them.*[11]

Nothing, however, in the letters or accounts of friends or family gives any hint of Hawthorne's far more bizarre decision—to go back, after graduation, to the room in his mother's house, where he remained with few interruptions for twelve years. Concerning these long years of seclusion, apprenticeship, trial, error, and modest success, speculation among critics has been so abundant as to be ludicrous. What is tangible is that Hawthorne published *Fanshawe* anonymously in 1828 but was so dissatisfied with it that he attempted to reclaim all of the copies; it was not until 1837 that *Twice-told Tales* appeared, although several short stories had been published in various albums and periodicals, still anonymously. In 1836 and 1837 he did some hack work for *The American Magazine of Useful, Entertaining Knowledge* and *Peter Parley's Universal History,* aided by Elizabeth Hawthorne, but was paid little, if anything.

The twelve years which Hawthorne always referred to as "solitary," "lonely," and "chilly" were certainly that. In his room, he read voluminously, wrote, burned what he wrote, and wrote some more. He took a few trips, often in his uncle's stagecoach, or walked alone. Tantalizing and provocative about this long seclusion are the suggestions, by Hawthorne and his sister Elizabeth, of his morbid reclusiveness. He borrowed books constantly from the Athanaeum Library, but always had his sister pick them up; he had his meals delivered to his room but left on a tray at his door; he went out only at night to mingle anonymously with a crowd or to watch a fire, which he loved; he always traveled incognito on short trips, although no one knew his name; he joined groups of old men in the parks of distant villages and eavesdropped on their reminiscences; he wandered about on the seashore near Salem, studying clouds and his footprints in the sand. These reports could describe a psychotic or neurotic personality or they could merely give us some insight into an apprentice writer learning his trade. Probably there was something of both in Hawthorne, for after he was snared by Sophia Peabody (who lived next door and was the victorious participant in a concerted effort by the Peabody sisters to "catch" the handsome young genius who needed, they assumed, to be taken out of himself), he displayed an immense reluctance to tell his family that he would be leaving the womb. It was not until a month before the wedding that he informed his sisters and mother of his marriage plans for July 1842, after a four-year engagement. Sophia was not received lovingly and family gossip indicates that she was roundly despised by the Hawthorne women.

Sophia, the invalid, plain of face but iron of will, had caught Hawthorne and apparently he loved being caught. However, from all we know of Hawthorne—his contempt for Margaret Fuller and her breed of transcendental ecstatics—and of the Peabody girls who worshipped diligently at the shrine of Emerson, whom Hawthorne could never tolerate, the forthcoming marriage seemed to be arranged in Salem, not in heaven. One should be convinced by the effusive love letters exchanged by Hawthorne and Sophia during their long engagement, while he was at Brook Farm attempting to find a home for them and while he was working at the Boston Custom House weighing and measuring coal. But the very archness and sentimentality of the missives in which Hawthorne calls Sophia his "Dove" and his "wife" and she christens him her "Lord" and her "husband" argue that one or both is going to be disappointed in the marriage.

After the wedding and the move to the Old Manse in Concord, where they were going to be heavenly poor together, Hawthorne and Sophia both kept the same notebook, so that each read the other's entries. Certainly, Sophia always sounds like a triumphant Cheshire cat who has swallowed a golden canary, but Hawthorne, valiantly trying to keep up the charade of the new Adam with his Eve in Eden, sounds a bit morose as he does the washing-up and the cooking so that Sophia will not ruin her pretty hands for doing her sketching.

Sophia rapturously produced three children, Una, Julian, and Rose, whom she considered perfect. The *American Notebooks* record Hawthorne's response to Una and Julian at play while his mother was dying, and his musing about the nature of children could be straight from Calvin's mouth:

> [Una] rushes from corner to corner of the room with the force and violence of a cannon-ball—or as if the devil were in her.

> This is the physical manifestation of the evil spirit that struggles for the mastery of her; he is not a spirit at all, but an earthly monster, who lays his grasp on her spinal marrow, her brain, and other parts of her body that lie in closest contiguity to her soul; so that the soul has the discredit of these evil deeds.

Una is describing grandmamma's sickness to Julian. "Oh you don't know how sick she is, Julian; she is sick as I was, when I had the scarlet-fever in Boston." What a contrast between that childish disease, and these last heavy throbbings—this funeral-march—of my mother's heart. Death is never beautiful but in children. How strange! . . . whereas, the death of old age is the consummation of life, and yet *there is so much gloom and ambiguity about it, that it opens no vista for us into Heaven.*[12]

That vista seems never to have appeared for Hawthorne.

Throughout the *American Notebooks,* the *English Notebooks,* and the *French and Italian Notebooks,* and from the writings of Hawthorne's contemporaries we get mostly equivocal feelings from Hawthorne about his marriage and children. Hawthorne loved his family, but the children's tantrums and clutter were difficult to abide for the privacy-loving bachelor who had married at thirty-eight and who had always required perfect quiet in order to write. During the European years, when almost every sight-seeing excursion was interrrupted or aborted by the whims of one of the children, or when Hawthorne was struggling unaided with a multiplicity of carpetbags and portmanteaus, his complaints of weariness become plaintive and pitiful.

From May 1850 until November 1851, the Hawthornes lived in Lenox, Massachusetts where the remarkable friendship between Hawthorne and Melville began, and ripened, only to wane within a few short years. Both men knew each other by reputation (Melville was fifteen years the younger). Melville published his ecstatic review of *Mosses,* in which he hailed Hawthorne as the new American Shakespeare. Certainly, it was the most auspicious literary friendship in America—Hawthorne was writing *The House of the Seven Gables* and Melville was in the midst of *Moby-Dick,* which was dedicated to Hawthorne. Melville's rapturous letters to Hawthorne (Hawthorne's to Melville have not survived) are filled with a frenzy and afflatus which may have terrified the shy, undemonstrative Salem Puritan into sexual anxiety. The friendship quieted after Hawthorne left Lenox.

During the European years Hawthorne was becoming weary (he aged from forty-nine to fifty-six through those years). Although he was not an old man even by nineteenth-century standards, the months of being saddled with Julian while Sophia lived in Lisbon for her health, the trials of traveling with an entourage, and the voracious sight-seeing with Sophia, who seemed determined to see every work of art in England, Paris, and Italy, made him wish, as we see in the notebooks and in his letters to intimate friends, for peace and for death.

The Calvinist faith that Hawthorne hardly knew he had was constantly being challenged by Old World sophistries and sophistication. The resulting confusion in his mind and heart was only exacerbated by his confused loyalties to an America of which he was an official representative and to whom he was certain he owed love and pride. But America was engaged in preparation for a searing internecine war and his dear friend, President Franklin Pierce, to whom he owed his position of consul general of Liverpool, was provoking the conflict by his unwavering anti-abolitionist stance and questionable dealings with the South. Hawthorne's letters at this time to his trusted friends, and even his restrained notebook entries, reveal a conflict of sensibilities, with a gradual change from hostility toward the English to a feeling that in England he had found his old home. Finally, his confusion made him state repeatedly that he had no desire to return to an America in turmoil or in peace.

The religious problems created by his travels were certainly even more serious for Hawthorne than his unsettled national loyalties. For a man who never went to church and who had an innate suspicion of undissenting creeds, it could only have been a guilty and reprehensible pleasure to find that he had fallen in love with English cathedrals and little Norman and Saxon churches. He even felt a sharp, personal resentment against Cromwell and the Covenanters for ruining so many ancient religious buildings. Hawthorne, who constantly refers to himself and Sophia as Puritans in the notebooks, was having a crisis of conscience over convictions he had never acknowledged; at the same time, he displayed a sneering contempt for the watered-down Anglicanism that was now the guardian of these magnificent shrines. All of his submerged Calvinism revolted against splendor and luxury in places of worship—he had thought the New England meetinghouse was the ideal of religious architecture—but his highly developed aesthetic sense and his love of the antiquated and venerable caused him no small discord in his heart of hearts.

Hawthorne's Puritan convictions, although tacit, dictated the moral center of his best tales and novels. This center Calvinistically placed fallen man in the position of having to sin repeatedly and necessarily while remaining accountable and responsible for the ineluctable taints—

repeating over and over the original Fall from Eden to which there was no way back. This moral center, which provided the singular, arresting, apodictic dramatic tension of Hawthorne's best works, was now at hazard in the perturbed, disquieted mind and heart of the author.

But the worst was yet to come. When the Hawthornes left England for the Continent, Hawthorne was desolated. He had no regrets at leaving the consular duties which he despised, but he had begun to love England and fantasized spending the rest of his life, pampered and rich, in a charming English manor house. The weeks in France were agony for him, but despite his illness, weariness, and his vexed and unsettled psyche, all of his American patriotism returned in amazing strength. England had become his old home, but France was totally alien: here there were no historical consanguinities, no nostalgia for a forgotten past. He hated the climate, the French, the food, and the humiliating role of a foreigner unacquainted with the language.

Italy, if anything, was worse. The journey was horrendous; Hawthorne was ailing; the family were fearful of bandit attacks during their nocturnal drive to Rome; their living quarters were inadequate; the language was unspeakable; the food inedible; the ubiquitous Catholicism was revolting and abhorrent; Rome was damp and frigid. In the early pages of the *Italian Notebooks,* Hawthorne voiced a longing for England and America, for the honest, arctic New England winters with white snow, not the damp, bone-racking chill of Italy. But gradually and mysteriously everything changed. The weather improved, the sight-seeing went on unabated, and Hawthorne, despite his Puritanic revulsions from the vortex of the papal "Anti-Christ," made pilgrimage after pilgrimage to St. Peter's, the heart of the "whore of Babylon,"[13] entranced, repelled, enraptured, revolted, and finally blissfully elated. He wrote in his notebook on the morning of the departure from Rome that he never wanted to see Rome again, but "no place ever took so strong a hold of my being . . . , nor ever seemed so close to me, and so strangely familiar. I seem to know it better than my birthplace, and to have known it longer. . . . I cannot say I hate it—perhaps might fairly own a love for it."[14]

By the time Hawthorne returned to New England, he was a rather fragile oldish man, although just fifty-six. Certainly, the years abroad and the continuous sight-seeing of most of those years took their toll upon him. Still, Hawthorne had been a man of magnificent health when he left England: he prided himself that he could jump in the air as high as his shoulders; he could walk miles without wearying; the English diet agreed with him; he gained weight and ate heartily. What happened to him between the time he left England for the Continent and when he returned to Concord? New England certainly did not agree with him; he declined steadily, lost weight and strength, and died of unknown causes less than four years after coming back to the Wayside, his Concord home.

The speculations about Hawthorne's decline have always been a critic's grisly feast. Without any becoming delicacy, I join the crowd. In England Hawthorne endured heart pangs when he realized that Puritan though he called himself, he was a wayward son of his Calvinist ancestors in his delight in English churches and cathedrals. Also, he must have been guilt stricken to realize that he felt physically and psychically more comfortable in England than America. These phenomena were not easily accepted by a man who had steeped hiimself in American history and was obsessed with both the virtues and flaws of his ancestors.

Everything that Hawthorne experienced in England conspired to establish what was, to him, inadmissible—that the American ideal had gone rotten, that Americans were not morally superior to the English, that the *Civitas Dei* had become a not very pleasant, bustling, churning, avaricious, competitive, defiled, uncultivated, and dissolute nation. England was no better, but then she had never pretended to be.

The return to Concord from the cosmopolitan capitals of the world was traumatic for Hawthorne. Everything seemed so small, so parochial, so strange. In Europe Hawthorne had been a very important person, first as a highly placed government representative, consul general of Liverpool, and later as an admired and sought after literary figure, thought by many European critics to be the greatest American man of letters. Concord was still sleepy old Concord, with Emerson the uncrowned king. The Wayside was much too small after the vast rooms of Italy and England, and although repairs and additions were begun, they predictably took longer and were costlier than expected. Hawthorne, thinking of his tower room in the Villa Montauto on the outskirts of Florence, decided to have a third-story tower study erected on the house. The noise of carpenters and workmen was deafening and Hawthorne could only scamper to the woods for refuge.

Hawthorne's health had begun to decline in Italy during Una's illness. His worry about his daughter and perhaps his guilt about his early observations on her demonic, elfin qualities thrust him into a vast weariness. Even the return to England did not revive him entirely, since he was engaged in writing and revising *The Marble Faun*. And the sea voyage home, which his family hoped would give him new life, had only a temporary salubrious effect.

Hawthorne probably had a severe organic illness. The symptoms Sophia secretly described to Hawthorne's publishers James T. Fields and William Ticknor and to Pierce, and Hawthorne's own acknowledgment of them in his letters to his closest friends (always with the warning that they were not to be mentioned to his family), suggest a wasting disease, perhaps a malignancy of the digestive tract. His daughter Rose says he slowly starved to death and lost weight rapidly near the end of his life.

But, most of all, it seems that *Hawthorne wanted to die*. Unhinged completely from his reluctant and tentative Calvinism, which in America he did not have to question or analyze, Hawthorne seemed able to rest his body and soul only in Europe, and especially England. After Italy there were only small vestiges left of what had been an unconsciously assenting Calvinism. Roman Catholicism was convenient and comforting, but nothing about it except these little eases attracted him; he felt only scorn for most Catholic clergy, and the concept of hierarchy revolted him. Anglicanism he viewed as a watered-down wisp of a religion that, like himself, had lost its moral center. He was more than ever disgusted by the easy optimism of the transcendentalists; agnosticism and atheism sickened him. What was left? *Doubts, doubts, doubts.* Unlike Melville, who troubled deaf Heaven with his bootless cries, Hawthorne was too repressed, too secretive, and too sensitive to cause his family pain, so he said nothing. But the festering uncertainties eroded his very bowels, as he remarks when he sees a young man in St. Peter's "writhing and wringing his hands in an agony of grief and contrition. If he had been a protestant I think he would have shut all that up within his heart, and let it burn there till it seared him." Hawthorne was "seared," in fact, incinerated, and the only way he knew to extinguish his anguish was in death. Beginning in Florence in 1858, the journal entries note such agonies as this: "taking no root, *I soon weary of any soil that I may be temporarily deposited in.* The same impatience I sometimes feel, or conceive of, *as regards this earthly life; since it is to come to an end, I do not try to be contented, but weary of it while it lasts."* On the return trip to England from Italy in 1859, the Hawthornes passed through Valence and Lyon, but Hawthorne was too exhausted and soul-sick to be interested in the scenery: "a thousand . . . objects, that ought greatly to interest me, if I were not so weary of being greatly interested. Rest, rest, rest! There is nothing else so desirable; and I sometimes fancy, but only half in earnest, how pleasant it would be to be six feet underground, and let the grass grow over me."[15]

Sometimes Hawthorne tried to explain, even to himself, the roots of his consuming death wish, but not very satisfactorily. He notes on the journey to Geneva on the way back to England: "I deem it a grace of Providence when I have a decent excuse to my wife, and to my own conscience, for not seeing even the things that have helped to tempt me abroad. *It may be disease; it may be age; it may be the effect of the lassitudinous Roman atmosphere; but such is the fact.*"[16] The apparently good Calvinist made a dutiful pilgrimage to Geneva, but the seat of Calvinism had become ashes for him.

Death now seemed an escape for Hawthorne, not only an escape from illness, war, weariness, and unresolved religious doubts, but also from the financial worries that had plagued him most of his life. On his return to America, he was uncomfortably aware of how costly life on the Continent had been, how little of the "fortune" that he had hoped to make as consul had materialized, how much had been spent and still had to be used for additions to the Wayside, and most of all, how unable he was to resume the writing that seemed the only hope for providing enough money for his family.

Hawthorne again took up the sketch he had made in England and Rome of an American claimant returning to England to establish his rights to an English estate. He began writing within a month of his return, but the story would not yield to his imagination and the three fragments, published posthumously, "The Ancestral Footstep," "Etherege," and "Grimshawe," are painful evidence of his loss of control over his material. What is lacking is a moral center. After *The Marble Faun,* in which Hawthorne had raised the question of the *felix culpa,* he had opened a hole through which all of the moral and dramatic tensions of his earlier work drained away, leaving no mortal conflict in the compulsory reenactment of the Fall. The hopeful possibility of good emerging from evil was a doctrine that Hawthorne could neither accept nor wholly reject. England had gone a long way toward undercutting Hawthorne's Calvinism with its seductive Norman and Saxon churches and magnificent Gothic cathedrals; Rome, city of the soul, with all its voluptuous beauty and a religion that Hawthorne felt catered to all human needs, was the

Siren that lured him to the brink of despair. When Hawthorne lost the Calvinism that he did not even know he had, there was nothing to take its place but Melvillean doubts. Hawthorne's artistic imagination, which had thrived on the Calvinist tenets of depravity, reprobation, and damnation, could not survive in an atmosphere of forgiveness, mediation, and hope.

The valiant yet hopeless struggles to write that Hawthorne underwent before his death are made unbearably vivid by his agonized marginal notes in his last manuscripts (the *Elixir of Life* manuscripts). Depressed because of illness, the war, inflation, the expense of educating his children, and particularly because of his inability to write, Hawthorne finally abandoned the romances.

Certainly, by this time Hawthorne was aware of his approaching death and welcoming it, but excessively considerate, as always, of Sophia and his family, he wanted nothing to upset them. Morbidly suspicious of doctors since his youth, he consulted none; perhaps he was afraid that he might be cured. Sophia, the eternal featherheaded optimist, kept thinking that a change of scene or a trip to the seashore would restore Hawthorne's health, and she refused to acknowledge what all of his friends could see, that he was dying. Finally she arranged for Hawthorne to travel with former president Franklin Pierce and to have an interview in Boston with Dr. Oliver Wendell Holmes, the most eminent physician of his day and one of Hawthorne's literary acquaintances. Holmes saw that Hawthorne was extremely ill (May 11, 1864) but did not suppose him near death. Pierce and Hawthorne took their journey by carriage, arriving at Plymouth, New Hampshire, the evening of May 18. Pierce noticed that Hawthorne had difficulty raising his legs and hands at that time, and early the next morning discovered that Hawthorne had died peacefully in his sleep.

And so on May 19, 1864, shortly before his sixtieth birthday on July 4, Hawthorne died of unknown causes while on a trip to regain his health. The Hawthornean ironies persist even in his death, and perhaps the subtlest one is that he died away from Sophia.

### III

My understanding of Hawthorne's submerged Calvinism, which ordains the irony of his best writings, is rooted in Calvin's extraordinary *Institutes of the Christian Religion,* the only systematic theology of the Reformation.

There is no assurance that Hawthorne ever read the *Institutes* themselves, but his Puritan ancestors certainly read Calvin, as well as the Belgic Confession, the Heidelberg Catechism, the Canons of Dort, and the Westminster Confession, all derived from Calvin's teaching. Whether Hawthorne read the *Institutes* or not is unimportant; what is significant is that Calvin's major tenets were completely ingrained in him—through his inheritance, his obsession with Puritan history, his eager reading of the lives and sermons of Puritan divines (both English and American), and his childhood churchgoing. He proudly nominated himself "Puritan," "Calvinist," and "heretic," especially in the entries of his *English* and *French and Italian Notebooks.*[17]

In "The Custom House," one of Hawthorne's most personal essays, he speaks of his Puritan ancestors with a complicated mixture of pleasure and pain. He is convinced that as he walks the streets of his native Salem, with which he had a love-hate relationship all of his life, he breathes in the dust of these early Puritans who "have mingled their earthly substance with the soil, until no small portion of it must necessarily be akin to the mortal frame wherewith, for a little while, I walk the streets." Not only does he inhale the dust of his ancestors, but he also speaks of the "moral quality" that haunts him and which "was present to my boyish imagination, as far back as I can remember." His accounts of his distinguished ancestry (on the Hawthorne side) continue the ambivalence, with shame felt for their cruelty coupled with pride in their importance. The earliest ancestor receives special mention: "*grave, bearded, sable-cloaked and steeple-crowned* progenitor,—who came so early with his *Bible and his sword,* and trode the unworn street with such a stately port, made so large a figure, as a man of war and peace,—a stronger claim than for myself, *whose name is seldom heard and my face hardly known.* He was a soldier, legislator, judge; *he was a Ruler in the Church;* he had all the *Puritanic traits,* both good and evil." Hawthorne sadly remembers that his first progenitor was "a bitter persecutor, as witness the Quakers." The son of this dubious worthy was even more infamous: he "inherited the persecuting spirit, and made himself so conspicuous in the martyrdom of the witches, that their blood may fairly be said to have left a stain upon him. So deep a stain, indeed, that his old dry bones, in the Charter Street burial-ground, must still retain it, if they have not crumbled utterly to dust!" Hawthorne, always concerned about damnation, wonders whether these two relentless Calvinists made any peace with God, or whether it occurred to them that they had done anything unusual.[18]

Hawthorne accepts responsibility for any shame or execration that might have accrued to these early zealots: "At all events, I, the present writer, as their *representative, hereby take shame upon myself* for their sakes, and pray that any curse incurred by them—as I have heard, and as the dreary and unprosperous condition of the race, for many a long year back, would argue to exist [the theme of *The House of the Seven Gables*]—may be now and henceforth removed."[19] Revealing his Calvinist conviction of Special Providences, Hawthorne believes a curse was put upon the early Hawthornes (or Hathornes) and he now prays God that it be removed.

Although Hawthorne longed for fame as a writer and went through a stern and protracted apprenticeship, he was not entirely persuaded that it was an honorable profession; he was often distressed about his coolness toward the human beings he observed, used, spied and eavesdropped upon as raw material for his tales. He saw himself simultaneously as an artist and as a violator of the human heart and was absolutely certain of the disapproval that his writing would occasion in his Puritan ancestors:

> Doubtless, however, either of these stern and black-browed Puritans would have thought it quite a sufficient retribution for his sins, that, after so long a lapse of years, the old trunk of the family tree, with so much venerable moss upon it, should have borne as its topmost bough, an idler like myself. No aim, that I have ever cherished, would they recognize as laudable. . . . "What is he?" murmurs one gray shadow of my forefathers to the other. "A writer of story-books! What kind of a business in life,—what mode of glorifying God, or being serviceable to mankind in his day and generation,—may that be? Why the degenerate fellow might as well have been a fiddler!" . . . And yet, let them scorn me as they will, strong traits of their nature have intertwined themselves with mine.[20]

The strongly Calvinist traits of Hawthorne's ancestors that have "intertwined themselves" with his nature are the basic tenets of the *Institutes,* and these constitute the essence of Hawthorne at his greatest and most ironic.

The first and most important of Calvin's dogmas contains and subsumes all of the others: God is totally sovereign; man is totally depraved.[21] In this concept of God's omnipotence and man's complete inability are implied the doctrines of predestination (election and reprobation), the lack of freedom of the will, and limited atonement (Christ died only to save the elect). Calvin's clarion declaration of God's supremacy over all human thought and action and of God's vast displeasure which amounted to detestation and abomination of man since Adam's Fall, is the bulwark of this reformed faith. According to Calvin, Adam, unlike his progeny, had free will and unimpaired intellect; he could have chosen to obey God, but, tempted by the devil and Eve, he fell when he ate the fruit to obtain the godlike knowledge of good and evil. The first words of the New England primer state: "In Adam's fall, we sinnéd all." After the Fall of Adam and the accompanying fall of nature, man becomes a puny, defiled creature incapable of good and totally dependent upon an affronted, outraged God for his every breath. Every motion of man's life must therefore be directed to this omnipotent being: "For so long as a man has anything, however small, to say in his own defence, so long he deducts somewhat from the glory of God."[22] "It must, therefore, be regarded as an universal proposition, that who so glories in himself glories against God" (Vol. II, 69). "When duly imbued with the knowledge of him, *the whole aim of our lives* will be to revere, fear, and worship his majesty, to enjoy a share in his blessings, to have recourse to him in every difficulty, to acknowledge, laud, and celebrate the magnificence of his works, *to make him,* as it were, *the sole aim of all our actions*" (Vol. I, 329). No wonder Hawthorne is conscious of his "unworthiness" in the eyes of his Puritan ancestors (how could writing "story-books" glorify God?), and quite probably in his own estimation of himself.

The corollary of the doctrine of God's total sovereignty—the total depravity of man—is the one which haunted Hawthorne and on which he based, in an ironic mode, his most impressive tales and romances. Concerning mankind's depravity, Calvin wrote exhaustively and terrifyingly, because in Calvin's moral economy, even though God knew from before the beginning of time that Adam would fall, each of the descendants of Adam bears his own and Adam's guilt from the Fall, rendering each person obnoxious to God. Mankind continues to sin necessarily. The turn of the screw, however, is that man also sins culpably and responsibly, even though because of Original Sin he has no choice *but* to sin. On Original Sin and the total depravity of man Calvin is eloquent, soul-affrighting, and formidable:

Original sin, then, may be defined a hereditary corruption and depravity of our nature, extending to all parts of the soul, which first makes us obnoxious to the wrath of God, and then produces in us works which in Scripture are termed works of the flesh. . . . Two things, therefore, are to be distinctly observed—viz. that being thus perverted and corrupted in all parts of our nature, we are, merely on account of such corruption, de-

servedly condemned by God, to whom nothing is acceptable but righteousness, innocence, and purity. . . . For when it is said, that the sin of Adam
has made us obnoxious to the justice of God, the meaning is not, that we,
who are in ourselves innocent and blameless, are bearing his guilt, but that
since by his transgression we are all placed under the curse, he is said to
have brought us under obligation. . . . the other point—viz. that his
perversity in us never ceases, but constantly produces new fruits, . . .
those works of the flesh . . . just as a lighted furnace sends forth sparks and
flames, or a fountain without ceasing pours out water. . . . For our nature
is not only utterly devoid of goodness, but so prolific in all kinds of evil,
that it can never be idle. . . . Meanwhile, let us remember that our ruin is
attributable to our own depravity, that we not insinuate a charge against
God Himself, the Author of nature. . . . It is plain that this wound was
inflicted by sin; and, therefore, we have no ground of complaint except
against ourselves. . . . Let it stand, therefore, as an indubitable truth,
which no engines can shake, that the mind of man is so entirely alienated
from the righteousness of God that he cannot conceive, desire, or design
anything but what is wicked, distorted, foul, impure, and iniquitous; that
his heart is so thoroughly envenomed by sin, that it can breathe out
nothing but corruption and rottenness; that if some men occasionally make
a show of goodness, their mind is ever interwoven with hypocrisy and
deceit, their soul inwardly bound with the fetters of wickedness. (Vol. I,
217–20, 291)

With these dreadful imprecations resounding in his subconscious, no
wonder Hawthorne could create such monsters of depravity as Judge
Pyncheon, Chillingworth, Mistress Hibbins, Rappaccini, Wakefield, and
Ethan Brand. The way in which the unconscious Calvinism ordains the
ironic mode is perhaps best illustrated in brief (the rest of this study will
examine the novels and major short stories in detail) in "Roger Malvin's
Burial." After Reuben Bourne is wiled into opting for the human choice
of life over certain death, he is under a compulsion to fail: his marriage
gives him no comfort, his farm collapses, and he is forced back into the
wilderness with his wife, Dorcas, and his only son, Cyrus, the one person
who gives him joy. Through an unconscious coercion he arrives at the
place in the forest beneath a rock gravestone where he had abandoned his
dying father-in-law, Roger, eighteen years before. Starting at a noise, he
shoots and kills Cyrus; then, Dorcas falls senseless over her son's body,
which has dropped on the bones of his unburied grandfather. Over this
horrifying pile of human detritus falls a blasted branch of an oak tree, once

the sapling to which Reuben had attached his blood-soaked handkerchief as a vow to Roger to return and bury his bones. Ending this barbarous Old Testament-like tale of vengeance, exacted by a fiercer Jehovah than the God of Abraham, is the bland statement that Reuben is now able to pray. The conclusion is really impertinent unless we see it as Calvinist-ordained irony that dramatizes the conflict between the depraved nature of all men (Reuben is the archetype of Calvin's Everyman) and the merciless, appalling righteousness of God, demanding from sinners the full price of their envenomed nature—not less than everything.

As Calvin rages at man's iniquity, we can see the seeds for *The House of the Seven Gables,* the inherited curse that Hawthorne feared for himself and bestowed in his romance upon the Pyncheons: "We must therefore understand . . . that a curse from the Lord righteously falls not only on the head of the guilty individual, but also on all his lineage . . . and [will] be followed in turn by succeeding generations, forming a seed of evil-doers" (Vol. I, 332–33).

In "Fancy's Show Box" poor old Mr. Smith, self-righteously drinking his excellent wine, is visited by a horrid trio of Fancy, Memory, and Conscience, who accuse him of seduction, murder, and heinous fraud. Mr. Smith is infuriated, asserting vehemently that he has committed no such outrages, but Conscience strikes daggers in his heart and Memory insists that he may have contemplated them. In the sketch, Hawthorne raises the grave question of whether we are guilty not only of sins of commission, but also of those merely entertained in the mind. He concludes ironically: "Man must not disclaim his brotherhood, even with the guiltiest."[23] This attitude is the purest Calvinism, as illustrated in Calvin's discussion of the Ten Commandments. Concerning the sixth— "Thou shalt not kill"—Calvin comments: "To be clear of the crime of murder, it is not enough to refrain from shedding man's blood. If in act you perpetrate, if in endeavor you plot, if in wish and design you conceive what is adverse to another's safety, you have the guilt of murder" (Vol. I, 347). On the seventh commandment, "Thou shalt not commit adultery," Calvin is just as positive: "And let not a man flatter himself, that because he abstains from the outward act he cannot be accused of unchastity. . . . Let not your mind burn within with evil concupiscence, your eyes wanton after corrupting objects, nor your body be decked for allurement; let neither your tongue by filthy speeches, nor your appetite by intemperance, entice the mind to corresponding thoughts" (Vol. I, 349–50).

Another Calvinist trait is Hawthorne's distrust of his own human desires throughout his life: should he be a writer and pry into the secrecy of the human heart; should he be so enamored with England; should he admire the nude statues in Rome; should he return to America; should he retain his loyalty to Pierce with the reality of the Civil War going on about him? His characters also constantly face prickly moral decisions— Young Goodman Brown, Robin, Dimmesdale, Holgrave-Maule, Zenobia, Miriam, ad infinitum. Calvin's answer is clear: "We hold that all human desires are evil, and we charge them with sin not in as far as they are natural, but because they are inordinate, and inordinate because nothing pure and upright can proceed from a corrupt and polluted nature. . . . Wherefore he seems to me to have made most progress who has learned to be most dissatisfied with himself" (Vol. I, 518, 526).

Calvin's doctrine of predestination is difficult: it is difficult to understand and, once understood, difficult to accept. Calvin agreed that before time began God decreed that some few men were elected to salvation, not because in his foreknowledge God knew they would merit it—because man deserves only reprobation—but, out of his free mercy, he chose them. At some time in their lives, those chosen for election become regenerated through the Holy Spirit. Those who are not chosen are the reprobate, who will be damned, as all men deserve damnation after the Fall of Adam. Knowledge of election or reprobation is not given by God to individual people, so those who might think they are elected because of a conversion, or an exemplary life, or feelings of regeneration, are the most likely to be hypocrites—the whited sepulchres—those who assume election and in reality are reprobates. Why certain individuals are chosen for election or reprobation is one of God's mysteries, not open to the corrupted intellect of puny man. The reprobates give glory to God in their deserved damnation, as do the elect by their unmerited salvation.

Calvin is completely sure of himself in explaining this intricate doctrine: "By predestination we mean the eternal decree of God, by which he determined with himself whatever he wished to happen with regard to every man. All are not created in equal terms, but some are preordained to eternal life, others to eternal damnation; . . . as each has been created for one or another of these ends, we say that he has been predestinated to life or death" (Vol. II, 206). God so arranges things "by his sovereign counsel," Calvin argues, that "individuals are born, who are doomed from the womb to certain death, and are to glorify him by their destruction" (Vol. II, 231). Thus, when God elects one and rejects another, it is owing not to any respect to the individual, but entirely to his own mercy, which is free to display and exert itself when and where he pleases. . . . The Lord therefore may show favour to whom he will, because he is merciful; not show it to all because he is a just judge. . . . [Scripture] does not . . . tempt us to pry with impious presumption into the inscrutable counsels of God, but rather to humble and abase us, that we may tremble at his judgment, and learn to look up to his mercy. (Vol. II, 234–35)

The elect never cease sinning because human nature is under a compulsion to sin, but the "faults of the saints are indeed venial, not, however, in their own nature, but because, through the mercy of God, they obtain pardon" (Vol. I, 362); hence, "even saints cannot perform one work, which if judged on its own merits, is not deserving of condemnation" (Vol. II, 180). In this "gulf of perdition God leaves those whom he has determined one day to deliver until his own time arrive; he only preserves them from plunging into irremediable blasphemy" (Vol. II, 250).

This complex doctrine of predestination caused Calvin considerable pains to explicate. It is distinctly his, however, and I have therefore lingered over it. Hawthorne seems to have assented completely to this doctrine, but he was far more interested in the fate of the reprobate than the elect. Ernest of "The Great Stone Face" is one of the few characters in Hawthorne whom we can deem elected. To the very end, Ernest looks for "some wiser and better man than himself."[24]

Concerning reprobation, Calvin was eloquent and his doctrine of man predestined to damnation because of God's decree, despite any futile human struggles, appealed strongly to Hawthorne's dark imagination and suggested his best plots. Calvin justifies this damnatory doctrine:

However universal the promises of salvation may be [in Scripture], there is no discrepancy between them and the predestination of the reprobate, provided we attend to their effect. We know that the promises are effectual only when we receive them in faith, but on the contrary, when faith is made void, the promise is of no effect. . . . His mercy is offered to all who desire and implore it, *and this none do, save those whom he has enlightened.* Moreover, he enlightens those whom he has predestinated to salvation. . . . *Illumination itself has eternal election for its rule.* (Vol. II, 256)

The refusal of reprobates to obey the word of God "when manifested to them, will be properly ascribed to the malice and depravity of their hearts, provided it be at the same time added, that they were adjudged to this depravity, because they were raised up by the *just but inscrutable judgment of God, to show forth his glory by their condemnation*" (Vol. II, 253). God's vengeance on the reprobate is described with great relish:

> *Tophet* is ordained of old. . . . He hath made it deep and large; the pile thereof is fire and much wood; the breath of the Lord, like a stream of brimstone, doth kindle it. . . . His indignation is like a raging fire, by whose touch all things are devoured and annihilated. . . . Unhappy consciences find no rest, but are vexed and driven about by a dire whirlwind, *feeling as if torn by an angry God,* pierced through with deadly darts, terrified by his thunderbolt, and crushed by the weight of his hand; so that it were easier to plunge into abysses and whirlpools than endure these terrors for a moment. How fearful, then must it be to be thus beset throughout eternity! (Vol. II, 275–76)

Calvin worries that language fails to describe the horrors of damnation; however, he manages quite successfully to scare the hell out of the reader. The expression "Tophet" for hell, which Calvin used and which is used in the King James version of the Bible, is one that Hawthorne savored and used on numerous occasions. Michael Wigglesworth's poem "The Day of Doom" (1662) which, in rhymed dog-trot Calvinism, gives magnificent images of the delight that the elect take in the writhings of the reprobate—whether they be mother, father, husband, wife, or child—was also certainly familiar to Hawthorne. It is not surprising, then, that Hawthorne is able to convey to the reader a profound sense of dread, fright, and panic for those of his characters who are most certainly damned—like Chillingworth, or the man of adamant, or Ethan Brand.

Calvin's doctrine that denies the freedom of man's will follows from his concept of man's total depravity. "The will, because inseparable from the nature of man, did not perish, but was so enslaved by depraved lusts as to be incapable of one righteous desire" (Vol. I, 233). Since man was "corrupted" by the Fall, he sins "voluntarily . . . not by violent compulsion, or external force, but by the movement of his own passion; and yet such is the depravity of his nature, that he cannot move and act except in the direction of evil. If this is true, the thing not obscurely expressed is, that *he is under a necessity of sinning*" (Vol. I, 254). Man is "so enslaved by the yoke of sin" that he cannot "of his own nature aim at good either in wish or actual pursuit," and "though he sins necessarily," he "nevertheless sins voluntarily" (Vol. I, 265). Hawthorne's villains all seem to be under the force of Calvin's dictum. Chillingworth tells Hester: "'By thy first step awry thou didst plant the germ of evil; but, since that moment it has all been a dark necessity.'"[25] Rappaccini and Baglioni seem to labor under such a "dark necessity," as do Goodman Brown, Wakefield, and Judge Pyncheon.

The tenet of limited atonement, which grows naturally out of the doctrines of predestination and reprobation, is the simple but daunting statement that Christ died only for the elect. The reprobate do not share in the infinite treasures of Christ's death and resurrection. It is not that these mercies are not sufficient, but they are withheld from the damned because before the beginning of time God has chosen those who are to be his own. Christ shows "that many are called, but few chosen" (Vol. II, 245–46). "He who selects those whom he is to visit in mercy does not impart it to all" (Vol. II, 255). In "Egotism; or, The Bosom-Serpent" Hawthorne shows that mercy can come even to one who seems surely damned, but the endings of such works as "Young Goodman Brown" and *The Scarlet Letter* occur in the gloom and smoke of the fiery pit of hell.

One of the most shocking, terrible, and fearful of Calvin's doctrines is that of infant damnation. The Fall of Adam, Calvin holds, "infected his whole seed. Paul could never have said that all are 'by nature the children of wrath,' if they had not been cursed from the womb" (Vol. I, 215–16). Thus, all men, "descending from an impure seed, come into the world tainted with the contagion of sin. Nay, before we behold the light of the sun we are in God's sight defiled and polluted" (Vol. I, 214). Even "infants bring their condemnation with them from their mother's womb; for although they have not yet brought forth the fruits of their un-righteousness, they have its seed included in them. *Nay, their whole nature is, as it were, a seed of sin, and, therefore, cannot but be odious and abominable to God*" (Vol. I, 474).

Hawthorne's accounts in the *American Notebooks* of his elder daughter's playing fantastic and suspiciously demonic death games as his mother lay dying say that he suspects her of being an elf-child, not a child of his flesh. The fearsome "unbreeched fanatics," the Puritan children in "The Gentle Boy" who deal little Ilbrahim mortal blows, argue Hawthorne's belief in infant depravity, as does *The Scarlet Letter*'s goblin child, Pearl, and the fiendish Puritan children who taunt her. There is, too, the "little child of strength" in "The Artist of the Beautiful" who crushes the butterfly that is the artist's life work.[26]

Calvin's next major point of dogma, the inerrancy of Scripture, reinforces the great reformer's emphasis upon the Word and the necessity of the preaching of the Word and nothing else. Only the Bible, which in no way can be in error, may be preached. "Nor is it sufficient to believe that God is true, and cannot lie or deceive, unless you feel firmly persuaded *that every word which proceeds from him is sacred, inviolable truth"* (Vol. I, 474).

Hawthorne's ministers, the Reverend Mr. Wilson and Dimmesdale of *The Scarlet Letter* and the Reverend Mr. Hooper of the "Minister's Black Veil," are all dedicated to preaching and proclaiming the inerrant Word, but Hawthorne deals ironically with the temptation to hypocrisy to which this great position of spiritual authority can lead.

The Calvinist tenets of irresistible grace and the perseverance of the saints grow, as do all of the others, out of the first great dogma, the absolute sovereignty of God and the total depravity of man. If man has been elected by the sovereign God before all time, then sometime in his lifetime, not *necessarily* at birth or even during his early life, God will call that elected individual to himself through the mediation of Christ's suffering and death, and the call will be irresistible. The elected one will answer the call: he has no choice, nor does this election have anything to do with his worthiness or works, which count for naught. He will then persevere in faith until his death, although he will continue to sin, as man sins voluntarily and necessarily, but never will he commit an "irremediable blasphemy." There are many fake elect, however, because the *"human heart* has so many recesses for vanity, so many lurking places for falsehood, is so shrouded by fraud and hypocrisy," it *"often deceives itself.* Let those who glory in such semblances of faith know that, in this respect, they are not a whit superior to devils" (Vol. II, 478).

In his mandates, Calvin effectively withdraws the mediations between God and man provided by the Roman Catholic church, against which he protested—the sacraments, the mediation of the Virgin and the saints, the Mass, indulgences, a sacramentally ordained clergy, and man's ability to cooperate *freely* with God's grace and the inexhaustible merits of Christ's *infinite,* not *limited,* atonement for man's sin. Calvin's vision places man naked and alone in an awful confrontation with the sovereign God, who will not be mocked. The examen of conscience which Calvin prescribes led some to excesses or unreasoning despair (see the *Personal Narrative* of Jonathan Edwards, the diary of Wigglesworth, the diary of Samuel Sewall, the anxiety-ridden poetry of Edward Taylor), and gave

others a groundless, hypocritical conviction that they were the saved, the
elect, God's people.

Hawthorne is mostly concerned with the hypocrite, first of all himself. He constantly questions his motives in writing and spying, his
self-adjudged coldness of heart and desire for solitude, his conscientious-
ness as surveyor and consul, his reluctance to go sight-seeing as much as
his Calvinist conscience tells him he must; and, finally and most ironically, he examines his constant catechizing of himself. His novels and tales
abound with sactimonious Pharisees: Judge Pyncheon, Dimmesdale,
Westervelt, Baglioni, the Puritan and Quaker populace of "The Gentle
Boy," all pretending to be members of the elect.

The reformed religion of Calvin retained only two of the seven sacraments of the Catholic church and these, baptism and the Eucharist, did
not, Calvin thought, have their former efficacy. Baptism did not remit
Original Sin and the Eucharist was not the true body and blood of Christ
under the appearance of bread and wine (Vol. II, 513, 517).

About the Eucharist, Calvin has a great deal to say, much of it
venting his distress and fury over the celebration of the Lord's Supper as
the central part of the Roman Catholic Mass. He acknowledges the Eucharist as a sacrament given "by the hand of his [God, the Father's]
only-begotten Son—viz. a spiritual feast, at which Christ testifies that he
himself is living bread on which our souls feed" (Vol. II, 557). Calvin
considers the Eucharist a mystery about which he will "freely confess" that
he is "unable to comprehend with my mind" (Vol. II, 561). This does not
prevent him, however, from arguing with Luther that the Eucharist is not
"transubstantiation," as the Catholics hold, or a "hypostatic union," as
Luther maintained, but *something else.*" He directs most of his rage
against the Mass, seeing it as an "abomination" which has so "intoxicated
all the kings and nations of the earth, from the highest to the lowest" and
"so struck them with stupor and giddiness, that, duller than the lower
animals, they have placed the vessel of their salvation in this fateful
vortex." He continues to thunder that "Satan never employed a more
powerful engine, to assail and storm the kingdom of Christ. This is the
Helen for whom the enemies of the truth in the present day fight with so
much rage, fury, and atrocity; and *truly the Helen with whom they commit
spiritual whoredom,* the most execrable of all. . . . I am unwilling to meddle with their obscene impurities, which are daily before the eyes and faces
of all" (Vol. II, 619).

Hawthorne maintained throughout his life a similar mistrust and suspicion of the Mass, in fact a suspicion of any ceremonial liturgy that departed at all from the stark pulpit-centered-plain-meetinghouse preaching of the Word to which he was accustomed. When, in Italy, he found himself in the cathedrals, basilicas, and churches in which these ceremonies were taking place, he was embarrassed and discomfited. The best literary use that Hawthorne made of this ritual is the black mass that he describes with such infernal, diabolical detail in "Young Goodman Brown."

Calvin dismissed the remaining five sacraments of the Catholic church with the epithet "unscriptural." Against penance, the sacrament that most intrigued Hawthorne, Calvin argues lustily and at length. His main point, next to the assertion that it is not scriptural, is that no priest can dare to set himself up as a vessel through which Christ dispenses absolution of sin: "such is the rudeness and ignorance of priests, that the greater part of them are in no respect fitter to perform this office than a cobbler to cultivate the fields, while almost all the others have good reason to suspect their own fitness" (Vol. I, 553). Calvin believed that man should confess his sins only to God.

Hawthorne was interested, from early in his life, in the public penance of which Calvin approved. This type of confession was demanded of all offenders by the minister in conjunction with the magistrates in the early Puritan theocracy of New England. Punishments ranged from some hours in the stocks, to lashings, to public ignominy on the pillory, to death. *The Scarlet Letter* takes its structure from the three pillory scenes, and the concepts of penance and penitence are crucial to the novel. When he was in Rome, Hawthorne was attracted by what he saw as the human convenience of the Catholic church, and he never tired of watching penitents go to the confessionals of St. Peter's, each to a priest who spoke his own language. This spying on penitents became almost obsessional with Hawthorne, who lingered in different Roman churches, clocking the time spent by the penitent in the confessional box, which he thought was an indicator of the seriousness of the penitent's sin; if it were an hour or more, he was convinced that the sinner was indeed no small-time offender. His decision to make one of the most dramatic scenes of *The Marble Faun* take place in St. Peter's, where Hilda goes to a confessional to pour out her feelings of guilt, signals his new fascination with private confession.

For Calvin, who adopted Luther's teaching that *man is justified by faith alone,* faith is a gift of God. Works are of no merit unless they are preceded by faith, and even then are of no consequence in the scheme of the redemption of the elect. It should follow that once one has been given the gift of faith, he will be inclined to all sorts of good works. With the gift of faith, God expects of man numerous good works, but although necessary, they count for nothing. Calvin pleads, "Let us willingly presume so far on his [God's] truth *as to cast away all confidence in our works,* and trusting in his mercy, venture to hope" (Vol. I, 507). Man *"is justified freely by faith alone"* (Vol. I, 509); those who believe that "repentance precedes faith instead of flowing from, or being produced by it, as the fruit by the tree, have never understood its nature" (Vol. I, 510).

In *The Scarlet Letter* Hawthorne has Hester try to comfort Dimmesdale in the forest. In despair over his seven years of agony, she offers him the comfort of *good works:*

> "You have deeply and sorely repented. Your sin is left behind you, in the days long past. Your present life is not less holy, in very truth, than it seems in people's eyes. *Is there no reality in the penitence thus sealed and witnessed by good works?* And wherefore should it not bring you peace?"
>
> "No, Hester, no!" replied the clergyman. *"There is no substance in it! It is cold and dead, and can do nothing for me! Of penance, I have had enough! Of penitence there has been none!"*[27]

Dimmesdale is too good a Calvinist to be comforted by the efficacy of good works.

Calvin teaches that God is both transcendent and immanent. Although the author of the whole world, he is, because of foreknowledge and his predestination of every man, present at man's every breath. Also immanent, through the permission of God, is the archenemy of God and humanity, the devil, who attempts to foil man's every effort toward faith and righteousness and win another soul away from the Almighty. God "arms the devil, as well as all the wicked, for conflict, and *sits as umpire,* that he may exercise our patience" (Vol. I, 190–91). Although Hawthorne grumbled at his poverty and his inability to write, for the most part he accepted what happened to him and his family as if it were part of the Providence of a transcendent yet immanent God. He even allowed Sophia to scratch upon the window of the Old Manse with her wedding diamond, "Man's accidents are God's purposes."

The Calvinist dogma of the immanence of the devil in the world admirably served Hawthorne's purposes as a writer. "The tendency of all that Scripture teaches concerning devils," Calvin writes, "is to put us on our guard against their wiles and machinations, that we may provide ourselves with weapons strong enough to drive away the most formidable foes." We must be "prepared for the *contest*. . . . Being forewarned of the constant presence of an enemy the most daring, the most powerful, the most crafty, the most indefatigable, the most completely equipped with all the engines, and the most expert in the science of war," and not "allow ourselves to be overtaken by sloth, or cowardice, but, on the contrary, with minds aroused and ever on the alert, let us stand ready to resist; and knowing that this warfare is terminated only by death, let us study to persevere" (Vol. I, 150–52).

Hawthorne's use of devil imagery, devil characters, witchcraft, the demonic, and the supernatural are too numerous to recount. And all the scientific villains in league with the devil (Rappaccini, Chillingworth, Westervelt); the witches (Mistress Hibbins, the coven in "Young Goodman Brown," the witch of "The Hollow of the Three Hills"); Pearl, the elf-child; the "unbreeched fanatics" of "The Gentle Boy" suggest that the *supernatural* is the *natural* climate for Hawthorne's romances.

The doctrine of Special Providences follows logically from the tenet of an immanent God. If God is at all times present to every human being, he at all times decrees one's every act and thought. This immanence and total direction applies also to all of nature, animate and inanimate. Nothing, then, happens by coincidence, chance, or fate, but is ordered by the sovereign God.

In addition to the general Providence of God, Calvin speaks of extraordinary and startling happenings as Special Providences. In the American Calvinism in which Hawthorne was steeped, a conspicuous Special Providence was associated with Anne Hutchinson. After being banished from the settlement at Massachusetts Bay for her "heresy" of proclaiming that God had communicated to her the names of the elect and the reprobate (including some ministers among the reprobate), she was on her way to Rhode Island to seek sanctuary with the "renegade" Roger Williams when she was set upon by a band of Indians and scalped. Her gruesome death only confirmed to the faithful of Massachusetts Bay that they had been absolutely correct in their treatment of her and that God had struck her down in this horrible way by a Special Providence. God ordains all things; he "so overrules all things that nothing happens without his counsel" (Vol. I, 174). "What, then, you will say, does nothing happen fortuitously, nothing contingently? I answer, it was a true saying of Basil the Great, that Fortune and Chance are heathen terms; the meaning of which ought not to occupy pious minds. For if all success is blessing from God, and calamity and adversity are his curse, there is no place left in human affairs for Fortune and Chance" (Vol. I, 179).

This doctrine, as much as any of Calvin's, led to the rank abuses which gave the Puritans a bad name. Although Calvin warns that judgment is for God alone, he did counsel neighbors to report each other to the magistrates and ministers if moral irregularities were observed, and in this way petty jealousies were often manifested—witness the witch trials at Salem. Calvin himself often thundered through the streets of Geneva; he arrested the chief magistrate's wife for dancing and once caught his brother's wife and her hunchbacked servant in "flagrante delicto." The problem was that the successes or failures of an individual became public knowledge and depraved human beings could not refrain from making moral judgments about one another.[28]

Special Providences are part of the plot of many Hawthorne stories which might be considered fortuitous or coincidental: Chillingworth returns from captivity just in time to see Hester on the pillory; Phoebe leaves for the country and Judge Pyncheon threatens Hepzibah and Clifford; Zenobia and Priscilla are revealed to be half-sisters; Wakefield happens to return home one rainy night twenty years after his departure. *Deus ex machina* was for the Calvinist a Special Providence.

Calvin's tenet of the absolute and sole judgment of God on the state of a man's soul, his election or reprobation, his secret sins and the unpardonable sin, was often flouted by believers. Although Calvin foresaw the dangers and raged and roared against the presumptuous, some of the earliest heretics against pure Calvinism were those who declared, as did Anne Hutchinson, that man could distinguish between the elect and reprobate. Calvin warned that we take an "envenomed delight" in both "prying into and exposing our neighbor's faults" (Vol. I, 353–54).

Calvin's definition of "the unforgivable sin" is precise: "he sins against the Holy Spirit who, while so constrained by the power of divine truth that he cannot plead ignorance, yet deliberately resists, and that merely for the sake of resisting" (Vol. I, 528). Those who believe "in conscience that what they repudiate and impugn is the word of God, and yet cease not to impugn it, are said to blaspheme against the Spirit, inasmuch as they struggle against the illumination which is the work of the Spirit" (Vol. I, 529).

Although Hawthorne's Ethan Brand is the quintessential perpetrator of this one unforgivable sin, Hawthorne's definition of the sin differs from Calvin's and Brand's to some extent. For Hawthorne, the unforgivable sin, as defined in the *American Notebooks*, "might consist in a want of love and reverence for the Human Soul; in consequence of which, the investigator pried into its dark depths, not with a hope or purpose of making it better, but from a cold philosophical curiosity,—content that it should be wicked in whatever kind or degree, and only desiring to study it out. Would not this, in other words, be the separation of the intellect from the heart?"[29] Hawthorne was enormously afraid that he himself might be guilty of the unpardonable sin because, desiring to be a "Paul Pry," he perhaps took "envenomed delight" when he spied, peeped, and eavesdropped on his own neighbors and created characters whose secret hearts he could violate.

The Calvinist dogma on the church and church discipline[30] probably concerned Hawthorne least, except for the emphasis Calvin placed upon the preaching of the Word as the central function of the church and its ministers, and his stern dicta about the "blasphemous" uses of images, statues, elaborate music, gorgeous vestments, sacred vessels of gold and jewels, in short, the entire Roman Catholic liturgy and its setting, the magnificent churches and cathedrals (Vol. I, 92, 96).

Hawthorne had a difficult time when he first went to England. After not having been inside a church since he was a boy in Salem—and then in the bare Presbyterian meetinghouse—he felt guilty about his newly acquired taste for churches and magnificent cathedrals. He went to look, not to worship, except for one rather disastrous family expedition to the services at Chester cathedral, during which Julian "gaped aloud" and Hawthorne was bored with the bland homily of the Anglican minister. But what disturbed Hawthorne most was his awestruck admiration for the glories of the Gothic cathedrals, for their magnificent stained-glass windows and the "images" themsleves. By the time he went to the Continent (after four and one-half years in England), Hawthorne was fulminating against his boyhood hero, Cromwell, and the destruction he wreaked on churches, cathedrals, and abbeys. Once Hawthorne reached France, and then Italy, he permitted his guilty admiration for "Papist" beauty to burgeon unchecked. Although at times he felt ashamed of himself, he continued to be obsessed with churches and cathedrals, occasionally quieting his Calvinist conscience with some critical remarks on the papacy and the corrupt clergy of a "dead" religion. But Hawthorne returned to America a broken Calvinist, and having found nothing to take the place of the religion of Geneva, he spent the last four years of his life afflicted with doubts and skepticism.

I have been at some pains to compress within a few pages the major tenets of the greatest and most influential (as far as the direction of American religious thought goes) of the theologians of the Reformation, John Calvin. This summary is only that and is, therefore, sketchy, although quotations from the voice of the terrifying cleanser of Geneva give some of the flavor of that stern divine.[31]

Calvin, who had his quarrels with the Swiss, French, and English reformers and a special argument with Luther and the German Protestants (especially about the Eucharist), was the only sixteenth-century dissenter to construct a complete and systematic theology. The *Institutes* remain a masterpiece of legalism, argument, humanistic thought, rhetoric, and conviction that blasts even a twentieth-century reader with such a potent frontal attack on religious flabbiness and smugness that he will never be the same.

The Calvinist inheritance was the very essence of Hawthorne's murky, glowering imagination. Before his tacit Calvinism was crumbled by his European experience, it provided the matrix of his art and dictated the ironic mode that galvanizes his greatest tales and novels. This study will proceed roughly in chronological order through Hawthorne's writings, probing his theological certainties and uncertainties, his elected isolation, his alienation—all of which dictated the ironic substance and texture of his novels and tales, whose most memorable characters are all hell-bent for damnation.

THE SCARLET LETTER

# "A" Is for Apple

*"And be the stern and sad truth spoken, that the breach which guilt has once made into the human soul is, never, in this mortal state, repaired."*

I

Although Peter de Vries has said that if Hester Prynne lived in the twentieth century she wouldn't get an *A* for adultery but only a *C-*, the hellfire lighted by Hawthorne in *The Scarlet Letter* burns on in perpetuity. Not only are twentieth-century plain readers still devouring this novel, but the far-from-plain critics of our day are threatening to write as much about it as has been written about *Hamlet.* So why another reading of *The Scarlet Letter?* "Evil can only produce evil," says Hawthorne, and so I join the ranks.

The novel was written in circumstances that would seem inauspicious: Hawthorne had been dismissed (because of a change in political administration) as surveyor of the Custom House in Salem; his mother was dying in the room above the one in which he wrote; his "study" had been converted into a nursery for Una and Julian. He probably began writing this romance in September 1849, and completed it on February 3, 1850.[1] It was published on March 16, 1850, a red-letter day for American literature. Within six months 6,000 copies had been printed in three editions; the work has never been out of print.

Many reviewers praised the book warmly, although a few carped at its "unsavory" subject matter, even though the adultery takes place before the romance begins. The Custom House essay, in which Hawthorne takes mild revenge on his political enemies and tries to relieve the magnificently sombre tone of his romance and to establish, however patently, verisimilitude for Hester's story, was a great success with his readers. Some even preferred it to *The Scarlet Letter,* as Hawthorne had predicted they would.

"The Custom House" is a fascinating autobiographical essay. In keeping with his modesty, Hawthorne apologizes for his "autobiographical impulse" (3), which has already overcome him twice—the first being his description of life in the Old Manse in his volume of short stories, *Mosses from an Old Manse*. Like his disciple, Henry James, Hawthorne always hoped for at least one sympathetic and appreciative reader, one who would "understand" him "better than most of his schoolmates and lifemates" (3): "it may be pardonable to imagine that a friend, a kind and apprehensive, though not the closest friend, is listening to our talk; and then, a *native reserve* being thawed by this genial consciousness, we may prate of the circumstances that lie around us, and even of ourself, *but still keep the inmost Me behind its veil*" (4). There is no danger that, with all his charm, Hawthorne is going to make any rents in the veil of his innate reticence about himself. But we are given some "hints and guesses": his pride and shame in his distinguished Puritan ancestors; his affinity with these "steeple-crowned" progenitors and his Puritan past; his instinctive clinging to Salem "as if the natal spot were an earthly paradise" (11); his desire to break this unhealthy relationship with Salem which seems to have a mysterious hold over him—"my doom was on me"—as if it were "the inevitable centre of the universe" (12); his resolve to leave Salem and become "a citizen of somewhere else" (44); and his desire to be remembered by future generations as a writer. Hawthorne's love-hate relationship with his own historical past; with himself as artist; with Salem, his birthplace and his doom; and with the story he proceeds to tell, is the warp and woof of his richest ambiguity and the intricate and recondite fabric of his greatest romance.

I would like to suggest an unraveling of *The Scarlet Letter* which illuminates the text and shows the consistency of Hawthorne's tragic vision of human life. The perennial questions about Hawthorne arise because of his notorious ambiguity, part of which results from his inability or refusal to push to its logical extremes his dreadful knowledge of human nature. What he does instead is to suggest throughout a work, but especially at the end, the possibility of alternate choices, an ironic and, sometimes maddening, device. Whether or not Hawthorne was doctrinally a reluctant Calvinist matters little; certainly he was unconcerned with dogmas or sects. But the black flower of Calvin's doctrine of total depravity—of man's necessary yet culpable sinning—stimulated Hawthorne's imagination as no Emersonian Rhodora could. Hawthorne's best tales, in fact, dramatize pitiful sinners' attempts "to spit from the mouth the withered apple seed" of the lost Eden. That these attempts are futile, that the corrupt seed grows rankly and with malignant haste and finally chokes the doomed sinners—this vision is Hawthorne's personal tragic-ironic apocalypse.

Roger Chillingworth speaks the lines that crackle around the doomed Hester and Dimmesdale and light up their agony with a dull red glow: "My old faith, long forgotten, comes back to me, and explains all that we do, and all that we suffer. By thy first step awry, thou didst plant the germ of evil; but, since that moment, it has all been a dark necessity" (174). Seen as the culmination of this dark necessity, the ending of the novel is tragic, as Hawthorne himself predicts in chapter 1: it is "the darkening close of a tale of human frailty and sorrow" (48). Hester, Dimmesdale, and Chillingworth are seared in the hellfire that is kindled by the original adultery and then stoked by their continuing and necessary sins. In Hawthorne's grim world, after the first excursion into evil, no return to innocence is possible, only a wallowing in ever-widening circles of graver sins: from the lesser sins of the flesh, down the circles of the inferno to spiritual pride and the frozen heart.

Chillingworth, initially a kind but cold man, takes on the godlike role of avenger and becomes, by his own admission, a fiend. Arthur Dimmesdale holds lovingly to his sin for seven years, becomes completely self-absorbed while his reputation as a saintly priest grows, and then knowingly and deliberately consents to evil with Hester in the forest. He even rejoices that he will be able to preach the Election Sermon before he leaves in open adultery. He dies after the sermon, but not before announcing himself as the one sinner of the world (in an ultimate example of inverted spiritual pride) and as saved, a proclamation which makes him, by his own Puritan standards (and most likely, by Hawthorne's) a victim of both hubris and damnation. Dimmesdale's final selfishness is evidenced by his hedging about Hester's chances for redemption, "'I fear!'" "'I fear!'" (256). He is right to fear, for Hester, a dark, luxurious, and passionate beauty, wanders in the labyrinths of her mind; she is capped and lettered in her uniform of a Puritan social worker, and after Dimmesdale's death *humbly* announces a new religion and revelation, with herself as John the Baptist.

If what has been done has a "consecration of its own" (195), the new revelation of the "surer ground of mutual happiness" (263) which Hester foresees between man and woman must be that adultery does not count.

The picture of Hester turned village do-gooder and amateur psychologist of the human heart, however winning to the sociological critics, is palpably disgusting to Hawthorne himself. The obvious irony is that the outcast, exiled, sinful Hester becomes the village caretaker and nurse; the deeper irony is that she is yet damned.

No one escapes the Hawthornean irony. Certainly Hawthorne suggests that those who sit in judgment on Hester, Dimmesdale, and Chillingworth—the Puritan magistrates and crowds (and even, perhaps, the reader)—are hypocritical, self-righteous, and uniformly wrong in their judgments.

Nor does Hawthorne, as author, simply condemn the characters, for on a superficial level he is just as delighted with Hester as are his most romantic readers (those who see the scarlet letter as her red badge of courage or even as a token of her red-letter day). But with his tragic view of human nature, Hawthorne is also compelled to demonstrate the devastation sin wreaks in the human personality. Hester is marvelous when she is passionate and loving (although sinful, as Hawthorne reminds us), but when she tries to justify her sin ("What we did had a consecration of its own" [195]); when she lies to Pearl in the forest about the significance of the letter, although she announces that she has held fast to truth; when her deepest reason for not telling Dimmesdale about Chillingworth is her hope of being reunited with the minister, she prattles like a moral imbecile. She offers Dimmesdale an Arminian explanation for the reality of his penitence—evidence signed and witnessed by his good works. But no true Calvinist would accept the Arminian heresy that good works— charity—could atone for one sin, let alone a multitude. Dimmesdale rejects the heresy of good works—"It is cold and dead, and can do nothing for me" (192)[2]—but then completely out-heresies Hester when he speaks of his own resurrection, his putting on of the new man, not in Christ but in the strong Hester; by her, he is "risen up all made anew" (202).

Hawthorne is not dismayed at the joys and excitement and life-giving quality of human love, although he is suspicious of it, but shows that forbidden, adulterous love has the power to make its participants forget their God—the Calvinist Jehovah who is vengeful and jealous. Just as in "Roger Malvin's Burial," where Reuben Bourne's opting for life costs not less than everything, so in *The Scarlet Letter* the lack of reverence for each other's souls or the choice of love, comfort, and pleasure by Hester and Dimmesdale has to be paid for at an unbelievable price, the Pearl of great price. Dimmesdale must live a life of humiliation, self-absorption, suffering, and spiritual pride; Hester, isolated and miserable for seven years, becomes an Antinomian Anne Hutchinson, by Puritan standards the worst thing that could happen to her; Chillingworth becomes a vengeful devil. And all for what? Pearl is made a human being by their awesome sacrifice of both temporal and eternal life, so that she will "grow up amid human joy and sorrow" (256). Three souls are lost so that the Pearl may become a fragile human child.

Perhaps we are drawn to Hawthorne because of the metaphysical shudder: Hawthorne always sees the skull beneath the skin.[3] In his greatest tales and novels we see reenacted again and again the Fall of man, the loss of Eden, which brought "death into this world and all our woe." But unlike Milton, the early Puritan, Hawthorne makes no attempt to justify the ways of God to man. His own horrible and sorrowful vision of the God of Abraham, the God who demands blood sacrifice, is the grim climate of his art. And paradoxically, as we shall see, this tragic vision was sustaining for Hawthorne as an artist. By the time he came to write *The Marble Faun* (1860), after almost two years in Italy and five in England, the rigors of his New England conscience had mellowed enough to allow him to consider at least the possibility of the *felix culpa* and true penitence. But Hawthorne was not at ease with this new dispensation. When he lost his vision of human nature as damned and hopeless, he also lost his artistic integrity and was never able to finish another novel. The tension was gone, because the old drama of the expulsion from Eden lost all of its horror if there were any way back in. Without his almost tactile sense of sin and guilt, Hawthorne had nothing left to say, as the abortive romances mutely testify.

In *The Scarlet Letter* we have a mutation of the Fall, with the disobedience taking the form of sexuality, as in Milton's *Paradise Lost,* but with a distinctive Hawthornean difference. Prynne-Chillingworth, as the Calvinist Jehovah-devil-God, sends Hester to the Eden of the New World. Lonely and passionate, the Lilith-Eve-Hester seduces Adam, or A.D., Arthur Dimmesdale. The outraged God-devil-Chillingworth comes to take vengeance for their original sin and the necessary result is, of course, death and damnation, with the murky ever-glowing scarlet letter—the token of sin—providing the only light.

Although most critics would not agree with such a reading, many would admit that the most obvious fact about *The Scarlet Letter* is its dramatization of the ironic conflict between appearance and reality. Romantic or sentimental readers, who see Hester and Dimmesdale as saved, ignore the fact that, if Hester is truly the able angel her community judges her to be and Dimmesdale the most powerful and saintly preacher in Boston, it is because their sin, unrepented, has made them prosper. Yet Hawthorne's dark Calvinist art could certainly not permit such a sunny view of the wages of sin. In truth, Hawthorne's crowds are almost always wrong. Fickle, protean, and cruel, they are remarkable for their obliquity. At the beginning of the novel, when all of our sympathies are engaged by the resplendent, proud Hester standing on the pillory, abandoned to the obscene exposure and violation of the crowds, we hate their monstrous sadism with her. We witness, too, their mindless glorification of the fainthearted Dimmesdale. We do not trust them when they allow Hester to move among them, forcing her to give up her dignity as isolato. We suspect their labeling of her as able angel; we suspect their canonization of Dimmesdale. Do we, then, at the end of the novel, join them as a congregation for Hester's new religion?

Hester, indeed, retains her dignity as an isolato, but at an unbearable price. The final scaffold scene is terrible in many ways, but perhaps most terrible because we suffer the corrosive separateness of the main figures. Dimmesdale is selfishly intent on dying in triumphant ignominy, and thus irritated by Hester's pleading for a reunion: "'Hush, Hester, hush'" (256); Hester is concerned about being promised an eternity with Dimmesdale and tries to call him back from death for assurance; Chillingworth is devastated because his victim is escaping him; and little Pearl, at last sincerely tearful, experiences one more trauma as the child born out of wedlock. Abused by young and old Puritans alike all of her seven years, Pearl is finally witness and participant in her father's awful death—this, her birthright as a human being, in Hawthorne's dreadful economy of salvation.

## II

Hawthorne's third-person narrator frequently offers the reader alternate explanations and interpretations of events as a way of avoiding the literal and suggesting the infinite complexity of human action.[4] Because Hawthorne thus habitually shrinks from committing himself, his voice is ironic. The irony has many levels. In "The Custom House," Hawthorne's concession to verisimilitude, we have a deliberately jolly narrator who gets great satisfaction out of pinioning his contemporaries. He makes the following comment, with remarkable clarity from the master of evasion, about Hester's angelic activities: "taking upon herself, likewise, to give advice in all matters, especially those of the heart; by which means, as a person of such propensities inevitably must, she gained from many people the reverence due to an angel, but, I should imagine, was looked upon by others as an intruder and a nuisance" (32). Hawthorne does not indicate clearly whether he wants the reader to think of Hester as an angel or an intruder. Yet the very fact that he offers the alternative of intruder (a Chillingworth-like activity for the aging Hester) weakens the statement about Hester's angelic qualities.

Although the narrative voice is far less lightsome in *The Scarlet Letter*, the reader continues to have the same problem of belief. In chapter 1 Hawthorne presents the reader with a rose from the wild rosebush in front of the prison, saying, "It may serve, let us hope, to symbolize some sweet moral blossom, that may be found along the track, or relieve the darkening close of a tale of human frailty and sorrow" (48). The reader is never again given anything even as solid as this symbolic moral blossom. After describing the interview between Hester and Mistress Hibbins, the narrator hedges, "if we suppose this interview . . . to be authentic, and *not a parable*" (117); in describing Hester's improved reputation with the crowd after seven years, "it is to the credit of human nature, that, *except where its selfishness is brought into play,* it loves more readily than it hates" (160); again on Hester, "society was inclined to show its former victim a more benign countenance than she cared to be favored with, or, *perchance, than she deserved*" (162); about the minister's encounter with Mistress Hibbins after his return from the forest, "old Mistress Hibbins, the *reputed* witch lady, *is said* to have been passing by" (221); and after the death of Dimmesdale and concerning the scarlet letter on his breast, *"The reader may choose among these theories"* (259).

The authorial voice of Hawthorne is much like the twentieth-century non-directive counselor, who avoids patent guidance to the patient but directs him anyway by the tone of voice he employs in repeating what he thinks the patient has said. Hawthorne usually refuses to be explicit or even leading, but the voice's alternative explanations, which involve not only the supernatural (such as Mistress Hibbins and the scarlet letter in the flesh of the minister's breast) but also the narrator-author's view of the characters, accumulate weight by their very repetition. In a subtle closure of aesthetic distance, however, moralizing authorial comments occur often in the forest scene and after, as Hawthorne becomes as explicit as he can be in his disapproval of Hester's and Dimmesdale's decision to leave together. We have the famous statement about sin: "And be the stern and sad truth spoken, that the breach which guilt has once made into the human soul is never, in this mortal state, repaired" (200–201). The weight of the narrative voice and the unvarying tone of that voice— solemn, melancholy, infinitely regretful—convinces us of Hawthorne's gloomy vision of life, a vision which necessitates the tragic conclusion of *The Scarlet Letter.*

Hawthorne set this, his most successful novel, in the Puritan era. The Puritan setting is certainly congenial to Hawthorne's blackness, as his most sensitive reader, Melville, was quick to point out. Although Hawthorne says in "The Custom House" that his Puritan ancestors would have nothing but scorn for him, he also boasts that "strong traits of their nature have intertwined themselves with mine" (10). Hawthorne makes his aesthetic distance from Puritan times and judgments explicit in the early part of the novel, especially in the first pillory scene, by his savage description of the crowd's watching of Hester; however, that distance dissolves almost imperceptibly as the novel continues. In the first part of the novel, it is comparatively simple to distinguish the Puritan ethic and its judgment of Hester from Hawthorne's. But by the time we are in the forest with Hester and Dimmesdale, having already been led through the labyrinths of Hester's mind and Dimmesdale's heart (in "Hester at her Needle" and "The Interior of a Heart"), Hawthorne's narrative voice becomes more insinuating about the latitude of Hester's thinking and the extravagances of Dimmesdale's feeling. Then the aesthetic distance between the nineteenth-century Hawthorne and a seventeenth-century Puritan divine is narrow indeed. In fact, there is a telescoping of the distance between Hawthorne as objective narrator, "telling" a story which took place two hundred years before, and Hawthorne as Puritan moralistic judge of his characters' actions. By the end of the novel, it seems that Hawthorne really speaks as the Puritan would, if a Puritan had the knowledge of the interior Hester and Dimmesdale that Hawthorne has. I am not suggesting that Hawthorne is a mouthpiece for Calvinist orthodoxy, but that the blight of man's evil, which Calvin reasoned about, was known to Hawthorne. It is this dark knowledge that compels the triple damnations of *The Scarlet Letter.*

The manner in which the aesthetic distance between Hawthorne and the characters and events of Puritan times gradually moves from objectivity to stern Calvinist judgment constitutes one of the most superb artistic achievements of the novel. It can pass undetected by a casual reader, but once noted, it is the signal clue to my interpretation of the novel as a masterpiece of Calvinist-ordained irony. For a third of the novel, Hawthorne's voice is strident against Puritan rigidity: concerning the beadle who led Hester to the scaffold—"This personage prefigured and represented in his aspect the whole dismal severity of the Puritanic code of law" (52); in regard to making an exhibition of Hester on the pillory—"There can be no outrage, methinks, against our common nature . . . no outrage more flagrant than to forbid the culprit to hide his face for shame" (55); about John Wilson, the elder clergyman who accuses Hester—"[he] had no . . . right . . . to step forth . . . and meddle with a question of human guilt, passion, and anguish" (65). In the second third of the novel (up to the second pillory scene, Dimmesdale's midnight vigil), Hawthorne examines the rebellious character of Hester, the capricious elf-child, Pearl, the growing demonism of Chillingworth, and the embattled interior of Dimmesdale's heart. The last third of the novel shows us "Another View of Hester" (chapter 13)—"The scarlet letter had not done its office" (166)—and the fateful interview between Hester and Dimmesdale in the forest. Here the words of Chillingworth to Hester, "By thy first step awry, thou didst plant the germ of evil; but, since that moment, it has all been a *dark necessity*" (174), reach an apodictic climax.

Hawthorne's authorial voice is infinitely sorrowing and doleful as it becomes more and more directive: "She [Hester] had wandered, without rule or guidance, in a moral wilderness; as vast, as intricate and shadowy, as the untamed forest. . . . Her intellect and heart had their home . . . in desert places . . . Shame, Despair, Solitude! These had been her teachers . . . and they had made her strong, *but taught her much amiss*" (199–200); "But Arthur Dimmesdale! *Were such a man once more to fall, what plea could be urged in extenuation of his crime? None*" (200). As Hester and Arthur decide to leave together, Hawthorne's voice condemns them: "It was the exhilarating effect . . . of breathing the wild, free atmosphere of an *unredeemed, unchristianized, lawless region*" (201). When Dimmesdale rejoices that he will be able to preach the Election Sermon before they leave together in their adulterous union, Hawthorne comments: "We have had, and may still have, worse things to tell of him; but none, we

apprehend, *so pitifully weak"* (215–16). Dimmesdale's demonic journey
from the forest back to his dwelling is one of Hawthorne's great scenes;
here, the closure of aesthetic distance between Hawthorne and his characters is complete. When Dimmesdale asks himself "'Have I *then sold myself . . . to the fiend,'*" Hawthorne responds: "The wretched minister! *He
had made a bargain very like it!* Tempted by a dream of happiness, he had
yielded himself with *deliberate choice,* as he had never done before, *to what
he knew was deadly sin.* And the *infectious poison of that sin had been thus
rapidly diffused throughout his moral system"* (222). On the day of the Election, Hester is described as already dead: "Her face . . . showed the
marble quietude. . . . It was like a mask; or rather, like the *frozen calmness
of a dead woman's features;* owing this dreary resemblance to the fact that
*Hester was actually dead,* in respect to any claim of sympathy, and had
departed out of the world with which she still seemed to mingle" (216).

After the bitter irony of Dimmesdale's dying public confession in
which he proclaims his own salvation but says he fears Hester's doom,
Hester and Pearl disappear. When Hester returns years later, she has
become a female Dimmesdale, but preaches a "new" revelation and "new"
truths. By this point, Hawthorne's authorial voice allows no possibility of
salvation for Dimmesdale or Hester.

The remarkable singleness of tone of *The Scarlet Letter*—sombre,
sorrowful, woeful, and anguished—has been universally acclaimed.
Hawthorne was concerned, however, that the unrelieved baleful climate
would displease some readers, and so he appended the more lightsome
"Custom House" to relieve it. In a letter to James T. Fields, he indicated
that the magnificent prose was a natural voice for him: "The Scarlet Letter
being all in one tone, I had only to get my pitch, and could then go on
interminably."[5] The diction that Hawthorne could write "interminably"
is dense, close, and dangerous for the unwary reader because of its deceptive lucidity. Only when Hawthorne was writing dialogue for Pearl,
the elfin child, did he encounter any difficulties. Granted that writing
speeches for a pixy seven year old would be arduous, Hawthorne had
particular problems with Pearl's chatter. Pearl's reply to her mother,
when the child refuses to cross the brook until Hester puts the scarlet
letter back on her breast and conceals her hair under her Puritan cap, is an
instance: "'Yes; now I will. . . . Now thou art my mother indeed! And I
am thy little Pearl!'" (211). The talk of the little Puritan children who
taunt Pearl is equally maladroit: "'Behold, verily, there is the woman of
the scarlet letter and, of a truth, moreover, there is the likeness of the

scarlet letter running along by her side! Come, therefore, let us fling mud at them!'" (102). If Hawthorne's daughter, Una, was the model for Pearl and these Puritan children, it is no wonder that Hawthorne questioned whether Una was his own child or a demon offspring.

### III

The symbolism in *The Scarlet Letter* is ubiquitous and provocative. There are all the mirrors and brooks in which the characters cannot bear to look because, in them, they see their real selves; the labyrinths of Hester's mind which her latitudinarian ideas cannot solve; the wild rose that we, as readers, hold and for which Pearl cries; the apple trees in the governor's garden (a new Eden) reputed to have been planted by the mythic first settler; the forest of natural, wild, and heathen evil; and the clearing of man-made, urbane, and civilized evil. There is the wild demonic laughter that only makes the tale more melancholy. And as the informing symbol of the novel, there is the scarlet letter itself, glowing ominously about Hester, Dimmesdale, Chillingworth, Pearl, and the Puritan crowd.

The mirror image in which a glass or brook or shield reveals the real and usually unsuspected horrid self to the viewer is one of Hawthorne's favorites; he uses it repeatedly in *The Scarlet Letter* and in other novels and short stories. Calvin uses the image in a similar way: "Thus the Law is a kind of mirror. As in a mirror we discover any stains upon our face, so in the Law we behold, first, our impotence; then, in consequence of it, our iniquity; and, finally, the curse, as the consequence of both."[6] Hester sees iniquity and a curse in the mirror of Pearl's eyes: "Once, this freakish, elfish cast came into the child's eyes, while Hester was looking at her own image in them . . . and, suddenly, . . . she fancied that she beheld, not her own miniature portrait, but another face in the small black mirror of Pearl's eye. It was a face, *fiend-like, full of smiling malice,* yet bearing the semblance of features that she had known full well" (97). When Pearl is to be catechized, at the age of three, by the governor and the ministers, she becomes entranced by a suit of armor, which serves as a mirror. Pearl urges her mother to look at herself: "Hester looked . . . and she saw that, owing to the particular effect of this convex mirror, the scarlet letter was represented in exaggerated and gigantic proportions, so as to be greatly the most prominent feature of her appearance. In truth, she seemed absolutely hidden behind it" (106). Later, Pearl's anger is reflected in the brook when she sees that her mother has cast away the scarlet letter. Dimmesdale also sees terrors in the mirror:

> He kept vigils . . . sometimes, viewing his own face in a looking glass, by
> the most powerful light which he could throw upon it. He thus typified
> the constant introspection wherewith he tortured, but could not purify
> himself. . . . Visions seemed to flit before him . . . more vividly, and
> close beside him, within the looking-glass. Now it was a herd of diabolic
> shapes, that grinned and mocked at the pale minister, and beckoned him
> away with them. (144–45)

Chillingworth, as fiend, is not free from the torture of his *real* self: "The
unfortunate physician, . . . lifted his hands with a look of horror, as if he
had beheld some frightful shape, which he could not recognize, usurping
the place of his image in a glass" (172).

In his own voice in "The Custom House" Hawthorne gives explicit
directions for the writing of a romance; firelight, moonlight, and a mirror
are necessary:

> This warmer light [firelight] mingles itself with the cold spirituality of the
> moonbeams, and communicates, as it were, a heart and sensibilities of
> human tenderness to the forms which fancy summons up. It converts them
> from snow-images into men and women. Glancing at the looking-glass, we
> behold—deep within its *haunted* verge—the smouldering glow of the half-
> extinguished anthracite, the white moonbeams on the floor, and a repeti-
> tion of all the gleam and shadow of the picture, *with one remove farther from
> the actual,* and nearer to the imaginative. (36)

Hawthorne holds this haunted mirror up to nature.

Labyrinth and maze imagery is used by Hawthorne to describe the
tortuous deeps of the minds of Hester and Dimmesdale. Calvin was also
fond of the image: "We should consider that the brightness of the Divine
Countenance . . . is a kind of labyrinth,—a labyrinth to us inextricable,
if the Word do not serve us as a thread to guide our path." And concerning the mind he writes: "let us remember that the human mind enters a
labyrinth whenever it indulges its curiosity," and also, "This evil
. . . must . . . be attributed to the School men, who have . . . drawn a
veil over Christ, to whom, if our eye is not directly turned, we must
always wander through many labyrinths."[7] Hester's mind is likened many
times to a labyrinth: "But Hester could not resolve the query [when Pearl
denies that the Heavenly Father sent her and questions where she comes
from], being herself in a *dismal labyrinth of doubt*" (98–99); "Hester
Prynne . . . wandered without a clew in the *dark labyrinth of mind*" (166).

In speaking to Chillingworth, Hester despairs of any solution to her triangular problem: "'There is no path to guide us out of this *dismal maze!* . . . There could be no good event for him [Dimmesdale], or thee [Chillingworth], or me, who are here wandering together in this *gloomy maze of evil,* and stumbling, at every step, over the guilt wherewith we have strewn our path!'" (173–74). Hawthorne devotes a whole chapter, "The Minister in a Maze," to describe the labyrinthine journey of evil that Dimmesdale makes, as he returns to Boston after conspiring in the forest with Hester to depart, in an adulterous union, for foreign shores.

Hawthorne uses flowers and weeds in obscene juxtaposition to suggest the admixture of evil in everything apparently beautiful. In front of the prison, described metaphorically as the Black Flower of civilization, in which Hester is initially confined, is an array of ugly weeds, "burdock, pig-weed, apple-peru, and such unsightly vegetation" (48) whose very names increase their offensiveness. Opposite the weeds is the "wild rose-bush, covered, in this month of June, with its delicate gems" (48), the rosebush that was rumored to have "sprung up under the footsteps of the sainted Ann Hutchinson" (48). The garden outside of Governor Bellingham's window attracts Pearl, but it, too, is an amalgam of flowery beauty and vegetable vulgarity: "Cabbages grew in plain sight; and a pumpkin vine, rooted at some distance, had run across the intervening space, and deposited one of its gigantic products directly beneath the hall-window; as if to warn the Governor that this great lump of vegetable gold was as rich an ornament as New England earth could offer him. There were a few rose-bushes, however, and a number of apple-trees" (106–07). Pearl cries for a red rose. Later she affirms to the governor and minister "that she had not been made at all, but had been plucked by her mother off the bush of wild roses, that grew by the prison door" (112), thus linking Hester further with the Antinomian Anne Hutchinson. I will discuss this link later.

The equivocal relationship of forest and clearing, so important to Hawthorne, often becomes a metaphor in *The Scarlet Letter.* The forest houses the "natural" evil—the Black Man, his cohorts, and their blasphemous covens; it is the favorite playground for the elf-child, Pearl; the scene of the adultery and the subsequent meeting place for Hester and Dimmesdale, who plan another adultery. Hester perceives "the mystery of the primeval forest," and in her mind "it imaged not amiss the moral wilderness in which she had so long been wandering" (183). But the

clearing is hardly better: it is the place of more "civilized" evil, of pillo-
ries, scaffolds, hypocrisy. The forest is the threatening, lowering habitat
of the devil; the clearing is the home of ruthless, smug, self-aggrandizing
human fanatics.

In "My Kinsman, Major Molineux," Hawthorne's most successful
device of horror is the use of laughter, grim, sadistic, and mirthless, to
signify the fearsomeness of Robin's journey into the Inferno-city; the
mocking laughter becomes more shrill until the climactic point, when
Robin joins in against his kinsman and laughs loudest of all. In another
tale, after Goodman Brown despairs, he laughs loud and long. Even in
"The Minister's Black Veil," the complexity of the Reverend Mr. Hooper's choice of the black veil is emphasized again and again by his gently
glimmering smile. In *The Scarlet Letter* over three dozen references to
smiles and laughter seem to have diabolic associations. Little Pearl laughs
much of the time, but her laughter is capricious and cruel, often directed
at Hester and the scarlet letter, making Hester wonder whether Pearl is a
human child. Roger Chillingworth's laughter is also fiendish, for when he
smiles "the spectator could see his blackness all the better for it" (169).
Dimmesdale laughs bitterly at himself during his scourging, "smiting so
much the more pitilessly, because of that bitter laugh" (144). He responds to his own visions of horror at midnight on the pillory with a
"great peal of laughter" (152), which is answered immediately by Pearl's
airy laugh. He smiles solemnly to Chillingworth (after he has discovered
Chillingworth is Hester's husband) and says ironically that he will pray for
him; thus, one devil will pray for another. Mistress Hibbins invites Pearl
to go for a ride with her some fine night to see her father, the Prince of the
Air, and then laughs "so shrilly that all the market place could hear her"
(242). Hester does not smile until she tosses away the scarlet letter, but
then displays a "radiant and tender smile" for Dimmesdale. In the forest
Hester and Dimmesdale smile together over Pearl, Hester a tender smile
and Dimmesdale an unquiet one. Then all of Hester's smiles stop
together, except for the one that Doom has for her. When she learns that
Chillingworth will accompany her and Dimmesdale on the voyage, her
spirit sinks "on beholding this dark and grim countenance of an inevitable
doom which . . . showed itself, with an unrelenting smile, right in the
midst of their path" (245). Hawthorne, thus, uses smiles and laughter
cogently throughout *The Scarlet Letter* to produce a gradually accelerating
sense of horror that culminates in the unrelenting smile of doom, a smile

most chilling and abhorrent. The appalling laughter that is humorless and dumbfounding is the apotheosis of Hawthorne's use of his ironic voice.

In *The Scarlet Letter* Hawthorne found a metaphor, as Melville did in the white whale, which is equal to all the demands his magnificent, fecund, grisly imagination could make. Never for a moment is the reader allowed to forget the smoking, glittering, singeing *A,* whose smouldering fire sears his eyes, ears, nose, throat; in fact, every part of his body— exposed or clad. When Hawthorne found the letter enclosed in an old document in the custom house, he claims to have "experienced a sensation not altogether physical, yet almost so, as of burning heat; and as if the letter were not of red cloth, but red-hot iron" (32). On Hester's breast "was that SCARLET LETTER, so fantastically embroidered and illuminated. . . . It had the effect of a spell, taking her out of the ordinary relations with humanity, and inclosing her in a sphere by herself" (53– 54). When Hester returns to prison after the humiliation of the pillory, "It was whispered . . . that the scarlet letter threw a lurid gleam along the dark passageway of the interior" (69). Chillingworth realizes the inevitability of Hester's fall which results in her wearing of the letter: "'from the moment when we came down the old church-steps together, a married pair, I might have beheld the bale-fire of that scarlet-letter blazing at the end of our path'" (74).

The letter imparts to Hester knowledge of others' secret sin that she prefers not to have: "she felt . . . then, that the scarlet letter had endowed her with a new sense. She shuddered to believe . . . that it gave her a sympathetic knowledge of the hidden sin in other hearts" (86). "The vulgar . . . averred that the symbol was not mere scarlet cloth, tinged in an earthly dye-pot, but was red-hot with infernal fire, and could be seen glowing all alight, whenever Hester Prynne walked abroad in the night-time" (87–88). Hawthorne does not discredit this notion of a phosphorescent letter, but writes: "And we must needs say, it seared Hester's bosom so deeply, that perhaps there was more truth in the rumor than our modern incredulity may be inclined to admit" (88).

Pearl, the elfin child, in her first infant awareness, identifies the scarlet letter with her mother and, as she grows older, persists in touching it or pelting it with flowers, despite the infinite "torture inflicted by the intelligent touch of Pearl's baby-hand" (96). Hester is so obsessed and beset by the letter that she clothes Pearl in crimson velvet: "It was the scarlet letter in another form; the scarlet letter endowed with life!" (102).

In her defiance of the governor and clergy who might take Pearl from her, Hester cries, "'Pearl punishes me too! See ye not, she is the scarlet letter?'" (113).

Dimmesdale, in his midnight vigil on the pillory, sees a meteor in the sky, which he immediately identifies, with his hands on his breast, as *this* scarlet letter: "beheld there the appearance of an immense letter,—the letter A,—marked out in lines of dull red light" (155). In his cosmic egotism, Dimmesdale interprets his sighting of the meteor as a kind of Special Providence intended for him alone; the general populace interprets the A as angel, signaling the death and election of Governor Winthrop.

Although the pariah of the community, Hester performs good works: she nurses the ill, sews burial shrouds, feeds the poor, becomes a self-ordained sister of mercy. The attitude of the people thus gradually changes towards her and her scarlet letter: "Elsewhere the token of sin, it was the taper of the sick-chamber" (161); "many people refused to interpret the scarlet A by its original signification. They said that it meant Able" (161). Some of the populace went further: "the scarlet letter had the effect of the cross on a nun's bosom" (163). But Hester was not pleased by this change in attitude. What Hawthorne finally tells us is that, despite its ominous power, "the scarlet letter had not done its office" (166). Despite Hester's latitudinarian wanderings of mind, she opposes any attempt by the magistrates to remove her stigmata: "'It lies not in the pleasure of the magistrates to take off this badge. . . . Were I worthy to be quit of it, it would fall away from its own nature'" (169).

Hester's once enforced and now elected alienation from society encourages her intellectual speculations. From a woman of the heart—passionate and luxurious—Hester becomes a woman of the head, and in the process loses her femininity. In the forest with Dimmesdale, Hester becomes womanly again for a short time. She flings the scarlet letter aside: "'With this symbol, I undo it all, and make it as it had never been'" (202). But her freedom is short-lived, as Pearl will not approach her until she replaces the letter: "She had flung it into infinite space!—she had drawn an hour's free breath!—And here again was the scarlet misery, glittering on the old spot. *So it ever is, whether thus typified or no, that an evil deed invests itself with the character of doom*" (211).

After the death of Dimmesdale, who exposes what is probably a scarlet letter branded into his breast, Hawthorne pretends to abandon the symbol: "We have thrown all the light we could on the portent, and

would gladly . . . erase its deep print out of our own brain; where long
meditation has fixed it in very undesirable distinctness" (250). But Hester
is as married to the letter as Dimmesdale was to his sin, and so when she
returns to her border cottage in Boston years after Dimmesdale's death,
she wears the scarlet letter. And the last sight Hawthorne gives to the
reader is that of the unshared graves of Hester and Dimmesdale, with a
tombstone that serves for both of them: "ON A FIELD, SABLE, THE LETTER
A, GULES" (264). Neither the reader nor Hawthorne, it seems, can "erase
its deep print" (259).

IV

Hawthorne's fondness for what Q. D. Leavis calls "public dramas,"[8] those
great, solemn, ritualistic spectacles that take place on a height, is never so
artistically managed as in the three pillory scenes that constitute the
beginning, middle, and end of *The Scarlet Letter*. Never again was Hawthorne able to structure a novel in this lean, taut, economical, and relentless way. Indeed, the tortured triangle of Dimmesdale, Hester, and
Chillingworth forms the scarlet *A* of the novel, which is composed of
Hester at its apex, since she is related through carnal knowledge to both
Dimmesdale and Chillingworth; Pearl as its bridge; and Chillingworth
and Dimmesdale as its vectors. These converge in the capital letter *A,*
which is the diagram of the novel as it is plotted in the three pillory
scenes. In the sunlight of the first pillory tableau, Hester has the principal
role "where she was made the common infamy, at which all mankind was
summoned to point its finger" (78). In this ritual set piece all mankind is
present, but only Dimmesdale and Chillingworth know anything; the
crowd below looks and sees not, hears and understands not.

The second pillory scene is Dimmesdale's parodic reenactment of
Hester's pilloried shame. It takes place in the moonlight and, instead of
the silence of the "thousand unrelenting eyes" (57) that fastened on Hester, there is the sound of Dimmesdale's shriek and his loud, mirthless
laugh. Hester, Pearl, and later Chillingworth join the minister on the
pillory in a pantomime of the earlier horror, and fallen nature, rather than
the Puritan crowd, comments on Dimmesdale's counterfeit confession by
burning a meteoric scarlet letter in the heavens.

From this point on, the third pillory scene is decreed, necessary, and
ineluctable. We only wait uneasily to see how and when it will come
about. The wages of sin is death and Puritan morality insists on public

confession. Dimmesdale's personal conscience tortures him for concealing his sin and his symbolic conscience torments him in the person of Chillingworth, the avenging God-devil who will not be mocked. Before the fury of the final scaffold scene and the ultimate horror for Dimmesdale and Hester, there is the delusory and chimerical scene in the forest. To toughen his theme of miserable humanity exhorted by the Calvinist Jehovah to suffer rigors that flesh cannot bear, Hawthorne has Hester and Dimmesdale meet in the forest under the aegis of nature—"the wild heathen Nature of the forest, never subjugated by human law, not illumined by higher truth" (203)—and here again, beguiled and cozened by the cheating promise of life, human affection, and sympathy, they ritually reenact the Fall a second time.

Like the first, the final pillory scene is played before all mankind; magistrates, commoners, Indians, and mariners assemble for the Election Day festival and are again given more than they bargained for. All who were present at the first pillory scene, except the compassionate young Puritan matron, who has died, gather again at the end. The procession halts at the foot of the pillory and again the crowd witnesses but does not comprehend the ritual drama. The actors take their ordained places and the last blasphemy is pronounced by Dimmesdale as he proclaims his own salvation (257).

Hester's continuing heresy of salvation through good works, compounded by her belief in the coming revelation of new truth, is the perennial delusion of a human being who tries to bargain with the Calvinist God, who accepts no payment except one's life. The lurid glow of the scarlet letter is the light at the end of the novel that is "gloomier than the shadow" (264), illuminating only layers of mystery and meaning. No wonder Hawthorne's voice "heaved" as he read the end of this tale to Sophia, who took to her bed with a headache.

## V

Although Hawthorne's characters in *The Scarlet Letter* are ritual figures, they nonetheless have a real life of their own. Hester is certainly Hawthorne's triumph. We are introduced to her in "The Custom House," when Hawthorne supposedly finds the faded scarlet letter and the ancient manuscript detailing her story. In the novel she appears before the reader when the prison door is flung open to reveal a beautiful, tall, elegant woman with lustrous dark hair and eyes, valiantly covering her shame with pride and dignity, and with scorn and a haughty smile for the greedy-eyed multitude. From the time of Hester's public abasement on the pillory, when she has all of the reader's sympathy, Hawthorne relentlessly develops her character so that she moves in her isolation, from the passionate, generous woman of the prodigal heart to the severe, joyless, do-gooding, unsexed zealot, who, at the end of the novel, announces new truths and a private revelation. The ruinous effect of sin and the Fall from Eden is recounted by Hawthorne in microscopic detail, as he probes Hester's mind and heart. Alone and alienated from love and friendship, with only her elfin child for companionship, she sinks into the quicksand of her untutored and freely speculative thoughts.

The scaffold of the pillory "was a point of view that revealed to Hester Prynne the entire track along which she had been treading, since her happy infancy" (58). From this unhappy height, Hester sees her entire past life, pleasantly uneventful until her marriage to the deformed old scholar, down to her present dreadful reality. We witness the bravery and audacity with which Hester faces her accusers, refuses to name the father of Pearl, and survives the racking interview with her husband, Chillingworth.

As Hester proceeds intrepidly to establish a home for Pearl in a remote cottage and to earn a meagre survival by her needlework, Hawthorne hints slyly at the iron chain which holds her in Boston. She could have left the town of her obloquy, but "there dwelt, there trode the feet of one with whom she deemed herself connected in a union, that unrecognized on earth, would bring them together before the bar of final judgment" (80). Although Hester compels herself to believe that "here . . . had been the scene of her guilt, and here should be the scene of her earthly punishment," this motive is only "half a truth, and half a self-delusion" (80).

However, her great skill at needlework, which Hawthorne believes is "the art—then, as now, almost the only one within a woman's grasp" (81), keeps her enough in the public gaze so that she is constantly tortured by the rich, the poor (whom she succors), and particularly the Puritan children. She comes to believe that the scarlet letter reveals to her the secret sins of others, and she begins to lose faith in the innocence of everyone: "Such loss of faith is ever one of the saddest results of sin" (87).

The magistrates and ministers decide, when Pearl is three, to remove her from her mother so that she can have a careful, Christian upbringing.

Hester responds like a lioness guarding her young, demanding that Dimmesdale speak for her: "'Look thou to it! I will not lose the child! Look to it!'" (113). Although Hester is often inclined to agree with the general opinion that Pearl is a "demon offspring," her child, both her torture and her comfort, is all she has.

The years pass and Hester becomes invaluable to the people of Boston; she cares for the sick and watches over the dying. Yet, by the scarlet letter, Hester's femininity is dessicated: "the light and graceful foliage of her character had been withered up by this red-hot brand, leaving a bare and harsh outline, which might have been repulsive" (163); "even the attractiveness of her person had undergone a similar change" as a "sad transformation" occurred and some "attribute had departed from her, the permanence of which had been essential to keep her a woman" (163). Hester's movement from passionate woman of the heart to the "marble coldness" of the woman of the head, desexes her: "her life had turned in a great measure, from passion and feeling, to thought" (164). And her thoughts are dangerous—"She assumed *a freedom of speculation . . .* which *our forefathers,* had they known of it, *would have held to be a deadlier crime than that stigmatized by the scarlet letter"* (164). Except for Pearl, "she might have come down to us in history, hand in hand with Ann Hutchinson . . . might . . . have been a prophetess . . . might, and not improbably, would, have suffered death from the stern tribunals of the period, for attempting to undermine the foundations of the Puritan establishment" (165). And thus, Hawthorne adumbrates the close of Hester's life when, without Pearl, she does indeed become a heretic, an unwomanly woman preacher (the "apostle of her own unquiet heart," like Catherine in "The Gentle Boy"), which is even more revolting to Hawthorne than a female scribbler.

In her loneliness and isolation Hester begins wondering whether any women should ever have been born: "Was existence worth accepting, even to the happiest among them? As concerned her own individual existence, she had long ago decided in the negative, and dismissed the point as settled. A tendency to speculation, though it may keep woman quiet . . . yet makes her sad. She discerns . . . such a hopeless task before her" (165). Hawthorne finally heaps all of his knowledge of Hester's vast moral deterioration into that famous, one sentence paragraph, *"The scarlet letter had not done its office"* (166). At one point, Hawthorne asks a typical, rhetorical question: "Had seven long years, under the torture of the scarlet letter, inflicted so much of misery, and wrought out no repentance? (177). Certainly the implied answer is yes. Hester has descended the circles of the Inferno from the "generous" sin of passion, to adultery, and to presumptuous, pharisaical, judgment of Chillingworth's sin as worse than her own.

On her way to meet Dimmesdale, Hester lies to Pearl about the meaning of the scarlet letter, "'I wear it for the sake of its gold thread'" (181), though she later admits that she met the Black Man once and the scarlet letter "'is his mark.'" She then enters the moral wilderness of the forest. Here, as one ghost greeting another,[9] she proposes the Arminian heresy of good works to comfort Dimmesdale, although he rejects it: "'Is there no reality in the penitence thus sealed and witnessed by good works? And wherefore should it not bring you peace?'" "'No, Hester, no! . . . There is no substance in it!'" (191–92). After Hester has made Dimmesdale forgive her for concealing Chillingworth's identity, they both rejoice that Chillingworth's sin has been blacker than theirs, and Hester speaks her great romantic excuse: "'What we did had a consecration of its own'" (195). Hester's heresy has now become well defined and encompasses her whole being, thus emblemizing Hawthorne's tragic view that the first excursion into evil, the first fall, must lead to successive and more deadly sins. She urges Dimmesdale to leave Boston, give up his name, begin anew, and "'Preach! Write! Act! Do any thing, save to lie down and die!'" (198). She eagerly promises to go away with him in what is now a fully conscious adulterous union and "Then, all was spoken!" (198).

Now Hawthorne analyzes Hester's "latitude of speculation," the region of "desert places" (199). The scarlet letter has been "her passport into regions where other women dared not tread" (199), regions that had, however, been trod by Anne Hutchinson. In fact, the similarities between Anne Hutchinson and Hester are in some ways remarkable.[10] Both were residents of Boston; both came afoul of the Rev. Mr. Wilson. Anne Hutchinson, a dark, handsome woman, worked as a nurse, as does Hester, and gathered the women together to preach her new revelation, as Hester does at the end of the novel. Anne Hutchinson did have a husband, yet, like most husbands of celebrated women "we may conclude" him to have been, Hawthorne comments, "a mere insignificant appendage of his mightier wife." Unlike Hester, Hutchinson was never accused of adultery, yet her dependence on inner light, inspiration, and emotionalism in religion is similar to Hester's emotional justification of her sin. And, finally, Anne Hutchinson was brought to trial for "traducing the ministers."[11]

Hester was taught by shame, despair, and solitude and "they had made her strong, but taught her much amiss" (200). At this point, Hawthorne's voice is totally directive. When Hester throws away the scarlet letter in an attempt to undo the past, we are certain of Hawthorne's dark apocalypse, even as Hester's sex, youth, and beauty return and she is convinced the ocean will swallow the scarlet letter that the forest cannot hide. When she resumes the red token to satisfy Pearl, her beauty and womanhood wither, never to return.

On Election Day Hester waits for Dimmesdale, and the scarlet letter reveals her "under the moral aspect of its own illumination" (226) with a face of "marble quietude," a "mask" or even the "frozen calmness of a dead woman's features" (226). When Dimmesdale appears and seems so absorbed and remote, she hardly knows him "in that far vista of his unsympathizing thoughts" (239) and "she could scarcely forgive him" (240). Shamed more by the crowd than at any time since she first put on the scarlet letter, Hester learns that Chillingworth is party to her plan to escape with Dimmesdale, and at last she sees the countenance of inevitable doom smiling at her.

Hester accepts the dying Dimmesdale's call to her from the pillory "slowly, as if impelled by inevitable fate and against her strongest will" (252). Her question to Dimmesdale, who is eaten alive by his spiritual pride, is sharp with her own fear, "'Shall we not spend our immortal life together?'" (256). In her reasoning they should be able to spend eternity together, "'Surely, surely, we have ransomed one another, with all this woe'" (256), but this again is the heresy of works, which affronts the Calvinism in which Dimmesdale believes.[12] Dimmesdale rejects Hester's heterodoxy finally and completely, "'The law we broke!—the sin here so awfully revealed!—let these alone be in thy thoughts! I fear! I fear!'" (256), and then, ironically, he announces his own salvation, a heresy of which even Hester had not dreamed.[13]

Many years after the death and damnation of Dimmesdale, Hester returns to New England. Hawthorne says she returns to "a more real life. . . . Here had been her sin; here, her sorrow; and here was *yet to be* her penitence" (262–63). Hawthorne never says that such penitence occurs. Women come to Hester with their problems, those of "wounded,

wasted, wronged, misplaced or erring and sinful passion" (263) and demand to know "why" they are "so wretched" (263). Hester comforts and
counsels them and, still the heretic, assures them "of her firm belief" that
*"a new truth would be revealed,* in order to establish the whole relation
between man and woman on a surer ground of mutual happiness."
Although earlier in life Hester "had vainly imagined that she herself
might be the destined prophetess," she knows now that "any mission of
divine and mysterious truth" will be confided to a woman "lofty, pure,
and beautiful," not one who is sorrow- or sin-stained, but one who can
show "how sacred love should make us happy, by the truest test of a life
successful to such an end" (263). So proudly clasping her scarlet letter,
Hester persists as the precursor of the prophetess. She preaches of the
coming happy life of love, which for Hawthorne seems to be the hopeless,
sinful, utopian dream of her labyrinthine mind, the dream of a new
sexuality. Here Hester has assumed Dimmesdale's office as preacher, but
in her own dispensation—her heterodoxy is so like that of Margaret
Fuller's that it would mortally offend not only every Calvinist, but every
orthodox Christian. Hawthorne makes sure that Hester goes to her grave
damned under the sombre light of the scarlet letter.

Dimmesdale, attenuated and pale, clutching his sin to his heart, is
much more bloodless than Hester and we are more easily convinced of his
selfishness and pride. After the first pillory scene and under the wary eye
of Chillingworth, Dimmesdale's health declines while his eminence as a
divine burgeons. Unlike Hester, Dimmesdale is no heretic until he becomes possessed: "In no state of society would he have been what is called
a man of liberal views; it would always be essential to his peace to feel the
pressure of a faith about him, supporting, while it confined him within its
iron framework" (123).

He is much weaker than Hester, and although handsome, "with a
white, lofty and impending brow, large, brown, melancholy eyes, and a
mouth which, unless when he forcibly compressed it, was apt to be
tremulous" (66), he lacks both moral and physical courage. In the first
pillory scene, his plea to Hester to reveal her partner in sin is calculated to
appeal to her generosity of heart. She responds, as he knows she will, by
refusing to name him. But she threatens him with the revelation of their
partnership in sin when the magistrates and elder minister try to take
Pearl from her, and under this duress, he pleads eloquently for her.
Dimmesdale envies Hester because he feels she suffers less than he, since

she must wear her scarlet token openly, while he must conceal his pain and "cover it all up" in his heart, where, Hawthorne implies, his searing pain and guilt have carved a scarlet letter all his own. This secret wound compels him always to press his hand over his heart.

Dimmesdale, in his rich, sweet voice, tells his congregation again and again of his own pollution, but they only say amongst themselves that this poor, suffering, emaciated man is a saint on earth. His fasts, vigils, and scourgings cannot purify him, and he, the "untrue man," becomes, like the universe, a shadow: "To the untrue man, the whole universe is false,—it is impalpable—it shrinks to nothing within his grasp" (145).

Hawthorne shows that Dimmesdale is too infirm and craven for crime: "Crime is for the iron-nerved, who have their choice to endure it, or, if it press too hard, to exert their fierce and savage strength for a good purpose, and fling it off at once! This feeble and most sensitive of spirits could do neither, yet continually did one thing or another, which intertwined, in the same inextricable knot, the *agony of heaven-defying guilt and vain repentance*" (148). Even Dimmesdale's moonlit counterfeit confession on the pillory is cowardly; he shrieks aloud and then trembles lest he be discovered. He interprets the meteoric *A* in the sky only in terms of his own egotism: he "had extended his egotism over the whole expanse of nature, until the firmament itself should appear no more than a fitting page for his soul's history and fate" (155). In his inverted spiritual pride, he sees the meteor as a cosmic acknowledgment of him and his adultery alone, although Hester is with him.

Dimmesdale's question to Hester in the forest, "'Art thou in life?'" (189), indicates that he has been so completely self-absorbed in playing with his sin that he is unaware of whether Hester is alive or dead. In his total self-regard, he not only forgets his partner in sin but his God as well. However, after refusing to be comforted by Hester's heretical statement that good works can atone for sin, he does admit: "'Of penance I have had enough! Of penitence there has been none!'" (192).

He presumptuously tells Hester how happy she is because she wears her letter openly while his "'burns in secret.'" His hysterical response to Hester's revelation of the identity of Chillingworth leads Hester to believe that he is mad and that, hereafter, there could only be "that eternal alienation from the Good and True, of which madness is perhaps the earthly type" (193). Dimmesdale finally forgives Hester for her silence about Chillingworth and they both heretically delight in the fact that

Chillingworth is a worse sinner than they are: "'he has violated, in cold blood, the sanctity of a human heart. Thou and I, Hester, never did so!'" (195). We realize that this is patent self-deception. But, still a Puritan, Dimmesdale's only response to Hester's great romantic alibi for their sin is, "'Hush, Hester!'"

After Hester assuages his greatest concern, that Chillingworth will reveal their secret sin, Dimmesdale selfishly asks her to "'Think for me, Hester! Thou art strong. Resolve for me!'" (196). The voice of the narrator becomes insistent here to determine what possible extenuation there could be for Dimmesdale's second fall: "None! . . . And be the stern and sad truth spoken, that the *breach which guilt has once made into the human soul is never, in this mortal state, repaired*" (200–201). Dimmesdale soon revives at the thought of escaping with Hester: "It was the exhilarating effect— upon a prisoner just escaped from the *dungeon of his own heart*—of breathing the wild, free atmosphere of an *unredeemed, unchristianized, lawless region*" (201). And Dimmesdale blasphemously feels that he has put on the new man, he is resurrected in Hester: "'I seem to have flung myself . . . down upon these forest-leaves, and to have risen up all made anew'" (201–02). Trembling still, Dimmesdale is terrified to meet Pearl (he confesses that children fear him and weep bitterly if he takes them in his arms), and her washing off of his unwelcome kiss does nothing to reassure him. After making sure that he and Hester will not leave until he can preach the Election Sermon, Dimmesdale hurries back to the village.

Hawthorne's account of Dimmesdale's journey ("The Minister in a Maze") is a triumphant dramatization of his vision that the evil-hearted see only evil. Dimmesdale, risen up a new man in Hester, has sudden strength and, diabolically, he leaps and bounds through the paths to the town, convinced that everything and everyone else has changed. But it is he who is transformed: "The minister's own will, and Hester's will, and the fate that grew between them, had wrought this transformation . . . nothing short of a total change of dynasty and moral code" (217). He is constantly "incited to do some strange, wild, wicked thing . . . with a sense that it would be at once involuntary and intentional" (217). He wants to utter a blasphemy about the communion supper to the deacon; give an unanswerable argument against the immortality of the soul to an old devout widow; drop a "germ of evil" in the "tender bosom" of a young virgin; teach wicked words to Puritan children; and exchange improper jests and oaths with a drunken seaman. He wonders whether he is mad or

possessed and then Mistress Hibbins shows she knows what he has done in
the forest. He wonders whether he has sold his soul to the devil and the
narrator answers for him: "he had made a bargain very like it. Tempted by
a dream of happiness, he had yielded himself, with *deliberate* choice, as he
had never done before, to what he knew was deadly sin" (222). When he
sees the pages of his unfinished Election Sermon, Dimmesdale knows his
old self is gone and "Another man had returned out of the forest" (223).
He has become wiser and has a "knowledge of hidden mysteries" that his
former simple self did not have, and "A bitter kind of knowledge that!"
(223). Dimmesdale, the new man, has become a devil and a devil-
worshipper. After telling Chillingworth he needs no more drugs and then
eating with a ravenous appetite, he writes feverishly all night on his
Election Sermon and "fancied himself inspired," as indeed he is—by
Satan.

On the day of the Election, Dimmesdale still has his great diabolic
energy but seems withdrawn. Mistress Hibbins proclaims that Dimmesdale is signed and sealed to the Black Man, but the narrator declares that
his demonic preaching has never been so eloquent or so awe-inspiring, and
"never, on New England soil, had stood the man so honored by his mortal
brethren as the preacher" (250).

As Dimmesdale crawls up the scaffold steps to the pillory, exhausted
by his sermon, he calls for Hester's strength, "'but let it be guided by the
will which God hath granted me!'" (253). After completely shriveling
Hester by asking, "'Is not this better . . . than what we dreamed of in
the forest?'" (254), he addresses the people of New England with a great
shriek and tremor: "'behold me here, *the one sinner of the world!'" (254).*
Not content to be a great sinner, Dimmesdale has to be *the one sinner of the
world.* Thus, the rigid Puritan speaks his dying words of incomparable
spiritual pride and bares his breast to the multitude, triumphantly. Selfish in death, as in life, he gives Hester no assurance of God's mercy to
her. He is sure only of God's mercy for himself, when he declares that
without all of the agonies he has endured, *"I had been lost forever"* (257).
But he dies damned, proclaiming his own election, the greatest heresy of
all for a Calvinist.

Most of the people of New England did not believe the minister any
more when he proclaimed himself the one sinner of the world than they
had ever believed him when he told of his sins Sabbath after Sabbath.
Hawthorne, however, does not hesitate to damn the minister. When the

narrator tells us of the attempts by Dimmesdale's devotees to explain his dramatic death as parabolic, the narrative voice proclaims unequivocally that "proofs, clear as the mid-day sunshine on the scarlet letter, established him [Dimmesdale] a false and sin-stained creature of the dust" (259). With tragic apprehension, the reader quakes in pity for Dimmesdale's triumphant ignominy and in fear for his soul, which, according to Dimmesdale's own doctrine, has been delivered to the devil. Ironically, in the forest Hester says to Dimmesdale, "'Do any thing, save to lie down and die!'" (198), and yet this is precisely what the poor, weak minister does.

That Chillingworth is damned everyone agrees. We first know of him when Hester, on the pillory, has a flashback of her life. When a personage similar to Hester's memory of Chillingworth suddenly appears in the gaping crowd, fixing his eyes penetratingly upon her while a "writhing horror twisted itself across his features, like a snake gliding over them" (61), the reader becomes nearly as apprehensive as Hester, as the snake image, of course, suggests diabolism.

We are not surprised, then, when Chillingworth, as he chooses to call himself now, turns up at the prison to minister to Hester and her infant, after the horrendous ordeal of their public exposure. Hester soon learns that her husband is not going to settle for any ordinary revenge. His purpose is darker, and although Hester will not give him the name of her partner in adultery, he assures her, "'Sooner or later, he must needs be mine!'" (75). Exacting a vow from her never to reveal his identity, Chillingworth leaves her, smiling like the Black Man.

Chillingworth never becomes entirely a cardboard villain, but he is clearly a devil figure who becomes more and more fiendish as the novel progresses. He becomes an intimate and confidante of the minister and, ironically, the people of Boston rejoice that their beloved, saintly pastor has his private physician to safeguard his obviously failing health. Even early in the novel Chillingworth's external appearance has changed; his features have grown uglier, and "his dark complexion seemed to have grown duskier, and his figure more misshapen" (112).

The physician manages to get a room in the same house with Dimmesdale and keeps him under observation at all times, administering potions and tormenting him with subtle accusations that secret guilt is the foundation of his disease. Chillingworth, in his search for "truth," has become a monster—driven by a "fierce . . . necessity. . . . He now dug into the poor clergyman's heart . . . like a sexton delving into a grave . . . likely to find nothing save mortality and corruption. Alas for his own soul, if these were what he sought!" (129). This image recalls Hawthorne's description of the unforgivable sin, the cold and clinical violation of another's heart. Chillingworth admits to Hester that he has become a fiend when she tells him that she must reveal his true identity to Dimmesdale. She asks him for forgiveness, but he denies having the power to pardon: "'My old faith, long forgotten, comes back to me, and explains all that we do, and all we suffer. *By thy first step awry, thou didst plant the germ of evil; but since that moment, it has all been a dark necessity'"* (174). This is pure Calvinism, but Chillingworth has assumed the role of devil-God who judges sinful man. This assumption of the role of religious anti-hero, the Satan-Jehovah, is consummated when he tries passionately to persuade Dimmesdale to come down from the pillory: "'I can yet save you!'" (252).

Following the death of his victim, Dimmesdale, Chillingworth "withered up, shrivelled away, and almost vanished from sight, like an uprooted weed that lies wilting in the sun" (260). There is no one to mourn Chillingworth, the God-devil, who blasphemously preordained another Fall and swept his victims with him into the pit.

Despite all of Hester's heresies, she is a good enough Puritan to know "that her deed had been evil; she could have no faith, therefore, that its result would be for good" (89–90). Pearl, supposedly modeled on Hawthorne's daughter, which was for poor Una a dubious distinction, is a nauseating child, forever taunting her mother about her scarlet letter and cavorting about elfishly. Much has been written of Pearl and about her symbolic function in the novel. Yet nothing has been said about the enormous price paid for Pearl's humanity. Before Dimmesdale's death, Pearl is portrayed as an elf, a witch-child, a demon offspring, as wilder than the wild Indian, as a child of the Lord of Misrule, a bird of scarlet plumage, a fairy skipping, as dancing and frisking and shimmering like a diamond, and as the living scarlet letter. She is the abrasive and sorrowful reminder of Hester's sin. Her laughter is diabolic and the only other human being except Hester and Dimmesdale that she seems to converse with is Mistress Hibbins, the witch who knows all about Pearl and senses the evil connection between them.

Pearl refuses to be catechized as a Christian child and announces that she "had not been made at all, but had been plucked by her mother off the bush of wild roses that grew by the prison door" (112). Interestingly, the wild rosebush is reputed to have "sprung up under the footsteps of the sainted Ann Hutchinson" (48), whose antinomian heresy was to believe that God inspired her to distinguish "between the chosen of man and the sealed of heaven,"[14] in other words, to determine the elect from the reprobate. To presume knowledge of election is what Calvin called the "immense abyss."[15] All of this knowledge Anne Hutchinson accomplished by inward vision and great latitude of mind. If the wild rosebush is the offspring of Anne Hutchinson, it is not so difficult to identify Pearl as the blossom of the wild rosebush which Hester produced through her relationship with Dimmesdale, and which she justifies, heretically, as "consecrated."

Pearl's relationship with nature differs from that of the other characters: "The great black forest . . . became the playmate of the lonely infant" (204). Pearl finds the choicest berries; birds do not fly from her; squirrels and foxes play with her and recognize "a kindred wildness in the human child" (205). Unable to relate to the fallen human beings of her community, Pearl is at home only with "wild heathen Nature" (203).

The humanity of Pearl is achieved at a prodigious cost—not less than everything. Hawthorne says Pearl "wanted . . . a grief that should deeply touch her, and thus humanize and make her capable of sympathy" (184). The grief comes and is incalculable; her mother has been forced all of Pearl's life to be the object of scorn and calumny in the community and has been exiled from its midst except as nurse or seamstress; Pearl has had to be jeered at by the Puritan children and adults and present at every scorching pillory scene; and finally, her father must die in pride, publicly shrieking his "triumphant ignominy" and be damned for the Pearl of great price. But Hawthorne's irony does not slake—the final irony is that Pearl, through Chillingworth's will, is the richest heiress of the New World and "had the mother and child remained here, little Pearl, at a marriageable period of life, might have mingled her wild blood with the lineage of the devoutest Puritan among them all" (261). "Human kind cannot bear very much reality," and so Hawthorne has Pearl escape the recently corrupted Eden of the New World and mingle her wild blood with an aristocrat of the Old World and the old dispensation.

Although Hester, Dimmesdale, Chillingworth, and Pearl are the major characters in the novel, Hawthorne's crowds become almost an equally important ritual figure. They do not function, however, as a chorus for the author's view because they are almost always wrong in their judgment of the characters. They feel, for example, that Hester becomes an Able-Angel; the reader knows she is stumbling into spiritual pride. The crowd is convinced that Dimmesdale is the holiest and purest minister in New England; the reader knows he is a whited sepulchre. Most members of the crowd are convinced that Chillingworth is using his physician's skills to help Dimmesdale recover his health; the reader knows that Chillingworth is tormenting Dimmesdale. It seems, in fact, that Hawthorne's most scathing and savage irony is reserved for the crowds and their smug, self-righteous presence.

At the beginning of *The Scarlet Letter,* the men are masked by their beards and steeple-crowned hats and some of the women are hooded (this same description of the crowd occurs in Hawthorne's sketch of Anne Hutchinson). The general impression is of furtiveness and covert hostility. Then Hawthorne describes the women more precisely as coarse beef-and-ale wives, terrifyingly vicious toward Hester. Their hostility to Hester is manifested in their eagerness for her to receive the death penalty. They envy her beauty and resent her hauteur. They are fearful of her and suspicious of their own husbands, since the paternity of little Pearl is a mystery they surely do not want solved too close to their own homes. The men are surly and curious about Hester, but not as menacing as the women, who feel Hester has shamed their sex. Only one young wife has compassion for Hester, but Hawthorne makes sure that she dies young, so that she does not appear in the final scene. Tenderness of heart does not survive long in the harsh Calvinist climate of seventeenth-century New England.

The cruelty of the crowd towards Hester worsens after her first pillory exposure, but then softens as she becomes needed as a seamstress and nurse in the village and assumes a humility she does not feel. However, even the poor, whom Hester feeds, revile her. By the time Pearl is seven, Hester has "general regard" in the community, but Hawthorne again warns us about the judgment of the crowd: "Society was inclined to show its former victim a more benign countenance than she cared to be favored with, or, perchance, than she deserved" (162).

In a perversion of Calvin, all of the crowd are more and more convinced that Dimmesdale is a saint because he wears his face of sanctity "to the multitude." After his midnight vigil on the pillory, Dimmesdale ironically "preaches a discourse which was held to be the richest and most powerful, and the most replete with heavenly influences, that had ever proceeded from his lips . . . more souls than one, were brought to the truth by the efficacy of that sermon" (157). Ferociously, Hawthorne describes the crowd, which he holds in Shakespearean contempt: "Into this festal season of the year . . . the Puritans compressed whatever mirth and public joy they deemed allowable to *human infirmity;* thereby so far dispelling the customary cloud, that, for the space of a single holiday [the Election], they appeared scarcely more grave than most other communities at a period of general affliction" (230).

The crowd is rapturous over Dimmesdale's demonically inspired Election Sermon: "According to their united testimony, never had man spoken in so wise, so high, and so holy a spirit, as he spoke that day; nor had inspiration ever breathed through mortal lips more evidently than it did through his. . . . It was as if an angel . . . had shaken his bright wings over the people for an instant . . . and had shed down a shower of golden truths upon them" (248–49). When Dimmesdale mounts the pillory for his last great scene, the crowd believes a miracle could take place: "nor would it have seemed a miracle too high to be wrought for one so holy, had he ascended before their eyes" (252).

After the minister's death on the pillory, the multitude can only emit a "murmur that rolled so heavily after the departed spirit" (257). There were any number of conflicting stories, many of them flattering to Dimmesdale. When Hawthorne says that one of the "morals that press upon us from the poor minister's miserable experience" is "Be true! Be true! Be true! Show freely to the world, if not your worst, yet some trait whereby the worst may be inferred" (26), he is undoubtedly thinking of the crowd, the New England world, and their quixotic judgments: "When an uninstructed multitude attempts to see with its eyes, it is exceedingly apt to be deceived" (127).

Misunderstanding Dimmesdale's life and his death, the crowd at the end of the novel is just as wrong about Hester as they were when they condemned her in the first pillory scene. Now she is seen as the angel of the new revelation; instead of putting her to death for her heresy, which Hawthorne suggests they would have done had they understood, the crowd has elevated her to angel. Thus, Hawthorne's manipulation of the crowd is another manifestation of his belief in man's depravity and his Calvinist-ordained irony.

## VI

Hawthorne was aware that in *The Scarlet Letter* he had written "positively a h—l-f-d story, into which I found it almost impossible to throw any cheering light,"[16] yet the closure of aesthetic distance between his narrative voice and the action of the novel may have been unconscious. His judging of characters and their actions by a submerged Calvinist morality decrees the irony that pervades this greatest of Hawthorne's novels.

In *The Scarlet Letter,* the fearsome, damnatory dogmas on the grim reformer of Geneva pervade the work, and it would be easy to acknowledge that, since Hawthorne was writing a romance set in Puritan times, he was merely being true to history. It is possible to make this assumption in the early part of the novel when the narrative voice is critical of Puritan severity and rigidity, and throughout the novel when the narrator specifically pinions the capricious, mercurial crowd. However, to ignore the enlarging solemn and judgmental voice of the narrator as he delves into the minds and hearts of his increasingly sinful characters is to evade and wink at Hawthorne's rueful and unavowed allegiance to Calvinist tenets. More than any other American artist, Hawthorne reaped a golden harvest from the Calvinist vision: the soul-grilling tension between sinful, guilty man and his infinitely requiring, threatening, and menacing God.

In "The Custom House" we read of Hawthorne's anxiety over the opinion his Puritan ancestors would have of him and his vocation. He is certain that they would condemn him completely as a "writer of story-books," an idler, no better than a fiddler. They would murmur: "'what mode of glorifying God . . . may that be?'" His answer, "And yet, let them scorn me as they will, strong traits of their nature have intertwined themselves with mine" (10), suggests how seriously he valued their standards and beliefs. Hawthorne's discomfort with his desire for fame as an author is totally Calvinistic.[17] Instances of Hawthorne's completely assimilated, native Calvinism and of the irony that results from his inability to acknowledge it fully abound in the novel.[18]

Hawthorne begins and ends this, his greatest work, with a view of the cemetery near the prison, ironically the first two apportionments needed in the New Eden. Hester moves out of the community prison, only to enter the prison of her labyrinthine mind and finally, the prison of the grave. Dimmesdale, with Chillingworth in relentless tow, elects quarters adjacent to the burial ground, and wonders, as he contemplates the graveyard during his agonies of self-attack, whether grass will grow on his grave. Finally, he is able to abandon the prison of his own body for the grave which, in our last view of the cemetery, we see as sunken, not grassy, and shadowed by the slate tombstone bearing the scarlet letter. *The Scarlet Letter* has, as Hawthorne tells us in chapter 1, "the darkening close of a tale of human frailty and sorrow" (48).

Part of the ambiguity of the novel's ending derives from Hawthorne's allowing us to judge the characters as human beings, as very fallible but, at least, in Hester's case, attractive. At the same time, he implies the damning judgment on them that, in his rigorous way, he makes us feel they deserve. The crowd does not judge Hester and Dimmesdale accurately because they do not know the real story as we do. If we were to judge the characters as the crowd does, there would be no ambiguity in the novel. The fact that Hawthorne sees his characters ironically as damned does not make us feel less sorry for them; rather we are unspeakably sorry for them.

The critic Austin Warren says he is at a loss to interpret why the theme of Dimmesdale's Election Day Sermon is "the high destiny of New England."[19] It seems to me that in his sermon (as reported by Hawthorne) Dimmesdale shows eloquently and prophetically that the high destiny of New England is its role as the New Eden, "for the newly gathered people of the Lord" (249). How ironic is this "high destiny" when even its most saintly minister and its new angel, Hester Prynne, have just ritually reenacted the Fall of man and the expulsion from Eden! Hawthorne's most heartfelt, regretful, and tragic conviction is that poor humanity is indeed damned.

And so, *A* is for Apple, the apple bitten to the core, "the fruit whose mortal taste brought death into this world and all our woe, with loss of Eden." And Dimmesdale and Hester, as nineteenth-century Adam and Eve, are able to escape the pain of postlapsarian existence only by death and damnation. Still Hawthorne and his readers dream vainly of innocence—of Adam and Eve guileless in Eden, "the unraised hand calm, the apple unbitten in the palm."[20]

THE HOUSE OF THE SEVEN GABLES

# *"An Uncontrollable Mischief"*

---

I

In 1850, on beginning *The House of the Seven Gables* less than six months
after the publication of *The Scarlet Letter,* Hawthorne determined to write
a sunny romance with a happy ending.[1] He was appalled always at what
he considered his hell-fired stories, especially *The Scarlet Letter,* which he
tried to rescue from its wonderfully grim singleness of tone by the personal preface of "The Custom House." Desperate for money and popular
success and determined not to give Sophia another sick headache (which
she got when he read her the last of *The Scarlet Letter*), Hawthorne valiantly tried to become the cheery narrator of a tale of inherited guilt and
sin. And yet, ironically, despite Hawthorne's preference for *The House of
the Seven Gables, The Scarlet Letter* has always outsold it, and readers have
always shown a preference for his more obviously sombre and tragic work.

In his preface Hawthorne explains that the Romance, "as a work of
art, sins unpardonably, so far as it may swerve aside from the truth of the
human heart" (21). Writing rapidly (the composition of *The House of the
Seven Gables* took only five months), he realized as he came to the end of
the novel that, even given the latitude of the Romance, it was difficult for
him not to "sin unpardonably." Despite the novel's *apparently* happy
ending—with the union of Holgrave-Maule and Phoebe Pyncheon and
the departure of the young couple, along with Clifford and Hepzibah,
from the old seven-gabled house to the idyllic country home—there is,
beneath the sunshine, the prevailing ironic *reality* of Hawthornean gloom.
Some of his readers might have been deceived about this ending, but
Hawthorne was not and he wrote to his publisher James T. Fields
(November 29, 1850) as he was trying to finish the book, "It darkens
damnably towards the close, but I shall try hard to pour some setting
sunlight over it" (xxii). This setting sunlight only illuminates Hawthorne's failure to answer his own question:

> We are left to dispose of the awful query, whether each inheritor of the
> property—conscious of wrong, and failing to rectify it—did not commit

68

anew the great guilt of his ancestor, and incur all its original responsibilities. And supposing such to be the case, would it not be a far truer mode of expression to say, of the Pyncheon family, that they inherited a great misfortune, than the reverse? (20)

The plot, resolved by an embarrassingly patent "happy ending," only signifies that Hawthorne is answering his own query with a tacit yes.

Hawthorne's letter to his friend Evert Duyckinck (April 27, 1851), written a couple of weeks after the publication of *The House of the Seven Gables,* expresses his frustration: "In writing it, I suppose I was illuminated by my purpose to bring it to a prosperous close; while the gloom of the past threw its shadow along the reader's pathway" (xxii). The shadow of the past is at once Hawthorne's glory and his failure. In the Hawthorne moral economy—Calvinist and damnatory—no sunshine is possible. The guilt of the fathers does descend upon the progeny and the final inheritance of money and country house here is an ill-disguised evasion of the theme of the novel. The characters move away from the house, the moral focus-locus of the story, but will continue to live on the judge's blood money at a country house built with the same tainted money which Hepzibah has eschewed all of her impoverished life. The death of the judge has no salvific effect on his money and the departure from the old house is not a redemptive act but a violent wrenching of the structural center and integrity of the romance. There is no expiation of the ancestral crime; the house remains intact. We are left with the central characters now materially prosperous but morally static, including Holgrave-Maule who has made an instantaneous conversion from giant transcendentalist roamer to placid country squire. The novel ends in "setting sunshine," but the afterglow is ominous and frightening when we realize that the four main characters will continue to live on the cursed inheritance. At least Hawthorne saved the novel from melodrama by not burning down the house of the seven gables (much as he liked fires) or making it split apart, as Poe does his house of Usher.

Therefore, at the end of the novel, despite the pastoral setting, the contented clucking of the Pyncheon chickens and the benevolent presence of Uncle Venner, the sensitive reader is aware that Hawthorne's query— "What is there so ponderous in evil, that a thumb's bigness of it should outweigh the mass of things not evil, which were heaped into the other scale!" (231)—has not been answered but only postponed. We fear, as Hawthorne does his best, with his multiple Eden references to make us fear, that we are going to be mute witnesses to another Fall enacted by the witless but sunny Phoebe and the daguerreotypist descendant of the wizard Maule. *The House of the Seven Gables* ends in horror, not happiness, no matter how carefully Hawthorne tried to disguise it with his manipulative ending. Indeed, he only gets everyone out of the old oaken house to a new Eden ripe for cataclysm.

Clifford, the old sybarite, a selfish, childlike seeker after beauty, will finally wither in the new Eden. Hepzibah, still scowling under her turban and now accepting the money she has refused for over thirty years, will stay in the shade of the garden after her life of useless sacrifice and—wonderful irony—keep hidden from the brother for whom she suffered so much because he cannot bear the sight of her. Phoebe, Eve-like and uncomprehending, will sing in the garden with her cold, reserved Adam-Maule until her little paradise is rocked by another Fall. We have no confidence that Holgrave's newest mask as country squire will be more permanent than his earlier ones of teacher, transcendentalist, dentist, peddler, author, daguerreotypist, and social reformer. In mining for his identity, Holgrave has struck gold, which, in Hawthornean terms, is always the equivalent of blood and evil. Uncle Venner gives up his freedom to become the object of the calculated and rather patronizing benevolence of the Pyncheon-Maules, for which he probably will have to feel and express more gratitude than the almshouse would exact. Ned Higgins, Hawthorne's representative of childhood depravity, has been paid off by Hepzibah to people his interior with a menagerie such as Noah took into the ark.

Dixey, an interested observer of the scene, watches with a friend the changing fortunes of the occupants of the house. "'Old Maid Pyncheon has been in trade . . . and rides off in her carriage with a couple of hundred thousand. . . .' 'Pretty good business!' quoth the sagacious Dixey. Pretty good business!'" (318–19). This is hardly a comment that the thunder-smitten Hawthorne would want the reader to share even though he tried to write himself out of the black hole that his heart dictated—a tragic ending—to please the public, to please his wife, to sell more books, to do "pretty good business."

## II

A careful examination of the text of *The House of the Seven Gables* enforces my conviction that Hawthorne attempted to gloss over his tragic view that the sins of the fathers are visited upon the children, generation after generation. Much as he would have liked to write a romance that was sunny, his ingrained but mostly submerged Calvinism ordained for him the dark necessity of showing ironically the human condition as depraved and unredeemed. His reluctance to admit openly the sombreness of his own belief occasions the false heartiness, the rushing over and away from the decreed despairing ending, and a stopping short of the inevitable ugliness. Hawthorne hurries over the abandonment of the house, the structural and moral center of the novel, in the last few paragraphs. This is a superficial device to move the characters out of the gloom of the house to the bright countryside. Yet, the deeper irony occurs when the reader remembers, as he is bound to, the unresolved question of inherited sin and guilt. Thus, the novel is seriously flawed because the authorial voice, almost chirping at the reader in some parts, forsakes the characteristic gravity of the first half of the last chapter ("The Departure") and becomes again, at the very end, deliberately and deceitfully fulsome and exuberant.

The authorial voice in *The House of the Seven Gables,* unlike that of the rueful Jeremiah who gathers moral weight in *The Scarlet Letter,* is confiding and cosy. Hawthorne wants to take the reader into his confidence with his opening description of the house with which he has been acquainted since youth. He memorably sketches the building of the house by the iron Puritan Colonel Pyncheon, who insensitively built his mansion over the property of the wizard Maule (the Maule whom he had helped to convict) apparently without taking seriously Maule's curse on him from the gallows, '"God will give him blood to drink"' (8). Concerning the colonel's choking to death in his own blood upon the completion of this house, Hawthorne offers the reader his usual alternate explanations, a device used in *The House of the Seven Gables* as frequently and as ambiguously as in *The Scarlet Letter.* At the end of Hawthorne's account of the Pyncheon family from the time of the witch trials, his question about the subsequent responsibility of the Pyncheons for the evil done to the Maules is still ringing in the reader's ear. Hawthorne then takes up his tale some thirty years before his present (about 1820) with the contemporary characters, the prosperous and evil Judge Pyncheon, the thirty-years-imprisoned Clifford, the starving and lonely Hepzibah, the boarder Holgrave, and the country cousin Phoebe.

In *The House of the Seven Gables,* Hawthorne's authorial voice is far more in the tradition of the nineteenth-century English novel than in that of *The Scarlet Letter,* and at the end of the first chapter he postures a bit: "And now—in a very humble way, as will be seen—we proceed to open our narrative" (29). The coyness and archness of the narrative voice continues throughout the bulk of the novel. He refuses to watch Hepzibah dressing: "Far from us be the indecorum of assisting, even in imagination, at a maiden lady's toilet!" (30). He then poses, but rather irritatingly and patronizingly both to Hepzibah and the reader, his usual series of rhetorical questions: "Will she now issue forth over the threshold of our story?" (31), etc. Even though the omniscient third-person voice is used throughout the novel, Hawthorne cannot resist his usual qualifications: his everready "possibly" and "perhaps" and his familiar "we recollect" and "we are loitering faint-heartedly on the threshold of our story" (34).

Hawthorne does not seem comfortable in the role of confidant and he makes his reader share his discomfort. He even appeals to Heaven to "forgive us for taking a ludicrous view of her [Hepzibah's] position" and then continues to laugh at her, despite saying that she "was a deeply tragic character" (37). His laughter at Hepzibah is a vain and heavyhanded attempt at humor similar to that which mars some of his sketches and short stories. Hawthorne is at his best when he uses laughter in a sinister and diabolic way. Although he confesses to the reader that it is a "heavy annoyance to a writer" to "represent nature," there is still a strange reluctance on the part of the reader to conspire with Hawthorne's laughter "that so much of the mean and ludicrous should be hopelessly mixed up with the purest pathos" (40–41). He further appeals to the reader:

> How can we elevate our history of retribution for the sin of long ago, when, as one of our most prominent figures, we are compelled to introduce—not a young and lovely woman, . . . but a gaunt, sallow, rusty-jointed maiden, . . . with the strange horror of a turban on her head! . . . Her great life-trial seems to be, that, after sixty years of idleness, she finds it convenient to earn comfortable bread by setting up a shop, in a small way. Nevertheless, if we look through all the heroic fortunes of mankind, we shall find this same entanglement of something mean and trivial with whatever is noblest in joy or sorrow. *Life is made up of marble and mud.* (41)

We should be interested in Hawthorne's problem of "marble and mud," but the skill of the narrative commentary of *The Scarlet Letter* seems at this point to have deserted Hawthorne and we are forced to agree with him that it is a "heavy annoyance" to us as readers, as well as to him as a writer, to be cozened into his artistic problems in this confessional way.

Hawthorne retains this rather amused detachment from his characters throughout the first nine chapters, but he is not so detached from his readers. In chapter 10 he speaks directly to the reader: "The author needs great faith in his reader's sympathy; else he must hesitate to give details so minute, and incidents apparently so trifling, as are essential to make up the idea of this garden-life" (150). These explicit claims on the reader's sympathy become rather wearisome and Hawthorne's determinedly light-hearted tone further tries our patience. The intrusive and coy author is not found in *The Scarlet Letter* or nearly as frequently in *The Blithedale Romance* and *The Marble Faun,* and we become particularly distracted when he begins to lecture to his characters. Clifford cries out for his happiness at the end of chapter 10 and Hawthorne admonishes him: "Alas, poor Clifford! You are old, and worn with troubles that ought never to have befallen you. You are partly crazy" (157). These painfully playful asides to the characters and the reader exhibit Hawthorne at his most unskillful. They abound throughout the novel.

The device of having Holgrave read Phoebe a story he has written describing Alice Pyncheon in the clutches of her greedy father and the wizard descendant of the original Maule is obvious but fairly satisfying. It is necessary, of course, to connect Holgrave with the Maules as well as to explain his mesmeric powers—powers which he is tempted to use on Phoebe but resists, thereby avoiding the unforgivable sin of violating the human heart. However, Holgrave's voice is identical with Hawthorne's. Holgrave's tale within a tale is inserted without artistic subtlety, but it serves to make Phoebe aware of Holgrave's nature as a cold, clinical observer. Holgrave watches Clifford and Hepzibah, says Phoebe, as if he is in a theater—with their tragedy played for his own amusement (217). By using Holgrave in this way, Hawthorne is working toward the mastery that he displays in *The Blithedale Romance,* where Coverdale functions as both narrator-observer and participant.

Beginning with chapter 15 Hawthorne abandons some of his playfulness and makes some extremely direct judgments on his characters. He speaks harshly, for example, of Judge Pyncheon's "miserable soul" and the "splendid rubbish" in his life (230). In the sixteenth chapter, "Clifford's Chamber," the voice of the narrator seems far more sure of itself and consistent than in the previous chapters of *The House of the Seven Gables.* The aesthetic distance between the narrator and Hepzibah is maintained skillfully, even though the reader is actively sympathetic with the terrified Hepzibah, who delays calling Clifford to the judge's summons. The authorial voice here is melancholy and regretful as Hawthorne describes the agony of Hepzibah, who feels the weight of the "dreary past . . . upon her heart" (240), her isolation from the world, her inability to pray to what has become for her a generalized Providence whose "vastness made it nothing" (245).

Had Hawthorne been able to maintain the assurance and mastery of what seems to be his natural voice—rueful, melancholy, forlorn, and regretful—*The House of the Seven Gables* would have been a better novel. To attempt to tell a story of greed, wizard's curses, hypocrisy, inherited guilt, and secret sin and maintain a buoyant and playful tone would be daunting to any author—more so to Hawthorne who took so seriously all the ills to which fallen man is heir. Thus, in the best parts of this work, the narrative voice is not sniggering, confiding, and insinuating to the reader, who resents such intimacy, but is cool and measured with an ironic undertone as damnatory of the human condition as that found in *The Scarlet Letter,* the best tales, and *The Blithedale Romance.*

Chapter 17, "The Flight of Two Owls," is brilliant, for here the narrative voice is controlled, confident, and firm as it relates the unreality of the journey of a temporarily reborn Clifford and a terrified Hepzibah. Describing Clifford on the train, Hawthorne can afford to indulge all of his ironic genius in Clifford's wild and erratic comments on the great spiraling progress of humanity epitomized by the railroad. The mindless Clifford confidently expounds all of the boundless optimism about the perfectibility of man that Hawthorne's neighbors, Emerson, Thoreau, and Alcott, propagated and which so disgusted and disaffected Hawthorne. But in the next chapter, "Governor Pyncheon," Hawthorne loses his control again. Even though this famous set piece has been inordinately admired by some critics, it is much too obvious, self-indulgent, and ultimately embarrassing. Certainly the idea is admirable—to sketch the busy activities planned by the now mortally stricken judge. But after Hawthorne has charged Judge Pyncheon to go about his business and taunted him with rhetorical questions over sixty times, we become acutely weary and irritated. Hawthorne knows that he is exploiting this situation: "We are tempted to make a little sport with the idea" (279); "indulging our fancy in this freak, we have partly lost the power of restraint and guidance" (280); "we were betrayed into this brief extravagance by the quiver of the moonbeams" (281). What Hawthorne has been betrayed into by this archness is an obvious and heavy-handed irony unlike the artistic, deep, subtle undertone of irony which is his most characteristic and successful mode.

In the next two chapters, 19 and 20, Hawthorne returns all of his characters to the house and we have a sense that he is once more in control, maintaining a suitable aesthetic distance and narrative voice. This artistic management of the romance continues halfway through the final chapter. In chapter 20 he brings Phoebe and Holgrave together with a profusion of prelapsarian imagery that is always ominous, since we are sure that in Hawthorne's tragic vision of man, the postlapsarian world follows inevitably. In the first half of the final chapter, the narrative voice is infinitely sorrowing and adroitly ironic as Hawthorne meditates, Hamlet-like, on the transience and evanescence of posthumous reputation: "The sudden death of so prominent a member of the social world, as the Honorable Judge Jaffrey Pyncheon, created a sensation . . . which had hardly quite subsided in a fortnight" (309); "of all the events which constitute a person's biography, there is scarcely one . . . to which the world so easily reconciles itself, as to his death" (309); "the public, with its customary alacrity, proceeded to forget that he had ever lived. . . . The honorable Judge was beginning to be a stale subject, before half the county-newspapers had found time to put their columns in mourning, and publish his exceedingly eulogistic obituary" (309–10). This admirable, temperate, and highly effective irony is followed by a masterful revelation of the previously implied innocence of Clifford and the vicious criminality of the judge. Hawthorne has the revelation occur almost naturally as the town gossips about the judge after his death when it is safe for the ordinary citizens to speculate about the scandals of this repulsive character's early life. Then is pronounced, in Hawthorne's most solemn authorial voice, a sentence most similar to the famous passage in *The Scarlet Letter*. In *The Scarlet Letter* Hawthorne describes the guilt of Hester and Arthur in this way: "*And be the stern and sad truth spoken, that the breach which Guilt has once made into the human soul is never, in this mortal state, repaired*" (200–201). In *The House of the Seven Gables,* Hawthorne again speaks pontifically, but more wearily while reflecting on the evil of Judge Pyncheon and the irreparable harm done to Clifford: "*After such wrong as he had suffered, there is no reparation. . . . It is a truth . . . that no great mistake, whether acted or endured, in our mortal sphere, is ever really set right*" (313).

If Hawthorne had remembered his own words for the next five pages and had not been so intent on setting everything right, *The House of the Seven Gables* would have been a more successful novel than it is, flawed though it might be with its alternating tone of playfulness and gloom. But undoubtedly tired of the story and driven by his conviction that he should write a sunny romance, he manufactured a clumsy *deus ex machina* ending which violated his theme and implicit intention. In so doing he buried the irony, not irreparably but apparently, beneath Alice's posies, still blooming in the deserted old house of the seven gables.

But the wily Hawthorne was probably partially aware of the bitter Calvinist irony of the so-called happy conclusion. Clifford, Hepzibah, Phoebe, and Holgrave are locked together in total isolation from the real world in their new Eden which was built with accursed and bloody money, and the simple Uncle Venner, now esteemed by the witless Clifford as a philosopher-sage, may witness an entirely new paradise lost.

## III

The images and symbols of *The House of the Seven Gables* lack the centrality and ambiguity of the great *A* of *The Scarlet Letter,* but they are nonetheless intriguing and provocative. The central symbol—the house—is also the structural and moral center of the romance, as well as its main character, and will be discussed in the section on structure.

Certainly the most dominant symbol (after the house itself) is that of the Garden of Eden which compounds the ambiguity of the apparently sunny ending. Hawthorne does not attempt to disguise or bury this symbol—in fact, chapter 20 is called "The Flower of Eden." The ruined garden of the Pyncheons, examined by Phoebe in chapter 6, emblemizes the blight besetting man east of Eden. It is also, appropriately enough, the site of the infamous seventeenth-century Salem witch trials in which Matthew Maule, the original owner of the land on which the seven-gabled house stands, was hastened to his death by the conniving of the greedy Puritan, Colonel Pyncheon. Hawthorne's account of the witch trials indicates his own ambivalence about them. Even though he has assumed the guilt of his own unrepentant ancestor-judge in "The Custom House" and even though he says that Matthew Maule "was one of the martyrs to that terrible delusion which should teach us, among its other morals, that the influential classes, and those who take upon themselves to be leaders of the people, are fully liable to all the passionate error that has ever characterized the maddest mob" (7–8), he seems to be as dismayed as many of those early citizens of Salem that Colonel Pyncheon would build his house "over an unquiet grave" where "the terror and ugliness of Maule's crime, and the wretchedness of his punishment, would darken the freshly plastered walls, and infect them early with the scent of an old and melancholy house" (9).

As is usual in Hawthorne, we are faced with the question of belief: he damns the mobs and the magistrates for "passionate error" in the hanging of witches, and yet the theme of *The House of the Seven Gables* depends on the psychological reality of our belief (even within the latitude of the Romance) in the wizardry of the Maules and their power over the Pyncheons. This diabolic sorcery manifests itself in Holgrave through his mysterious use of mesmerism. Although Hawthorne may not have subscribed consciously to the Calvinist doctrine of total depravity, he was unable to accept (until seven years abroad) even the remotest possibility of good coming from evil. Consequently, during the composition of *The House of the Seven Gables,* despite his resolve to go against his own sombre grain and drench his romance in sunlight, the undertone of evil propagating evil constantly vies with the determinedly cheerful authorial voice and displays itself repeatedly in the imagery and symbolism.

The allusions to the expulsion of Adam and Eve from Eden mount throughout the novel until we are prepared to witness another frightful catastrophe, perhaps not as cosmic as the first, but just as damning to the characters in the novel. In the last paragraph of the book, Phoebe, Holgrave-Maule, Clifford, and Hepzibah, "chatting and laughing very pleasantly together," are off to the pastoral Eden, while Maule's well throws up a "succession of kaleidoscopic pictures, in which a gifted eye might have seen foreshadowed the coming fortunes of Hepzibah, and Clifford, and the descendant of the legendary wizard, the village-maiden, over whom he had thrown love's web of sorcery" (319). Meanwhile the Pyncheon-elm "whispered unintelligible prophesies." As careful readers we are brought up short, amidst the chattering and laughing, to remember the brackish waters of Maule's well on which only the chickens thrive, which causes "intestinal mischief" to everyone else, and in whose waters Clifford would see the "dark face" and be miserable. We also remember that the ancient elm has one branch of bright gold—but Hawthorne has reminded us that it resembles the golden branch that was the passport of

Aeneas and the sibyl to Hades. Thus, even in the apparent sunniness of the final paragraph of the novel, we seem to be warned ironically and subtly that the future of the new Adam-Holgrave-Maule and Eve-Phoebe may be frightfully involved with dark faces and prophecies of hell and damnation.

The Eden imagery occurs frequently in *The House of the Seven Gables* (over ten allusions), but viewed functionally and collectively, it is damning to the characters. In the tenth chapter, "The Pyncheon Garden," Hawthorne describes this garden minutely. Phoebe had discovered earlier that "The black, rich soil had fed itself with the decay of a long period of time. . . . The evil of these departed years would naturally have sprung up again, in such rank weeds (symbolic of the transmitted vices of society) as are always prone to root themselves about human dwellings" (86). She had also found that the rare white rosebush in the garden had to be viewed from a distance to look "as if it had been brought from Eden"; a closer look showed that the blossoms "had blight or mildew at their hearts" (71). The entire garden is "the Eden of a thunder-smitten Adam, who had fled for refuge thither out of the same dreary and perilous wilderness, into which the original Adam was expelled" (150). The recognition of love between Phoebe and Holgrave is an Edenic one. "They transfigured the earth, and made it Eden again, and themselves the two first dwellers in it." But the new Eden does not last: "how soon the heavy earth-dream settled down again!" (307). Thus, Hawthorne's faith in the transfiguring power of human love, even though he probably partially believed that Sophia had rescued him from his shadowy room and total isolation, is never absolute nor constant. Even old Uncle Venner, who is going to dwell in the new garden of the country house, wants to provide the apple for the fall of the new Eden: "'I suppose I am like a Roxbury russet [earlier called a "frost-bitten apple"]—a great deal the better, the longer I can be kept'" (318). The question then is how long Uncle Venner, the russet, can be kept before he is consumed, thus yielding knowledge of both good and evil.

The "ponderosity" of evil is certainly one of the major themes in the novel, but Hawthorne also uses it skillfully as symbol. In the preface Hawthorne states his moral, "that the wrong-doing of one generation lives into the successive ones, and, divesting itself of every temporary advantage, becomes a pure and uncontrollable mischief" (2), but then virtually withdraws the moral because he says he cannot flatter himself that a romance will teach anything except "through a far more subtile process than the ostensible one" (2). Hawthorne pursues this "more sub-tile process symbolically, often with a favorite device of his: the mirror. The interior life of the old house is contained in the dim looking glass— all the characters are shown as they really are. The Maules by a "sort of mesmeric process . . . could make its inner region all alive with the departed Pyncheons; not as they had shown themselves to the world, nor in their better and happier hours, but as doing over again some deed of sin, or in the crisis of life's bitterest sorrow" (21). In the chapter on Governor Pyncheon, the looking glass "is always a kind of window or door-way into the spiritual world" (281). Judge Pyncheon never looks into the mirror, for fear of seeing his real self or, more frighteningly, the spiritual world, but contents himself with "what purports to be his im-age, as reflected in the mirror of public opinion" and in that way "can scarcely arrive at true self-knowledge" (232). But the narrator tells us "that a daily guilt might have been acted by him, continually renewed, and reddening forth afresh, like the miraculous blood-stain of a murder" (229). The judge cannot escape "a thumb's bigness" of evil. The weight of evil perpetuated by the Pyncheons can never be vitiated: "no great mis-take, whether acted or endured, in our mortal sphere, is ever really set right" (313). And so the story that Hawthorne maintains must not be impaled by its moral, "as by sticking a pin through a butterfly," suffers from his efforts to defy theme and moral and be "sunny." Thus, the beautiful "butterfly" that loses its life, "causing it to stiffen in an un-gainly and unnatural attitude" is the imposition, the "impaling," of a tragic theme, the "uncontrollable mischief" resulting from the wrongdo-ing of successive generations, with a beautiful but inappropriately light-some "butterfly," the superficially happy ending (2). The negation of the brightness is accomplished unwillingly by Hawthorne through the for-tunate intrusion of his Calvinist-ordained irony that requires another paradise lost.

Through dreams, which Hawthorne wisely predicts modern psycholo-gy will systematize, the Maules tyrannize the Pyncheons: "The Pyn-cheons . . . haughtily as they bore themselves in the noonday streets of their native town, were no better than bond-servants to these plebian Maules, on entering the topsy-turvy commonwealth of sleep" (26). The grandson of wizard Maule, young Matthew "was fabled . . . to have a strange power of getting into people's dreams, and regulating matters there according to his own fancy" (189): using this power, he destroyed Alice Pyncheon by gaining control of her mind.

The heaviness of guilt accumulates in the romance despite the narrator's chirping voice until the reader becomes aware of a most uncomfortable pressure. It is the pressure of moral disease which is handed down generation by generation. Hawthorne's "query" as to "whether each inheritor of the property . . . did not commit anew the great guilt of his ancestor" (20) haunts us, making us doubt the possibility of any happiness for the characters we have come to know. Hepzibah can have no ultimate faith in righting a wrong by moving to Jaffrey Pyncheon's country house, for when she reflects on his resemblance to his Puritan ancestor, she thinks: "'He has proved himself the very man to build up a new house! Perhaps, too, to draw down a new curse!'" (59). Even sunny Phoebe Pyncheon, who thinks so little, recognizes the resemblance of Judge Pyncheon to the evil colonel:

> A deeper philosopher than Phoebe might have found something very terrible in this idea. It implied that the weaknesses and defects, the bad passions, the mean tendencies, and the moral diseases which lead to crime, are handed down from one generation to another, by a far surer process of transmission than human law has been able to establish. (119)

At the end of the novel we foresee the moral blight that threatens the children of Phoebe and Holgrave, even if Phoebe does not.

Satan, who tempted the first dwellers in Eden to their ruin, skulks about the characters of *The House of the Seven Gables* in symbolic form. He appears, for example, under Clifford's arched window as the organ grinder's monkey with an "enormous tail, (too enormous to be decently concealed under his gabardine,) and the deviltry of nature which it betokened" (164). And every representative of mankind casually passes by the hideously tailed beast-Mammon "without imagining how nearly his own moral condition was here exemplified" (164). Again, the tragic view of the fallen and diseased human condition which is Hawthorne's most characteristic and regretful conviction ironically and heavily undermines the sunny tale he thinks he relates.

The weight of moral ruin seems to annihilate any possibility of happiness for Hepzibah and Clifford. Hawthorne suggests this Bunyanesque burden with a favorite image: the heart as dungeon. On the day following Clifford's return from his long imprisonment, Hepzibah's "unwonted joy shrank back, appalled . . . and clothed itself, in mourning; or it ran and hid itself . . . in the dungeon of her heart" (101–02). When Hepzibah and Clifford attempt to join the crowd going to church, they realize that the house is their self and their jailor: "At the threshold, they felt his pitiless gripe upon them! For, what other dungeon is so dark as one's own heart! What jailor so inexorable as one's self!" (169). The irony is rich here: Clifford comes to the dungeon of the house from a thirty-year stay in the civil dungeon of the jail.

The Calvinist belief in the depravity of children is often suggested by Hawthorne. In the *American Notebooks* he speculates about his own daughter Una's abrupt and fiendish changes of mood and wonders if she has something of the devil in her; in *The Scarlet Letter,* the elf-child Pearl is thought to be an offspring of Satan, as are her childish Puritan tormentors; Ilbrahim, the gentle boy, is tormented and almost killed by the little "unbreeched fanatics." The children in *The House of the Seven Gables* are not any more palatable. Ned Higgins, the consumer of gingerbread menageries, is cannibalistic and filled with devilish impatience. The children who follow the organ grinder and his monkey are "shrewd" (a dangerous word in Hawthorne—cf., the "shrewdness" of Robin in "My Kinsman, Major Molineux") and the youths that Hepzibah fears might make sport of Clifford are described as children of Satan: "Satan . . . the father of them all!" (247).

Hawthorne is suspicious of all excessively sensual appetites. Even the delicate, beauty-loving Clifford becomes coarse when he eats: "He ate food with what might almost be termed voracity, and seemed to forget . . . everything else around him, in the sensual enjoyment" (107). Judge Pyncheon is a man of strong and vicious desires; as he attempts to kiss Phoebe, she draws away from him: "The man, the sex, somehow or other, was entirely too prominent" (118). Again concerning the judge's sexuality, Hawthorne, speaking of the judge's "marital deportment," indicates that "the lady got her death-blow in the honey-moon" (123). There are numerous other allusions to the animal appetites of the judge, but the quotations I have used are singular in Hawthorne. As a shy, nineteenth-century man, Hawthorne makes only rare, specific references to sex (one interesting exception is Coverdale's speculating about the virginity of Zenobia), but the "prominent" sex of the judge and his sexual exploits on his honeymoon are not only suggestive but specific, and lead us to imagine that there was perhaps sexual as well as spiritual slavery in the power that Matthew Maule had over Alice Pyncheon. Certainly he violated her human heart, Hawthorne's unforgivable sin, but what are we to make of this: "She felt herself too much abased, and longed to change natures with some worm!" (209)? She finally achieves death, which even the sunny authorial commentator can speak of only as "the great final remedy" (166).

The symbolic use of laughter and smiles as tragic or diabolic, managed so well in *The Scarlet Letter,* "My Kinsman, Major Molineux," and "Young Goodman Brown," becomes rather obvious and less effective in *The House of the Seven Gables.* Hawthorne comments that Clifford's tearful response to the ugliness of the organ grinder's demonic monkey is a sign of weakness "which men of merely delicate endowments—and *destitute of the fiercer—deeper, and more tragic power of laughter*—can hardly avoid" (164). The authorial voice is guilty of sniggering at Hepzibah's clumsiness and ugliness, and in chapter 15, "The Scowl and the Smile," contrasts the goodness of Hepzibah with her scowl and the evil of the judge with his "dog-day smile of elaborate benevolence, sultry enough to tempt flies to come and buzz in it" (282). But there is no truly subtle and sinister irony in the characters' smiles except for Matthew Maule's "dark" smile in his bargaining with Alice Pyncheon's father for what turns out to be her soul (208). Maule has a "certain *peculiar* smile" as does the eye of Heaven on the Pyncheon garden: "The eye of Heaven seemed to look down into it . . . with a *peculiar* smile" (87). Hawthorne usually excels in his use of such neutral words as peculiar to suggest endless possibilities of evil, but there is a dearth of them in *The House of the Seven Gables.* Maule's dark and peculiar smile is suggestive enough of evil, but what are we to make of the peculiar smile of the eye of Heaven? It is reminiscent of the narrator's comment on Hepzibah's prayer falling back on her like lead, convincing her that Providence was unconcerned about individual agonies "but shed its justice, and its mercy, in a broad, sunlike sweep, over half the universe at once. Its vastness made it nothing" (245). This perception of man's Lilliputian importance in a vast cosmos of indifference is one thing which causes so many critics to label Hawthorne patronizingly as "modern" or "pre-modern." Certainly his vision *is* more like that of Kafka or Camus than that of Dickens or Thackeray. His dark Calvinism inevitably redeems much of the nineteenth-century author-narrator's playing with the characters, asking them silly rhetorical questions and thumpingly and heavy-handedly pulling the reader into the story.

As the scowl and the smile are indicative of merely the surface appearance and not the reality of the person wearing them, so Phoebe, innocent and rather mindless, begins to doubt, after her first encounter with the judge, whether eminent men can possibly "be otherwise than just and upright men" (131). Because Phoebe does not have "a wider scope of view, and a deeper insight," her universe would be thrown into chaos by this idea and so she smothers her intuitions "in order to keep the universe in its old place" (131). But Hawthorne does not feel it necessary to harness the universe and, in his delving beneath the "dog-day" smile of the judge, he compares his exterior to a palace, all splendid halls and costly marble but having in some nook or closet "a *corpse, half-decayed, and still decaying* . . . beneath the show of a marble palace, that pool of stagnant water, foul with many impurities, and perhaps tinged with blood—that secret abomination, above which, possibly, he may say his prayers, without remembering it—is this man's miserable soul!" (230). This description of the judge's palatial interior, containing not only a stinking corpse but certainly his miserable soul, is recovered later in the novel when he is lying dead in the abandoned old seven-gabled house. The exterior of the house reveals nothing ominous: "So little faith is due to external appearance, that there was really an inviting aspect over the venerable edifice. . . . Its windows gleamed cheerfully in the slanting sunlight" (285). An imaginative person passing by "would conceive the mansion to have been the residence of the stubborn old Puritan, Integrity, who, dying in some forgotten generation, had left a blessing in all its rooms" (285). Instead, in reality we get the Puritan resident, Predestination.

All of the characters are masked: Hepzibah, with her scowl disguising a tender heart; Clifford, appearing old and wrinkled but having only a childish intelligence; the judge, with his dog-day smile concealing murderous rapacity; Phoebe, the sunshine girl gradually initiated into evil; and Holgrave, apparently a harmless daguerreotypist, habitually masking "whatever lay near his heart" (301), which is a Maule-heart. Maule's well epitomizes all of the deceptive qualities of appearance and reality best. Its fountain is "paved . . . with what appeared to be a sort of mosaic-work of variously colored pebbles . . . wrought magically" (88), but in reality it contains brackish and poisonous water like the fountain in "Rappaccini's Daughter."

Hawthorne's customary use of heights on which to enact public dramas (as in *The Scarlet Letter* and "Roger Malvin's Burial") seems limited in

*The House of the Seven Gables* to Clifford's arched window through which he observes the world in little: the organ grinder and his monkey and the accompanying children; political processions; the omnibus "typifying that vast rolling vehicle, the world, the end of whose journey is everywhere and nowhere" (160); the people passing back and forth, and the churchgoers. Clifford is impelled to jump into the political procession, but is restrained by Phoebe and Hepzibah. Clifford and Hepzibah are each an isolato, doomed not to be citizens of the world. By the end of the novel, Phoebe no longer goes back and forth to church, nor does Holgrave continue his itinerant life, nor does Uncle Venner go from door to door in search of scraps for his pig. All of these characters are isolated and insulated from the real world in the judge's country house, built with blood money and apparently destined, until the necessary, emergent Fall from this new Eden, to a life as insubstantial as the soap bubbles that Clifford blows out of his window.

Time in *The House of the Seven Gables* is more a destroyer than a preserver. Clifford "with a mysterious and terrible Past, which had annihilated his memory, and a blank Future before him, . . . had only this visionary and impalpable *Now,* which, if you once look closely at it, is *nothing"* (149). Holgrave, before his transformation into conservative country squire, wishes to annihilate "the moss-grown and rotten Past" (179). On the train, Clifford prophesies a better future "in an ascending spiral curve" (259), but the narrator tells us that Clifford has a diseased intelligence. His rantings resemble only too transparently the dreamy and visionary transcendental chatter that Hawthorne heard constantly from his wife and her sister, as well as from Thoreau, Emerson, Channing, and Alcott. If the past is evil, the present nothing, and the future only an optimist's dream, time is tyranny indeed, as Hawthorne suggests so vividly in describing the only sound in the room of the dead judge, the ticking of his watch: "this little, quiet, never-ceasing throb of Time's pulse, repeating its small strokes with such busy regularity, in Judge Pyncheon's motionless hand, has an effect of terror, which we do not find in any other accompaniment of the scene" (277). As Hawthorne comments, time, the destroyer, allows no great mistake to be set aright: "Time, the continual vicissitude of circumstances, and the invariable inopportunity of death, render it impossible" (313).

With all this imagery and symbolism contradicting the light, sunny narrative voice and collectively striking doom and gloom, it is no wonder

that Hawthorne wrote Fields that "it [*The House of the Seven Gables*] darkens damnably toward the close" (xxii).

## IV

The structure of *The House of the Seven Gables* is not as neat as that of *The
Scarlet Letter,* which has the three great pillory scenes at the beginning, the
middle, and the end. Hawthorne does attempt a patterned beginning and
end which he manages so well in some of his best tales: we have the
seven-gabled house at the opening of the novel and at the end.[2] But there
is a glaring inconsistency in *The House of the Seven Gables* because at the end
the house is deserted by those who have made it their home. It remains,
therefore, like themselves, unredeemed, but also abandoned.

The plot of *The House of the Seven Gables* is quite simple. It has little
action: the characters leave and return to the house; but there is no
resolution to the question posed by Hawthorne at the opening. We are
never directly told that the guilt of the fathers descends upon the progeny
and becomes an "uncontrollable mischief." But, nevertheless, the reader
expects a cosmic disaster to take place in the country house.

The uses to which Hawthorne puts the house in *The House of the Seven
Gables* constitute an artistic triumph. The house operates functionally
throughout the novel as the dominating symbol of both Pyncheon greed
and inherited guilt; it is also the structural center of the book, the locus to
which the characters keep returning; it is even the story's main character.
But despite this superfluity of meaning and importance, Hawthorne un-
dercuts the symbolic value of the house and its structural centrality by his
calculatedly bright and cheerful authorial voice which coexists with the
gathering weight of doom and gloom, the inevitable result of his sombre
and grave moral intention. The final blow to the house as structural and
symbolic center is dealt when Hawthorne wrenches all of the important
characters away from the house and sends them off to the country. The
house, as central character, is little diminished by this barbarous separation. However, the theme and intention that demonstrate the "pure and
uncontrollable mischief" resulting from inherited guilt, the symbolic
function of the house as both exterior and interior reflection of nearly two
hundred years of accumulating evil, and the architecture of the Romance's
structure, which is built on the house—all are seriously violated by this
apparently happy ending. Close reading of Hawthorne's ambiguity and

irony reveals that the ending is truly tragic because all the characters are deceived about their planned happiness in a new rural Eden country house built by the same blood money that constructed the old house. But the Hawthornean complexity is too mechanical, the authorial voice in the last half of the last chapter too hurried and bright not to damage the total effect seriously. Hawthorne, that master of artistic ambiguity, fails purposely to bring off his usual sorrowing and regretful tone, and while the expected multi-leveled interpretation of his work continues to provoke the reader, the triumph of ambiguity as art, which is the Hawthorne hallmark in his best fiction, is seriously compromised in *The House of the Seven Gables*.

In the novel are countless references to the house, and its signal importance grows and expands until its intricacies and variations make it the most intriguing and complex character in the novel. In the beginning Hawthorne devotes many pages of loving description to its establishment on the land of the wizard Maule who, from his gallows height, had cursed the original Pyncheon. This Pyncheon, it is implied, was a principal in the damning of Maule as a wizard during the Salem witch trials. Colonel Pyncheon's hunger for Maule's land even shocked the insensitive Puritans of the time, and he compounded the horror by constructing his house over an accursed site, "an unquiet grave." But "the Puritan soldier and magistrate was not a man to be turned aside . . . either by dread of the wizard's ghost, or by flimsy sentimentalities of any kind" (9). The house was constructed magnificently by the leading architect of the day, Thomas Maule, the son of the hanged man.

Hawthorne tells us at the beginning of the novel that the house was part of his childhood and had "always affected me like a human countenance" (5). This emphasis on the humanity of the house gathers significance throughout the novel. When the house is completed, and the whole town is invited to the religious and festive celebration, we see it with the eyes of the townspeople: "There it rose, a little withdrawn from the line of the street, but in pride, not modesty" (11). Its exterior was "ornamented with quaint figures, . . . drawn or stamped in the glittering plaster" and "On every side, the seven gables pointed sharply towards the sky, and presented the aspect of a whole sisterhood of edifices, breathing through the spiracles of one great chimney" (11). Sunlight came into the hall and chamber, but "the second story, projecting far over the base, and itself retiring beneath the third, threw a shadow and thoughtful gloom into the lower rooms" (12). Time is inevitably involved with the house: "On the triangular portion of the gable that fronted next the street, was a dial . . . on which the sun was still marking the passage of the first bright hour in a history, that was not destined to be all so bright" (12).

Down through the generations, the Pyncheons "clung to the ancestral house, with singular tenacity of home-attachment" (20). Hawthorne believes that although the legal tenure of the house was obvious, "many, if not most, of the successive proprietors of this estate, were troubled as to their moral right to hold it" (20). For Matthew Maule "trode downward from his own age to a far later one, planting a heavy footstep, all the way, on the conscience of a Pyncheon" (20).

By the original will Hepzibah is given a life estate in the old house but is "wretchedly poor." However, she refuses all help from the judge "either in the old mansion or his own modern residence" (24). It is especially puzzling, then, that Hawthorne has Hepzibah, Clifford, and Phoebe happily inherit Judge Pyncheon's bloody money and move away in an apparently carefree way to his modern country estate. There is no suggestion by Hawthorne that the curse has in any way been expiated. It would be as difficult to argue that Phoebe's marriage to Holgrave-Maule vitiated the curse on the house any more than did Alice Pyncheon's enslavement and eventual death by the fiendish demands of wizard Maule's grandson, Matthew.

At the outset of the novel, Hawthorne describes the house as a living character with a heart. The human imagery associated with the house and the structural unity it provides the novel, which is named for it, endow the structure with more important, fascinating, and enigmatic qualities than are given to any of the other characters:

> But as for the old structure of our story, its white-oak frame, and its boards, shingles, and crumbling plaster, and even the huge, clustered chimney in the midst, seemed to constitute only the least and meanest part of its reality. So much of mankind's varied experience had passed there—so much had been suffered, and something, too, enjoyed—that the very timbers were oozy, as with the moisture of a heart. *It was itself like a great human heart, with a life of its own, and full of rich and sombre reminiscences.* (27)

Whenever Hawthorne begins to identify something or someone with a human heart, the reader should be aware of the ambiguities and ambivalences that Hawthorne always suggests about that organ—the heart uncorrupted and innocent as that of Adam and Eve in the prelapsarian Eden is inextricably linked with the heart as a foul cavern of duplicity and horror. Both possibilities are present in the heart of the seven-gabled house. In front of it stands the ancient Pyncheon-elm, "sweeping the whole black roof with its pendent foliage. It gave beauty to the old edifice, and seemed to make it part of nature" (27). In the yard on either side of the house behind a "ruinous wooden fence" is a huge growth of weeds: "an enormous fertility of burdocks, with leaves, . . . two or three feet long" (27). The beauty of the elm and the ugliness of the harsh-sounding burdock weeds suggest the cryptic quality of the house as heart, and Hawthorne further extends and complicates the imagery by telling of the green moss of decay on the roof and of Alice's posies also growing there out of the "dust of the street and the decay of the roof" (28). Richly symbolic of Hawthorne's faltering attempt to gladden and lighten the dark tale of inherited guilt and greed is his conclusion about the house: "it was both sad and sweet to observe how Nature adopted to herself this desolate, decaying, gusty, rusty, old house of the Pyncheon family; and how the ever-returning Summer did her best to gladden it with tender beauty, and grew melancholy in the effort" (28). The pervasiveness of melancholy, which is Hawthorne's natural tone, clings to this novel and refuses to be lightened even by his most determined efforts at heartiness and cheer.

Throughout the novel the importance of the house as character, structural center, and symbol is expanded and enriched. Hepzibah worries about young Phoebe's staying in the house because "it lets in the wind and the rain . . . but never lets in the sunshine" (74). Phoebe, though, cheers up the house: "the battered visage of the House of the Seven Gables, black and heavy-browed as it still certainly looked, must have shown a kind of cheerfulness glimmering through its dusky windows, as Phoebe passed to-and-fro in the interior" (81).

The ailing house improves with the presence of Phoebe: "The grime and sordidness . . . seemed to have vanished, since her appearance there; the gnawing tooth of the dry-rot was stayed, among the old timbers of its skeleton-frame; the dust had ceased to settle down so densely from the antique ceilings" (136). Because of Phoebe's wholesome effect upon the decaying condition of the house, one wonders whether Hawthorne had intended to have Phoebe Pyncheon be the salvific force in the novel and then abandoned the idea since Phoebe, as Pyncheon or even Pyncheon-

Maule, could hardly have redeemed all of the sins of the fathers. Yet his final decision to have the characters abandon the house does not solve the problem he has posed of inherited guilt becoming an "uncontrollable mischief."

Hepzibah refuses Judge Pyncheon's offer to move her and Clifford to his country house: "'Clifford has a home here!'" She continues (and this is again difficult to reconcile with the ending and the happy departure to the country house): "'It would never suit Clifford'" (128). And yet, when Hepzibah and Clifford try to join the churchgoing crowd and cannot, Clifford says: "'We have no right among human beings—no right any-where, but in this old house, which has a curse on it, and which therefore we are doomed to haunt'" (169). Again we wonder how the fate of Clifford and Hepzibah as doomed ghosts could be changed by inheriting Judge Pyncheon's doomed money and house.

Phoebe, on leaving for a final goodbye to her mother before assuming what we expect to be permanent occupancy of the old house, wonders "how it came to pass, that her life of a few weeks, here in this heavy-hearted old mansion" has come to seem "a more important centre-point of remembrance than all which had gone before" (219). Wherever she looked in the house and whatever she touched "responded to her consciousness, as if a moist human heart were in it" (219). The heart of the house has taken hold of Phoebe's heart we are told, and yet at the end she leaves it cheerfully. We wonder if she has left her heart in the house, an unlikely but certainly a Hawthornean touch.

When Clifford and Hepzibah flee the house abortively in their terror over the death of Judge Pyncheon, Hepzibah sees the house everywhere while she is whirling away on the train: "This one old house was every-where" (258). Again we are left to try to imagine how Hepzibah, at the judge's country house, will be freed from her conviction that the house is omnipresent.

With Judge Pyncheon dead in Colonel Pyncheon's old chair, the house begins "to sing, and sigh, and sob, and shriek" (277) as if its heart is broken. The heart image persists as the organ grinder, along with the long-tailed monkey and the procession, halt in front of the house, empty now except for the dead judge: "But, to us, who know the inner heart of the seven gables, as well as its exterior face, there is a ghastly effect in this repetition of light popular tunes at its door-step" (294). Just to be sure that we get the point of house as heart, Hawthorne concludes the paragraph with another heart image: "The gloomy and desolate old house, deserted of life, and with awful Death sitting sternly in its solitude, was the emblem of many a human heart, which, nevertheless, is compelled to hear the trill and echo of the world's gaiety around it" (295).

To the returning owls, Clifford and Hepzibah, the house looks welcoming even though it holds the dead judge in the oaken chair: "'Thank God, my brother, we are at home!' 'Well!—Yes!—thank God!' responded Clifford. 'A dreary home, Hepzibah! But you have done well to bring me thither!'" (308).

In the last chapter, "The Departure," the four characters decide to remove themselves from the dismal old house to the judge's country dwelling without apparently a thought of their previous aversion to the old man's tainted money, nor their earlier feeling of necessary commitment to the haunted house-heart. Ironically, Holgrave's only regret is that the judge did not build his country house of stone instead of wood.

The last mention of the house comes after the Pyncheon-elm whispers "unintelligible Prophecies" and the deserted Maule's well shows kaleidoscopic pictures that "fore-shadowed the coming fortunes" of Hawthorne's characters. Uncle Venner fancies he hears Alice Pyncheon giving a farewell touch upon her harpsichord as she floats "heavenward from the House of the Seven Gables" (319). Earlier in the novel we are told that Alice's playing usually occurs "when one of the Pyncheons was to die" (83). All of this ambiguity certainly countervails Hawthorne's laughing and chattering group heading for the judge's country house in a handsome green barouche. We are left to meditate on the abandoned house and the preparation for another Fall from Eden in the splendid garden of the country estate.

Hawthorne's usually exquisite style, limpid and deceptively lucid, is marred in *The House of the Seven Gables* only by his frequent interruptions as grimly cheerful and confiding narrator. In the descriptions of the house, and especially in the remarkable images of the house as heart, the style is confident and masterly, as displayed in the unself-conscious and modest use of internal rhyme, alliteration, assonance, balance, repetition, and parallelism.

The house itself is a towering achievement, living, breathing, palpitating, shivering, and groaning. It is a melancholy fact that the house undergoes two violations at the end: as structural center it is deserted and as the novel's central symbol it is left abandoned to its dry rot and unredeemed heart.

V

Next to the solemn, ponderous, and omnipresent house, the central characters of *The House of the Seven Gables* lack development, but are not without interest. None of them, except Holgrave-Maule, is significantly different at the end of the novel and his transformation is only one of a series of metamorphoses that he has undergone throughout his short lifetime.

Hepzibah is a loving creation by Hawthorne when he is not laughing at her inappropriately in his breezy authorial voice. Gaunt, scowling because of her myopic, weak eyes, clumsy, turbaned, and looking like the embodiment of the east wind, she has devoted thirty years of her life to waiting for Clifford's release from prison. Her loneliness, her pathetic clinging to her idea of a lady until she tortuously flouts such ideas to open the cent-shop, her unswerving devotion to Clifford even when he cannot bear to look at her, and her kindness to Phoebe, all combine to give her many of the qualities of the tragic heroine. Hawthorne, however, chooses not to exploit these tragic qualities. She remains at the end of the novel what she was at the beginning, doggedly devoted to Clifford but doomed to sit in the shade of the garden of the country house, out of Clifford's view because he cannot stand to look at her and because her eyes cannot stand the light of day.

Clifford, the lover of the beautiful, is released after thirty years in prison as little more than a shell of a man, impotent, sorely weak in his wits, and childlike in his need for food, toys, warmth, shelter, and love. Unable to fit into the real world of churchgoers and railroad travelers, he blows soap bubble worlds from his arched window, sits in the garden arbor, and cries for his happiness. Not capable of feeling gratitude for Hepzibah's devotion ("He owed her nothing. A nature like Clifford's can contract no debts of that kind" [109]), Clifford has to content himself with the catering and pampering given to a spoiled but much-loved child. This sensitive sybarite has lost his health, vitality, and intelligence and can only be comforted, not by Hepzibah whose ugly face he abhors, but by Phoebe, the mindless child who, like a small twittering bird, soothes his troubled soul. The character of Clifford is undeveloped because he is an undeveloped child and so we get a flat portrait rather than a flesh and blood human being.

Judge Pyncheon is a typical Hawthorne villain, the supreme hypocrite. To know him is to despise him. Disguised by a sultry smile of dog-day benevolence—"very much like a serpent" (119)—he is a ruthless politician, a greedy criminal, imperious, crafty, and relentless. Patron of the temperance society, he privately overindulges in costly wines and spirits. He is the same from the beginning of the novel to his death in the traditional manner of the cursed Pyncheons, choking on his own blood that God has given him to drink.

Phoebe, probably modeled on Sophia Hawthorne whom Hawthorne used to call by that name, is all sunshine and as unreal as the gentle boy, Ilbrahim, "the domesticated sunbeam," in Sophia's favorite story. All heart and no head, Phoebe sings like a bird, cannot believe in the reality of evil, and is terrified of Holgrave's ideas and mysteries because she does not understand ideas or mysteries. She is happy to be needed and finds her playmate and soulmate in Clifford, for they are both children. She is one of Hawthorne's light, sunny, and unbelievable heroines—women of the hearth, not of the head,[3] women busy about the house and suffering up to their limited capacities from the evil they do not recognize. Phoebe does not change in the novel but goes off sunnily at the end, no doubt loving Hepzibah, Clifford, Holgrave, and Uncle Venner in equal portions and totally unaware that she is probably destined to play Eve to Holgrave-Maule's Adam.

Holgrave-Maule is a consistently inconsistent character who promises to be interesting and complex but is never allowed to be:

> At almost every step in life, we meet with young men of just about Holgrave's age, for whom we anticipate wonderful things, but of whom, . . . we never happen to hear another word. The effervescence of youth and passion, and the fresh gloss of the intellect and imagination, endow them with a false brilliancy, which makes fools of themselves and other people. (181)

In his varied career he has been a country schoolmaster, a salesman, the political editor of a country newspaper, a peddler, a dentist, a minor official on a packetship, which enabled him to visit Europe, a member of a community of Fourierists, a lecturer on mesmerism, and now, at the age of twenty-two, he is a daguerreotypist as well as an author who has had some stories published. In many ways he resembles Hawthorne who always feared that the artist in him made him a clinical observer of life rather than a participant. Holgrave is accused by Phoebe of being a calm and cool observer of Hepzibah and Clifford, not really wishing them well but viewing them as if they were actors in a theatre. Holgrave admits that

this is true: "'A mere observer, like myself, (who never have any intuitions, and am, at best, only subtle and acute,) is pretty certain to go
astray'" (179). His ideas of getting rid of the past and all its institutions
and traditions, particularly that of building houses for posterity, are
secondhand Emerson. In fact, Hawthorne seems to enjoy having Holgrave
pontificate his ideas only to forsake them in a moment. Ironically, Holgrave's conversion from giant transcendentalist is so complete that
Hawthorne's scorn for Emersonian optimism, with its basis in the belief
in man's infinite perfectibility, is evinced by his indicating that Holgrave
has "read very little" and although he "considered himself a think-
er . . . had perhaps hardly yet reached the point where an educated man
begins to think" (180). But Holgrave has ambition, a "personal ambition,
hidden—from his own as well as other eyes" (181), and so when he is
instantly converted from daguerreotypist-reformer-author to country
squire we see him as a run-of-the-mill, eye-on-the-main-chance young
man seeking a happy combination of wife and money and freedom from
toil. This Maule has struck gold, like the golden branch of the ancient
elm, but we wonder if it is the equivalent of blood for the young mesmerist, even though he refrains from a complete violation of Phoebe's heart
when she is under his spell. We wonder if he is destined in his next
transformation to be the new Adam to Phoebe's Eve in the garden of the
country estate.

The rather Dickensian Uncle Venner, whose lifelong ambition to go
to the poor farm is thwarted by the charity of the Pyncheon-Maules who
establish him in a gingerbread cottage in their new country garden to
amuse Clifford, seems to have been put in the position of having to be
grateful for calculated benevolence, something that would not be required
even by the county almshouse. Uncle Venner is nicely done as the kindly
simpleton who seems a distinguished philosopher to the mindless Clifford
and Phoebe. He provides color and saltiness even though he remains a flat
character. Ned Higgins, voracious, greedy, and impatient, along with the
shrewd children who follow the organ grinder and his too-long-tailed
monkey, are types of child depravity that the Calvinist Hawthorne continued to observe. They are miniatures of Hawthorne's view of fallen humanity preying on each other and forever unsatisfied. Dixey and his friend
function as the crowd-chorus and are typical of Hawthorne's crowds,
misinformed, unsympathetic, fickle, and heartless.

Even though Hawthorne's characters are not fully developed, we do not easily forget the turbaned Hepzibah, the childish Clifford crying for his happiness, and the pharisaical Judge Pyncheon. Unfortunately, the stunted Pyncheon chickens are more memorable than sweet Phoebe. Ned Higgins, emerging cannibal, is more of an original than Holgrave-Maule, who changes and fades as fast as his daguerreotypes. Hawthorne's most developed characters are those doomed by his Calvinist vision: Hester, Zenobia, Miriam, Ethan Brand, Goodman Brown, Robin.

## VI

At the conclusion of what Hawthorne called his favorite novel, the reader is left unsatisfied, not because of the ambiguity but because of the apparent violation of Hawthorne's statement that "no great mistake, whether acted or endured, in our mortal sphere, is ever really set right" (313). Hawthorne is in haste here to make everything right and Clifford, Hepzibah, Phoebe, and Holgrave-Maule are whisked out to Judge Pyncheon's country estate "chatting and laughing very pleasantly together" (318).

Of course the grim Hawthornean irony remains with the foreshadowing and Delphic pictures in Maule's well and the "unintelligible prophecies" whispered from the Pyncheon-elm (319). The sensitive reader is convinced that the garden of the country estate, built by the cursed blood money of the serpent Judge Pyncheon, is only tempting Phoebe-Eve and Holgrave-Maule-Adam to another ineluctable Fall.

Our unease does not come from the Calvinism that dictates the irony but from Hawthorne's rejection of his own remarkable unity of structure—the house—which is abandoned with its heart wrenched out of it. We are also disturbed by the unevenness of tone in the authorial voice, which vacillates between a cheerful, bright, confiding, and conspiratorial one that plays with the characters and the reader, and the customary Hawthornean lament filled with rue, regret, and ruin. Hawthorne's mistrust of his own melancholy and ironic response to human nature compels him to perjure himself into a sham sunlit world even while his heart longs for the shadows.

THE BLITHEDALE ROMANCE

# The *"Triumphant Ignominy"* of Paul Pry

I

Following the favorable reception of *The House of the Seven Gables* (January 1851), Hawthorne contemplated a new romance with less trepidation than usual. As he had done for *The Scarlet Letter* and *The House of the Seven Gables,* Hawthorne spent five months writing, and as on the other occasions, he was heartily sick of his novel before he had quite finished.[1] Though he was determined, as he wrote Horatio Bridge, to make this new novel "even more genial than the last," neither his friends nor the reading public found *The Blithedale Romance* "genial." It was not possible for Hawthorne to be sunny even when he was determined to write against his natural bent for gloom and melancholy.

His preface to *The Blithedale Romance* contains the specific disclaimer that Brook Farm as setting was "merely to establish a theatre, a little removed from the highway of ordinary travel, where the creatures of his [Hawthorne's] brain may play their phantasmagorical antics, without exposing them to too close a comparison with the actual events of real lives. . . . These characters . . . are entirely fictitious" (1–2). Nonetheless, the first impact of the romance on the reading public was that of a tantalizing guessing game. Which character, the readers wondered, was Margaret Fuller, Emerson, Ripley, Alcott, Brownson? After the speculations began to subside among the transcendental circles, *The Blithedale Romance* became Hawthorne's most neglected novel until the critics of the past twenty years began to interest themselves in it.

While some of the scholars only revived the game of trying to identify the *Blithedale* characters with historical personages, a speculation that is as endless as it is fruitless, others found evidence in the novel of Hawthorne's serious involvement with socialism. But since *The Blithedale Romance* neither celebrates nor damns socialistic principles, these critics became annoyed with Hawthorne and labeled the novel a failure. It is futile for sociological critics to chide Hawthorne for not being a propagandist. To him, Brook Farm was a possible expedient that would provide a home for him and Sophia and permit them to marry. He went with expectation, certainly, and with good will and a financial investment he could ill afford, but soon came to see his companions as "brethren in affliction." After a few weeks of work on the manure pile, which he ironically called the "gold mine," he concluded that "a man's soul may be buried and perish under a dungheap or in a farrow of the field, just as well as under a pile of money."[2] Before the end of September 1841, he knew he could not spend the winter there, and was convinced he could not find a permanent home at Brook Farm. Like Coverdale, he often left to go back to Salem or Boston for a respite from the reformers, and his last notebook entry (October 27, 1841) suggests his final appraisal of Brook Farm as "essentially a daydream, and yet a fact" (2). To fault Hawthorne for not providing a history of one of the more interesting utopian experiments in nineteenth-century America is to misunderstand what Hawthorne was trying to accomplish in *The Blithedale Romance*. In his preface he expresses "an earnest wish" that someone of that early and distinguished group would write the history of Brook Farm. He makes it very clear that he himself intends no such thing.

More recent critics have commented on the novel's remarkably innovative use of the narrator-participant and have noted the sophistication of Hawthorne's dramatic and technical achievement. But despite the spate of articles and scholarly dissections, *The Blithedale Romance* is still Hawthorne's most enigmatic, ambiguous, multi-leveled, and crafty romance.

In *The Blithedale Romance,* as in his other novels, Hawthorne is not a political propagandist, a historian, a sociologist, or anything but a writer concerned with the *usable truth of the human heart.* Undoubtedly, as he mentions to Sophia in his first letter from Brook Farm, he linked his arctic arrival (and Coverdale's) to the would-be New Jerusalem with that of the Mayflower Puritans who came to the American wilderness to establish the new Eden: "But I reflect that the Plymouth pilgrims arrived in the midst of storm and stept ashore upon mountain snowdrifts."[3] For the nineteenth-century Hawthorne, there was the central paradox of the Calvinist experiment in America: the coupling of a profound conviction of man's depravity with an earnest hope for a new Canaan. The corrupted American dream, corrupted because it became real through men of human frailty, was the paradigm for Hawthorne of his own experience at Brook Farm and of his "counterfeit Arcadia" of Blithedale. It had also informed his ironic vision of the New Jerusalem, foretold, in his Election Sermon, by the fallen Dimmesdale at the end of *The Scarlet Letter.*

Certainly part of Hawthorne's intention in *The Blithedale Romance* was to deal again, as he had in *The Scarlet Letter, The House of the Seven Gables,* and many of his more successful short stories (such as "Young Goodman Brown," "The Birthmark," "Rappaccini's Daughter"), with witchcraft, wizardry, and mesmerism. When Coverdale says in the fourth paragraph of the novel that the veiled lady and her accomplishments "have little to do with the present narrative," he is being deliberately deceptive since the slenderly Gothic plot depends on the mesmeric machinations of Westervelt over the nearly impalpable Priscilla. Hawthorne was at once fascinated and horrified at the despotic control that a malign individual could exert over the mind of another. While he was at Brook Farm, he wrote to Sophia forbidding her to experiment with mesmerism as a way to cure her headaches because he was alarmed over the possibility that one could thus lose dominion over one's quintessential privacy. His ambivalence about the very real power that one individual could exert over the mind of another was related to his understanding of his own vocation as an artist.

If Hawthorne's "unpardonable sin might consist in a want of love and reverence for the Human Soul; in consequence of which, the investigator pried into its dark depths, not with a hope or purpose of making it better, but from a cold philosophical curiosity,—content that it should be wicked in whatever kind or degree, and only desiring to study it out,"[4] then how many of Hawthorne's characters—Coverdale, Chillingworth, Matthew Maule, the "kind friend" in "My Kinsman, Major Molineux," and so many more—were not culpable? And was not Hawthorne himself guilty of violating the human heart to secure material for his art—through his incognitos, his eavesdropping, his icy scrutinizing of his fellow creatures? Hawthorne must have thought he was guilty of so horrible a sin, and his *Notebooks* and the letters reveal his ambivalence about his writing. Although he would have liked to be completely indolent, his Calvinist conscience kept reminding him that idleness is the devil's workshop. Political appointments, such as his surveyorships and later his consulship in Liverpool, gave him a legitimate excuse not to write, but he despised these jobs. His carefully written *Notebooks,* kept diligently while he was busy with his required duties and filled with ideas for future tales, betray his predicament: he could write in his natural voice of the terror of a threatening Calvinist Jehovah, demanding over and over again the ultimate sacrifice for human depravity, and be damned because he despised that angry God; or he could be sluggish and idle, letting his family starve, and be damned; or he could escape the demon in his inkstand and slave in dusty, tedious offices for paltry loathesome money—and be damned! Always underestimating his talent, never aware of his genius, he called himself a "fiction-monger." In *The Blithedale Romance,* Hawthorne discovered some palliative for his own anguished and sorrowing voice by creating the impotent, meddling narrator-participant Coverdale, behind whose shallow sarcasm he could alternately conceal and reveal himself.

Henry James, at least, was convinced that Hawthorne had written in *Blithedale* "the lightest, the brightest, the liveliest" of his novels. It is strange that James, the master of "setting traps for the unwary reader," should have been taken in by Hawthorne, whom he acknowledges so slightly and at times so patronizingly as a "natural, original genius" but provincial and bewildered. James's graceful essay on Hawthorne is notable for some extraordinary insights but also for his apparent blindness to his own prodigious debt to Hawthorne.[5] Nowhere is James's debt more obvious than in *Blithedale,* with Hawthorne's precocious use of Coverdale as narrator-participant. Certainly Winterbourne in *Daisy Miller* could hardly have existed without the example of the wintry, unreliable Coverdale, who as first American voyeur, peers and peeps and spies upon characters in the most dispassionate and glacial manner. For James, Zenobia is the only complete character in the novel and he relegates Coverdale to a minor role. But Coverdale is Hawthorne's most fascinating, ingenious, and original creation.

Presumably, Miles Coverdale is named for Miles Standish, the Puritan leader who sent John Alden to court Priscilla for him with understandable results. Six years after *The Blithedale Romance,* this legend was used in a long poem by Hawthorne's close friend, Longfellow. Miles Coverdale does not send a John Alden to his Priscilla, but a bird which flies past his hermitage. The bird is instructed to tell Priscilla that Miles is the only mortal who "really cares for her," but there is the usual Coverdale qualification; he cares not "for her realities . . . but for the fancy-work with which I have idly decked her out" (100). Coverdale is a masterly creation who dominates in a negative but effective way our impressions of the action and the characters in the novel. A true original, Coverdale, as cold, curious, meddling, unreliable narrator, solves all of the difficulties Hawthorne had with the authorial voice in *The House of the*

*Seven Gables.* By having Coverdale, a priggish, prying, unloving, self-deceived young man tell the story, Hawthorne frees himself from narrative constraint and allows himself the privilege of moving in and out of the character of Coverdale, while maintaining a constant ambiguity over the reader's problem of belief.

Coverdale remembers the story twelve years after the events. He characterizes himself as a frosty bachelor of thirty-eight. The reader perceives him as one who is victimized by the common delusion that he has experienced a hopeless, unrequited love. This great disappointment excuses him for the rest of his life from marriage or any other commitment, while he contents himself with every bodily and material comfort to heal his imagined unhappiness.

At the beginning of the novel Hawthorne's Coverdale, then, out of idleness and a mistaken idea of his own generosity, goes to Blithedale to reform the world. Ironically, *Blithe*dale is the scene of tragedy not *blithe*ness and Coverdale is there to "cover" the events for the reader, as through a glass darkly. Through Coverdale's selfishness, jealousy, and irresponsibility, Hawthorne reveals the impossibility of establishing a new Eden. Ironically, Coverdale, as representative of fallen humanity, blames all of the other characters for having self-interested motives in coming to Blithedale. Zenobia, the glamorous dark beauty with an exotic name, fills Coverdale with admiration for her magnificent, womanly splendor, but frightens him sexually by her proud self-possession. Hollingsworth, or Hollowworth, the single-minded philanthropist, bearish and glowering but sexually irresistible to women, overpowers Coverdale with his all-consuming egotism. When Priscilla, prissy, mindless, and tremulous, attaches herself like a leech to Hollingsworth, Coverdale watches almost dispassionately another reenactment of the Fall in the Blithedale Eden. Westervelt, the devil of the Western World who has a mysterious power over Zenobia (probably an early marriage), is the snake who is able to tempt Zenobia to abandon her intellect and throw Priscilla to him, while her heart and her money—the apple—go to Hollingsworth-Adam. Hollingsworth-Adam is also an inverted Puritan Jehovah who judges Zenobia as Lilith. When impoverished and unable to finance his grandiose scheme for the reform of criminals, he turns to the suddenly wealthy Eve-Priscilla and the Fall is complete, with the suicide of the abandoned Zenobia only heightening the stress.

Westervelt laments the suicide of Zenobia only because his victim has escaped him (like Chillingworth); Hollingsworth-Adam is doomed to live with his own great crime—his Fall and his crypto-murder of Zenobia—and has to abandon his plans to reform other criminals. The ostensibly meek Priscilla-Eve, with her negative aggression, has inherited the earth and the fallen Adam-Hollingsworth. This is indeed a paradise lost for which no Redeemer comes.

The irony in the novel is deep and penetrating. Our last view of the smirking Coverdale is searing. He is, finally, the greatest villain of all, the cold self-deceiver. By resisting any impulse toward love and generosity, he is the utterly homeless man who has allowed himself to become, unwittingly, the arch fiend. His final coy confession, "'I—I myself—was in love—with—PRISCILLA!'" (247), which at first strikes the reader as fatuous, is seen on further reflection to be Hawthorne's final irony—the complete self-cozening of Coverdale.

Thus the theme and intention of *The Blithedale Romance,* hardly "bright" as James called it, or "genial" as Hawthorne wanted it to be, is the enactment of another Fall from Eden, this time in the pastoral counterfeit Arcadia of depraved humanity's most yearned for, noble, and ultimately self-delusive ideal, utopia in nineteenth-century New England.

II

Probably Hawthorne's greatest accomplishment in *The Blithedale Romance,* and one of his greatest as an artist, is his solution to the novelist's omnipresent problems of establishing point of view, authorial voice, and aesthetic distance. He created a minor poet narrator-participant who, glacial, devious, consumed with impertinent curiosity, and yet determined to stand apart from any passionate involvement with his fellow creatures, resembles Hawthorne's unfalteringly Calvinistic view of himself as artist. The prismatic voice of Coverdale affects the reader in a variety of ways. By turns cold, calculating, offensive, self-pitying, unreliable, skeptical, meddlesome, sulking, and sadistic, he reveals himself as a complex, nasty, and still most necessary personage. In the last chapter he confesses that he has "made but a poor and dim figure in my own narrative" (245). What opulent irony, for while it is true that he never emerges from his cover to assume a precise shape, he is the main character in the novel and from his directive voice we must draw our judgments of the action and characters. The fact that he is often despicable does not lessen his significance, and his skewed reporting only provides Hawthorne with a more convincing device for offering the alternate explanations so necessary to his masterful ambiguity. Since Coverdale has two preeminent functions in the novel, as both authorial voice and major character, he will be discussed in this section in his more obvious role of narrator, and in Section V as a character.

Zenobia frequently accuses Coverdale of having no serious purpose in coming to Blithedale and of obtruding himself into her private life only to provide himself with material for a ballad. Despite Coverdale's disclaimers, *The Blithedale Romance* is indeed his ballad. He says in the last chapter ("Miles Coverdale's Confession") that he has given up poetry for the last ten years, but the romance itself, written twelve years after the events at Blithedale, has in it some of the prime ingredients of the ballad: a touch of the supernatural—the spells Westervelt casts over Priscilla and his mysterious power over Zenobia; a pinch of demonism—the devil figure, Westervelt, with his serpent cane; the demon lover—Hollingsworth, the diabolically egotistic philanthropist; a measure of ghastly tragedy—the suicide of Zenobia and the hideous inflexibility of her drowned body; and a soupçon of a refrain—the constant, jealous, petulant, self-pitying, and self-deceiving complaints of Coverdale.

Hawthorne achieves, through Coverdale, a remarkably ironic aesthetic distancing from the intrigues of the characters and the machinations of the action of *The Blithedale Romance.* Several removes from actual life are managed by having the characters involved in the mock life of the pseudo-Arcadia, Blithedale; by having Coverdale tell the story of this sham life; and by having Hawthorne hovering behind Coverdale, sometimes speaking through him or Hollingsworth, but much of the time lurking slyly and ironically behind his creation. The problem, then, that we observed in *The Scarlet Letter* of the omniscient narrator gradually making closure of the aesthetic distance is obviated in *The Blithedale Romance.* This novel also does not suffer from the artistic discrepancy created in *The House of the Seven Gables* by using an unnaturally brisk third-person omniscient authorial voice to tell a tale of inherited guilt and sin.

Coverdale cleverly tries to mask his intrusive shadowing and eavesdropping activity, like that of a clumsy amateur detective, by proclaiming that he is a chorus:

> My own part, . . . was singularly subordinate. It resembled that of the
> Chorus in a classic play, which seems to be set aloof from the possibility of
> personal concernment. . . . Destiny, it may be—the most skilful of stage-
> managers—seldom chooses to arrange its scenes, and carry forward its
> drama, without securing the presence of at least *one calm observer*. It is his
> office . . . to . . . distil, in his long-brooding thought, the whole moral-
> ity of the performance. (97)

Typically, Coverdale gives his inept, bumbling voyeurism a dignity and a
function that it does not have. A calm observer he is, but his calmness and
chilliness exclude him from a more vital role because he is also selfish,
jealous, and fundamentally a bore. The chorus in a classic drama has a
right to observe all the actions; Coverdale does not. He sulks and struts
like a spoiled child robbed of what he imagines to be his due: the focus of
all attention, center stage. Unloved and unloving, he adopts the vocation
of voyeur, with the reader as his confidant. Yet the reader, because of the
intriguing drama, does not object to Coverdale's invidious snooping but
only wishes he were more competent at his job of ferreting. The skill with
which Hawthorne manipulates this priggish reporter amazes those of us
who condescendingly assume that only a twentieth-century writer could
have such psychologically acute insights into the heart of the clinical
observer.

In telling the story of the veiled lady and Moodie-Fauntleroy, Hawthorne does not have the problem of trying to alter the style, as he did in
*The House of the Seven Gables* when Holgrave recounts to Phoebe the legend
of Alice Pyncheon. In *The House of the Seven Gables* Hawthorne solved the
problem by ignoring it and the voice of Holgrave does not differ from that
of the omniscient narrator. In *The Blithedale Romance* Coverdale tells all the
stories, so no artistic adjustment has to be made. Coverdale vexes the
reader by not getting to Blithedale in time for the great dramatic judgment scene at Eliot's pulpit, but Henry James's master, Hawthorne, knew
exactly what he was doing. He had a great scene which would have been
damnably difficult to write and ultimately unsatisfactory, and so he left it
out and instead showed the results of the crisis, through the reporting of
Coverdale, on the sensibilities of the participants. Even though the obtuse
Coverdale lacks sensitivity and empathy, he tells us what he sees; all of
Hawthorne's artistry is invoked because in this scene, as in so many others
that Coverdale describes in the novel, the reader learns far more about the
situation and the characters than Coverdale does. We despise Coverdale

for his induration as we make judgments that he is incapable of, but we need him to tell us the story and allow us to gloat over our superior moral insight and perception.

Coverdale is torn—as much as a clinical observer can be—by being left out of the passionate relationships of Zenobia, Hollingsworth, and Priscilla and so he tries to view them with godlike detachment. If he can be a god and judge mankind cruelly, then he will not have to feel slighted as a man. Coverdale is the true monster in the pastoral. Unlike *The House of the Seven Gables,* the tone of *The Blithedale Romance* is remarkably consistent—Coverdale never changes nor learns anything—but, rather than becoming a deity, is an incarnate Paul Pry.

### III

All the characters at Blithedale are deluded hypocrites, but Coverdale is the most deceived. The dominant imagery and symbolism of *The Blithedale Romance* is that of the deceptive quality of appearance and reality. This imagery, which is functional to the theme, accumulates ambiguity and equivocation because of the unreliability of Coverdale as narrator. The characters also sham behind their names: Coverdale covers up what he pleases and constantly conceals himself while eavesdropping on the others but reveals himself to the reader; Zenobia conceals herself behind the name of an oriental princess—her other name, Coverdale says, is well known, but it is never revealed; Priscilla, apparently without a last name until near the end (Fauntleroy-Moodie), hides behind the veil of her own evanescence; Hollingsworth, with no first name, discloses himself to be of hollow worth; Moodie has assumed a name appropriate to his character; and Westervelt embodies the demonism of the entire Western world.

Not only are the characters cloaked (and yet sometimes paradoxically revealed) in their names, they are also screened by the roles they assume in the "counterfeit Arcadia" (21). No one is what he appears to be. There is not only the veil of the veiled lady, Priscilla, but also the eye patch behind which old Moodie tries to hide as he skulks about furtively. The handsome Westervelt's false teeth warn Coverdale of a deeper "moral and physical humbug," and suggest that "his wonderful beauty of face . . . might be removable like a mask" (95).

The using up of old clothes by the Arcadians suppresses what identities they have: when they finally adopt a kind of blue smock uniform, anyone might be anyone. When Coverdale returns to Blithedale and stumbles on the masquerade, it is "as if Comus and his crew were holding their revels" (209). All but Hollingsworth, Silas Foster, and Priscilla are in costume, mask over mask, and Coverdale is startled by an Indian chief, the goddess Diana, Shakers, shepherds, grim Puritans, Cavaliers, "Moll Pitcher, the renowned old witch of Lynn," and many more "vassals" of the Queen of the Masquerade—Zenobia (209–11). Like the Merrymounters (in "The Maypole of Merrymount"), the Blithedalers are self-deceived and seem to be spoiling for Eliot of Eliot's pulpit to apply the whips and stocks of Puritan reality to the daydreams of a carefree worldly utopia of human progress.

Hollingsworth imagines himself a god who could prey upon the naïveté of the reformers for his own selfish purposes. That monumental self-deception explodes with Zenobia's sudden knowledge, after he has rejected her in favor of the now wealthy Priscilla: "'You are a better masquerader than the witches and gipsies yonder; for your disguise is a self-deception'" (218). But since there is no one but the reader to show Coverdale the realities and since the reader cannot do so, Coverdale, like Prufrock, pursues a death in life. We see the real ogre of *The Blithedale Romance* twelve years after the tragedy of Blithedale: "Being well to do in the world, and having nobody but myself to care for, I live very much at my ease, and fare sumptuously every day" (246).

Eden imagery (found in all of Hawthorne's novels because the Fall is always reenacted) pervades *The Blithedale Romance,* functioning as an ironic contrast to the mock deceptive Eden of Blithedale. Coverdale's excursion to Blithedale begins unprosperously enough in an April blizzard. Presaging trouble in Eden, Coverdale complains of "our exploded scheme for beginning the life of Paradise anew. Paradise, indeed! Nobody else in the world . . . nobody, at least, in our bleak little world of New England—had dreamed of Paradise, that day, except as the pole suggests the tropic" (9–10). When Zenobia greets the crypto-Arcadians warmly, Coverdale condoles with Zenobia about women's work still being in the kitchen:

> It is odd enough, that the kind of labor which falls to the lot of women is just that which chiefly distinguishes artificial life—the life of degenerated mortals—from the life of Paradise. Eve had no dinner-pot, and no clothes to mend, and no washing-day.
>
> "I am afraid," said Zenobia . . . , "we shall find some difficulty in adopting the Paradisiacal system, for at least a month to come. . . . As for

the garb of Eden," added she, . . . "I shall not assume it till after May-day!" (16–17)

With his uncanny instinct for understanding psychological aberrations, Hawthorne has his voyeur, Coverdale, immediately undress Zenobia in his imagination, a task that would have been unnecessary in Eden:

> . . . these last words . . . irresistibly brought up a picture of that fine, perfectly developed figure, in Eve's earliest garment. . . . One felt an influence breathing out of her, such as we might suppose to come from Eve, when she was just made, and her Creator brought her to Adam, saying—"Behold, here is a woman!" (17)

But poor Coverdale is no match for Zenobia, a fully developed woman, much less an Eve or Lilith. As she sets the table for him in this mock Eden, she asks him:

> "Do you think you can be content—instead of figs, pineapples, and all the other delicacies of Adam's supper-table—with tea and toast. . . . And there shall be bread-and-milk, too, if the innocence of your taste demands it." (17–18)

Bread and milk slops seem to be the true food for Miles Coverdale, who vainly prides himself as a connoisseur of fine cuisine and spirits. Amateurs, dilettantes, and triflers can have no part of the rage in Eden; they may only peek through the bushes and hear the cosmic *non serviam.*

Priscilla, delivered by Hollingsworth out of the snowstorm and into the sham Eden, believes she is in paradise. Never recognizing Westervelt as a devil, or Zenobia as a Lilith, she naturally thinks of the iron Hollingsworth as a god. Nor does he ever disabuse her of that conviction, since he shares it.

The arrival of Westervelt signals loudly the devil to pay. No archangel fallen, he is still a most beautiful young man exposed only by his inauthentic brilliant teeth and his serpent stick. Coverdale suspects that under the mask of masculine splendor is "a wizened little elf, gray and decrepit, with nothing genuine about him, save the wicked expression of his grin" (95).

Once the devil has arrived in Eden, the wintry Arcadia heats up as Zenobia and Priscilla become rivals for the attentions of the would-be deity, Hollingsworth, who makes pseudepigraphical pronouncements (70–71). And so the Fall is decreed. Hollingsworth, at once a false god and an Adam, tries mercilessly with his tyrannical powers to make instant slaves of women and dallies with Zenobia and Priscilla until he makes his judgment of Zenobia under the aegis of Eliot's pulpit. Moreover, when he takes over Eliot's Calvinist zeal (but only for self-serving purposes), he casts the now impoverished Zenobia-Lilith aside and embraces the *nouveau riche* Eve-Priscilla. Superficially, we have a god-Adam, Hollingsworth, filled with self-adulation, and an innocent Eve-Priscilla. But Hawthorne's irony makes us see a self-ordained deity in Hollingsworth and a parasitic Priscilla, whose triumph over Zenobia is completed by passionately aggressive meekness.

As Priscilla humbly backs up, she pushes Zenobia over the wall of Eden and into the rash suicide which is Zenobia-Lilith's final revenge against the false god-Adam Hollingsworth. This dreadful and final hostile act of Zenobia destroys the iron man and changes him from a deity into a debilitated "murderer" clinging to the arm of the triumphant Eve-Priscilla. That the necessary duplication of the Fall—necessary because of Hawthorne's tragic vision of corrupted human nature—should take place in a mock Eden, peopled by self-deluded devotees of progress who hope to reform the world, redoubles the thrust of Hawthorne's bitterness. But, as usual, Hawthorne screens the barbarousness of his vision through veils of ambiguity and through the equivocation of his dubious narrator-observer-participant.

There is no heartfelt laughter in this joyless Eden, but the symbolism of laughter and smiles, although less prominent than in some tales, functions in *The Blithedale Romance* as it always does in a Hawthorne story—the laughter and smiles are devilish, tragic, and more devastating than tears. When he first meets Zenobia, Coverdale thinks her laugh "mellow, almost broad . . . but not in the least like an ordinary woman's laugh" (16). Later, the competition between Zenobia and Priscilla for Hollingsworth's affection becomes more devious: Zenobia's smile is "mischievous" when at the conclusion of her rendering of the legend of the veiled lady she throws the veil over Priscilla. After Coverdale crassly gets entrance to the boarding house in the city to continue his spying, Zenobia smiles "but, as I thought, with a good deal of scornful anger underneath" (162). From this point on the menace in Zenobia's smiles and laughter becomes more obvious. Coverdale reports that Zenobia laughs when she tells him she has been on trial before Hollingsworth for her life. But Coverdale sees no mirth as he sees in Hollingsworth "the grim portrait of a Puritan magistrate, holding inquest of life and death in a case of witch-craft; [or]—in Zenobia, the sorceress herself, not aged, wrinkled, and decrepit, but fair enough to tempt Satan with a force reciprocal to his own" (214). As Hollingsworth summons Priscilla to him, Zenobia smiles at the revenge Hollingsworth has taken, but it is a smile of dreadful defeat (219). After Hollingsworth and Priscilla have left, Coverdale watches Zenobia sob tearlessly and when she regains some composure she becomes aware that, of course, Coverdale is there watching her. It is then that she accuses him, smiling, of "turning this whole affair into a ballad" (223), a deadly barb which is lost on Coverdale, whose emotions, he says, have been so tortured and overwrought that he falls asleep for several hours!

Coverdale's smiles and laughter reveal his selfishness, his petulance, and finally his demonic self-delusion. When Priscilla arrives at Blithe-dale, Coverdale smiles at her distress out of "the iron substance of my heart" (29); he laughs even louder than Westervelt at Hollingsworth and at "our especial scheme of reform, which . . . looked so ridiculous that it was impossible not to laugh aloud" (101); he smiles at Zenobia's feminist convictions, saying that "what amused and puzzled me, was the fact, that women, however intellectually superior, so seldom disquiet themselves about the rights or wrongs of their sex, unless their own individual affections chance to lie in idleness, or to be ill at ease" (120–21). Here we suspect that Hawthorne, who believed that women should attempt no more than needlework, is ironically concurring. To taunt Zenobia, Cover-dale laughs at Hollingsworth and makes the reader laugh ironically at him when he says, on his last trip back to Blithedale to snoop further, "I laughed with the bitterness of self-scorn, remembering how *unreservedly I had given up my heart and soul* to interests that were not mine" (205). The masked Arcadians hear his burst of laughter and then truly and finally recognize him for what he is: "'The voice was Miles Coverdale's,' said the fiendish fiddler, with a whisk of his tail and a toss of his horns. 'My music has brought him hither. He is always ready to dance to the devil's tune'"(211).

Beautiful flowers grew in Eden, and in the mock Eden of Blithedale the multiple flower images assume a sexual function. Zenobia, the gorgeous dark beauty with the mysterious past, wears an exotic hothouse flower in her hair, a new and fresh one each day. Coverdale thinks it "an outlandish flower—a flower of the tropics, such as appeared to have sprung passionately out of a soil. . . . This favorite ornament was actually a subtile expression of Zenobia's character" (45). He also associates it with carnal knowledge and speculates salaciously and endlessly on Zenobia's sexual experience: "Zenobia has lived, and loved! *There is no folded petal, no latent dew-drop, in this perfectly developed rose!*" (48). Poor feeble Coverdale. Only in his wildest daydreams could Zenobia have "unfolded" herself to him. Both terrified and fascinated, our shrinking voyeur has to content himself with undressing Zenobia in his imagination to quiet his castration terror. In town, Zenobia's natural flower is transfigured to one "exquisitely imitated in jeweller's work" (164), which highlights the chameleon quality of Zenobia.

Priscilla appears first at Blithedale as "a flower-shrub that had done its best to blossom in too scanty light" (27); later, as she grows healthier, Zenobia says, "The best type of her is one of those anemones" (59). Spring flower that she is, Priscilla must in Coverdale's mind be virginal and even after he discovers that she is and has been under the devil Westervelt's power as a mesmerized veiled lady, he is positive "she had kept, as I religiously believe, her virgin reserve and sanctity of soul, throughout it all" (203). As a "pure, pale flower" (224), Priscilla is no threat to Coverdale's questionable virility. Zenobia's marriage gift to Priscilla via Coverdale of her jewelled flower ironically symbolizes Priscilla's passage from virgin to sexual initiate.

The imagery of fire and hearth is juxtaposed ironically at the beginning of the novel with cold and snow imagery. The enterprise begins in a vicious April blizzard (itself a paradox, an irony, or an oxymoron) and Coverdale laments, as Hawthorne did, having to desert his comfortable coal grate fire for the unknown and untried Blithedale. Recalling Blithedale and its roaring short-lived fire, the aging narrator Coverdale tries to rake out his memories. The exhausted fire is now just "the merest phosphoric glimmer. . . . Around such chill mockery of a fire, some few of us might sit, . . . spreading out each a palm towards the imaginary warmth, and talk over our exploded scheme for beginning the life of Paradise anew" (9). The fires of the do-gooders are too abundant and burn out quickly as Silas Foster warns, "but whether he meant to insinuate that our moral illumination would have as brief a term, I cannot say" (25). The reader, of course, can say. Coverdale expresses his disillusionment with the transitory fire and the lofty enterprise in layers of irony: "*I rejoice that I could once think better of the world's improvability than it deserved*" (20). The fire dies as rapidly as do the schemes of the Arcadians for the reformation of humanity. The dreary snowstorm also is "a symbol of the cold, desolate, distrustful phantoms that invariably haunt the mind . . . to warn us back within the boundaries of ordinary life" (18). Priscilla appears to be "some desolate kind of a creature, doomed to wander about in snowstorms" (27), but the imagery surrounding her arrival suggests the tension that will flourish between her and Zenobia. Zenobia, a creature of the fire, hovers about it and the glow in her cheeks makes Coverdale "think of Pandora, fresh from Vulcan's workshop and full of the celestial *warmth* by dint of which he had tempered and moulded her" (24). Priscilla, "*melted* in quietly amongst us" (25) and the watery Priscilla is symbolically set at odds with the fiery Pandora-Zenobia, the all-endowed woman made by Vulcan in his evil smithy (the self-absorbed blacksmith, Hollingsworth) as the god's revenge on mankind for the gift of fire by Prometheus. Pandora-Zenobia, the underworld goddess, finally opens her box after the crisis of Eliot's pulpit. By exchanging roles with Priscilla, Zenobia electing death by water, she wills to Priscilla her jewelled flower, which is, in essence, a Pandora's box containing all the ills that have ever since afflicted mankind. Priscilla becomes the feeble fire, only warm enough to sustain the guilt-stained Hollingsworth: Zenobia goes to her watery death, and the contamination of Eden by evil and violent death burns and drowns man's foolish hopes of earthly paradise. The irony is as searing as Vulcan's smithy, and the water and fire interchanged by Priscilla and Zenobia combine with the ingredients of the "salubrious" country air to destroy the fourth element, the fallen earth, where man can only reenact the Fall in Eden.

The head-heart symbolism, so pervasive in Hawthorne's fiction, becomes in *The Blithedale Romance* confounded with mesmerism and magnetic power, and this coupling serves to increase the ironic effect. Hollingsworth's magnetism causes Zenobia to violate her own heart when, in her love for Hollingsworth, she abandons her feminist convictions and agrees with his view of women. Women who act independently from men, says Hollingsworth, should have all men gather "to scourge them back within their proper bounds" (123). Priscilla has no head to lose; she tells Coverdale that she never thinks at all (75)—and so she gives ("the gentle parasite" [123]) her heart completely to Hollingsworth. Even Coverdale is tempted to be Hollingsworth's slave and commit himself to discipleship in Hollingsworth's religion of self, which is ironically expressed through his "selfless" reform of criminals. Too much a self-deluded egotist to be anyone's follower, however, Coverdale refuses. Zenobia, after she has been judged by Hollingsworth and tossed aside, regrets most that "a great and rich heart has been ruined in your breast" (219). Coverdale, admitting that his "dog-kennel of the heart" (90) has been devoted "too exclusively" to the study of others, "making my prey of people's individualities" (84), finally partially recognizes his own monstrosity—but only momentarily: "That cold tendency, between instinct and intellect, which made me pry with a speculative interest into people's passions and impulses, appeared to have gone far towards unhumanizing my heart" (154). He continues to violate human hearts in his cold voyeurism, and these occasional confessions seem to derive from Hawthorne's own *mea culpa*. Westervelt, the professional mesmerist, profaner of hearts, and devil figure, is annoyed at Zenobia's suicide since she has wasted her mind because of her heart— "that troublesome organ" (240).

The surface irony of Coverdale, terrified of mesmerism (198) yet making prey of human hearts in as casual a manner as a mesmerist, gives way to the deeper and more perturbing irony of Coverdale-Hawthorne's excuse for continuing the voyeurism: Hollingsworth, Zenobia, and Priscilla "stood forth as the indices of a problem which it was my business to solve" (69). And yet as soon as death (Zenobia's) becomes part of the problem Coverdale is blubbering in fright that the devil might get Zenobia's soul or, more terrifying, that she has struggled against Providence, or, most intimidating of all, that she will be sent to hell by an angry God and be damned forever, if—unspoken horror of nihilism— there is a God. The dread of nothingness, ill-concealed by Coverdale in the last chapter when he tells of his life since Zenobia's death—"Nothing, nothing, nothing!" (245)—only accentuates the ludicrousness of his self-delusion and presages the philosophical uncertainties of Hawthorne-Coverdale.

Death imagery saturates *The Blithedale Romance,* but it functions most effectively and ironically when it is used to adumbrate the ghastly drowning of Zenobia. The novel begins in April and although the snowstorm makes it the cruelest month, spring does come, bringing apparent life to the dead land. As the novel ends in September and the promise of winter and death is fulfilled, Zenobia's ostensibly light-hearted reception of the snow-covered Hollingsworth and Priscilla—"'the sable knight Hollingsworth and this shadowy snow-maiden, who, precisely at the stroke of midnight, shall melt away at my feet, in a pool of ice-cold water, and give

me my death with a pair of wet slippers!'" (33)—is remembered as
Coverdale awakens at midnight. Horrified, he summons Hollingsworth
and Silas, who finds Zenobia's soaked French slipper embedded in the
mud. As the summer passes, Coverdale speculates paradoxically to Hollingsworth that Blithedale will never be "'a real . . . system of human
life, until somebody has sanctified it by death'" (130). He wonders who
will be the first to die and wants to choose "the rudest, roughest, most
uncultivable spot, for Death's garden-ground; and Death shall teach us to
beautify it, grave by grave. By our sweet, calm way of dying . . . the
final scene shall lose its terrors; . . . it may be happiness to live, and bliss
to die" (130). This shallow, fatuous optimism about blissful death is
juxtaposed with the nightmarish hooking of Zenobia's rigid body from
the black river. Earlier, when Coverdale trespassed in Zenobia's city apartment and savagely taunted her about Hollingsworth's tenderness for Priscilla, he noticed that her face in the mirror (as is often the case in
Hawthorne, this is a prophetic mirror) was "very pale;—as pale, in her
rich attire, as if a shroud were round her" (167). The details of the
recovery of Zenobia's body—including Hollingsworth's hooking her in
the breast, the attempts to straighten her rigid legs and hands, and the
gruesome procession back to the house with Zenobia's body on a rail fence
bier—certainly rank among Hawthorne's great artistic accomplishments,
but Hawthorne-Coverdale's anxiety about the possible damnation of
Zenobia's soul is the touch not only of a great writer but of a crypto-
Calvinist. The funeral, unlike the ones planned by the Arcadians to
express their "eternal hopes," conforms "with the old fashion" (238–39)
yet lacks any religious representative or comfort: "We all stood around the
narrow niche in the cold earth; all saw the coffin lowered in; all heard the
rattle of the crumbly soil upon its lid—that final sound, which mortality
awakens on the utmost verge of sense, as if in the vain hope of bringing an
echo from the spiritual world" (239). This novel is hardly as "bright" as it
appeared to Henry James.

IV

The structure of *The Blithedale Romance,* while not as tight as that imposed
by the three great pillory scenes of *The Scarlet Letter* or the central house-
heart of *The House of the Seven Gables,* until the wrenching ending, has a
circular simplicity that is pleasing. The main characters move from the
unreal city to the unreal country, and back to the city before converging at

Blithedale for the great tragedy of Zenobia's suicide after which they scatter to cottage and city. The patterned beginning and ending in Coverdale's snug and elegant apartments in Boston enclose the action and supply the tacit comment that nothing about Coverdale has changed.

The four main characters, all seemingly unattached, thirty years old or younger, and at loose ends, set out for Blithedale ostensibly on a mission of reform and dedication. We soon learn that they are all homeless creatures looking for a home: Hollingsworth, seeming to come straight from his anvil, seeks a patron (or patroness), disciples, and the Blithedale property as a home for his project of reforming criminals; Zenobia, the beauteous and dark exotic, presumably weathy orphan, and ardent feminist, looks for a home where she can expend her tremendous energy and benevolence; Priscilla, the nearly impalpable seamstress oppressed by urban blight, searches for a home and a sister; Coverdale, prosperous bachelor dilettante, tries to acquire a home in which he will be worshipped and adulated, and, if it is not too much trouble, perhaps do someone some good. The great irony is that not one of the four is what he seems and that no one finds a home at Blithedale, except Zenobia in her grave. The novel's structure, then, only points out that the journey of the reformers to Arcadia occasions no reform but only an ordained tableau of the first Eden, with paradise destroyed, not regained.

The action of the plot is fairly complex but determined by the corrupted human beings who are the characters. Apparently abandoning the evil, dissipation, frivolity, and polluted air of the city to go to a rural Arcadia, which is to form the nucleus of the new Eden of progress and community, the four main characters find in the pastoral Blithedale the evils of jealousy, competition (the neighboring farmers are viewed as business rivals by the Blithedalers), violation of the heart, and, finally, engulfing egotism and death. The plot creaks at times with rusty Gothicism: discovered relationships (Zenobia and Priscilla as daughters of the same father); mesmeric spells (the spiritual captivity of Priscilla to the mesmerist-devil Westervelt and Zenobia's probable early marriage to him); and the sisterly love rivalry (the openly aggressive pursuit by Zenobia of the messianic Hollingsworth and the negatively aggressive meekness of Priscilla who ultimately wins Hollingsworth).

Some critics have complained that the suicide of Zenobia is contrived, unmotivated, and melodramatic and that it was included in the novel only so that Hawthorne could fictionalize a similar event in which he was involved, an incident which he records, in detail, in his notebooks. This seems mere caviling. Although one of the most awesome and terrorizing scenes that Hawthorne ever wrote, it is not intended to be melodramatic. The suicide of Zenobia and its consequences are necessary to put the proper blight on Blithedale, where the Fall of man is ritually reenacted, and to put Hawthorne's quietus on the deceptive dreams of fallen man for new truth and progress. Zenobia's moral is not, therefore, incidental but required by Hawthorne's Calvinism:

> *"There are no new truths,* much as we have prided ourselves on finding some. A moral? Why, this: —that, in the battle-field of life, the downright stroke, that would fall only on a man's steel head-piece, is sure to light on a woman's heart, over which she wears no breastplate, and whose wisdom it is, therefore, to keep out of the conflict. Or this: —that the whole universe, her own sex and yours, and Providence, or Destiny, to boot, make common cause against the *woman who swerves one hair's breadth out of the beaten track.* Yes; and add . . . that, *with that one hair's breadth, she goes all astray, and never sees the world in its true aspect, afterwards!"* (224)

Zenobia, unlike the damned Hester who prates of "new truths," is finally undeceived and recognizes that despite the Blithedalers' desire for human progress, *"there are no new truths."* She also acknowledges the "truth" of *The Scarlet Letter* that one step astray leads to the breach in the ruined wall—reprobation.

While *The Scarlet Letter* opens with the prison that adjoins the cemetery and closes with the prison of the grave, the penultimate chapter of *The Blithedale Romance* places us beside Zenobia's grave at Blithedale and the final chapter in Coverdale's quarters twelve years later. We see these sumptuous apartments as Coverdale's prison, the prison of the totally selfish and self-deluded voyeur who thinks he has been in love. For Nathaniel Hawthorne graveyard and prison are man's inheritance east of Eden, no matter what utopia he projects for himself.[6]

## V

In the cast of characters of *The Blithedale Romance* we have the typical Hawthornean devil-villain, Westervelt, but with the difference that Westervelt, from a distance at least, is a beautiful man; Priscilla, the pale mesmeree, more diaphanous than most of Hawthorne's variations on Sophia but triumphant; Silas Foster, the shrewd Yankee with his mind on his pigs and his dung heap; Old Moodie, a sidewise, covert, one-eyed skulker; and the splendid creations of Hollingsworth, Zenobia, and Coverdale.

Coverdale, a Hawthorne manqué, is the most intriguing and important character in the novel. Because his pride is stung when Zenobia, Hollingsworth, and Priscilla do not recognize him as a superior creature, and because he is not sought after, pursued, and made much of, he becomes not only the most contemptible spy but sadistic, derisive, and taunting to the very characters he longs to have admire him. His jealousy, pique, and voyeurism give a density and a multi-leveled significance to everything he reports and the reader alternates between despising him and being annoyed with him because he is such an inefficient and nugatory peeper. Artistically, he is surely one of Hawthorne's most prodigious achievements.

Coverdale's selfishness is shown early on when he is asked by Old Moodie if he will do him a "very great favor," as Coverdale goes to Blithedale the next day: "'A very great one!' repeated I . . . although I was ready to do the old man *any amount of kindness involving no special trouble to myself*" (7). The irony of Coverdale's setting out for Blithedale to labor in the vineyards for the reform of the world, and yet being unwilling to do anything that would involve any special trouble to himself, points up the half-mocking comment the man makes about himself at the very end: "were there any cause, in this whole chaos of human struggle, worth a sane man's dying for, and which my death would benefit, then—*provided, however, the effort did not involve an unreasonable amount of trouble—methinks I might be bold to offer up my life*" (246–47). There has been no real change in Coverdale; perhaps he is even more selfish and self-indulgent twelve years after Blithedale. So, when he coyly confesses, blushing and turning away his face, that he was in love with Priscilla, we are amused and also angry that he is still so comfortable in his self-delusion, and, though self-indulgent, fiercely judgmental of others.

Modern psychiatrists describe voyeurism as if they had invented it. An isolated individual who fears women and doubts his sexual adequacy, the voyeur gets a heightened sexual response both from peeping and from the danger of being caught. The voyeur's peeping gives him satisfaction without risk of rejection or failure, reassuring him of his potency, and serving as an outlet for aggressive hostile drives, since peeping is a stealthy act and probably makes the voyeur feel superior to the people he is watching. This description could have come from someone who had just read *The Blithedale Romance,* as well as from a psychological dictionary. Coverdale undresses Zenobia in his imagination, speculates on her lost virginity, and then feels cheated; he has to convince himself over and over that Priscilla retained her virginity in her enslavement to Westervelt so she would be worthy of his (Coverdale's) love; he also has sexual fantasies about his hermitage with its "grapevine, of unusual size and luxuriance," marrying the trees "with a perfectly inextricable knot of polygamy" and he imagines it as a perfect place to spend a honeymoon, "had it ever been my fortune" to have one. He thinks of it as "my one exclusive possession . . . , it symbolized my individuality, and aided me in keeping it inviolate," and fantasizes his appearing before the community "with shoulders bent beneath the burthen of ripe grapes, and some of the crushed ones crimsoning my brow as with a blood-stain" (98–99). The sexual connotations are obvious and rather pathetic, especially when we consider Coverdale's confession of love for Priscilla at the conclusion of the novel. Filled with self-love, he could never have loved Priscilla, nor would he have wanted her clinging to him like his grapevines, because this would have cost him "special trouble." Zenobia's legend of the veiled lady and of Theodore's everlasting woe and regret is the Keatsian Romanticism of "La Belle Dame Sans Merci," and Coverdale immediately identifies himself with the deprived lover fated to "waste life in a feverish quest" (114), a much more felicitous view to take of himself than the true one of impotent voyeur. Our last view of Coverdale as a totally self-indulgent, sybarite bachelor accentuates the caustic irony of his vast self-deception.

It is ironically amusing that Sophia, who industriously crossed out of Hawthorne's notebooks all allusions to smoking and drinking or to her children's natural functions, should have been so delightfully and transcendentally oblivious to these sexual references, except for altering "breast" to "bosom." It is equally pleasant to think of the ways in which Hawthorne got his sly revenge. The Sophia-like characters are all somewhat fatuous—dear Phoebe (Hawthorne's pet name for Sophia) is a witless sunbeam; Priscilla, apparently meek, is single-mindedly aggressive about getting Hollingsworth; and Hilda, the Dove in *The Marble Faun* (another pet name for Sophia), is an inflexible, uncharitable prude.

After Coverdale's recovery from the cold that he had feared would take his life, he feels reborn: "In literal and physical truth, I was quite another man" (61). Ironically, despite his belief in his resurrection ("I had a lively sense of the exultation which the spirit will enter on the next stage of its eternal progress, after leaving the heavy burthen of its mortality in an earthly grave . . . " [61]), he is the same man. He feels some qualms about "prying into his [Hollingsworth's] character" but adds pathetically: "I could not help it" (69). His resurrection has been only into a more determined snoop, especially as he now views the three characters— Zenobia, Hollingsworth, and Priscilla—as figuring "so largely on my private theatre" (70). Besides relegating his friends to characters in a drama enacted solely for his own amusement, Coverdale admits "making my prey of people's individualities, as my custom was" (84), which seems as much as anything to be Hawthorne's private-public confession of *his own* secret guilt. Hawthorne's suspicion was that his own art pandered to his inclination to violate the human heart, coldly and curiously. Thus, by his own definition of it, he himself was guilty of the unforgivable sin.

After Coverdale returns to the city from Blithedale and amuses himself looking out the third floor window at the "backside of the universe" (148), he convinces himself that the fronts of residences are "a veil and a concealment. Realities keep in the rear" (149). In taking this backside view of the universe, he is convinced that what he sees of Zenobia, Priscilla, and Westervelt in the back window of their apartment is reality and he is dreadfully affronted when Zenobia drops the window shade to cut off his view. After admitting that he longs for a catastrophe, he cannot imagine, in his sadistic voyeurism, why Zenobia and Hollingsworth have not selected him as their observer (161).

But Zenobia gets brief revenge when Coverdale decides to call on Zenobia and Priscilla since she (Zenobia) has deprived him of his view of their activities. Coverdale mocks Zenobia by asking her whether Hollingsworth has ever seen Priscilla in her lovely dress and Zenobia warns him, "'It is dangerous, sir, believe me, to tamper thus with earnest human passions, out of your own mere idleness, and for your sport. I will endure it no longer! . . . I warn you!'" (170). Coverdale virtuously responds with the usual defense of the interfering busybody: "'It is an uncertain sense of some duty to perform, that brings my thought, and therefore my words, continually to that one point'" (170). Zenobia's answer contains a most insightful view of Coverdale's character:

> "Oh, this stale excuse of duty! . . . Bigotry; self-conceit; an insolent curiosity; a meddlesome temper; a cold-blooded criticism, founded on a shallow interpretation of half-perceptions; a monstrous scepticism in regard to any conscience or any wisdom, except one's own; a most irreverent

propensity to thrust Providence aside and substitute one's self in its awful place—out of these, and other motives as miserable as these, comes your idea of duty! But beware, sir! With all your fancied acuteness, you step blindfold into these affairs. For any mischief that may follow your interference, I hold you responsible!" (170–71)

A sensitive man, as Coverdale thinks he is, would have been destroyed by this angry but tellingly accurate accusation. But Coverdale merely bows to Priscilla and, Pilate-like, says of the responsibility Zenobia charges him with, "'I wash my hands of it all'" (171).

Coverdale washes his hands of any responsibility which he may incur as interfering mischief-maker but does not refrain from further prying. He seeks out Old Moodie to extract more information, which he dignifies by the term "my subsequent researches" (181). When he returns to Blithedale, Zenobia reminds him of his function in the novel: "'This long while past, you have been following up your game, groping for human emotions in the dark corners of the heart'" (214). We are made more and more aware, through Zenobia's view of him and our cumulative knowledge of him, that Coverdale has become monstrous.

Later, in the search for the drowned Zenobia, Coverdale seems terrified of Silas Foster's remark, "'I half thought it was the Evil One on the same errand as ourselves—searching for Zenobia!'" (233). Momentarily we may wonder if he is concerned with the responsibility with which Zenobia has charged him, but detail after detail convince us that if there are damned souls in *The Blithedale Romance* (Zenobia, Hollingsworth, Westervelt), certainly the one at the bottom of the pit is Coverdale. We recall his unkindness to the drowned Zenobia—he muses that she would never have drowned herself if she knew how ugly she would look. He is curious to pry more information out of Westervelt at Zenobia's funeral; he makes a trip to gloat over the crushed Hollingsworth. He finally damns Hollingsworth: "I see in Hollingsworth an exemplification of the most awful truth in Bunyan's book . . . from the very gate of Heaven, there is a by-way to the pit!" (243). Yet, at the end of the book, he says smugly: "I exaggerate my own defects" (247). The irony is that he lives still veiled by his self-delusion. Coverdale, like Hawthorne at Brook Farm, says farewell to the pigs when he takes his first leave of Blithedale. He has quite a kinship with the swine. He is as indolent as they are; he roots about as they do, looking for morsels of gossip or private knowledge, but unlike them, he does not deserve or get the dignity of slaughter.

It is fascinating to wonder where Hawthorne got his models for his

rich, mysterious, proud, voluptuous, dark women—out of fancy or experience. His imagination must have been sorely taxed to create the
sumptuous, opulent, and carnal Hester, Zenobia, and Miriam, surrounded as he was in Salem, Concord, Lenox, and Brook Farm by the
Peabody sisters, his own sisters, the Alcott "girls," and other attenuated
"progressive" ladies who worshipped Emerson and spoke oracularly of
transcendental intuitions and the genius of the heart and intoned Fuller-
isms about the enslavement of women and the coming of "new truths."
From their pictures, all of these "real" women look like genial horses.
Certainly, Hawthorne's inspiration for his most interesting women was
not Sophia. For anyone who could write in her maiden notebook, "We
had an exquisite visit from Waldo last night. It was the warbling of the
Attic bird . . . Mr. Emerson is Pure Tone,"[7] had to be, if not murdered,
transformed into Phoebe, Priscilla, and Hilda. But whatever the source of
his dark women, they (like Melville's exotic Isabelle in *Pierre*) attain a
significant flesh and blood existence in the novels. When Zenobia bursts
onto the scene upon Coverdale's arrival at Blithedale, he is overwhelmed,
as his breathless description makes apparent:

> Her hair—which was dark, glossy, and of singular abundance—was put
> up . . . without . . . other ornament, except a single flower. It was an
> exotic, of rare beauty . . . yet enduring only for a day. . . . She was,
> indeed, an admirable figure of a woman, just on the hither verge of her
> richest maturity, with a combination of features which it is safe to call
> remarkably beautiful. . . . Preferable . . . was Zenobia's bloom, health,
> and vigor, which she possessed in such overflow that a man might well
> have fallen in love with her for their sake only. (15–16)

Coverdale recognizes her as a true woman, not as an unsexed reformer:

> . . . the eye might chastely [we wonder how chastely] be gladdened with
> her material perfection. . . . The native glow of coloring in her cheeks,
> and even the flesh-warmth over her round arms, and what was visible of her
> full bust—in a word, her womanliness incarnated—compelled me some-
> times to close my eyes, as if it were not quite the privilege of modesty to
> gaze at her. (44)

But Zenobia, a true Hawthorne creation, suffers great conflict between her head and her heart. We regret that this "complete woman" is so
taken in by Hollingsworth's appeal to her heart that she abrogates all of
her considerable intellectual qualities, becoming an abject slave to

Hollingsworth's bearish ego and even embracing his outdated chauvinist views (outdated even for the nineteenth century) on the role of women (122–23).

Zenobia's honesty about herself after Hollingsworth has cast her aside for the now wealthy and adoring Priscilla is startling. She does not want pity but sees what has happened to her "'as a woman's doom'" (223). She gives Coverdale her jeweled flower for Priscilla and does not begrudge Priscilla her victory, but when she gives her hand to Coverdale he finds it cold and deathlike. When Coverdale kisses her hand, she acknowledges the gesture like a queen: "'And so you kiss this poor, despised, rejected hand! . . . You have reserved your homage for the fallen'" (227). Her next words, which warn of her intention, are lost on the benighted Coverdale: "'When you next hear of Zenobia, her face will be behind the black-veil; so look your last at it now'" (227–28). Zenobia, convinced now that there are no new truths, throws herself into the dark river, perhaps the river Styx. Coverdale's vitriol ends with Zenobia's tragedy as he meditates on her grace and the decay of her once beautiful but now inflexible, marblelike body, which is not sculptured for posterity but for sending up a crop of weeds. And yet Zenobia, as one of Hawthorne's greatest creations, outlives the bitter epitaph of Coverdale. In the last chapter, when Coverdale shows us his meaningless, selfish life, we remember Zenobia. Even in death she is far more alive than the mean-spirited and self-deluded Coverdale, who survives her to immortalize her in his ballad of Blithedale.

Hollingsworth, the obsessed blacksmith and man of iron who imagines himself a philanthropist, is one of Hawthorne's most dazzling creations and one of the few characters in Hawthorne who *apparently* repents of the godlike control he exerts over others. We find him, at the end of the novel, fallen from his dominance, unmanned and dependent on the wispy Priscilla. I say *apparently* repentant because in his new role we are not sure whether he is trying to reform his own nature (instead of rehabilitating criminals) or whether he has now become a Dimmesdale-like compulsive who is going to play with his sin for years. We also suspect that Zenobia is indeed haunting Hollingsworth as she has promised, for, as Coverdale tells us, "I knew . . . whose vindictive shadow dogged the side where Priscilla was not" (243).

Hawthorne figures in the character of Hollingsworth, as well as in Coverdale. As noted, Hawthorne's motives for going to Brook Farm were mixed, to say the least. Unconvinced that human progress was possible, he went to Brook Farm more for practical than idealistic reasons. He saw the utopian project as providing a possible home and he invested a thousand dollars in the project that he could ill afford. Hawthorne's disenchantment came even more rapidly than Coverdale's, and, although he may have stayed a month longer than Coverdale, he had long before detached himself from the community. Later he even went to court to try to regain his investment. Yet, his Calvinist conscience quite possibly convinced him that he, like Hollingsworth, was exploiting Brook Farm for his own private advantage not only to find a home, but also, like Coverdale, to exploit the Brook Farmers by observing them in order to write about them.

Hawthorne endows Hollingsworth with more magnetism than Westervelt and Priscilla, the actual mesmerist and medium. Hollingsworth is more successful than they because he extends his "spell" over Zenobia and Priscilla, and almost succeeds in getting the uncommitted Coverdale to become his disciple. Seen initially by Coverdale and the others at Blithedale as a tender, grave, Christ-like figure, Hollingsworth soon reveals himself to Coverdale and later to Zenobia as the devil-god who demands, because of his delusion of total sovereignty, absolute obedience and obeisance.

When Coverdale quotes Fourier to Hollingsworth, Hollingsworth becomes outraged and makes a judgment that he repeats later at Eliot's pulpit:

> "I never will forgive this fellow! *He has committed the Unpardonable Sin! For what more monstrous iniquity could the Devil himself contrive, than to choose the selfish principle—the principle of all human wrong, the very blackness of man's heart, the portion of ourselves which we shudder at, and which it is the whole aim of spiritual discipline to eradicate—to choose it as the masterworkman of his system?"*
> (53)

And yet Hollingsworth, unknown to himself, has chosen just this same selfish principle for his master plan of reforming criminals and working in the blackness of their hearts. In damning Fourier, Hollingsworth is unconsciously damning himself.

In the middle of the book, in the chapter named "A Crisis," Hollingsworth makes his bid for Coverdale's discipleship. Hollingsworth's self-delusion and egotism have by this time convinced him of his divine powers and, as Anti-Christ, uses Christ's words to beguile Coverdale into enslavement: "'Do not forsake me,'" he says and then commands him, "'Be with me . . . or be against me! There is no third choice for you!'" (133, 135). At Coverdale's refusal, Hollingsworth vomits Coverdale out of his mouth as one of the lukewarm.

Before the novel ends, Hollingsworth, as false Calvinist Jehovah, has judged Zenobia and gone off with Priscilla. In this reenactment of the Fall, Hollingsworth is both pseudo-Yahweh and Adam, tempted both by the conviction of his own divinity and the very real devil-Westervelt. He casts off Lilith-Zenobia and, defiant as the first Adam, goes off with Eve-Priscilla to another part of the garden. After Zenobia's suicide he and Priscilla are peered at by Coverdale as the shamed inhabitants of the real postlapsarian world. The scene at Eliot's pulpit, which Coverdale comes upon immediately after the "primal eldest sin," is chilling and frightening. Coverdale sees it as a witch trial: "I saw in Hollingsworth all that an artist could desire for the grim portrait of a Puritan magistrate, holding inquest of life and death in a case of witchcraft" (214). Zenobia does not accept the verdict or the entire burden of guilt but points to Hollingsworth as "judge, jury, and accuser" all in one. Hollingsworth does not deny his God-role: "As I have unquestionable right of judgment . . . *I have already judged you, but not on the world's part*" (215). The suicide of Zenobia and her haunting of him are required before Hollingsworth surrenders his role as deity.

Zenobia's final recognition of Hollingsworth as cold monster completes the remarkable characterization:

> "It is all self! . . . Nothing else; nothing but self, self, self! The fiend, I doubt not, has made his choicest mirth of you . . . . I see it now! I am awake, disenchanted, disenthralled! Self, self, self! . . . You are a better masquerader than the witches and gipsies yonder; for your disguise is a self-deception." (218)

Hollingsworth's fierce, vengeful stabbing for Zenobia's drowned body and his postmortem wound in her heart inspires the reader with pity and fear. Zenobia has drowned herself in complete awareness of the fact that her death is not a ritual sacrifice to a god; the tragic waste of her life and love is offered in shame and fury to a man who is all self.

The final question about Hollingsworth is whether Zenobia really avenged herself on him by her suicide. The last pathetic picture of the man-who-would-be-God, weakly leaning on Priscilla, is the answer. Not only has Zenobia exorcized Hollingsworth's self-assumed deity, she has unmanned him.

Compared with the forceful characterization of Zenobia and Hollingsworth and the complex depths of Coverdale, Priscilla seems a poor and weak creature, just another Hawthornean woman of the hearth—pale, submissive, and fugitive. But with Priscilla, Hawthorne accomplishes another corrosive irony. She is meek, certainly, but like the meek she inherits the earth—or her view of all the earth, anyhow, which is embodied in Hollingsworth. She does this through the most successful of strategies, negative aggression. Little vapid Priscilla, constructor of silk purses, no doubt mesmerically out of sow's ears, has triumphed and, as Hollingsworth's guardian, has ironically and successfully *imprisoned* that great self-deluded reformer who wanted to free from prison and reform the criminals of the world.

When Priscilla arrives at Blithedale, she is dovelike, "wan, almost sickly . . . like a flower-shrub that had done its best to blossom in too scanty light" (27), but she soon becomes healthy and cheerful, unthinkingly worshipping Hollingsworth and adoring Zenobia. Coverdale would like her to worship him, but she pays little attention to him.

Although Zenobia never dreams of it at first, Priscilla becomes a formidable rival for Hollingsworth's affections. Priscilla is Zenobia's evil fate—and a parasite "whose impalpable grace lay so singularly between disease and beauty" (101). Hollingsworth is Priscilla's god— "Hollingsworth could have no fault. That was the one principle at the centre of the universe" (220). She, the meek, inherits Hollingsworth, who is not so big as the earth nor so deep as a well, nor so wide as a church door, but for Priscilla, 'tis enough, 'twill serve.

A variation on the Hawthornean devil-villain, Westervelt appears to be young and handsome until Coverdale discovers his sham teeth. A wizard, with Priscilla as his familiar and veiled lady, he enjoys center stage, and his hold over Zenobia tempts her and Hollingsworth to deal with him, thus precipitating the Fall. His response to Zenobia's suicide is annoyance with the waste of her talents; our fears are that he or his devilish superior has her in his clutches.

Old Moodie, a superficial Coverdale, wastes his fortune, becomes a criminal, and then attempts concealment by hiding behind an eye patch and by shrinking into any available corner. He is the true father of

Priscilla because like her he tries to control people by shrinking and hiding. Still with his hands on the pursestrings, he judges Zenobia. Easily overcome by Coverdale's trickery and superior wine, he confides his story to the one person in the novel who will be sure to tell all. He is one of Hawthorne's more successful minor character creations, a snapper-up of unconsidered trifles.

The canny follower of *Poor Richard's Almanack,* Silas Foster, is always the voice of shrewdness and Yankee thrift, traits that seemed to have displeased Hawthorne. He is what the Blithedalers are fated to become, Hawthorne suggests, if they allow themselves to be buried under the manure pile of physical labor. Silas can make nothing of Zenobia's suicide because he thought she had plenty of money and was sure to get a husband.

In this novel there is no worldly crowd to misinterpret characters and events except the community of Blithedalers. These maskers are fated to be, not the reformers of the world, but only members of the Hawthornean brotherhood of evil.

### VI

As in *The Scarlet Letter* and *The House of the Seven Gables,* Hawthorne uses *The Blithedale Romance* to create the possibility of a new Eden but with it inexorably comes another Fall. At the end of the romance we are troubled, as we are at the end of *The Scarlet Letter,* with the possibility of the damnation of the characters we have come to know. We fear with Silas Foster that the devil has taken Zenobia's soul, since her frantic message to Hollingsworth via Coverdale, "'Tell him he has murdered me! Tell him that I'll haunt him!'" (226), seems to be endorsed by Hollingsworth's last words to Coverdale: "'Ever since we parted, I have been busy with a single murderer!' . . . and I knew what murderer he meant" (243). Hollingsworth's fate is unknown; we are not sure that as with Dimmesdale there has been enough of penance but no penitence. Westervelt, like Chillingworth, is a true fiend and of his damnation we are sure, but not discomfited. Coverdale is an enigma; still culpably self-deluded, smug, and self-righteous, the voyeur who aspired to be idolized (as Priscilla and Zenobia idolized Hollingsworth) is well along the primrose path. Priscilla, the guardian of the enfeebled Hollingsworth, is "saved," but a heaven of Priscillas is too daunting to be contemplated.

Some feminist questions are inevitable in *The Blithedale Romance* because Hawthorne was concerned with a group of idealistic reformers and was surrounded by them on all sides—Elizabeth Peabody; his own sister, Elizabeth Hawthorne; Margaret Fuller. Coverdale thinks of himself as a liberated man, even more so than Zenobia, because she allows herself to be infatuated with that great enemy of women's freedom, Hollingsworth. Hollingsworth, the archetypal chauvinist, would "'scourge them back within their proper bounds!'" (123). Priscilla adores what Hollingsworth says and is the perfect type of witless woman. Zenobia begins as a battler for the equality of women: "'How can she [any woman] be happy, after discovering that fate has assigned her but one single event, which she must contrive to make the substance of her whole life?'" (60). She complains that women are not allowed to speak but only to write a little. She says a great deal more until she becomes aware of Hollingsworth's disapproval; then she abandons her "cause," proving herself the most romantic and emotional of any of her sisters by drowning herself because she has been spurned by the unworthy man she loves. How did Hawthorne stand on the women's rights issue? Just a few of his statements clarify his stance: Hester, at her needlework, "It was the art—then, as now, almost the only one within a woman's grasp—of needlework" (81); in a letter to James T. Fields (December 11, 1852), "All women, as authors, are feeble and tiresome. I wish they were forbidden to write on pain of having their faces deeply scarified with an oyster-shell"; in a letter to William Ticknor (January 6, 1854), "But inkstained women are, without a single exception, detestable";[8] in the *American Notebooks* about Sophia, "She has . . . the love . . . for flowers, without which a woman is a *monster*" (319). There are many more passages, but all in the same vein; Hawthorne was not an advocate of women's rights, and wished that women would stay at home by the hearth and sew. This attitude toward women is typically Calvinist. Calvin granted that women were necessary to prevent men from burning, but the terrifying reformer hurtled through the streets of Geneva, arresting the magistrate's wife for dancing, and arranging a raid on his brother's house to take his sister-in-law in *flagrante delicto* with the servant.

In describing the Lyceum hall where Priscilla is being exploited by Westervelt, Hawthorne comments on the Puritanism of his time: "here, in this many-purposed hall, (unless the selectmen of the village chance to have more than their share of the puritanism, which, however diversified with later patchwork, still gives its prevailing tint to New England character,) here the company of strolling players sets up its little stage . . . " (196). Hawthorne's Puritanism has no patchwork and its prevailing tint defines the ironic mode of *The Blithedale Romance*—a tale told by a hypocrite (Coverdale) who judges all of the characters except himself as would any Puritan magistrate. Calvin speaks eloquently on this point as if he were skewering Coverdale: "Such is the *envenomed delight* we take both in *prying into* and *exposing our neighbor's faults.* . . . Let *hypocrites* now go, and *while keeping depravity wrapt up in their heart,* study to lay God under obligation by their works. In this way they will only offend him more and more."[9]

As artistically challenging and provocative as anything Hawthorne wrote, *The Blithedale Romance* is a magnificent book and deserves more readers than it has had. Rich, intricate, and pithy, as deeply textured as a Persian rug and with as anfractuous a pattern beneath the apparently simple structure, it emerges as another rueful, despairing, and infinitely sorrowing record of Hawthorne's Calvinistically ironic and tragic vision of damned humanity.

TWICE-TOLD TALES

# "Lamplight on the Wall
# of a Sepulchre"

---

I

In his typically self-belittling way, Hawthorne writes in his preface to the 1851 edition of *Twice-told Tales* that he is surprised that they gained what little popularity they did:

> They have the pale tint of flowers that blossomed in too retired a shade—the coolness of a meditative habit, which diffuses itself through the feeling and observation of every sketch. . . . We have allegory, not always so warmly dressed in its habiliments of flesh and blood, as to be taken into the reader's mind without a shiver. Whether from lack of power, or an unconquerable reserve, the Author's touches have often an effect of tameness. . . . The book . . . requires to be read in the clear, brown, twilight atmosphere in which it was written; if opened in the sunshine, it is apt to look exceedingly like a volume of blank pages. (5)

Perhaps the most interesting comment that Hawthorne makes in his 1851 preface, after nine years of supposedly idyllic marriage, is: "They [the tales] are the memorials of very tranquil and not unhappy years"—this after two children (Una and Julian) and with another child (Rose) due to arrive in two months. Hawthorne appears to be looking back at those much conjectured about twelve years in his third floor chamber of the Manning house with something very like regret. Once dislocated from that "dismal and squalid chamber"[1] where fame was won, he was restless, never wanted to stay in one place very long, and was perhaps surprised that there was so little joy in his life, no matter where his temporary home was. He was always searching for "the realm of quiet," where he could be "a citizen of somewhere else" ("The Custom House").

The writing of *Twice-told Tales* was, as far as we know, at least a twelve-year effort, during which period he also wrote *Fanshawe* (1828), the unfortunate novel he tried to have recalled.[2] In addition, there were other tales, probably historical, such as the "Tales of the Province House," which Hawthorne said he burned.[3] As it is, we still have a rather mixed bag written between 1825 and 1839, about a third of which are set in the colonial period, a setting congenial to Hawthorne's artistry in the great novel, *The Scarlet Letter,* and in some of his finer stories, including "The Grey Champion," "The May-Pole of Merry Mount," "The Gentle Boy," "The Minister's Black Veil," and "Young Goodman Brown." But this was not an infallible formula for Hawthorne. In some of the tales, such as "Howe's Masquerade," "Edward Randolph's Portrait," and "The Prophetic Pictures," the use of history, instead of providing a mere stepping-off place for Hawthorne's journey into the minds and hearts of his characters, becomes the story itself. Even though we are prepared for twice-told tales by the title of the collection, they seem sometimes just vapid retellings of legends without the imposition of the Hawthorne badge of irony and ambiguity.

The best of these tales create a sense of isolation through a blending of theme, intention, setting, atmosphere—the characteristic amalgam of the tragic-ironic vision. "The Ambitious Guest," one of Hawthorne's best-known allegorical stories, has elements of the greatness of his best tales, but its greatest appeal is its sustained ironic tone. In this story is the bitter irony of a nameless young man being convinced, as is John Marcher in James's "Beast in the Jungle," that he has been born for a great destiny:

> . . . his whole life . . . had been a solitary path; for, with the lofty caution of his nature, he had kept himself apart from those who might otherwise have been his companions. . . . The secret of the young man's character was, a high and abstracted ambition. He would have borne to live an undistinguished life, but not to be forgotten in the grave (327).

In the anonymity of a hospitable tavern in the Notch of the White Hills, the nameless hero shares his dreams, grows quickly fond of the tavern keeper's young daughter, and encourages the family to share with him their modest dreams. The father wishes for a safer house, but a slate gravestone "'and something to let people know, that I lived an honest man and died a Christian'" (329). The young stranger at once agrees that it is everyone's nature "'to desire a monument, be it slate, or marble, or a pillar of granite, or a glorious memory in the universal heart of man'" (329). The grandmother wants to be arranged carefully in the coffin clothes she has fashioned. The young man then muses that all, old and young, dream of graves and monuments, and pities (in a nice, but rather obvious adumbration) the mariners who are buried in the ocean, "that wide and nameless sepulchre" (332). The final irony occurs when all rush out to the refuge and are destroyed, while the house is left untouched by the avalanche.

Even though the story lacks the urbanity, the skillful ambiguity, and the complexity of many of the later tales, the stinging bitterness of Ecclesiastes is appropriately administered to the ambitious youth by the narrator: "Then shall the dust return to the earth as it was: And the spirit shall return unto God who gave it. Vanity of vanities, saith the preacher; all is vanity" (Eccles. 12:7–8).

The alienation and isolation of the reclusive Hawthorne permeates "Foot-prints on the Sea-shore" (1838). This great lover of solitude confesses that he cannot keep himself in health and vigor "without sometimes stealing from the sultry sunshine of the world, to plunge into the cool bath of solitude. . . . When . . . the yearning for seclusion becomes a necessity within me, I am drawn to the sea-shore. . . . I bound myself with a hermit's vow, to interchange no thoughts with man or woman" (451). The sketch abounds with Hawthorne's delight in isolation and his love of the sea as he follows his own tracks, idly plays with seaweed, examines a live horseshoe, writes in the sand, clambers up over crags, and encounters "one huge rock . . . on which the veins resemble inscriptions, but in an unknown tongue" (455). This is reminiscent of the giant rock gravestone, "upon which the veins seemed to form an inscription in forgotten characters" of the earlier "Roger Malvin's Burial" (1832) in *Mosses from an Old Manse* (338). Here the "I" persona discovers remains of dead animals and birds, huge bones, and he wonders where the hulks of sunken ships, corroded cannons, corpses and skeletons of perished seamen are buried. Withering foliage sheds itself upon the waves, and as the day draws to an end, he is haunted by the past. He tries to interpret the mysteries of the "sea's unchanging voice" (460) and calls out aloud: "what joy for a shy man to feel himself so solitary, that he may lift his voice to its highest pitch without hazard of a listener!" (460). But he fears that in the dusk "gloomy fantasies" (461) will haunt him as the sea grows melancholy and his wandering spirit finds no resting place "and comes shivering back" (461). Hawthorne is convinced that his solitary day at the seashore will preserve his individuality as he goes back to the crowded streets: "but yet shall not melt into the indistinguishable mass of human kind. I shall think my own thoughts, and feel my own emotions, and possess my individuality unviolated" (461). Unlike Wakefield, Hawthorne determines to use his solitude to preserve his uniqueness, not to lose it. Again we are faced with another Hawthorne question—solitude, necessary to him, preserves his separateness from "the indistinguishable mass of human kind," and yet this very isolation causes him pain because he fears that his reclusiveness is somehow unnatural and even sinful. Calvin himself had the same problem. By nature a reclusive scholar, he was pressured into a public life of leadership through his conviction that his friend, Farel, who exhorted him to action, was speaking to him as a Special Providence and voice of God. Hawthorne, the crypto-Calvinist, prefers isolation, but fears that his withdrawal from the mainstream of life is a selfish choice that will lead him to damnation.

Of all the sketches and tales of *Twice-told Tales,* none is more typical of Hawthorne's themes, intention, irony, or of his tragic-ironic view of himself as isolated than the sketch, "The Haunted Mind," which should be examined in some detail. A singularly poetic, pre-Freudian sketch, "The Haunted Mind" (*The Token,* 1835), is a remarkably accurate reflection of Hawthorne's ambivalence. Although yearning for the comfort of a healing belief in connubial joy, Hawthorne's haunted Calvinist mind continuously summons up to his half-awake "passive sensibility" ghastly specters of a "funeral train" (306) of evil, mockery, and horror.

The sketch begins with his awakening at midnight from an hour of dream-filled sleep. Hawthorne describes the strange state of suspension between sleep and waking that we all have experienced as an "intermediate space" between yesterday and tomorrow, "where the business of life does not intrude; where the passing moment lingers, and becomes truly the present; a spot where Father Time, when he thinks nobody is watching him, sits down by the way side to take breath" (305). It is winter and the window glass "is ornamented with fanciful devices in frost work . . . each pane presents something like a frozen dream" (305). The winter scene presents itself to Hawthorne in a series of alliterative pictures—from white spired steeple to frosty sky, snow-covered roofs, "frozen street, all white, and the distant water hardened into rock" (305–06)—all making him shiver "less from bodily chill than the bare idea of a polar atmosphere" (306). Yet, the thoughts of the drowsy, delicious warmth of many blankets is only momentarily comforting. For the gloom-stricken mind of Hawthorne next conjures up the "hideous" idea of the dead, "lying in their cold shrouds and narrow coffins, through the drear winter of the grave" (306) and he cannot persuade his "fancy that they neither shrink nor shiver, when the snow is drifting over their little hillocks, and the bitter blast howls against the door of the tomb" (306). He identifies with the dead who are wrapped as he is, but in shrouds, not blankets. Hawthorne's terror increases as he begins paragraph five with no ambiguity or qualification: "In the depths of every heart, there is a tomb and a dungeon, though the lights, the music, and revelry above may cause us to forget their existence, and the buried ones, or prisoners whom they hide. But sometimes, and oftenest at midnight, those dark receptacles are flung wide open" (306). This is the time, Hawthorne avers, "when the mind has a passive sensibility, but no active strength; when the imagination is a mirror, imparting vividness to all ideas, without the power of selecting or controlling them; then pray that your griefs may slumber, and the brotherhood of remorse not break their chain. It is too late! A funeral train comes gliding by your bed" (306). In this soul-affrighting funeral train, all sequestered abstractions assume bodily shapes and specters: Passion; Feeling; Sorrow; fondest Hope; and "a sterner form . . . with a brow of wrinkles, a look and gesture of iron authority . . . Fatality, an emblem of the evil influence that rules your fortunes; a demon to whom you subjected yourself by some error at the outset of life, and were bound his slave forever, by once obeying him. . . . Shame" (307). Hawthorne's Calvinist conscience, now undisguised and forthright, summons up the preconscious terrors of the fiery pit of hell—a hell deserved by mankind whether guilty of great crime or not, for only one step awry is necessary—and that was accomplished by Original Sin: "Sufficient without such guilt, is this nightmare of the soul; this heavy, heavy sinking of the spirits; this wintry gloom about the heart; this indistinct horror of the mind, blending itself with the darkness of the chamber" (307).

The panic slowly dissipates and Hawthorne attempts to alleviate the horror of "these night solitudes" by imagining the comfort of a "tenderer bosom" sharing the bed (307–08). Even though this imaginary intimate has "no existence but in that momentary image" (308), he hopes her influence, through light not gloom, can control this state "on the borders of sleep and wakefulness." Again, the imagery is powerful and alliterative: "wheeling of gorgeous squadrons, that glitter in the sun . . . glimering shadow of old trees . . . the sunny rain of a summer shower . . . the sunny trees of an autumn wood [winter is dispelled] . . . the brightest of all rainbows, over-arching the unbroken sheet of snow . . . dancing radiance . . . twittering flight of birds in spring" (308). But all of this sunshine cannot melt the Dantean ice of this last circle of hell.

In the last two sentences Hawthorne tries to salvage his haunted mind from total despair: "Your spirit has departed, and strays like a free citizen, among the people of a shadowy world, beholding strange sights, yet without wonder or dismay. So calm, *perhaps,* will be the final change; so undisturbed, as if among familiar things, the entrance of the soul to its Eternal home!" (309). Making a Herculean effort, Hawthorne attempts to mitigate the very real agony of fear: he tries to believe in marital comfort, sunshine, rainbows—of simplicities not mysteries. But the dooming shroud of death, the fiendish magnetism of the grave, and the threat of hellish retribution combined with the great "perhaps" of the last sentence are what is searingly remembered from this formidable sketch of the haunted mind. Calvin himself has no more eloquent or baleful words for the naked vulnerability of fallen humanity than Hawthorne's picture of those demonic nightmares that come, unbidden and unrelenting, to Adam's cur offspring.

This sketch dramatizes, in seminal and explicit form, the tragic themes that preoccupied the mind of Hawthorne from his earliest writing to his last feeble efforts in the abortive romances and in the pathetic letters of 1860–64 after his return from Europe. Here we find Hawthorne's obsession with death and the grave and his lack of confidence in a glorious life hereafter; with the world's iciness which becomes an emblem of fallen man's enduring but not prevailing in a distorted natural world, doomed to be forever hostile; with the oft-repeated metaphor of the heart as dungeon, spelled out in all of its horror as the dark receptacle of secret sin, guilt and grief; and with the Hawthornean breed of Calvinism, which perfectly declares itself in Hawthorne's conviction that Adam's Fall from innocence is inevitably reenacted by every man and "is never in this mortal life repaired."[4] Hawthorne's tragic vision of man, which he never totally acknowledges, gets some prescriptions for a cure: take a good dose of connubial intimacy—this will ease, but only temporarily, the loneliness and fear, and will transform the wintry scene to an autumn wood; then try to imagine death, "the final change," not as terrifying but gentle. Needless to say Hawthorne's patient remains critically ill. Indeed, as a finite human being, he is a dying animal. Hawthorne never accomplished the resigned and secure faith of one of his most notable descendants in the Calvinist line, T. S. Eliot, who comes to a recognition:

> *The whole earth is our hospital*
> *Endowed by the ruined millionaire*
> *Wherein, if we do well, we shall*
> *Die of the absolute paternal care*
> *That will not leave us, but prevents us everywhere.*[5]

## II

In the prefaces to *The House of the Seven Gables, The Blithedale Romance,* and *Twice-told Tales* we have grown accustomed to what might be called Hawthorne's introductory tone of voice. It is a rueful, self-deprecating, apologetic, ironic voice, and yet with all of its apparently confiding and conversational sonance, we learn nothing private or personal. As Hawthorne himself says in "The Old Manse": it is "so reserved, even while they [the sketches] sometimes seem so frank" (*Mosses from an Old Manse,* 34). But Hawthorne was as artful as he was honest, and we doubt his belittling of himself just as we must recognize the irony of his attempting to show the simplicity of his writing: "They [the sketches and tales] have none of the abstruseness of idea, or obscurity of expression. . . . They never need translation. . . . Every sentence . . . may be understood and felt by anybody, who will give himself the trouble to read it, and will take up the book in a proper mood" (6). If this is so, then there is no mystery in "The Minister's Black Veil," "The Hollow of the Three Hills," or "The White Old Maid." But as generations of readers know, mystery *is* there and we must read every sentence with care and "take up the book in a proper mood."

The veil that Hawthorne mentions so often, the one he keeps between himself and the reader, can only be rent with considerable pain. The narrative voice in many of the tales and sketches in *Twice-told Tales* is apparently Hawthorne's own, but in many cases this does not clarify his meaning. In "The Village Uncle" published in 1835, when Hawthorne was thirty-one, the narrative voice is that of an old man reminiscing about the past, yet he seems to much resemble Hawthorne: "a hermit in the depths of my own mind; sometimes yawning over drowsy volumes, . . . a scribbler of wearier trash than what I read; a man who had wandered out of the real world and got into its shadow, where his troubles, joys and vicissitudes were of such slight stuff, that he hardly knew whether he lived, or only dreamed of living" (311). The assumption of various voices is the grand prerogative of the fiction writer, of course, but we often lose our way in a Hawthorne tale when we make the casual assumption that each voice is Hawthorne's own. We must recall the dictum that the "kindly" stranger gave to Robin in "My Kinsman, Major Molineux": "'May not a man have several voices, Robin, as well as two complexions?'" Our only hope is to be most wary readers.

Hawthorne often talks to the reader confidingly, as in "Foot-prints on the Sea-shore," or takes him by the arm. Unless the voice is melancholy and rueful, however, we suspect an affected persona, particularly, because of Hawthorne's Calvinist vision, if the tone is cheerful and hopeful. It is much more difficult to judge the aesthetic distance between Hawthorne and his reader and his material in the short sketches and tales than it is in the novels, where the sheer length of our association with him reveals more about him than perhaps he cares to have revealed. Many critics have uncovered two Hawthornes—the sombre recluse and the family man of cheer and kindness—but both may be delusive, for there is also the icy-hearted clinical observer and the man who sees and consorts with devils. In "Dr. Heidegger's Experiment" we are surely tempted to see the narrator as Hawthorne himself, who watches the four aged guests drink the water of youth and commit over again all their infantile follies. In *Twice-told Tales,* Hawthorne provides as frequently as in the novels his alternate explanations for events to avoid committing himself. Perhaps it is best to take the most revelatory of Hawthorne's sketches of the veiled face behind the veiled voice and see whether we can catch a glimpse, even if only in "the clear, brown, twilight atmosphere" (5), of the narrator of "Sights from a Steeple." The sketch is of signal importance because of the revelations made by its narrative voice. All of the speculations by Hawthorne critics vis-à-vis his personal life are only increased by the character of Hawthorne lurking in a church steeple, seeing but unseen, peeping through his pocket spyglass at the people below, and wishing for devilish help to "uncover every chamber, and make me familiar with their inhabitants!" (192).

This is the mysterious, hidden Hawthorne so intriguing to biographers and general readers. A sketch such as this unnerves those critics—Hoeltje, Wagenknecht,[6] et al.—who find Hawthorne a sociable, friendly man who has been maligned by the critics that see him not only as reclusive, secretive, and wary, but also as endlessly curious and slyly snoopy about everyone else. But anyone who clung to his room in his mother's house for the better part of twelve years (while he was twenty-one to thirty-three), refusing to eat with the family, going out only at night and then mostly to fires, sending his sister to the library for him, and taking summer walking trips through New England incognito, even though he was not known to anyone, is not the ordinary young college graduate of 1825. This study is not intended to psychoanalyze Hawthorne, an endeavor as foolish as it is meaningless. However, certain of his personal characteristics did have a profound influence on his writing, especially on his intention, symbolism, attitude toward the artist, and unorthodox orthodoxy. It seems, therefore, a barren enterprise not to acknowledge him as one of the great New England eccentrics. He did not stand out as a personal anomaly because he was surrounded by much more chromatic fantastics, such as Thoreau, Margaret Fuller, and Bronson Alcott, but he, at least, managed to draw some wonderment from Louisa May Alcott, who found something to exclaim about when he did his disappearing act into the woods: Hawthorne, in his red carpet slippers, disappeared whenever anyone appeared who looked as if he might want to talk with him, especially if it were Bronson Alcott.

At the beginning of "Sights from a Steeple" Hawthorne lyricizes about the cloudlike state of his isolated station in the steeple, high above the earth yet far from heaven. The reader expects a rhapsodic exercise on cloud formations, but the first of the nine paragraphs ends with a bitterly ironic simile from this twenty-seven-year-old disappointed author: "Bright they [clouds] are as young man's visions, and like them, would be realized in chillness, obscurity and tears. I will look on them no more" (192).

Elaborating on his role as a clinical, detached observer, Hawthorne states: "The most desirable mode of existence might be that of a spiritual-ized Paul Pry, hovering invisible round man and woman, witnessing their deeds, searching into their hearts, borrowing brightness from their felic-ity, and shade from their sorrow, and retaining no emotion peculiar to himself" (192). The incompatibility of Hawthorne's desires for himself is obvious—he wants to know everything about everyone, leeching onto their emotions and prying into their hearts, but retaining the inviolability of his own emotions.

This cold curiosity, this clinical observer's reporting horrors while not being moved by them, is epitomized in his creation, twenty years later, of Coverdale, the narrator-participant, and by many other characters in his

*Twice-told Tales* and novels: Holgrave-Maule in *The House of the Seven Gables;* the ironic narrative voice of "Sunday at Home," "David Swan," "The Hollow of the Three Hills," "The Ambitious Guest," "Chippings with a Chisel," "Night Sketches," "Foot-prints on the Sea-shore," and "The Threefold Destiny"; and the damning authorial voice of "Fancy's Show Box" and of the cold observer, Dr. Heidegger, in "Dr. Heidegger's Experiment." Hawthorne was never comfortable in the role that he espoused—that of Paul Pry—because he feared that, as an artist and clinical observer, he, too, was guilty of the unforgivable sin of violating the human heart.

Hawthorne is delighted by the varied scene observed from his ecclesiastical perch, but meditates on the various activities going on beneath him: "In some of the houses over which my eyes roam so coldly, guilt is entering into hearts . . . —guilt is on the very edge of commission . . . ; guilt is done" (196). As he views the deeds of his fellow men, from whom he is separated by the distance of the church steeple, he finds himself unable to express his thoughts: "There are broad thoughts struggling in my mind, and, were I able to give them distinctness, they would make their way in eloquence" (196). Hawthorne eschews generalizing on guilt, just as he remains comfortably and coldly detached from the antlike humanity he views from his height. The rain comes and the people hurry home, "all that have a home" (196), and we are struck once again by the isolation, alienation, and homelessness of Hawthorne's perch above and coldly removed from humanity.

Hawthorne hopes only for the rainbow of God's covenant with the world, for another world is unknown and, in its inscrutability, ultimately terrifying, but not as horrifying as the possibility always present in what Hawthorne does not say but only hints at—the dread of nothingness.

### III

One of the most successful uses of continuous and consistent symbolism—symbolism which is functional not peripheral, organic and not merely decorative—is the remarkable use of flowers in "The May-Pole of Merry Mount." In this fine tale, the flower imagery expands to encompass the theme—the quarrel between the exponents of the Maypole, the sporters with life, the "sworn triflers of a lifetime" (60), and the Puritans who prayed, worked, and fought the Indians, whose "festivals were fast-days," who had no dancing except around the whipping post, "the Puritan May-Pole" (61).

The Maypolers, who had scattered "flower-seeds" upon their arrival in New England, celebrate midsummer eve amidst "roses . . . of a more vivid hue than the tender buds of Spring" (54). The Maypole is decked in brightly colored banners but especially "garden flowers, and blossoms of the wilderness": "On the lowest green bough hung an abundant wreath of roses, some that had been gathered in the sunniest spots of the forest, and others, of still richer blush, which the colonists had reared from English seed" (55). The wild throng, masqued as all sorts of monsters and satyrs, dance joyfully about the Maypole to celebrate a marriage that is to take place between Edgar and Edith, the lord and lady of the May.

The wedding couple have "bright roses . . . in contrast with the dark and glossy curls of each, . . . scattered round their feet, or . . . sprung up spontaneously there" (56–57). The priest that is to marry them is "canonically dressed, yet decked with flowers, in heathen fashion, and wearing a chaplet of the native vine leaves" and seems "the wildest monster there" (57). When they are married "the wreath of roses, that hung from the lowest green bough of the May-Pole, had been twined for them, and would be thrown over both their heads, in symbol of their flowery union" (57).

Suddenly Edith's glance grows pensive and Edgar remonstrates, "'Is your wreath of roses a garland to hang above our graves, that you look so sad?'" (58). Edith is saddened by the thought that perhaps nothing in the future will be so bright as the present moment. "Just then, as if a spell had loosened them, down came a little shower of withering rose leaves from the May-Pole" (58). Hawthorne's comment is that "From the moment that they truly loved, they had subjected themselves to earth's doom of care, and sorrow, and troubled joy, and had no more a home at Merry Mount" (58). They have accepted the Calvinist ethic and must face deflowered, fallen nature and the blight of fallen, withered humanity.

Hawthorne leaves them to the drooping roses and their nuptials while he supplies the history of Merry Mount in terms of seasonal flowers. But the Puritans spy on the revelers and determine to punish them for their enormities. The feud is to be settled this midsummer eve: the armored Puritans attack the worshippers of the May who are routed by the "Puritan of Puritans . . . Endicott himself!" (63).

Endicott first addresses the "'priest of Baal. . . . But now shall it be seen that the Lord hath sanctified this wilderness for his peculiar people. Woe unto them that would defile it! And first for this flower-decked abomination, the altar of thy worship!'" (63). Endicott then smites down the Maypole with his sword: "it showered leaves and rose-buds upon the remorseless enthusiast; and finally, with all its green boughs, and ribbons, and flowers, symbolic of departed pleasures, down fell the banner-staff of Merry Mount" (63). Punishment is also doled out to the merrymakers: stocks, stripes, and severer penalties are promised, including branding and cropping of ears. The priest is destined for trial by the "Great and General Court," and as a final dreary sentence, the dancing bear is shot as a witch (64).

Endicott now must deal with the newly married couple. Moved by Edgar's plea to accept all the punishment himself and by Edith's identical wish, even though she is of "that sex, which requireth the stricter discipline" (65), Endicott smiles and "almost" sighs "for the *inevitable blight* of early hopes" (66). He agrees to have Edgar's curls cropped, but orders that both Edith and Edgar be treated "more gently than their fellows," as he sees a possible workman-warrior in Edgar and in Edith qualities "that may fit her to become a mother in our Israel" (66). Finally, Endicott, severest Puritan of all, acts:

> [He] lifted the wreath of roses from the ruin of the May-Pole, and threw it, with his own gauntleted hand, over the heads of the Lord and Lady of the May. It was a deed of prophecy. *As the moral gloom of the world overpowers all systematic gaiety, even so was their home of wild mirth made desolate amid the sad forest.* . . . But, as their flowery garland was wreathed of the brightest roses that had grown there, so, in the tie that united them, were intertwined all the purest and best of their early joys. (66–67)

And so, from the brightest garlands of the Maypolers, to the blossoms that decay when Edith recognizes marital responsibility, to the destruction of the Maypole and the placing of the rose garland about the necks of Edgar and Edith by Endicott, Hawthorne tells us a sobering tale. It is a tale of a Puritan triumph brightened, lightened, and finally approved by Hawthorne through the changing symbolism of flowers, flowers that ultimately signal the union of former revelers, now converted to a grave connubial love. The use of the single symbol of flowers, expanded like a metaphysical conceit to carry the major weight of theme and intention (which is Hawthorne's final approval of the Puritan conscience) in a tale of thirteen pages, is a remarkable artistic accomplishment even for Hawthorne, from whom we have learned to expect these prodigies.

Hawthorne's mirrors—images that reveal the true self—are heavily and fondly used throughout *Twice-told Tales*. Mirrors crack and splinter under the gaze of the Hawthornean gimlet eye, but even in the pieces are reflected the terrors of the ugly, veritable, depraved self.

But the most dominant form of imagery in *Twice-told Tales* is what we have come to expect in Hawthorne—an obsession with death, the grave, the shroud. Hawthorne's haunted mind turns "The Lily's Quest," a rather simple story of a young engaged couple's search for the proper site upon which to erect their Temple of Happiness, into a sombre elegy upon the vanity of human wishes. The short sketch, "Snow Flakes," shows Hawthorne only a sable hearse; "Edward Fane's Rosebud" is the intimate of death and "The White Old Maid" is a story death-ridden with murder and possibly vampirism.

Yet of all the *Twice-told Tales*, the one that can best exemplify Hawthorne's consummate use of the functional symbol is "The Minister's Black Veil." The story opens at the moment of greatest drama on the Sabbath. As the sexton rings the bell to summon the townspeople of Milford for the service, the Reverend Mr. Hooper appears. Everyone is terrified and bewildered because the young, gentle minister is wearing over his face a black veil—"two folds of crepe, which entirely concealed his features, except the mouth and chin" (38).

Hawthorne has the parishioners give the usual alternate explanations for Mr. Hooper's donning the veil, but the minister explains nothing to the congregation and no explanation is ever forthcoming, except that he tells his fiancée that he has taken a vow and that he is "'bound to wear it ever, both in light and darkness, in solitude and before the gaze of multitudes, and as with strangers, so with my familiar friends. No mortal eye will see it withdrawn'" (46). The results of the minister's wearing of the veil are various: he is more effective than ever when he preaches of secret sin; he is welcomed at funerals; he is feared at weddings; he perplexes an embassy of elders about his reason for wearing the veil; he loses his "plighted wife" because he refuses to remove the veil; children run from him in terror; he is known to have such an antipathy toward the veil that he will never look into a mirror; he becomes a most efficient clergyman, particularly with people "in agony of sin" (49); he attains a fabled reputation throughout New England; he summons enough strength on his deathbed, to keep a young minister from removing the veil; he dies veiled and is buried with the veil still upon his face.

The alternate explanations for Mr. Hooper's wearing of the veil explain nothing: "'He has changed himself into something awful, only by hiding his face'; 'Our parson has gone mad!'" (38); some purport to understand the mystery; another says his "'eyes were so weakened by the midnight lamp, as to require a shade'" (41); the doctor believes something is amiss with Mr. Hooper's intellect; a "superstitious old woman" swears that a maiden's corpse shuddered when he bent over it (42). However, all of the alternate explanations are powerfully suggestive of some great mystery that not one of the congregation is willing to explore.

Perhaps the most puzzling behavior of Mr. Hooper is his melancholy smiling. The first day that he puts on the veil he is avoided by the congregation, but he looks back at their terror-stricken faces as he goes into his parsonage: "A sad smile gleamed faintly from beneath the black veil, and flickered about his mouth, glimmering as he disappeared" (41). When the elders come to confront him about the veil and are unable to ask him anything, they "perceive the glimmering of a melancholy smile" (45). Elizabeth, his affianced, asks him to put aside his veil and tell her why he put it on but he smiles faintly as he tells her that in "'an hour to come . . . all of us shall cast aside our veils'" (46). She then pleads with him and implies that whispers are going about the village that he wears his veil "'under the consciousness of secret sin,'" and yet he smiles again, "that same sad smile, which always appeared like a faint glimmering of light, proceeding from the obscurity beneath the veil" as he answers: "'If I hide my face for sorrow, there is cause enough . . . and if I cover it for secret sin, what mortal might not do the same?'" (46). When Elizabeth finally refuses to be his wife, Mr. Hooper smiles again "to think that only a material emblem had separated him from happiness" (47). Even the "lawless wind" never blows aside his veil—"But still good Mr. Hooper sadly smiled, at the pale visages of the worldly throng as he passed by" (49). When the zealous young minister attempts to remove the black veil from the dying Father Hooper, he meets with unexpectedly strong resistance, "yet the faint, sad smile, so often there, now seemed to glimmer from its obscurity, and lingering on Father Hooper's lips" (52). Even in death Father Hooper is "a veiled corpse, with a faint smile lingering on the lips" (52). Laughter and smiles in Hawthorne are rarely cheerful and we have learned to read of them with misgiving, mistrust, and foreboding. The smiles of Mr. Hooper are especially melancholy and ironic; he knows something that his parishioners do not and we are forced to try to puzzle it out.

Hawthorne has warned us by his subtitle, "A Parable," that we must look for hidden meanings, and his frequent reference to the black veil as emblem is a further nudge to our sensibilities to find in the tale a meaning for the black veil. We are given many "hints and guesses, / Hints followed by guesses." When we, as well as the parishioners, first see Mr. Hooper in his veil, Hawthorne tells us that the veil "probably did not intercept his sight, farther than to give a darkened aspect to all living and inanimate things" (38). This reminds us of the Calvinistic definition of Original Sin. While Mr. Hooper stood in front of the church, the veil "threw its obscurity between him and the holy page, as he read the Scriptures; and while he prayed, the veil lay heavily on his uplifted countenance" (39). This further emphasizes the tremendous abyss between even the holiest of men and the awful sovereignty of God—fallen man's darkened intellect that vainly seeks to understand God's purposes. When Mr. Hooper tries to explain to Elizabeth the necessity of his wearing the veil, he insists that it is "'a type and a symbol. . . . This dismal shade must separate me from the world: even you, Elizabeth, can never come behind it!'" (46). He seems to be speaking of the terrible isolation of postlapsarian creatures whose minds are so darkened by Original Sin that they can never understand each other and are doomed, even in the most intimate of human relationships, marriage, to apartness and estrangement, each buried in the solitude of his own thoughts and feelings, which are inevitably, even though unwillingly, veiled from the other. Mr. Hooper appeals passionately to Elizabeth: "'Oh! you know not how lonely I am, and how frightened to be alone behind my black veil'" (47). After Elizabeth refuses to be his wife, he smiles, certainly ironically, and says that the crepe veil which separates them was only a "material emblem . . . though the horrors which it shadowed forth, must be drawn darkly between the fondest of lovers. . . . Thus, from beneath the black veil, there rolled a cloud into the sunshine, *an ambiguity of sin or sorrow,* which enveloped the poor minister, so that love or sympathy could never reach him" (47, 48). It now is clearer to the reader that Mr. Hooper's black veil, while certainly "real," is also a parabolic emblem of the divergence from good and the separateness of all the poor banished children of Eve.

Mr. Hooper lives to a great age and, as representative of the best of

Christian men, is "kind and loving, though unloved, and dimly feared; a man apart from men, shunned in their health and joy, but ever summoned to their aid in mortal anguish" (49). This account of the minister's life suggests the lonely God who, forsaken by men in their prosperity, is called upon desperately in the time of extremity.

Yet, Mr. Hooper's veil is an emblem of man's sin and masking of himself. And because the veil is material and not incorporeal, it "had separated him from cheerful brotherhood and woman's love, and kept him in that saddest of all prisons, his own heart" (50). Reiterating the theme of "The Haunted Mind," "in the depths of every heart, there is a tomb and a dungeon" (306), Hawthorne smiles ironically and Calvinistically with Mr. Hooper at those who would attempt to veil the horrors of the prison of the heart by masks of "lights, . . . music, and revelry" (306).

The Hawthornean view, Calvinist and desolating, is stated without ambiguity at the end of "The Minister's Black Veil"; Mr. Hooper's dying words, as he clings feebly to his black veil, characterize the disordered postlapsarian universe:

> "Why do you tremble at me alone? . . . Tremble also at each other! Have men avoided me, and women shown no pity, and children screamed and fled, only for my black veil? What, but the mystery which it obscurely typifies, has made this piece of crepe so awful? When the friend shows his inmost heart to his friend; the lover to his best-beloved; when man does not vainly shrink from the eye of his Creator, loathsomely treasuring up the secret of his sin; then deem me a monster, for the symbol beneath which I have lived, and die! I look around me, and, lo! on every visage a Black Veil!" (52)

The Reverend Mr. Hooper, by wearing a corporeal black veil, is parabolically attempting to show his pale-faced congregation (those pale faces that affright *him*) the masks all of us wear to hide from ourselves and others some inkling of our own depravity. Mr. Hooper is doomed to isolation and alienation from the pale-faced brotherhood of evil who refuse to acknowledge their evil. But he smiles gently and ironically at the culpable refusal of the mass of humanity to acknowledge their involvement in the horrors of secret sin.

Mr. Hooper commits no special sin; he is branded by the Original Sin that the Calvinist Hawthorne saw as the essential disfigurement of humanity. Mr. Hooper's gentle, ironic smile expresses his recognition that his emblem of this Original Sin—the black veil—is unrecognized by the congregation and even Elizabeth for what it really is. For the congregation and for all humanity, Hawthorne seems to be saying, it is easier to wear a mask of pale-faced conformity than to admit the mystery and horror of our involvement in Adam's Fall, to acknowledge our own black veil.

IV

Hawthorne's structuring of his better tales and sketches is the ordained action of the characters. "The Gentle Boy" illustrates an almost perfect ironic ordering of events that the characters dictate. "The Minister's Black Veil" opens *in medias res,* with the first appearance of the minister in his black veil, and unfolds slowly and inevitably as Mr. Hooper refuses to reveal his reason for wearing the veil. The tale covers the minister's lifetime, ending with the familiar ambiguity of his death. "The May-Pole of Merry Mount" proceeds after a detailed description of the Merry Mounters to the necessary confrontation with the Puritans and their conquest by religious zeal in which Hawthorne uses some equivocation to keep from a too obvious defense of Puritan righteousness. "The Wedding Knell," "The Great Carbuncle," "Dr. Heidegger's Experiment," "The Ambitious Guest," "Edward Fane's Rosebud," and "Lady Eleanore's Mantle" follow a smooth pattern, without any complicating devices of recognition or reversal—just the expected adumbrations, alternate explanations, and rhetorical questions. The endings are not unexpected and Hawthorne's moral conclusion is rather obvious; consequently, these are not great tales.

In "Mr. Higginbotham's Catastrophe" we have the opposite impediment to a structurally biddable tale: we know too much. A story that promises mystery with the tobacco peddler, Dominicus Pike, getting accounts of precise details of the murder of a wealthy man, spreading the news, being refuted, and finally going to the place of the murder just in time to prevent it, devolves into a prosaic tale of virtue rewarded. Hawthorne explains the enigma of Pike's preknowledge and so we have virtue or rather curiosity rewarded by material prosperity without even the wonted Hawthornean irony to redeem the tale from the commonplace.

But when Hawthorne gives rein to his grimly Calvinistic view of man's corrupt nature and allows his ironic mode to dictate the dramatic structure of his tales we have a masterpiece like "The Gentle Boy."[7] Even in Ilbrahim, Hawthorne's gentle boy, "sweet infant of the skies," the mortal taste of the fruit of that forbidden tree corrupts his heavenly nature and makes his heart elect as friend a "foul-hearted little villain." Nowhere does Hawthorne's obsession with the enigma of Original Sin show itself more poignantly than in his story of "this poor, broken-hearted infant" (93).

Hawthorne's acute psychological intuition of the ironic way in which mankind's Eden-wounds lead to heartbreak shapes all the characters in the story. Ilbrahim's father and mother, the Pearsons, and the old Quaker are victimized by a hostile society, and in turn they seek a victim—the archetypal victim—Adamic Ilbrahim. Caught in the dualism of masochism and sadism, Ilbrahim is "used" by the self-seekers. Damned to be their sweating selves, the isolated ones fasten on the innocent, who is led into evil by his own flawed nature. Implicit in the theme of fallen nature are the other favorite Hawthorne leitmotifs: isolation and estrangement; secret guilt; the historical past universalized; the search for a father and a home; the initiation into evil; and the loss of innocence.

The story is deceptively simple, but the irony could not be more specific. The story is divided into six sections—opening and closing with a historical account of New England religious history which provides a patterned beginning and end. Symbolically, the early scene of Ilbrahim clinging to his father's grave is repeated when the story ends with a vision of Catharine's new grave and Ilbrahim's "green and sunken grave" (105).

The significant physical violence in the tale occurs in the forest, the forest of primitive, unleashed, malevolent forces. Ilbrahim's father has been hanged in the forest, and in the forest-crowned amphitheater Ilbrahim is attacked by "the brood of baby-fiends." The "civilized" violence takes place in the clearing—the town—where hypocrisy and sham mask the bestial behavior. It is in the meetinghouse that the minister incites the Puritans to persecution of the Quakers, that Catharine hurls imprecations at her persecutors, and that Ilbrahim is given away by his mother to the Pearsons. In the Pearson home in the clearing, Ilbrahim dies broken-hearted. There is constant movement in the story; the characters go from the forest to the clearing, the wilderness, the desert, the prison. All places seem to be not a home but a prison, a prison of human misery, and all the characters are on a pilgrimage.

An analysis of the sections of the tale is necessary before the subtle meaning of the story is clear. The historical opening and closing is a favorite Hawthorne device. It becomes evident upon examination that Hawthorne is far less interested in the historical foundations of any given story than he is in using the device to create a superficial verisimilitude. Hawthorne establishes the links with the past, but once that has been done his intention is not historical but psychological. Source studies of Hawthorne stories usually throw light only on the first paragraphs, because Hawthorne uses the historical event to provide a stepping-off place into the realms of his art: dark fantasy, brooding imagination, and universal human guilt. Thus the historical opening and closing serve only ironically to emphasize the unhistorical timeless world where Hawthorne's "constant care is not to please but to remind of our, and Adam's curse."

The grave is the symbolic center of the story as is the gravestone in "Roger Malvin's Burial" and the pillory in *The Scarlet Letter.* Ilbrahim attaches himself to his father's grave and says: "My home is here" (72). (As in so many of Hawthorne's stories, the characters foresee their own fate.) Pearson promises Ilbrahim a new life and home; paradoxically, Ilbrahim, in going to Pearson's home, finds not life but death. When Tobias and Ilbrahim reach the Pearson home, the description of the house is more the description of a shut, warm grave than a living home. The attack on Ilbrahim occurs in the amphitheater behind the meetinghouse-grave and the death of Ilbrahim occurs back in the home-grave, even more coffinlike because of the diminished and impoverished state of the Pearsons. The last scene is the grave of Catharine and the "green and sunken grave" of Ilbrahim.

In the second scene Tobias takes Ilbrahim home to his wife, Dorothy, because he has been moved by compassion. But unlike those of the biblical Tobias, Pearson's motives are not pure. Pearson has been having religious difficulties; he has felt guilty about his own children, whose deaths his neighbors imputed to his worldly motives in coming to New England; he has tired of religious war under Cromwell; he has responded to an inward voice in rescuing Ilbrahim, an imperceptible stirring of Quaker feelings; and he is half convinced that he is a backslider, as his Puritan neighbors say he is, for befriending a Quaker heretic. These conflicts in Pearson lead him to a spiritual blindness as the biblical Tobias was subjected to physical blindness; Pearson is attracted to Quaker belief, and because he is, he hates himself and turns inward in a rage of self-attack. If, like that of the biblical Tobias, Pearson's blindess is a test of his virtue, he fails the test. Pearson grows bitter under his persecution; his son does not restore his sight. Pearson broods inwardly, his son perishes, and Pearson's "sight" is never recovered.

In the third section of the story—the events at the meetinghouse—imagery that was just suggested in part two is made explicit. We have learned that Pearson fought in the religious wars with Cromwell as a cornet of dragoons and was presently a lieutenant in the trainbands. Pearson's role as a military man in the strife of religious war with devils and heretics is adopted and expanded by Hawthorne into an elaborate military metaphor to symbolize the bellicose and contentious nature of Puritanism that brings not peace but the sword. Biblical authority sanctions the imaginative concept of actual warfare with the devil, and Calvin complacently expands and accentuates it.[8] Hawthorne, however, uses the military imagery to suggest the psychological subtleties of religious belief clothed in a uniform of external authority which conceals ravening doubts and compulsions to sadistic behavior. The worshippers are summoned to religious exercises by the beat of a drum. The people respond at once in a disciplined, mechanical way. "At the first sound of that martial call to the place of holy and quiet thoughts, Tobias and Dorothy set forth" (78). Hawthorne's irony is apparent in the juxtaposition of "martial call" and "holy and quiet thoughts." With the "thundering summons" in their ears, the congregation forms a "formidable phalanx" at the door to indicate their fury at the Pearsons' audacity in bringing the little heretic Ilbrahim to church. The ploys of battle continue during the service; the Puritan minister denounces the Quakers and warns of the "danger of pity." Ilbrahim's mother emerges from her muffled cloak to hurl down imprecations at her persecutors; "hatred and revenge now wrapped themselves in the garb of piety" (81). Religion is the name which fallen humanity has given to strife and warfare. If the Puritans are armored and equipped with weapons, then the Quakers are the eager martyrs goading them and seducing them into using their weapons. In the coffin-grave meetinghouse the vengeful, cruel, Calvinist Jehovah father figure in the guise of the Puritan minister wars with the fanatic, wild-eyed, unsexed, malignant mother figure in the guise of Catharine the Quaker. Pearson, wrapped in uneasy doubts, turns in on himself; Dorothy's "rational piety" superficially comforts her. The congregation, like all Hawthorne's crowds, is devious, fickle, capricious, and protean. Everything takes place over the head and on the heart of little Ilbrahim, the forgotten victim, the

lost cause. Catharine finally gives Ilbrahim away to the Pearsons and
Hawthorne describes the scene: "The two females, as they held each a
hand of Ilbrahim, formed a practical allegory; it was rational piety and
unbridled fanaticism contending for the empire of a young heart" (85).
Ironically, neither side triumphs, but instead, the "young heart" is
broken. The physical violence in the forest, where Ilbrahim's father was
hanged and the brutal attack was made on Ilbrahim by the children, is no
worse than this "civilized" violence of the meetinghouse. The physical
brutality is horrible in itself, but at least it cannot be totally disguised by
hypocrisy and religious fraud.

Catharine, leaving Ilbrahim with the Pearsons, goes in search of
further persecution, "the apostle of her own unquiet heart" (87). Hawthorne has described the battlefield, the combatants, the weapons of both
sides; in the actual warfare the spoils become the victim. Up to this point,
Ilbrahim has been "used" by adults; it is when he is "used" by his peers
that his heart is completely broken.

Ilbrahim is tempted to bestow his "residue of unappropriated love"
(90) upon an injured neighbor child. Hawthorne subtly endows the crip-
pled boy with the characteristics of the devil. The boy falls out of a tree;
his "countenance . . . impressed a beholder disagreeably" because the
mouth is distorted and the eyebrows are irregular and close together; there
is "an almost imperceptible twist of every joint"; the boy is sullen and is
thought to be "obtuse in intellect," yet later in his life "evinced ambition
and very peculiar[9] talents" (90); and finally Hawthorne suggests personal
and moral irregularities, shrewdness, and moral obliquity. Although
Ilbrahim is appalled at the boy's moral deviousness, he is the victim of his
own loving yet bent nature, and "nestled continually by the bed-side of
the little stranger" (91).

Ilbrahim's giving of his love makes him totally vulnerable. Later,
when he sees a group of Puritan children playing, he who had always
before elected a more secure isolation approaches them "with a look of
sweet confidence on his fair and spiritual face, as if, having manifested his
love to one of them, he had no longer to fear a repulse from their society"
(92). When Ilbrahim first sees the children, they are playing gleefully: "a
heavenly little band," their "light and airy voices" coming from their
"untainted bosoms," the "bliss of childhood" gushing "from its innocence" (92). When Ilbrahim approaches, Hawthorne describes eloquently
the fallen and depraved nature of children, according to Puritan
theology:[10] "all at once, the devil of their fathers entered into the un-

breeched fanatics, and sending up a fierce, shrill cry, they rushed upon the poor Quaker child. In an instant, he was the centre of a brood of baby-fiends, who lifted sticks against him, pelted him with stones, and displayed an instinct of destruction, far more loathsome than the blood-thirstiness of manhood" (92). Ilbrahim's "friend" calls to him to come and take his hand: "After watching the victim's struggling approach, with a calm smile and unabashed eye, the foul-hearted little villain lifted his staff and struck Ilbrahim on the mouth, so forcibly that the blood issued in a stream" (92). Ilbrahim no longer tries to defend himself. He is finally saved by a "few neighbors, who put themselves to the trouble of rescuing the little heretic" (93). Ilbrahim recovers physically after long, careful nursing, but spiritually he is broken and waits for death.

The sacrifice of the innocent victim occurs in a "forest-crowned amphitheater," a "public place";[11] it is a public sacrifice ritually enacted. Ilbrahim is the human sacrifice demanded by the youthful fiends under the direction of the twisted child who delivers the mortal blow with his devil's staff.[12] The horrifying contrast Hawthorne makes between the innocent children at their guileless play and their devilish and obscene attack upon Ilbrahim is one of his most explicit statements of the capriciousness of man's fallen nature. Ilbrahim is misled by his own wounds to seek friendship with a devil; his encounter with the devil and his "brood of baby-fiends" gives him his mortal wounds. Ilbrahim is betrayed by his own misbegotten and misplaced love, betrayed by the Judas words of friendship: "Fear not, Ilbrahim, come hither and take my hand" (92). Withered humanity cannot stand the affront of superior virtue; that virtue must be corrupted into shrewdness[13] or be destroyed. Ilbrahim refuses to fight back or acquire guile and so, because the blows were delivered under the guise of love—although love betrayed—they are mortal and he must die.

Hawthorne could find no more terrifying and moving symbol of the depravity of man than the hideous transfiguration of the children from blissful innocents to knowledgeable baby-fiends. Hawthorne's disciple Henry James later shows he has learned his lesson well in *The Turn of the Screw,* and in our own time Tennessee Williams has given children in *Suddenly Last Summer* the final obscenity of cannibals. With terrible irony Hawthorne seems to be saying that we move from our blighted, isolated selves to love and social involvement; but in this movement away from isolation we either become armored and shrewd or, like Ilbrahim, die.

The autumn wind of desolation that swept around Ilbrahim as he clung to his father's freshly turned grave becomes in the fifth section of the story a howling winter blizzard as Ilbrahim quietly seeks his own grave. The winter wind—"not so unkind as man's ingratitude"—blows home to Ilbrahim his wandering, distracted mother. The paradox of the mother who is yet "cold and wintry" indicates a woman who has abdicated her femininity for the role of prophet and fanatic. Ilbrahim dies in the wind, in this household of desolation, amid the self-seekers who have "used" him for their own purposes.

Since Pearson's adoption of Quakerism, fines, imprisonments, and "his own neglect of temporal affairs" (95) have made him poor. But as his possessions have waned, his spirit has not grown rich and comforted in his newfound religion. Pearson has only changed roles, not his heart; from the persecutor, he has become the persecuted, from the hunter, the hunted, and Hawthorne ironically suggests that even though this is an apparent reversal, it is difficult to tell the two states apart. Pearson still does not "belong"; he is isolated, estranged, embittered, full of self-pity. Like the biblical Tobias, he has been blinded, but he can only lament; Pearson's son does not consort with an angel who will restore his sight.

In the sixth section the historical narrative is resumed and we learn of Catharine's increased fanaticism after the death of her son. Gradually, however, the king's mandate has a mitigating effect upon the men of blood, and they begin to regard Catharine less in wrath than in pity. Less able to withstand pity than persecution, Catharine dies. Hawthorne's bitterest irony is reserved for the populace—all of selfish, blighted humanity is impaled on his final words:

> When the course of years had made the features of the unobtrusive mourner familiar in the settlement, she became a subject of not deep, but general, interest; a being on whom the otherwise superfluous sympathies of all might be bestowed. Everyone spoke of her with that degree of pity which it is pleasant to experience; everyone was ready to do for her the little kindnesses which are not costly, yet manifest good will; and when at last she died, a long train of her once bitter persecutors followed her, with decent sadness and tears that were not painful, to her place by Ilbrahim's green and sunken grave. (104–05)

Hawthorne's language is never more dispassionate and urbane than here, where he damns all lukewarm, unloving humanity to hell with his faint praise.

Ironically, the story of a gentle boy is a cruel and barbarous tale.

Sadistic Puritans and masochistic Quakers—all are whited sepulchers us-ing religion as a flail to enact primitive and primordial rites of chastise-ment and sacrifice. Both seek a victim—an Ilbrahim—to satisfy their lust for blood. But the victim must be as innocent as shriveled humanity can provide; and so it is a child, a lamb to be given to the slaughter. Haw-thorne records in his *American Notebooks* in 1836 that "There is evil in every human heart" (29) as if his own experience of life had only corrobo-rated Calvin: "if these are the hereditary properties of the human race, it is vain to look for anything good in our nature. . . . It cannot be denied that the hydra lurks in every breast."[14] The idea of the hydra in the heart, this Original Sin in the Calvinistic damnatory theology that Hawthorne could not embrace yet was unable to disavow, so conditioned his imagina-tion that his brooding fancy produced at its best—as in "The Gentle Boy"—a tale forlorn and sorrowing, where mankind is caught "spitting from the mouth the withered apple-seed."

It is only because Hawthorne yearns toward gentleness and innocence that his dry, remorseless indictment of universal human corruption is so moving. He is not resigned either emotionally or rationally to the effects of Original Sin, and his inquietude gives his work a deep, if negative, religious passion. What is it in the last paragraph of "The Gentle Boy" that makes his rhetoric so compelling but the juxtaposition of two ethics? Only one of these ethics is expressed—that of decent self-regard, in which compassion and love for others cross no threshold of pain. The implied ethic, which serves as ironic contrast, is of course the fundamental Chris-tian idea of love "costing not less than everything." The agony is that the Christian ethic appears impossible, so that the heart that desires it is forever frustrated.

"The Gentle Boy" is one more oblique statement of Hawthorne's tragic vision of depraved mankind in which a little child—Ilbrahim, the foreigner, the Samaritan—must die of the disease of humanity for which there is no cure. Hawthorne's horror and rejection of man's total depravity and his faltering acknowledgment of it result in the ironic perfection of his art. The story is a wry and anguished cry, "Damn, damned Human-ity!"

V

The most interesting character in *Twice-told Tales,* with the possible ex-ception of Wakefield, is Hawthorne himself, as the persona, or narrator-participant, of so many of the tales. He is the old, tedious village uncle;

the confidant of the gravestone chiseler overwhelmed by his own mortality; the hidden spy in the window of "Sunday at Home," who makes rather mocking comments on the Sunday Christians; the sober crypto-kidnapper of Little Annie in "Little Annie's Ramble"; the sham narrator who attempts to stop Wakefield's vagary; the nasal voice of the Town-Pump; the moral judge of the allegory of "The Great Carbuncle"; the philosophical observer of the "might-have-beens" of the sleeping "David Swan"; the Paul Pry of "Sights from a Steeple"; the almost silent narrator of the horror story, "The Hollow of the Three Hills"; the fifteen-year-old romantic of "The Vision of the Fountain"; the propounder of vexing theological questions in "Fancy's Show Box"; the cold Dr. Heidegger himself in his observations of the folly of ugly age trying to regain youth; the moralizing voice of the Province House stories; and the truly haunted insomniac of "The Haunted Mind." But nowhere in all these personae is Hawthorne the casual, carefree beholder. One of Hawthorne's delusions about himself, no doubt fostered by Sophia, his children, and his college friends with whom he used to play childish practical jokes, was that he was a humorist. Most of his attempts at the light touch are heavy-handed and his sportiveness often embarrasses the sympathetic reader and irritates the antipathetic one.[15] The result of all these complementary and conflicting poses and voices is complex, to say the least, but the outcome certainly demonstrates the infinite variety of Hawthorne's range and artistry and should give the lie to those critics who see Hawthorne only as a rather prim, vague, and occasionally felicitous nineteenth-century romantic writer. The overall impression from these stories is that of craftiness, infinite competence, alienation, and more than a touch of quiet desperation.

Few of the characters in this first set of tales are developed completely, a near impossibility in any short story, but there are some memorable and consistent creations: the veiled and smiling Father Hooper ("The Minister's Black Veil"); the spiritualized Paul Pry ("Sights from a Steeple"); the grim Endicott of the iron gauntlet ("The May-Pole of Merry Mount," "Endicott and the Red Cross"); the prideful Lady Eleanore ("Lady Eleanore's Mantle"); gentle Ilbrahim and the frustrated and embittered Tobias Pearson ("The Gentle Boy"), the Ur-scientist-villain, Dr. Heidegger ("Dr. Heidegger's Experiment"); the allegorical but pathetically arrogant searcher for immortality ("The Ambitious Guest"); and the eccentric old maid in her winding sheet ("The White Old Maid").

The most memorable characters of *Twice-told Tales* are the eccentrics, the anomalies. All of the Maypolers, in their mad revelling which resembles despair, excite our interest, as do the strange white old maid, faithful follower of funerals, and the bridegroom who appears in his shroud in "The Wedding Knell." Ralph Cranfield of "The Threefold Destiny," subtitled "A Faery Legend," promises to be exciting ("from his youth upward, had felt himself marked out for a high destiny" [473]), but he discovers the three marvellous events, after searching the whole world, in his own village and with his childhood sweetheart. Up until the rather prosaic ending, Ralph Cranfield with his conviction of his unusual fate seems to be an archetypal John Marcher for James's "Beast in the Jungle," and it is certainly possible that Cranfield was the germ of James's idea for his far more complex and beautiful tale.

But Hawthorne's resplendent creation is Wakefield. Certainly one of the most galvanizing and perturbing of Hawthorne's tales, "Wakefield" was almost completely ignored until the 1960s and even since, much of the critical speculation about it has been whether or not it is an anecdote or a story. Every attentive reader seems willing to concede that the character of Wakefield is a true original—neoteric and unique—but there is a constant undercurrent of dissatisfaction about the structure of the piece: it is too weak, too intellectual, too unstructured, in short, too sketchy.

I should like to argue, however, that Wakefield, amorphous, inchoate, and anomalous as he is, ordains a very real ironic structure—even an Aristotelian structure with an identifiable beginning, middle, and end, and a satisfactory ending at that.

Hawthorne begins his sixteen-paragraph story with a deceptively ingenuous bid for verisimilitude. He recounts having read in an old magazine or newspaper the story of "perhaps the strangest instance, on record, of marital delinquency . . . in the whole list of human oddities" (130). He summarizes the story briefly, places it in London, and makes the ending more specific than his story's will be: "he entered the door one evening, quietly, as from a day's absence, and became a loving spouse till death" (130).

Ordinarily, a summary of a story in the first paragraph would mean defective art, eliminating all possibility of suspense or even curiosity about the rest of the tale, but Hawthorne only whets our interest to hear more than this bare-bones outline. He does this by suggesting the strangeness of the character of Wakefield (an interesting name since, far from Wakeful, he seems to be rather stuporous, or, in another sense, to be perhaps keeping a wake or vigil over his own death as the previously known character, Wakefield). Hawthorne points out that "We know, each for himself, that none of us would perpetrate such a folly, yet feel as if some other might" (131). We are caught because we immediately begin speculating, as Hawthorne does, about the bizarre character of Wakefield and wondering if we know anyone who might do the same thing Wakefield did.

Hawthorne invites us to continue our own meditations or ramble with him "through the twenty years of Wakefield's vagary" (131), promising that "there will be a pervading spirit and a moral, even should we fail to find them, done up neatly, and condensed into the final sentence" (131). Now our guard is up because the sly ironist has promised us a spirit and a moral in the last sentence "even should we fail to find them." The cagey Hawthorne has set his first trap for the unwary reader.

The third paragraph tells us both much and little about Wakefield: he is "in the meridian of life"; his never violent matrimonial affections are sobered and habitual; he should have been the most constant of husbands because of his sluggishness; he is intellectual, but lacking vigor, his mind is engaged in "long and lazy musings" to no purpose; he rarely expresses thoughts in words; he lacks any imagination; his heart is cold but not depraved; his mind is not feverish nor original, so how could he "entitle himself to a foremost place among the doers of eccentric deeds?" (131). This is the second of nine rhetorical questions that Hawthorne poses to the reader in this short tale in order to puzzle and challenge our understanding of the character of Wakefield, since he has just given us a series of characteristics that are inherently contradictory: Wakefield is sober; he should be constant because of his sluggishness but is not; he is intellectual, but muses to no purpose, for he is inarticulate and lacks imagination; his heart is cold but not depraved or wandering; his mind has no originality but he does something extraordinary. Despite these paradoxes of his nature, none of his acquaintances would have expected anything memorable from him, only "the wife of his bosom might have hesitated" (131).

Mrs. Wakefield has not analyzed her husband's character but is "partly aware" of a "quiet selfishness," of a "peculiar sort of vanity" (again the alert sounds because Hawthorne's use of the neutral word "peculiar" is usually ominous), of a "disposition to craft" (keeping petty secrets), and "lastly . . . [of] what she called a little strangeness" (132).

After Wakefield says goodbye to his wife, telling her he will be back for supper Friday evening, he partly opens the door and Mrs. Wakefield sees him through the crack "smiling on her" for a moment. As we know, smiles or laughter in Hawthorne are not to be trusted—certainly not as connoting happiness or good spirits—for they most often signal craftiness, ironic melancholy (the Reverend Mr. Hooper's smile in "The Minister's Black Veil"), or downright demonism (Westervelt's smile in *The Blithedale Romance*). Mrs. Wakefield finds her husband's smile haunting her throughout the next twenty years: "that smile recurs, and flickers across all her reminiscences of Wakefield's visage" (132), and she fancies that it is "strange and awful." She sees in her imagination this strange smile "frozen" on his face in a coffin; or "if she dreams of him in Heaven, still his blessed spirit wears a quiet and crafty smile" (133). The "crafty smile" is the most potent initial indication we have of Wakefield's strangeness.

The story now turns to Wakefield himself, who is hurrying away, crossing and recrossing streets. Devious, breathless, and hardly able to believe he has not been followed or recognized, he finally arives at a small apartment, "previously bespoken" in the street next to his own (133). To arouse our interest, Hawthorne tells us that we have had to hurry to keep up with Wakefield as he pursues his journey of a block "ere he lose his individuality, and melt into the great mass of London life. It would be vain searching for him there" (133).

Hawthorne addresses Wakefield directly, and irritating as this authorial device can be, in this story it seems not only appropriate, but as if Hawthorne is expressing the views of the reader, who also wants to admonish Wakefield and tell him that he is a fool. Hawthorne castigates Wakefield for not knowing his own unimportance, tells him to go to bed and return the next day to his wife. He warns that "were she, for a single moment, to deem thee dead, or lost, or lastingly divided from her, thou wouldst be woefully conscious of a change in thy true wife, forever after" (133). We begin to realize that, even though Hawthorne has announced "our business is with the husband," the character of Mrs. Wakefield is going to assume great importance in the tale. She will, in fact, change significantly. Paragraph five ends with this deliciously ironic statement: "It is perilous to make a chasm in human affections; not that they gape so long and wide—but so quickly close again!" (133).

As Wakefield turns his project over in his mind, he becomes curious to know how his "exemplary wife" will respond to his absence and curious about "the little sphere of creatures and circumstances, in which he was a central object" (134). Hawthorne judges that "a morbid vanity . . . lies nearest the bottom of the affair" (134). The problem for Wakefield now is to find out how his absence affects those closest to him and yet not let them see him watching them. Confused and resorting to habit he wanders back to the very step of his house before he realizes where he is. Hawthorne addresses him: "Wakefield! whither are you going?" (134).

Wakefield hurries away and Hawthorne, with the firm and directive authorial voice he uses throughout the story, indicates that this is the crisis: "At that instant, his fate was turning on the pivot. Little dreaming of the doom to which his first backward step devotes him, he hurries away" (134–35). Wakefield feels sure someone has seen him, but after he is certain no one has recognized or followed him, he realizes that neither his house nor his wife looks the same. "In Wakefield," Hawthorne asserts, "the magic of a single night has wrought a similar transformation, because, in that brief period, a great moral change has been effected. But this is a secret from himself" (135).

At one point in Wakefield's first circuitous journey to the next block he hears a voice shouting "and fancied that it called his name" (133). For twenty years hereafter no one will call Wakefield by his name as he becomes the archetypal isolato, the one who loses his identity through a moral transformation that has been wrought in him by his frightened and confused decision to stay away from his home and become the anonymous disguised voyeur. Hawthorne's probing psychological insights into the increasingly grotesque character of Wakefield tacitly pose some fearful questions to the reader. If nobody calls us by our name for twenty years, do we really know who we are? Can a change of clothes, of residence, of name, shatter the fragile, brittle, and infirm personality that we have so carefully constructed? Is this created personality so delicate and vulnerable that it needs constantly to be supported by others? Are we really only a part of a "magnetic chain" that will close us out the minute we miss a step and therefore lose our place in the procession of life? Some modern readers may be startled or annoyed that in 1835 Hawthorne could address these existential questions and identity dilemmas that we arrogantly assume are creations of the twentieth-century age of anxiety and of the post-Freudian, nuclear age, an age threatening us with atomization, extinction, and nothingness.

The middle of this absorbing and disquieting tale (paragraphs nine through fifteen) is the account of Wakefield's twenty-year absence from his own tiny space in his little universe and his change to the anonymous voyeur whose only satisfactions are the little paps to his cold curiosity of peering and prying.

During these years, Wakefield assumes a new mask which transforms him into another man who wears old clothes and a reddish wig. Hawthorne regrets that he is not able to write a whole folio about this singular character to "exemplify how an influence, beyond our control, lays its strong hand on every deed which we do, and weaves its consequences into an *iron tissue of necessity"* (136–37). The omnipresent Calvinism, always operant in Hawthorne's thought, suggests for Wakefield, as for so many others of Hawthorne's characters,[16] that once there is a chink in the ruined wall of the soul, it is never in this mortal life repaired.

There is one great moment which occurs ten years after Wakefield's antic departure. Wakefield meets his wife face-to-face and she does not recognize him. At this point Hawthorne describes Wakefield as "meagre; his low and narrow forehead is deeply wrinkled; his eyes, small and lustreless, sometimes wander apprehensively about him, but oftener seem to look inward. He bends his head, but moves with an indescribable obliquity of gait, as if unwilling to display his full front to the world" (137). He skulks about like Chillingworth or like Old Moodie, who tried to hide himself behind his eye patch. But Mrs. Wakefield has prospered: "She has the placid mien of settled widowhood. Her regrets have either died away, or have become so essential to her heart, that they would be poorly exchanged for joy" (137). Lean Wakefield and "well conditioned" Mrs. Wakefield are pressed together by the crowd and look into each other's eyes.

As the throng moves away, Mrs. Wakefield continues soberly to church, and "throws a perplexed glance along the street," but evidently reassured, opens her prayer book and goes into the church. Wakefield, on the other hand, flies wildly to his lodgings and bolts the door. Hawthorne tells us that all at once the "miserable strangeness of life is revealed to him . . . and he cries out, passionately—'Wakefield! Wakefield! You are mad!'" (138).

Hawthorne concedes that "perhaps he was so." Wakefield had dissevered himself from the world and vanished "without being admitted among the dead" (138). No one in the crowd saw him; no one called him by his name. Hawthorne suggests that "it was Wakefield's unprecedented fate to retain his original share of human sympathies . . . while he had lost his reciprocal influence on them" (138). Hawthorne further suggests, in Wakefield, the separation of head and heart. Altered as he is, Wakefield would have no consciousness of his alteration "and still he would keep saying—'I shall go back!'—nor reflect, that he had been saying so for twenty years" (138). To Wakefield, who has dropped out of life to become a corporeal ghost and voyeur, the twenty years would seem no longer than the week he had intended to stay away. He still could imagine that, when he decided to return, "his wife would clap her hands for joy, on beholding the middle-aged Mr. Wakefield. Alas, what a mistake!" (139).

One evening twenty years after he left home, Wakefield is lurking about his house when a gusty shower falls. He peers through the window, voyeur to the last, and sees a warm, comfortable fire and his wife. Another rhetorical question is posed by Hawthorne: "Shall he stand, wet and shivering here, when his own hearth has a good fire to warm him, and his own wife will run to fetch the gray coat and small-clothes, which, doubtless, she has kept carefully in the closet of their bed-chamber?" (139). Hawthorne answers this question himself: "Wakefield is no such fool." So he heavily ascends the steps, unaware that twenty years have taken their toll on the suppleness of his legs. But Hawthorne, with the irresistibly involved reader's consent, tries to stop him: "Stay, Wakefield! Would you go to the sole home that is left you? Then step into your grave!" (139). But the unheeding Wakefield passes through the door and we catch a parting glimpse of "the crafty smile, which was the precursor of the little joke, that he has ever since been playing off at his wife's expense" (139–40).

Although Hawthorne suggests that Wakefield will quiz his wife unmercifully, he refuses to follow Wakefield across the threshold. He concludes his fantastic story with the moral he promised at the beginning: "Amid the seeming confusion of our mysterious world, individuals are so nicely adjusted to a system, and systems to one another, and to a whole, that, by stepping aside for a moment, a man exposes himself to a fearful risk of losing his place forever. Like Wakefield, he may become, as it were, the Outcast of the Universe" (140).

Certainly Wakefield's fate as the chthonian outcast of the universe is dreadful, but because the clever Hawthorne does not invade Wakefield's home and try for a great dramatic confrontation which could never be as satisfying as our fantasizing of the great scene, we have another Hawthornean character that must be reckoned with. Wakefield may, with his craft and cruelty, salvage what infinitesimal identity he had before his twenty-year disappearing act. But what of the widow Wakefield? She has felt every one of her tolerable twenty years and has passed comparatively effortlessly from her identity as Mrs. Wakefield to her identity as widow Wakefield. What now is in store for her? Certainly in having to dislocate herself from comfortable widow to duped and cozened wife, she is in great hazard of losing her identity completely. And what identity can she hope for? As the twenty-year butt of a crafty voyeur's jibe, what is to be poor Mrs. Wakefield's fate? She is truly the outcast of the universe.

Thus, in sixteen paragraphs Hawthorne has given us the strangest and most riddling of his tales. It is structurally impeccable, portraying two characters, one Wakefield, the sluggish actor, and Mrs. Wakefield, the acted upon, the undeserving victim of sadism and cruelty. It has also raised for the reader a succession of agitating and vexing metaphysical questions (the kind we expect from a Kafka or a Camus or a Beckett) that are destined to plague us forever.

## VI

The thirty-nine stories of *Twice-told Tales* are a galaxy of delights, but it becomes obvious the more one considers them that the greatest of the stories reinforce the thesis that Hawthorne's submerged Calvinism dictates the ironic mode, his most natural and effective voice. The stories or sketches singled out for detailed attention in each of the six parts of this chapter are uniformly baleful, anguished questionings of the most frightening dilemmas of human existence.

Hawthorne never ceases from this agonized questioning in his writings until the last months of his life, when weariness, failing health, and theological uncertainties make him long only for the rest of the grave. But in this first collection of tales there is the strange ambivalence concerning his Puritan inheritance—a singular blend of pride and shame. But Hawthorne is his own man. He is no idealistic dreamer of compensation and oversoul, as are Emerson and Thoreau. He is, rather, a powerful thunder-smitten Adam, feeling fully his fault in paradise lost and ruefully, dolefully trying to acclimate himself to this sorrowing world east of Eden. Without a knowledge of Hawthorne's quivering Calvinist conscience, it would be difficult to imagine an artistic sketch on the subject of "Fancy's Show Box": are we responsible not only for those sins we have committed but also for every "flitting phantom of iniquity" that we have only imagined?

For those critics who admire Hawthorne's art but dismiss him summarily as a non-thinker or a man incapable of examining a theological or philosophical question, "Fancy's Show Box" is a troublemaker. No Calvinist divine is more serious than Hawthorne as he meditates on the question of human guilt and responsibility in this sketch, and he is far from refreshed or reassured by his cogitations. In fact, no tale or sketch by Hawthorne gives us more access to the inquietude of his soul and the formidable, deep obliquity of his cavernous heart than does "Fancy's Show Box."

In the first paragraph of this nine-paragraph sketch, Hawthorne asks a series of questions which involve man's guilt and possible damnation, and they are posed in the Calvinistic terms that Hawthorne would have been familiar with from his childhood and from his constant reading of Puritan theological literature and sermons. The first question is "What is Guilt?" (220). Hawthorne answers this himself: "A stain upon the soul." He then considers if it is necessary for sinful deeds to be committed "physically . . . in order to give them their entire validity against the sinner" (220). This rhetorical question is followed by another more weighty one which asks if guilty thoughts "will . . . draw down the full weight of a condemning sentence, in the supreme court of eternity" (220). He deems that such thoughts can occur in a "midnight chamber" or "in a desert"; he also says that in "church, while the body is kneeling, the soul may pollute itself even with those crimes, which we are accustomed to deem altogether carnal" (220). Hawthorne is undoubtedly meditating on Matthew 6:28, "But I say unto you, that whosoever looketh on a woman to lust after her, hathe committed adultery with her already in his heart" (Geneva Bible). The paragraph concludes with the alarming sentence: "If this be true, it is a fearful truth" (220). [17]

Hawthorne then explores the subject of guilt for sins of the mind and heart which are not physically accomplished but only contemplated by his "imaginary example." He chooses the venerable Mr. Smith warming himself alone with a couple of glasses of wine. Mr. Smith, "whose silver hair was the bright symbol of a life unstained, except by such spots as are inseparable from human nature" (221)—that is, by natural depravity—

seems apparently comfortable alone, but Hawthorne warns that solitude will induce his thoughts to "stray into the misty region of the past, and the old man [will] be chill and sad" (221).

Suddenly, three figures come into the room where Mr. Smith is drinking his wine. We are alerted to the fact that Mr. Smith is in for a bad time, not only because the three menacing and portentous figures have mysteriously arrived, but because Hawthorne has indicated that Mr. Smith has a "shrewd" idea. Like the neutral word "peculiar" which Hawthorne uses to presage vicissitude, so "shrewd," in Hawthorne's vocabulary, usually connotes a mundane sophistication and lack of innocence that Hawthorne despises. In the chamber, Memory takes her place at Mr. Smith's right hand, Conscience on the left, "so as to be near his heart" (222), and Fancy puts her picture box and magnifying glass on the table.

Three main pictures are shown to Mr. Smith. The first is of a young man standing arrogantly and haughtily over a kneeling girl, "sinking under a weight of shame and anguish" (222). Mr. Smith finally recognizes himself as the youth and the girl as his first "cottage love." He is "scandalized" and protests that the girl married a young man, was an affectionate wife, and since has been a "reputable widow." But when Memory turns the pages of her book and reads a passage into Mr. Smith's ear—"it is a record merely of sinful thought" (223)—Conscience strikes a dagger blow of extreme torture into Mr. Smith's heart.

One of the pictures depicts a murder in which a young man lay on the floor with "a ghastly wound crushed into his temple" (223) and over him the young Mr. Smith. Outraged, Mr. Smith again protests, but Memory reads of a tipsy quarrel between Mr. Smith and his youthful friend which concluded with Mr. Smith throwing a bottle at his friend. The bottle missed but Conscience again "unveiled her face, struck a dagger to the heart of Mr. Smith, and quelled his remonstrance with her iron frown. The pain was quite excruciating" (224).

The final picture infuriates Mr. Smith; it shows him "stripping the clothes from the backs of three half-starved children." But Memory reads him a page recalling how he had been "grievously tempted by many devilish sophistries" to instigate a lawsuit against three orphans, heirs to a large estate, but his claim had proved "as devoid of law, as justice" (225). Conscience stabs him again and he gets "an ugly gash."

The last three paragraphs of this fanciful sketch examine some of the most difficult problems of belief that confront any Christian, let alone a reluctant Calvinist such a Hawthorne.

In the first of these paragraphs Hawthorne asks whether these secret sins of the mind of Mr. Smith, "so near akin to nothingness, give valid evidence against him, at the day of judgement" (225). The question is answered in a way that at first suggests that Hawthorne is blenching at the pure Calvinism of damnation: "there is reason to believe, that one truly penitential tear would have washed away each hateful picture, and left the canvas white as snow" (225). However, Mr. Smith, the Pharisee, is in no mood for the necessary repentance that would at least (according to orthodox Calvinism) put him in the proper attitude for regeneration.

The case of Mr. Smith is now taken up by Hawthorne in his most ironic mode and argued in a way that reveals him to be the uneasy stepson of Calvin and an author convinced that he would have been disavowed by his "stern and black-browed" ancestors. So Hawthorne argues for Mr. Smith's cause by comparing his situation with that of the writer of a tale: "A scheme of guilt, till it be put in execution, greatly resembles a train of incidents in a projected tale" (225). The author, in order to achieve realism, must make his tale seem "more like truth . . . than purely fiction." The prospective sinner plans a crime in a dreamlike state never certain it will be carried out: "in a dream, as it were, he strikes the death-blow into his victim's heart, and starts to find an indelible bloodstain on his hand" (225). The analogy continues as Hawthorne shows that a novel writer or dramatist, "in creating a villain of romance, and fitting him with evil deeds, and the villain of actual life, in projecting crimes that will be perpetrated, may almost meet each other, half-way between reality and fancy" (226). Hawthorne, now exposed as a younger Mr. Smith, is admitting culpability and guilt, but it is not "until the crime is accomplished, that guilt clenches its grip upon the guilty heart [here the novelist and prospective criminal seem to become one] and claims it for his own" (226). Then, Hawthorne admits, sin is felt and if not accompanied by repentance, "grows a thousand fold more virulent by its self-consciousness" (226). Hawthorne continues to identify writer and criminal by showing "that men often overestimate their capacity for evil." They (and we again assume artist and criminal are linked, not only in a similitude but in reality) can contemplate crime at a distance, take steps toward it, yet refrain at the last moment, for Hawthorne argues that "there is no such thing in man's nature, as a settled and full resolve, either for good or evil, except at the very moment of execution. Let us hope, therefore, that all the dreadful consequences of sin will not be incurred, unless the act have set its seal upon the thought" (226).

If the sketch ended here without the final paragraph, one could easily believe that Hawthorne had absolved both the writer, who creates villains, and the actual criminal, who plans a crime, unless the deed moves out of the mind of both into the reality of action—the completed novel or tale or the criminal act. However, as much as Hawthorne longs for a generous and all-forgiving God, he cannot conceive of the sovereign Jehovah condescending to man's infamy. We can almost hear the words of Calvin's *Institutes* refuting the faint hopes of Hawthorne:

> But God, whose eye nothing escapes, and who regards not the outward appearance so much as purity of heart, under the prohibition of murder [the bottle Mr. Smith throws at his friend], adultery [Mr. Smith and his cottage sweetheart], and theft [Mr. Smith's designs against the orphaned children] includes wrath, hatred, lust, covetousness, and all other things of a similar nature. . . . And let not a man flatter himself, that because he abstains from the outward act he cannot be accused of unchastity. . . . To be clear of the crime of murder, it is not enough to refrain from shedding man's blood. If in act you perpetrate, if in endeavor you plot, if in wish and design you conceive what is adverse to another's safety, you have the guilt of murder. (Vol. I, pp. 321, 347, 349, 352)

Apparently with the sombre logic of Calvin in his ears, Hawthorne begins his last paragraph with a great "Yet." "Yet," he admits, his framed "fancy work" has in it "some sad and awful truths." The conclusion is the pure Calvinism of *The Institutes,* unadulterated by two centuries of heterodoxy:

> Man must not disclaim his brotherhood, even with the guiltiest, since, though his hand be clean, his heart has surely been polluted by the flitting phantoms of iniquity. He must feel, that, when he shall knock at the gate of Heaven, no semblance of an unspotted life can entitle him to entrance there. Penitence must kneel, and Mercy come from the footstool of the throne, or that golden gate will never open! (226)

In an unsparingly rigorous and Calvinistic way, Hawthorne ironically unites humanity—the apparently good Mr. Smith, the wily but "guilty" novel writer, the conspiring criminal, and all of us—in a brotherhood of evil that dictates damnation unless there is humble penitence: "by repentance I understand regeneration [i.e., in Calvinist terms only the regenerate elect; the reprobate are damned completely and finally, no matter what their regrets], the only aim of which is to form in us anew the image of God, which was sullied, and all but effaced by the transgression of Adam" (Vol. I, p. 515). If the penitence is abject enough *and* we are of the regenerate elect, still we are incapable and helpless unless God— "Mercy"—comes to us. In and of ourselves we can do nothing—"the only end which he [the Lord] has in view is to bring us to an acknowledgement of our utter nothingness" (Vol. I, p. 286).

A fanciful sketch indeed! Good old white-haired Mr. Smith and Hawthorne, teller of tales, intentional criminals, and the rest of us— Pharisees and hypocrites—all are ironically reduced to Hawthorne's view of the true state of human nature: cringing, depraved, foul-hearted, loathsome creatures hoping against faint hope that the golden gate will open to us. And in this vision we are all doomed to hellfire despite the fact that our sins may *not* result in deed but only reside festering in our hearts and minds—all unless we have been abjectly penitent, regenerated, and elected from all time for salvation through God's sovereign mercy. For Hawthorne, this is a twice-told, many-times-told tale.

MOSSES FROM AN OLD MANSE

# *"The Life-Long Shiver"*

---

I

On July 9, 1842, seven months after the publication of the two-volume edition of *Twice-told Tales,* Hawthorne married Sophia Peabody. They moved to Concord to live in the Old Manse where they remained for three years. But, because Hawthorne was not prospering as a writer, they left in the autumn of 1845 to return to Salem and live in the Manning house with Hawthorne's mother and sisters. In the spring of 1846, Hawthorne was made surveyor of the Custom House in Salem, a political appointment finally managed for him by his friends.

Between July 1842 and August 1845, Hawthorne published in various periodicals and on June 5, 1846, *Mosses from an Old Manse* was published with his latest tales and sketches, plus nine older works; e.g., "Young Goodman Brown" and "Sketches from Memory" date from 1835.[1]

When Hawthorne was in England as consul general of Liverpool, James T. Fields sent him a copy of the 1846 edition of *Mosses* to review and correct for the second edition. After working on the 1846 copy, Hawthorne wrote Fields that it was "a very disagreeable task. . . . Upon my honor, I am not quite sure that I entirely comprehend my own meaning in some of these blasted allegories," but added later in the letter: "Yet certainly there is more in it than the public generally gave me credit for, at the time it was written" (522–23). Most of the reviewers preferred *Mosses from an Old Manse* to *Twice-told Tales* and the 1846 edition was reviewed memorably by both Poe and Melville.

It is interesting that in this remarkable collection, fifteen of the twenty-six tales and sketches are set in the probable present, five in the past, and six in a fantasy time. Three of the greatest tales, "The Birthmark," "Young Goodman Brown," and "Roger Malvin's Burial," occur in past times; two, in the fantasy world of unidentified time, "Rappaccini's Daughter" and "Earth's Holocaust"; and just one from the probable present, "The Artist of the Beautiful." There are many other tales and sketches that would be given first honors by other critics, but in my view, the past operates most creatively on Hawthorne's imagination. This is especially true in his novels: the greatest, *The Scarlet Letter,* is set in seventeenth-century Boston; *Blithedale,* in the present but at a remove from mid-nineteenth-century exigencies in the utopia of Brook Farm; *The Marble Faun,* in the present, but like "Rappaccini's Daughter," set in Italy to absent it from contemporary American political, historical, or sociological influences. Even the one novel of the present world—*The House of the Seven Gables,* Hawthorne's least successful—is isolated from ordinary events because of the sheltering house and the hereditary curse.

The subjects we have come to expect from Hawthorne—guilt, isolation, secret sin, initiation into evil, the Fall—are all found in *Mosses.* In "The New Adam and Eve" Hawthorne has the newly created Adam and Eve walking about Boston after Doomsday bewildered by the objects of man's vanity. We who are accustomed to the "world's artificial system" never know how much is natural "and how much is merely the interpolation of the perverted mind and heart of man" (247). Adam and Eve are confused by department stores and churches, sickened by law courts and prisons, puzzled by the Hall of Legislature, and confounded by the remains of an elegant banquet—except for the fruit. Adam gives Eve a red-cheeked apple "in requital of her predecessor's fatal gift to our common grandfather" (259). They play with money in a bank, and are completely puzzled by the "rich library of Harvard University" (264). Only by Eve's insistence does Adam leave his perusal of books and this "happy" influence of Eve ironically prevents another Fall: "the annalist of our poor world would soon have recorded the downfall of a second Adam. The fatal apple of another Tree of Knowledge would have been eaten. All the perversions and sophistries, and false wisdom mimicking the true; . . . all the wrong principles and worse practice, the pernicious examples and mistaken rules of life; all the specious theories . . . —the whole heap of this disastrous lore would have tumbled at once upon Adam's head" (265). Here Hawthorne has Eve prevent a second Fall, but his view of the postlapsarian world in which the new Adam and Eve wander is a truly tragic one.

The terrible isolation and alienation of the brotherhood of evil which so haunted Hawthorne reaches an apogee in "Young Goodman Brown." Young Goodman Brown, intent on just one night's demonism away from his Faith, thinks that afterward he can "cling to her skirts and follow her to Heaven" (75). Written fifteen years before *The Scarlet Letter,* this story presages what initiation into evil does to the perpetrator. In *The Scarlet Letter* Hester feels a sympathetic quiver in her scarlet letter when she encounters a person guilty of secret sin, and Dimmesdale, after his willful commitment to evil in the forest, is filled with an incredible energy and an almost unconquerable desire to corrupt everyone he meets. But Goodman Brown, who recognizes evil in everyone he meets after his diabolic excursion into the forest, ironically seems able to endure his own evil because he does not recognize it. Doomed, he becomes a grim isolato so that even "his dying hour was gloom" (90).

In "The Procession of Life" Hawthorne's tragic vision of humanity, classified and marching through life led by the dark rider on the pale horse, Death, chars the imagination through its riving irony. Hawthorne always seems to have some trouble with his endings, especially when his tragic vision has ordered an irony that he cannot bear to enunciate. And so, in the last sentence, we have a conclusion that seems at first reading fairly consoling: "But God, who made us, knows, and will not leave us on our toilsome and doubtful march, either to wander in infinite uncertainty, or perish by the way!" (222). However, as we consider the conclusion, there is not a great deal of solace in the thought of God's judgment on the members of a procession who have among them not one who is good.[2]

Hawthorne's 1844 sketch, "The Intelligence Office," epitomizes what we have come to see as the dominant theme of the Hawthorne question—the ambiguity of man's moral nature. These Hawthornean equivocations, when added up, usually are weighted on the side of the dark impulses of the heart, which is natural for this inheritor of Calvinist orthodoxy who sees utter depravity and viciousness at the root of all *semblances* of virtues—faith, hope, charity, and other expected marks of the loving Christian. Far from rejoicing in this evil, Hawthorne writes with tragic irony of the quandaries and quagmires of deluded mankind on its lifetime pilgrimage:

> But all the way, in a dark wood, in a bramble,
> On the edge of a grimpen, where is no secure foothold,
> And menaced by monsters, fancy lights,
> Risking enchantment.[3]

On the simplest and most obvious level, "The Intelligence Office" is Orwellian—a *1984* dominated by a Supreme Intelligence Officer who has the miserable records of every wish, desire, and activity of every man. But Hawthorne's lack of concern with *Realpolitik* diminishes it to another depravity of human nature. That Big Brother is watching our every move is not doubted by Hawthorne, but the Hawthornean Big Brother bears a much closer resemblance to a jealous Calvinist Jehovah than to a Stalinist reprobate. In the Hawthorne atlas there is true democracy: all men are sinners.

At a deeper level "The Intelligence Office" is like the creations of the tortured mind of Franz Kafka. The office is as dusty, cluttered, hidden, dreary, and barren as any of those in the miserable tenements found in Kafka, and the Intelligence Officer, turning over his huge folio and peering at it with his "mysterious spectacles," seems as menacing as the chief clerk who comes looking for Gregor Samsa. What is surprising (because of our complacent notion that the thinkers of the twentieth century discovered existential alienation and isolation) is that the comparisons just suggested are to twentieth-century writers and not to any of Hawthorne's contemporaries. Certainly there are enough mouldy offices in Dickens, but in them are underpaid clerks or sleek, cheating lawyers, not inscrutable and recondite dealers with the sinister and covert desires of the human heart. The Kafkaesque qualities of "The Intelligence Office," that seem to form such a direct DNA from Hawthorne to twentieth-century malaise, are what make this sketch memorable. These attributes are the climate of nightmare, but yet a waking one with all of the physical realities exact and in place: the element of the absurd, the antic, the bizarre that affects the reader as does electroshock, and the weighty guilt of unknown cause that plagues the characters and infects the readers so that even if we, like Joseph K., do not know what our crime is, we know we are accountable.

The whole idea of a central intelligence office for the ordinary citizen is repulsive, perhaps more for twentieth-century readers than those of the nineteenth century, since we are slowly learning that such intelligence, or spying, has become a way of life: bugging, wiretapping, hidden microphones, sudden revolutions in faraway places, cryptic murders, and spy organizations have made us all guilty and ashamed.

But the sketch begins innocently enough once we have accepted the idea. People come in and out of the office at first as if it were an employment agency, but soon the requests to the officer become outlandish. Suddenly, we are taken out of the ordinary into the metaphysical—the existential: the man who searches for his place in the universe. In Hawthorne's tragic and, in this tale, absurdist vision, no man has a place in the universe, nor can the intelligence officer find him one. As in "Wakefield," Hawthorne is dealing here with an outcast of the universe, but nine years after writing "Wakefield" he has made all men ousted D.P.s.

Another customer finds his lost jewel—a great pearl—and is rapturous. However, the officer tells him that, since it is the Pearl of Great Price: "'This pearl . . . is held upon a peculiar tenure; and having once let it escape from your keeping, you have no greater claim to it— nay, not so great—as any other person. I cannot give it back'" (327–28). Certainly, this is a reference to Matthew 13:45–46: "the kingdom of heaven is like unto a merchant man, seeking goodly pearls: who when he had found one pearl of great price, went and sold all that he had, and bought it." The seeker's desperate pleas go unheeded and he runs "madly forth into the world" (328). Hawthorne's Calvinist-ordained ironic mode is never more precise than here. The biblical allusion points out that the owner of the pearl is not of the elect, so that now in his necessary but culpable loss of the Pearl of Great Price—the kingdom of heaven—he must join the ranks of the reprobate: he will never recover the pearl or attain salvation.

The final request is made by a man who looks at the officer "with a glance of such stern sincerity, that perhaps few secrets were beyond its scope. 'I seek for Truth,' said he" (335). The agent says it is "'the most rare pursuit'" that has ever come to him but he cannot help. The miracle must be achieved by the man himself, but he suggests that Truth may be next to him, behind, or before him. The truth-seeker then demands to know who the Intelligence Officer really is. The answer is: "'I am no minister of action, but the Recording Spirit!'" (336).

As this trenchant sketch concludes, the reader is more convinced than ever that Hawthorne's epiphany of human depravity—"The Intelligence Office"—in which each human being follows the desires of his foul cavern of a heart, all of which are recorded forever in the Calvinist economy of election and reprobation, is tragic, ironic, sorrowing, but apocalyptic.

II

It is not surprising that Hawthorne is most artistic in the short stories and sketches in which he uses the omniscient third-person narrative voice, because with that apparently remote voice, he is able subtly to pinion man's foul heart forever. Of the twenty-six stories and sketches in *Mosses from an Old Manse,* sixteen are in the first person, two use a created persona, and the other eight have third-person omniscient authors. Among these eight are certainly five of Hawthorne's greatest accomplishments: "The Birthmark," "Roger Malvin's Burial," "Young Goodman Brown," "Rappaccini's Daughter," and "The Artist of the Beautiful." Hawthorne's own voice or persona is often charming and occasionally menacing, but in the shorter tales and the novels, except for the notable exception of the magnificent creation of Coverdale in *The Blithedale Romance,* Hawthorne seems more comfortable and skillful at the third-person remove. Using this persona, he is free to make moral judgments on the characters and events, to provide alternate explanations for the action, to ask persistent, but not identifiably personal, questions, and to insert more ironic and less obviously individual adumbrations.

Hawthorne's voyeurism spices some of the tales in *Mosses* that are told in his own voice. His role throughout the whole of "Earth's Holocaust" is that of voyeur. He admits he likes fires and so travels to the prairies of the West to watch a gargantuan bonfire. He meets there a strange spectator who, seemingly impelled by the same chilly curiosity as Hawthorne, is more knowledgeable about the result of the conflagration than Hawthorne. In part three of "Sketches from Memory," "The Canal Boat," Hawthorne encounters another voyeur and the result is amusing: "I caught the eyes of my own image in the looking-glass, where a number of the party were likewise reflected, and among them the Englishman, who, at that moment, was intently observing myself" (435). What a delicious skirmish, one voyeur peering at another.

But by far the most interesting and revelatory act of voyeurism in the whole of *Mosses from an Old Manse* comes later in the same section of the sketch. The passengers prepare to sleep in the cabin which separates the men and women by a crimson curtain, each passenger having a shelf to sleep upon. Hawthorne indicates his difficulty:

> My head was close to the crimson curtain—the sexual division of the boat—behind which I continually heard whispers and stealthy footsteps; the noise of the comb laid on the table, or a slipper dropt on the floor; the twang, like a broken harp-string, caused by loosening a tight belt; the rustling of a gown in its descent; and the unlacing of a pair of stays. *My ear seemed to have the properties of an eye; a visible image pestered my fancy in the darkness;* the curtain was withdrawn between me and the western lady, who yet disrobed herself without a blush. (435–36)

Now Hawthorne is completely awake, and feels "a feverish impulse to toss my limbs miles apart" (436). In his discomfiture, he falls from his berth and then goes ashore to look at a phosphorescent tree—describing it as "a frigid fire" or an emblem of that type of genius which "owes its brilliancy to moral rottenness" (438). When he finally recovers himself, the boat has left without him.

The explicit sexual quality of this voyeuristic experience could come from a twentieth-century novel, but it certainly animates what has been a rather dull trip on the canal for Hawthorne and the reader. Specific and graphic as it is, we can only wonder how it escaped the chaste Sophia unless she saw it as a transcendental experience of Emersonian compensation.

"The Old Manse," which serves the function of both sketch and preface to the collection *Mosses from an Old Manse,* took Hawthorne longer to write than his three novels, each written in about five months. Finding anything indelicate in "The Old Manse" is hopeless—the three years of the honeymooning couple, if we believe the sketch, were completely occupied by Hawthorne's (Mrs. Hawthorne is never mentioned) enjoying the scenery. However, this sketch is as interesting for what it does not say as for what it says. At one point, "Mine honored reader" is directly addressed and lest we believe that we have learned anything personal about Hawthorne in this sketch he assures us: "My conscience, however, does not reproach me with betraying anything too sacredly individual to be revealed by a human spirit, to its brother or sister spirit. . . . Has the reader gone wandering, hand in hand with me, through the inner passages of my being, and have we groped together into all its chambers, and examined their treasures of their rubbish? Not so" (32). Just so, but the omissions of which Hawthorne is so proud cannot help but tantalize the reader who is led, deluded, forgotten, and then affronted by an unexpected Hawthornean smugness which seems to say, "I've written thirty pages about myself and told you nothing." Hawthorne, perhaps, never reckoned with the twentieth-century reader who likes to fill in the blanks, considers the connotations of words, and pries into the hidden meanings of his artificially neutral prose.

To use one of Hawthorne's favorite figures of speech, the author of *Mosses* is humbly proud. Reserved, melancholy, and dubious about his chances of attaining literary immortality, Hawthorne criticizes himself before anyone else can. He is a great writer—a master—but he can never satisfy his perfectionist longing to be the American Shakespeare—and yet

Melville will call him that four years later. His natural detachment, diffidence, and love of mystery prevent him from dropping the veil about his face, but the careful reader, whom Hawthorne would contentedly mislead, detects behind that piece of crepe, the glimmering of Mr. Hooper's smile—ironic, mildly contemptuous, and, above all, secret.

## III

Such a plethora of symbolism exists in *Mosses from an Old Manse* that this discussion will of necessity be a random sampling. Hawthorne's concern with the deceptive quality of appearance and reality informs the entire collection, but this example from "A Select Party" illustrates his ambivalence. He speaks of the castle in the air wherein a man of fancy is giving a party. The castle is not visible to all:

> And . . . if the people of the lower world chanced to be looking upward . . . they probably mistook the castle in the air for a heap of sunset clouds, to which the magic of light and shade had imparted the aspect of a fantastically constructed mansion. To such beholders it was unreal, because they lacked the imaginative faith. Had they been worthy to pass within its portal, they would have recognized the truth, that the dominions which the spirit conquers for itself among unrealities, become a thousand times more real than the earth whereon they stamp their feet. (58)

Hawthorne continues to live his real life in his imagination.

In another story, the early "Passages from a Relinquished Work," Hawthorne represents symbolically his Calvinist view of his own life. He has run away from the rigid Calvinist God-guardian, adopted the profession of an "idler" (in Calvinist terms) and is unable to enjoy any of his successes because he is always accompanied by Eliakim, the successor of the line, and keeper of the key of David. Eliakim, his Calvinist conscience, is always with him urging him to suffer guilt and to repent for his indolence and lack of moral fiber. It is no wonder that Melville said of *Mosses:* "Certain it is, however, that this great power of blackness in him derives its force from its appeals to that Calvinistic sense of Innate Depravity and Original Sin, from whose visitations, in some shape or other, no deeply thinking man is always and wholly free."[4]

As in *Twice-told Tales,* the tales and sketches of *Mosses from an Old Manse* are drenched with Edenic imagery. The entire sketch of "The New Adam and Eve" dramatizes the cardinal differences between the real world of the mid-nineteenth century and the Garden of Eden. "Rappaccini's

Daughter," which will be explored later in this section, has an inverted Fall; in "Egotism; or, The Bosom-Serpent," the serpent is represented as the "symbol of a monstrous egotism" (274) which is pampered night and day by Roderick. In "The Artist of the Beautiful," the ideal butterfly that Owen finally creates is likened to those butterflies "which hover across the meads of Paradise" (470), not earthly ones which fade; the beautiful carved woman which Drowne (of "Drowne's Wooden Image") creates wears "the strange rich flowers of Eden on her head" (314); among the extraordinary items of the Wandering Jew's collection (in "A Virtuoso's Collection") is "a rose from Eve's bridal bower" and the "skin, with beautifully variegated lines, supposed to have been the garment of the 'spirited sly snake,' which tempted Eve" (479). In "Buds and Bird-Voices" Hawthorne dreams with the coming of spring of "the old, paradisaical economy of life" (149) in which there was no work, of "trees of beauty [which] are trees of Paradise, and therefore not subject to decay" (152), and mourns the age of the world since the Fall: "Why may we not be permitted to live and enjoy, as if this were the first life, and our own the primal enjoyment, instead of treading always on these dry bones and mouldering relics. . . . Sweet must have been the Springtime of Eden" (152). Yet he comforts himself: "Each human soul is the first created inhabitant of its own Eden" (152), and this yearning for prelapsarian beauty and innocence points to the tension and the drama of the Fall to which he bears witness over and over again. Edenic imagery is functional and organic in Hawthorne: he often finds the world ugly and degenerate because he compares it to the radiant splendor of our lost primal paradise.

Mirrors continue to absorb Hawthorne and show the real, not the apparent; the vain young man in "Mrs. Bullfrog" in a narcissistic impulse feels that he may have "to perpetrate matrimony with my own image in the looking-glass" (130); poor "Feathertop," on the verge of a successful courtship with Polly Gookin, is seen by her in the mirror in all his scarecrow reality and despairingly glimpses himself in the same looking glass: "a picture of the sordid patchwork of his real composition" (244). The whole sketch "Monsieur du Miroir" involves the fantasy of a young man who cannot escape himself because of his constant reflection in a mirror. It ends rather sombrely: "Thus do mortals deify . . . a mere shadow of themselves, a spectre of human reason, and ask of that to unveil the mysteries, which Divine Intelligence has revealed so far as needful to our guidance and hid the rest" (171).

Hawthorne's special brand of laughter—fiendish, tragic, and

diabolic—appears prominently in many of the tales of *Mosses from an Old Manse*. From the laughter that kills in "The Christmas Banquet," to the scornful laughter of the callous grandsire ("The Artist of the Beautiful"), over the crushing of Owen's butterfly, to the demonic, despairing laughter of Goodman Brown who has lost his faith, Hawthorne ironically freezes the reader with expressions that should provoke mirth and jollity.

Hawthorne's death obsession forms many of the images in these tales: all of the guests of "The Christmas Banquet" are dead or "living dead"; "The Old Apple Dealer" is described as a "corpse from which life has recently departed" (44); even in "Buds and Bird-Voices," Hawthorne's most lyric treatment of nature, a fall of snow makes him wonder "how this vast napkin was to be removed from the face of the *corpselike* world" (149); P. in "P's Correspondence" finds that men remind him of graves "and dry bones of people who . . . now can only clatter, clatter, clatter, when the sexton's spade disturbs them" (377). Hawthorne's necrotomy goes on and on, but certainly one of the most grisly accounts comes from the imagination of Reuben Bourne as he fancies the last hours of Roger Malvin: "Death would come, like the slow approach of a corpse, stealing gradually towards him through the forest, and showing its ghastly and motionless features from behind a nearer, and yet a nearer tree" (346).

There are many allegories in *Mosses from an Old Manse,* some "blasted" as Hawthorne describes them, such as "A Select Party," "The Hall of Fantasy"; some very well managed—"Feathertop," "Egotism; or, The Bosom-Serpent," "The Christmas Banquet," "A Virtuoso's Collection"; some incomparable—"Procession of Life," "The Intelligence Office," "Earth's Holocaust"; and one consummate masterpiece—"The Celestial Rail-road." "The Celestial Rail-road" is an allegory of an allegory, since it is modeled on Bunyan's *Pilgrim's Progress* and then, again, since it is a dream, it is a dream of an allegory of an allegory.

No story of Hawthorne's more stimulates the imagination and yet leaves the reader with as many unanswered questions as "Rappaccini's Daughter." One of the longest and most carefully wrought of the tales, enriched with Edenic imagery, echoes of Dante, and the choicest of Hawthorne's fanatasies and intimations of demonism and the supernatural, it is also an enigma, for no consistent and satisfactory reading has yet been made of all of its contradictions and paradoxes. The reading I suggest has consistency, but only demonstrates again the happy futility of trying to explain everything in Hawthorne.

The tale is a subtle variation on the Fall of man, made even more complex by the fact that it is a Fall in reverse. The crypto-Jehovah, Rappaccini, an earthly scientist who would be the creator of the world— in his false, poisonous Eden garden—chimerically creates first an Eve, the beautiful and poisonous Beatrice, who lures by her beauty, her loneliness, and her innocence an Adam already ripe for the Fall, the shallow, vain, and selfish Giovanni. Although already infected with the poison of Rappaccini, the would-be-God, Adam-Giovanni attempts to "cure" himself and Beatrice from the poison which renders them anathema to the rest of fallen humanity. Earnest to escape his doom, he persuades Beatrice-Eve to eat the apple—the fatal antidote supplied by the jealous, envious Satan-Baglioni, who wishes to revenge himself upon the Rappaccini-God, who far surpassed him in creating scientific wonders. Beatrice-Eve must die, as must all creatures since the original Fall, but in a reversal of both the biblical story and the Miltonic version which Hawthorne knew so well, she dies, accusing Adam-Giovanni: "'was there not, from the first, more poison in thy nature than in mine?'" (127).

Young Giovanni Guasconti (whose name—*guastare*—means to spoil, destroy, taint, infect) comes to Padua from Naples to study at the university. The first adumbration of disaster occurs when he takes a room in an old decayed mansion belonging to a family descended from an ancestor whom Dante had damned to his Inferno. The room gives onto the garden of the neighboring house, which belongs to the famous and dubious Dr. Rappaccini, a medical genius who deals in poisons as cures.

Giovanni is ambivalent toward the garden, filled as it is with botanic wonders, including some which are too highly colored, others which creep along the ground like serpents, and the central one, a purple, gemlike beauty, which stands in the pool of a ruined fountain. He is amazed to see the famous professor walking among his plants, hands covered with gloves and face covered with a mask when he approached the purple shrub. Rappaccini, the would-be Jehovah, is sallow and sickly, his face showing great intellect but no warmth. Giovanni is frightened that Rappaccini seems so wary of cultivating his garden, "that most simple and innocent of human toils, and which had been alike the joy and labor of the unfallen parents of the race. Was this garden, then, the Eden of the present world?—and this man, with such a perception of harm in what his own hands caused to grow, was he the Adam?" (96). As we read on, it becomes apparent that the answer to Hawthorne's rhetorical question must be no.

Rappaccini is not the Adam of the present world, but the sham Jehovah who created his poisonous garden of Eden and Eve-Beatrice. When Beatrice appears to care for the purple shrub, her "sister," Giovanni is overcome by her beauty, which has a Zenobia-like but virginal queenliness, "redundant with life, health, and energy . . . compressed, as it were, and girdled tensely, in their luxuriance, by her virgin zone" (97).

Giovanni is entranced by the beauty and mystery he sees and he questions another doctor—Baglioni (*bagliore* means to glimmer, dazzle), who wants to be his mentor—about Rappaccini and his daughter. The answers puzzle him, for he learns that Rappaccini had skill and prowess and yet, according to Baglioni: "'He would sacrifice human life, his own among the rest, or whatever else was dearest to him, for the sake of adding so much as a grain of mustard-seed to the great heap of his accumulated knowledge'" (99–100). Hawthorne informs the reader that Giovanni would have taken Baglioni's views "with many grains of allowance" had he been aware of the fiendish warfare between Rappaccini and Baglioni registered in "black-letter tracts" in the university records (100).

To Giovanni's questions about Beatrice, Professor Baglioni laughs (and laughs are dangerous in Hawthorne) and shows his malice and envy by suggesting that perhaps Rappaccini is training Beatrice to take Baglioni's place at the university. Giovanni, intrigued, returns to his room, having purchased on the way a bouquet which he tosses to the beautiful Beatrice, who is in the garden. A series of events do or do not take place as Hawthorne teases the reader with his alternate explanations. Perhaps a lizard dies at the feet of Beatrice, or a beautiful insect dies in her proximity. Ominously, Giovanni's flowers seem to wither as she disappears into her house.

Giovanni, who "had not a deep heart," is obsessed with Beatrice, not in love with her: "It was not love, . . . nor horror . . . but a wild offspring of both love and horror that had each parent in it, and burned like one and shivered like the other. . . . Blessed are all simple emotions. . . . It is the lurid intermixture of the two that produces the *illuminating blaze of the infernal regions*" (105). This distinct adumbration of Giovanni's damnation to a hell of love and horror gathers importance as the tale continues.

In his preoccupation with Beatrice, Giovanni again encouters Baglioni, who smiles at him as he guesses his plight (and again, we suspect any Hawthornean character who smiles). Baglioni assures Giovanni that

Rappaccini is using him in one of his experiments. Baglioni decides he must "save" Giovanni with the "arcana of medical science," but his motives are made obvious: "'it is too insufferable an impertinence in Rappaccini thus to snatch the lad out of my own hands.'" He is determined to outwit Rappaccini and Beatrice: "'I may foil you where you little dream of it!'" (108).

Giovanni is led rather unaccountably by the servant into Rappaccini's garden, where he begins to examine the awesome plants that are "no longer God's making, but the monstrous offspring of man's depraved fancy" (110). Beatrice appears and tells Giovanni that "'this garden is his [Rappaccini's] world'" (111), another affirmation of Rappaccini's assumption of the godlike role of creator of his own world. Beatrice begs Giovanni to believe not what he sees but only what he hears from her lips, for what he sees "'may be false in its essence'" (112). The only untoward occurrence in this first meeting with Beatrice is her passionate prevention of his picking a blossom from the purple shrub, which she says would be fatal to him. Beatrice and Giovanni begin to meet daily and appear to be lovers, but Beatrice never allows Giovanni to come close to her. If he is late she calls him and "down he hastened into that Eden of poisonous flowers" (115).

Baglioni makes another appearance, this time in Giovanni's room to warn him, first by a fable and then openly, of the danger Giovanni is in from the poisonous Beatrice and diabolically proud father. Baglioni's warning arouses all of Giovanni's suspicions, "which now grinned at him like so many demons" (118), and Baglioni leaves with him an "antidote" to Beatrice's poison. But Baglioni's fiendishness is exposed to the reader: "'We will thwart Rappaccini yet!' thought he, chuckling to himself'" (119).

Giovanni's faith in Beatrice is terribly shaken. He purchases a bouquet and, as he admires himself in the mirror just before going down to meet Beatrice, he sees that the flowers are withering. After killing a spider with his breath, he turns all of his fury on Beatrice, wishing his breath would slay her. In their ensuing confrontation Hawthorne mourns that Giovanni has not the high faith to see that the "real Beatrice was a heavenly angel" (122). Giovanni asks her where the purple shrub came from and she replies: "'My father created it,'" but she warns him of the awful doom that estranged her from all society until "'Heaven sent thee, dearest Giovanni'" (123). Giovanni with venomous anger accuses Beatrice of blasting him, making him as poisonous, loathsome, and deadly as she. She is broken and baffled until he demonstrates, by killing a swarm of insects with his breath, his own poisonous nature, which has always been there, but is now manifested.

Beatrice denies any complicity in this change in Giovanni: "'It is my father's fatal science! No, no, Giovanni; it was not I! . . . Not for a world of bliss would I have done it!'" (125). Giovanni becomes mournful now, for "they stood, as it were, in an utter solitude, which would be made none the less solitary by the densest throng of human life" (125). When Hawthorne poses this question: "Ought not, then, the desert of humanity around them to press this insulated pair closer together?" (125), we must answer "No, in thunder." This is because Giovanni wants to return to what he believes is the real world, leading Beatrice by the hand in a reversal of Dante's Beatrice (Beatrix—she who makes happy), who led Dante to paradise. Hawthorne echoes our no: "There could be no such hope. She must pass heavily, with that broken heart, across the borders of Time—she must bathe her hurts in some fount of Paradise, and forget her grief in the light of immortality—and *there* be well! But Giovanni did not know it" (126).

So Giovanni offers the antidote "'to those [herbs] by which thy awful father has brought this calamity upon thee and me'" (126). Beatrice drinks but warns Giovanni to wait for the result, as Rappaccini comes out and spreads his hands in a blasphemous benediction over them, assuring Beatrice that his science has turned Giovanni into a fittingly poisonous bridegroom for her. Beatrice asks faintly why Rappaccini has "'inflicted this miserable doom upon thy child?'" (127). Rappaccini, furious, tells her she has great power "'to quell the mightiest with a breath . . . Wouldst thou, then, have preferred the condition of a weak woman, exposed to all evil, and capable of none?'" (127). Rappaccini's vaulting ambition to be a devil-God and create devilish and powerful beings is not Beatrice's desire.

Beatrice, who whispers she would have preferred to be loved, not feared, is dying and going where she says the evil that her father tried to mingle with her being will vanish "'like the fragrance of these poisonous flowers, which will no longer taint my breath among the flowers of Eden'" (127). Turning to Giovanni, she cries out: "'Oh, was there not, from the first, more poison in thy nature than in mine?'" (127). Her accusation reverses the biblical version of the Fall, in which Adam accuses Eve.

Hawthorne's elegaic tone in speaking of Beatrice seems to confirm this reading that Rappaccini, aspiring to be the diabolic, sovereign creator-God but remaining only a man, has therefore created, in his daughter, something perverse: "And thus the poor victim of man's ingenuity and of thwarted nature, and of the fatality that attends all such efforts of perverted wisdom, perished there, at the feet of her father and Giovanni" (128).

Beatrice suffers death because of her father's—the devil-God's—perverted wisdom. For Rappaccini's presumption, a fitting Calvinist conclusion is provided; he has lost everything which he values and is himself damned. Calvin is explicit:

> And what can man do, man who is but rottenness and a worm. . . . Everything which our mind conceives, meditates, plans, and resolves, is always evil. . . . As the human mind is unable from dulness, to pursue the right path of investigation, and, after various wanderings . . . at length gets completely bewildered, so its whole procedure proves how unfit it is to search the truth and find it. . . . Hence, under the influence of a *vain curiosity,* it torments itself. (*Institutes,* Vol. I, pp. 39, 244, 234)

Baglioni, the tempter and devil who envies the self-made God-Rappaccini and wishes, out of his covetousness, to destroy Rappaccini's unnatural creation, has the last word: "'Rappaccini! Rappaccini! And is *this* the upshot of your experiment?'" (128).

Like Aylmer, Giovanni can stand no imperfection in the one he thinks he loves (and he has more cause since, after all, Beatrice is poisonous). But if Rappaccini is the God figure, he is a crypto-Calvinist Jehovah who has decreed election only for Beatrice and her lover, Giovanni. Rappaccini is defeated in his experiment. For Beatrice is the creation of the *true* God and of Rappaccini, the would-be God; even though one of the elect, she retains the poison of her Eve nature, her birthmark, which kills ordinary mortals. Giovanni-Adam cannot accept the extraordinary state of isolation that he must attain to love Beatrice. Unlike Dante, he will not permit her to lead him from the fallen world to paradise. So he uses the devil-Baglioni[5] and his fatal antidote to try to make Beatrice like himself—mortal, guilty, inconstant, fallible, and poisonous. Because Giovanni has no *faith* and even more poison in his nature than Beatrice, she can only die. Thus, the tragically ironic, inverted Fall is reenacted once more in the false Eden of the modern world, with no Redeemer to come.

IV

Hawthorne uses more set pieces, lists, and catalogues in *Mosses from an Old Manse* than in *Twice-told Tales* or the later *Snow Image*. Consequently, although the major tales are structured with Hawthorne's usual acuity and sense of culminating action, there are fewer tales to ponder. In "Rappaccini's Daughter" and "The Birthmark," both of which concern the death of an innocent and compliant young woman, the action is decreed by the determination of the scientist-God figure. In "The Birthmark," Aylmer alone is responsible for trying to perfect Georgiana; the tragic flaw of Aylmer's crypto-divine character is adumbrated throughout and the reader expects—especially after he learns the true meaning of the birthmark (Original Sin) and the contents of Aylmer's folio detailing his failures—the catastrophe that occurs. "Rappaccini's Daughter" is complicated by more mystery and more characters than the "The Birthmark," for Beatrice is not only the victim of her father's blasphemous zeal, but is also caught in the net of Baglioni's diabolic jealousy and by Giovanni's weak and shallow faith. Beatrice's death and transposed Fall from the Eden of the modern world thus become inevitable.

The meaning or moral of "The Artist of the Beautiful" certainly seems ambiguous, but structurally the tale is impeccable. The structure, which clarifies the meaning, is built upon five visits that seem to deliver a deathblow to the artist's dream, yet they only strengthen his ideal and his pursuit of the beautiful. These visits, then, form a kind of ladder upon which Owen ascends to a greater spiritual achievement after each apparent setback. When he has climbed the ladder again after the fifth visit, he is empowered to continue his work and attain his view of success. Thus, he can make the sixth visit himself and not collapse when his perceptible symbol of the beautiful—the butterfly—is ruined and ravaged.

The structure of "Young Goodman Brown" is apparently quite simple and circular—from town to forest to town—but a deeper structure, one dictating the gloomy ending, consists of a series of Calvinist principles which Young Goodman Brown acknowledges for everyone but himself. He believes that he, but no one else, can spend one night in the forest consorting with the devil and then return the next day, unblemished, to cling to the skirts of Faith "'and follow her to Heaven'" (75). After he accompanies the devil into the wilderness—the forest—Goodman Brown is unable to stop because of "the instinct that guides mortal man to evil"; here he admits that his will is not free. Goodman Brown casually assumes the election of all those "good people" whom he knows—Goody Cloyse, Deacon Gookin, the minister—but as Calvin warns, Goodman Brown learns they are hypocrites, whited sepulchres. Laughing in despair, Goodman says: "'Come, devil! for to thee is this world given'" (83); here he admits his total lack of faith. When Goodman Brown returns from the forest, he is a "desperate man," which in Calvinist terms tells us that he had been deluded about having faith;[6] his consenting to diabolism in the forest makes clear his reprobation. He returns to the clearing—i.e., the village—in despondency, terrified of every one else's sin: "he shrank from the bosom of Faith, and at morning or eventide, when the family knelt down at prayer, he scowled, and muttered to himself, and gazed sternly at his wife, and turned away" (89). At his death, "they carved no hopeful verse upon his tomb-stone; for his dying hour was gloom" (90). According to Calvin, only the reprobate, men unelected and without faith, can so despair. Thus, this remarkable story set in Puritan Salem is Hawthorne's study of the most contemptible of men: the hypocrite reprobate who says he will put off his faith for one night of evil and then resume it, who gives himself over to the devil and resulting despair, and who then saturninely judges as damned all those around him except himself. Hawthorne's Calvinism (which is the only explanation of his grave and solemn treatment of the darkling evil of witchcraft) ordains this story's ironic structure and tone.

Although Reuben Bourne, the non-hero of "Roger Malvin's Burial," is no more Hamlet-like than the next avatar of the human condition, conscience has made a coward of him as it has of so many of Hawthorne's characters. "Roger Malvin's Burial" is one of the most polished of Hawthorne's short stories, one of the ones most rewarding of close reading.[7] The focus of the story is clear; Hawthorne concentrates three-quarters of the story in the forest and directs our attention to the two most significant days in the life of Reuben Bourne:[8] the day in the forest on which he makes his promise and the day in the forest on which that promise is in some way fulfilled.

There is a circular structure to this tale; the story begins and ends in the forest. It seems obvious from the time that Malvin seeks to "wile" Reuben "to his own good" that the action assumes a dark necessity. In "Young Goodman Brown" there is an exact reversal, although the structure is still circular; the action moves from the clearing or community to the forest and back to the community. In both tales, however, Hawthorne's interest lies in the forest, the wilderness, and what happens there. Young Goodman Brown returns from the forest a blighted man and his life from then on is gloom; Reuben Bourne comes out of the forest a wounded youth who becomes a blighted man. Some "wounds" compelled Goodman Brown to go into the forest. His resemblance to his devil-companion is made explicit: "bearing a considerable resemblance to him . . . still they might have been taken for father and son." Goodman Brown is the son of the devil—guilty of Original Sin—and the blight of the forest remains with him forever. His own sin he is able to endure or perhaps deny, but the brotherhood of evil of which he learns in the forest overpowers him. Reuben does not fare as well even as the gloomed and doomed Goodman Brown. His wound from the forest blights his life, but not only *his* life is blighted. Hawthorne also makes it necessary for Reuben to blight his son completely by shooting him, to blight his wife by depriving her of her son, and then leaves Reuben standing weeping and praying over the grave of his son and father-in-law. How much does Reuben pay for his wounds? Everything. The last picture of the body-strewn rock-gravestone and Reuben in prayer seems far harsher a fate than that of Goodman Brown. Brown finally escapes into death; Reuben must live on with his blight.

The first section of the story is the historical paragraph. This is Hawthorne's customary technique, the link with the past—the bid for verisimilitude; but as subsequent action unfolds, it becomes apparent that, for Hawthorne, the historical event is not so much an acknowledgment of fact as a disclaimer of fact.[9] The historical event of the introduction is separate and remote from the Hawthornean events that follow. This is an ironic procedure in which the material of fact is absorbed, impregnated, and fructified to produce a mutation bearing no resemblance to its avowed parentage. In the instance of "Roger Malvin's Burial" the historical fact of the opening paragraph is Lovell's fight in the Indian Warfare of 1725. There were few survivors of a scouting party which battled twice their number of Indians. Hawthorne warns us that romance and imagination will be at work on the incident. He concludes the historical introduction by suggesting that some of the incidents to follow will be recognized by those who have heard these stories in oral tradition. Here Hawthorne is being ironic: some of the incidents will be recognized, despite the substitution of fictitious names, but these are not the important ones, only the historical ones; the incidents with which he is truly concerned, over which romance and imagination have brooded, will bear no resemblance to history or tradition.

The second section begins with a description of the actual events with which we will be concerned. The early sunbeams hover cheerfully in contrast to the two weary and wounded men on a bed of withered oak leaves. Hawthorne describes the rock beneath which the men lie as "not unlike a gigantic grave-stone" (338). Here he prefigures the tone of the story as well as the meaning. The gravestone is central to the story, and the significant events occur here: it is the symbolic center, as is the pillory in *The Scarlet Letter*. Although Hawthorne adumbrates the meaning of the rock gravestone, he by no means makes it clear; it is a rock "upon which the veins seemed to form an inscription in forgotten characters" (338). The meaning of the ritualistic sacrifice that takes place on the gravestone is something that has to be read in a forgotten language, with Hawthorne only suggesting or hinting at the glossary.

Significantly, the rock gravestone is surrounded by oak trees rather than the "pines, which were the usual growth of the land" (338). This oak of myth and legend figures with the rock gravestone as the center of the opening and closing scenes in the forest. The second paragraph of the tale, then, sets the tone and suggests the meaning, and we find as the story continues that Hawthorne returns to this ritual description.

In the debate between Roger Malvin and Reuben, in which Roger attempts to persuade Reuben to leave him, much is said that assumes significance in the light of Reuben's return to the forest. Roger speaks to Reuben with a "father's authority" and charges him to be gone. Reuben replies: "And because you have been a father to me, should I therefore leave you to perish and to lie unburied in the wilderness?" (340). It seems as if the answer to this question must be yes, and yet the price that is paid for not burying the father is everything—all that Reuben has. Reuben, wiled by Malvin, departs from him after having vowed by the blood on his handkerchief, which he affixes to the young oak sapling as a mark, to return either to save Malvin or bury him. Reuben keeps his oath, but he does not pay with his own blood, but with his son's blood. It is obvious that Reuben's wounds are not entirely physical, and that they are never healed.

The forest, in a sense, is "the undiscovered country from whose bourn no traveller returns" for Roger and Reuben. Roger cannot choose but to remain and die, but Reuben is "wiled" into a belief in life and turns his back on the undiscovered country. Ironically, where he goes—into the clearing—represents his choice not to "bear those ills we have" but to "fly to others that we know not of," although he believes he is choosing life, not death. Yet his choice of life leads him inexorably to death, the forest. In Hawthorne's ironic paradox, the choice for life fails because by it Reuben is guilty of "moral cowardice"—"thus conscience doth make cowards of us all"—and Reuben Bourne is his own bourn.

"The hidden strength of many another motive" (343) is powerfully suggested when Hawthorne describes Reuben's departure from Roger. He hurries, "for a sort of guilty feeling, which sometimes torments men in their most justifiable acts, caused him to seek concealment from Malvin's eyes" (345). This psychological insight is one which we would all acknowledge, but the one which follows and describes Reuben creeping back unseen to gaze on the desolate Roger "impelled by a wild and painful curiosity" (345) is the intuition of genius.[10] More and more Reuben is beginning to act like a human being, almost any human being, in the given situation, trying to do the noble and supererogatory act and being persuaded not to—failing in perfection but with an unaccountable masochistic desire to look back at the one who, in a sense, demands the perfection and yet persuades him against it. Reuben watches Roger behind the shelter of "the earthy roots of an uptorn tree" (345) on a morning in May. The ceremony of expiation will not be complete until Reuben returns to the shelter of the same tree in another May.

Reuben knows as he gazes surreptitiously at Roger that "Death would come. . . . But such must have been Reuben's own fate, had he tarried another sunset; and who shall impute blame to him if he shrank from so useless a sacrifice?" (346). Again Hawthorne adumbrates, for it is Reuben's fate to have death steal gradually towards him in the forest, but it comes to Reuben reincarnated in his son. There is no way in which we can answer the question and accuse Reuben if we acknowledge that, as fellow unheroic human beings, we would undoubtedly have done what Reuben did.

Section three, which concerns Reuben's eighteen years at the settlement in the clearing, is disposed of by Hawthorne in a few paragraphs. Hawthorne is eager to tell the reader but a few facts. Reuben is unable to explain to Dorcas his abandonment of her father in the wilderness and he is forced to suffer "from every tongue the miserable and humiliating torture of unmerited praise" (348). Reuben, because of his transformation into sadness and irritability, fails as a husbandman. He is also alienated from the society of the settlement. "To be brief, the world did not go well with Reuben Bourne" (351). A "ruined man," he must return to the forest ostensibly to seek a new homestead.

Part four begins the repetitive and ritualistic climax of the return to the forest. All the acts of the first scene and all of the scenery and props must be repeated to establish the totemistic, ceremonial, mythic, and compulsive sacrifice. The journey is begun early in May. The final act must occur on the same day as the first act.

Hawthorne's people wander in a real forest—alone in a wood, a gloomy wood astray—a post-paradisaical wilderness where there is guilt and blood sacrifice. Cyrus wonders why his father strays from the course of the previous autumn "into a region, of which savage beasts and savage men were as yet the sole possessors" (353) unaware that the savage propitiation must yet be made. Dorcas mentions the date, the twelfth of May, and Reuben is afflicted by his memory. Dorcas continues "in that mournful tone, which the tender-hearted appropriate to griefs long cold and dead" (355), with the comforting thought that her father died in Reuben's arms. Reuben sets out in another direction from Cyrus to hunt for game and is led like a sleepwalker in a circle until he comes to a place heavily timbered with oak trees. "Unable to penetrate to the secret place of his soul, where his motives lay hidden" (356), Reuben believes that he has been led by a supernatural voice and power and that it is Heaven's intent to let him expiate his sin. As in the beginning, Reuben is unable to understand his motives and trusts blindly that he is doing the right thing. He shoots where he sees a movement and hears a low moan which tells him he struck his target. Hawthorne then asks the question: "What were the recollections now breaking upon him?" (356).

What follows is a description of the thicket described in the first forest scene with the rock gravestone containing an inscription in forgotten characters. Reuben finds that he is standing as he did eighteen years before to the day, "behind the earthy roots of the uptorn tree" (356) from which he had gazed secretly at Roger Malvin. He notices in horror that the oak sapling had become a large tree whose topmost bough was utterly withered and dead. "Whose guilt had blasted it?" (357), asks Hawthorne. The easy answer is Reuben's, but had it?

With the reader quaking in pity and fear, Hawthorne shifts the scene in the next section back to Dorcas singing over the fire. The irony created by our knowledge and her ignorance of the event is a fine touch of horror. When she hears the shot, she is sure that Cyrus has slain a deer and the vision of the death of an innocent, gentle animal is mordantly effective. Dorcas searches for Cyrus, the triumphant hunter, and finds him dead at Reuben's feet. Reuben tells her that the rock is the gravestone of her father and son. As she sinks down insensibly to Cyrus, the withered branch falls over her, Cyrus, Reuben, and Roger's bones. Then Hawthorne tells us that Reuben's heart is stricken; the vow of the wounded boy is redeemed by the blighted man; the sin is expiated; the curse is gone; "and, in the hour, when he had shed blood dearer to him than his own, a prayer, the first for years, went up to Heaven from the lips of Reuben Bourne" (360).

If this ending is taken literally and seriously as an explanation of the story, as it is a great temptation to do in Hawthorne, it does make the "badly perverted nonsense" that some readers found. Hawthorne's language is so unpretentious and poetic, with such an effect of superficial clarity, that we often assume we know precisely what he is saying. But it would be a mistake to assume that such a careful artist as Hawthorne would write off a magnificent story with such an impertinent moral as occurs at the end of "Roger Malvin's Burial." Reuben nourished a secret guilt because he did not acknowledge his justifiable leaving of Roger, or his failure to return to fulfill his vow. Reuben must pay for his guilt—and what is the price required? Not less than everything. He must sacrifice his only son on the very spot where Roger died, and thus Reuben has atoned and is now able to pray. If this is not "perverted nonsense," what is it? It seems to me that the consistent symbolism of the tale builds up to the inevitable and compulsive sacrifice. What has been sacrificed, Hawthorne says ironically, is only that which is expected by the Calvinist Jehovah. Once Reuben has yielded to the desire for life, he must pay for this privilege not by his own death, in Reuben's case this would be too easy, but with his dearest love, his only begotten son.

The cruelty and sadism of the story are only partially masked in the telling. Reuben is "wiled" by Roger into a desire for life—life only brings him misfortune, sadness, irritability, and misanthropy. There is one subject for his love, his image, Cyrus. He has vowed by his blood to return to Roger to bring him aid or bury him. He will now bury him along with his own son. Roger has spoken to Reuben with a father's authority. Reuben obeys his father by leaving the forest for the clearing, but he does not fulfill his vow. He fails his father, as, in a sense, every human being wounded by Original Sin fails his God. Reuben hopes he will be able to expiate his sin by burying Roger's bones, but the necessary propitiation is far greater than this. A complete sacrifice is required by the flouted parental authority—the Puritan vengeful God. In a sense Reuben's disobedience to Roger is a reenactment of the Fall, Original Sin, with its Calvinist overtones of damnation.

In many ways Reuben is Everyman—every human being who fails his father; he obeys first and yet fails. Still Reuben denies between the rocks and is unable to tell the truth to Dorcas, who blithely assumes the heroism that he could not perform yet cannot deny. Reuben is the nonheroic man undermined by the poison of humanity, which keeps him a human being and not a god. Is it possible to cover up the dead bones, to redeem the dream of incorruptibility? Hawthorne ironically says no.

Not only does Reuben seem to be Everyman, but the structure of the tale is that of a morality play, a journey—forest to clearing to forest. The way up is the way down. In my beginning is my end.

The mystery deepens as Reuben, Dorcas, and the victim go back into the forest to assume their places in the final sadistic ceremony. None of the participants is entirely conscious of his role in the holocaust. Yet because of the inviolable nature of the sacrifice, Cyrus becomes the piacular offering mechanically as if the immolation had been ordained from the beginning of time. Once the forest has been reentered in May the characters move automatically into position for the final terrible tableau at the foot of the rock. The forest is the real situation, the mythic place of decision and payment of the consequences, like the sea in *Moby-Dick*.

The final ritualistic oblation is more horrible than the Abraham and Isaac story. Despite the revulsion one feels for the brutality, this Old Testament gesture to an unpropitiated God is not allowed to be made. Abraham passes his test, Isaac is delivered, and the sacrifice is animal and not human. Also God spoke to Abraham and requested the sacrifice. In "Roger Malvin's Burial" there is neither the clarity nor the personal element of the Old Testament trial; God does not speak to Reuben. Rather there is the automatic, predestined, wooden, even blind fulfillment of a destiny not understood and not merited. Who did not bury his father must bury his son.

Hawthorne further shrouds his story in the mists of archetypal symbol by surrounding the sacrificial altar with oak trees—not pines as he carefully points out. The oak is the most widely worshipped of all trees, and folklore about it is vast. Undoubtedly Hawthorne, an extremely self-conscious artist, wishes to suggest all possible extensions of the tree as emblem. All of the admixture of characteristics—pagan and Christian, mythic and real, good and evil—the oak is, as is the whiteness of the whale.

What happens to Reuben Bourne when he shoots his son is the worst thing that could happen. All of his preconscious terror is realized in this slaying: he has killed what he loved best with his own hand. It is Room 101 for Reuben Bourne.

It is now time to ask whether we can decipher the "inscription in forgotten characters" (356) that appears on Roger Malvin's and Cyrus' gravestone. Yvor Winters, in disposing of Hawthorne's short stories, says that they "seem incapable of justifying the intensity of the method."[11] It is certainly true that there is an intensity in the best tales and the novels, but if they do not justify this intensity, Hawthorne is an inferior artist. It seems to me, however, that the ambiguity which marks the ending of the greater works results from Hawthorne's unwillingness to push to the fullest extreme his tragic vision of life. This accounts for the lessening of intensity noticed at the end of the works and the subsequent feeling by the reader of being given an inadequate or equivocal moral or arbitrary conclusion. Yet this ambiguity also results from Hawthorne's reluctance to declare what he feels consciously or unconsciously to be a higher truth—that appearance and reality are much the same—that perhaps even good and evil are interchangeable.[12] Thus, the illegible stone reads that Reuben Bourne has paid the price for humanity—totally depraved humanity. In order to pray, all Reuben has to do is become isolated, lose his material and spiritual prosperity, and kill his only son. Consciously or unconsciously Hawthorne's dark imagination, his sickness of human life, his New England Puritan heritage, his fear of the price of expiation demanded by the Calvinist Jehovah, have betrayed him into irony. The human condition as Hawthorne felt it was no more savory than Melville's vision of it:

> What Cosmic jest or Anarch blunder
> The human integral clove asunder
> And Shied the fractions through life's gate?[13]

V

Except for those in the great tales discussed earlier, not many characters in *Mosses from an Old Manse* are developed or even memorable. But, since Hawthorne's scientific villains really are the most Stygian, Hadean, and delectably repellent characters in *Mosses from an Old Manse,* we will look at one of them: Aylmer. Although Aylmer in "The Birthmark" is one of the scientist-villains that both attracted and repelled Hawthorne, he is not a stereotype. Certainly he is shown to have gargantuan egotism and a conviction of himself as God. But unlike Chillingworth, who believes that "iron necessity" made him a fiend, or Rappaccini and Baglioni, who compete for diety and demonism, or Dr. Heidegger, who enjoys observing the idiocy of the old repeating the follies of their youth, Aylmer has a quality of idealism about his belief that suggests an ingenuous Emerson who has gone into the laboratory to demonstrate to skeptics the sameness of mind and matter, and the indwelling of divinity in every man. Aylmer wants his bride, Georgiana, to be perfect and, unable to settle for less, he determines to remove the birthmark on her cheek and thus improve on nature.

In many ways, it is easier to imagine an Aylmer in our particular segment of the twentieth century than in Hawthorne's time. In these days (predicted so accurately in 1932 by Aldous Huxley in *Brave New World*) of genetic engineering, organ transplants, nuclear medicine, and test-tube babies, the simple removal of a birth-mark seems like minor outpatient surgery. Although on the most simplistic level Aylmer's elaborate treatment of Georgiana seems ludicrously Gothic—he incarcerates her in a tapestried boudoir and uses fiery furnaces to churn out a distilled elixir to erase her birthmark—the deeper meaning of Aylmer's flagrant presumption is timeless.

"The Birthmark" is set in the latter part of the eighteenth century, during the age of reason, a time like our own, when discoveries in electricity, "and other kindred mysteries of nature, seemed to open paths into the region of miracle" (36). Soon after their marriage, Aylmer tells Georgiana that the small, red birthmark—shaped like a tiny hand in the center of her left cheek (the sinister side), which had been admired as a beauty mark by her other suitors—shocks him "'as being the visible mark of earthly imperfection'" (37). Georgiana is deeply hurt and tells her husband:

"'You cannot love what shocks you!'" (37). But Aylmer becomes obsessed
with the tiny hand:

> It was the fatal flaw of humanity, which Nature, in one shape or another,
> stamps ineffaceably on all her productions either to imply that they are
> temporary and finite, or that their perfection must be wrought by toil and
> pain. The Crimson Hand expressed the ineludible gripe, in which mortal-
> ity clutches the highest and purest of earthly mould, degrading them into
> kindred with the lowest, and even with the very brutes, like whom their
> visible frames return to dust. In this manner, selecting it as the symbol of
> his wife's liability to sin, sorrow, decay, and death, Aylmer's sombre
> imagination was not long in rendering the birthmark a frightful object.
> (38–39)

It is now clear that Hawthorne is not describing a slight cosmetic
imperfection or beauty spot. In fact, he has just given a perfect Calvinist
description of Original Sin; but Aylmer, the rational scientist, cannot
accept in his wife this "symbol of imperfection, . . . the spectral hand
that wrote mortality, where he would fain have worshipped" (39). Unable
to bear the agony of Aylmer's horrified gaze, Georgiana begs him to
remove the mark. Aylmer is rapturous because he has now been given a
fitting scientific challenge, never suspecting what Georgiana and the
reader know from the beginning, that the birthmark is Georgiana's link
to life and humanity. Aylmer assures Geogiana: "'I feel myself fully
competent to render this dear cheek as faultless as its fellow; and then,
most beloved, what will be my triumph, when I shall have corrected what
Nature left imperfect'" (41).

In Aylmer's attempts to become a god, the shudders that he feels at
the sight of Georgiana's birthmark are transferred to the reader, who
begins to fear for him. Interestingly enough, there is no pity, nor any
catharsis at the end, because Aylmer has not the stature of a tragic hero
aspiring to be a god. In place of consummate pride is the lesser flaw of an
overriding vanity. Aylmer would be godlike and worshipped, but he is
too pygmy-souled to be more than a lesser deity.

One day Georgiana finds a folio containing a detailed record of all of
Aylmer's experiments and discovers that

> his most splendid successes were almost invariably failures. . . . The
> volume . . . was yet as melancholy a record as ever mortal hand had pen-
> ned. It was the sad confession . . . of the short-comings of the composite
> man—the spirit burthened with clay and working in matter—and of the

despair that assails the higher nature, at finding itself so miserably thwarted by the earthly part. (49)

Georgiana has discovered her husband's birthmark, apparent but unacknowledged. Aylmer is not pleased that Georgiana has read his book, but she assures him: "'It has made me worship you more than ever'" (49). His response shows the obliquity of his understanding and his smug assumption of diety: "'Ah! wait for this one success . . . then worship me if you will. I shall deem myself hardly unworthy of it!'" (50).

Georgiana completely misreads Aylmer's character when she hints that, if the experiment fails, she can only die while he must live a life of remorse. She does not understand that she will be only another page in his folio. But she does realize that he will be forever dissatisfied and that, even should she live, she would not please him for more than a moment. One of the deepest ironies in this story is the fact that Georgiana, like so many of Hawthorne's pale, compliant women, does not resent the fact that Aylmer sees her only as an experiment; she longs to be a votary to Aylmer, and if that is not possible, she wants only to die. "'You are fit for heaven without tasting death!' replied her husband" (53). Aylmer, as a god, must have a wife of immaculate conception, freed of the birthmark of Original Sin and, therefore, not subject to death.

Georgiana drinks down the elixir and sleeps, watched over by Aylmer. He watches the birthmark shudderingly: "Yet once, by a strange and unaccountable impulse, he pressed it with his lips" (54). This atypical act, similar to Reuben Bourne's slinking back to spy on Roger Malvin saying his last prayers, is a fine Hawthornean touch. The god-man Aylmer salutes the mark that the sovereign God has placed upon Georgiana to signal what he believes to be his triumph over the blight that all men are heir to. But his victory is premature.

Georgiana wakes, sees in the mirror that the birthmark has waned and then speaks her last words to her husband: "'My poor Aylmer!' she repeated. . . . 'You have aimed loftily!—you have done nobly! Do not repent, that, with so high and pure a feeling, you have rejected the best that earth could offer. Aylmer—dearest Aylmer—I am dying!'" (55). The hoarse, chuckling laugh of Aminidab emphasizes the final irony of Hawthorne, the narrator, who says that Aylmer had not attained wisdom and "he need not thus have flung away the happiness" which could have been his. He had failed "to find the perfect Future in the present" (56).

Strangely, we have no pity for Aylmer, probably because Hawthorne has made him so real to us that we can see him recording another glorious failure in his folio and looking around for his next experiment. Georgiana's last words would have been cruel if Aylmer had any sensitivity. Since he has none, we leave him with the shudder induced by Hawthorne's searingly ironic portrait of another man who would be God.

## VI

Of the five greatest tales in *Mosses from an Old Manse* ("The Birthmark," "Rappaccini's Daughter," "Young Goodman Brown," "Roger Malvin's Burial," and "The Artist of the Beautiful") four have the peculiar Hawthornean blackness that Melville and the modern reader find so compelling. With the exception of "The Artist of the Beautiful," the weighty and dooming Calvinist view of man's moral nature dominates the theme, the characters, and the final impact of the tales and requires the ironic mode that Hawthorne found so congenial.

Even in the lightest sketch Hawthorne usually instills some of the death and grave imagery that so obsessed him. Much as Hawthorne labored to balance his most serious, grim, and implacable tales with pleasant sketches and fillers, the general impression left with the reader of *Mosses from an Old Manse* is much the same as T. S. Eliot's response to Hawthorne: "And as for the writer who to me is the greatest among them [nineteenth-century American writers], Nathaniel Hawthorne, it seems to me that there is something in Hawthorne that can best be appreciated by the reader with Calvinism in his bones and witch-hanging (*not* witch-hunting) on his conscience."[14]

The sketch "Earth's Holocaust" contains a composite of most of the themes that fascinated and haunted Hawthorne during his lifetime. This does not mean that the sketch has a more particular excellence than other Hawthorne tales and sketches—some of the tales are far greater accomplishments—but despite his fondness for lists, catalogues, and inventories, this sketch delivers a powerful thrust of irony, an irony of voice and action ordained by the Calvinism that proclaims the foul cavern of the human heart.

The sketch opens with the familiar words (but not familiar from Hawthorne), "Once upon a time," which naturally beguile the reader into expecting a children's fairy story. But we are soon disabused of this assumption. Hawthorne continues: "but whether in time past or time to come is a matter of little or no moment." In this equivocal period of time, the whole world is so "overburthened with an accumulation of worn-out trumpery" (381), that all of the inhabitants decide to have a general bonfire to get rid of it all. The irony is immediately apparent, for the site decided upon for the fire—the center of the globe—is chosen by the insurance companies so that no houses will be in danger from the flames.

Hawthorne decides to go—we know he loves fires—"Having a taste for sights of this kind, and imagining, likewise, that the illumination of the bonfire might reveal some profundity of moral truth, heretofore hidden in mist of darkness" (381). As materials are fed to the fire, the crowd grows as people come from all over the world to watch. The bonfire becomes more and more fascinating when we realize that the great reformers of the world seem to be in charge of selecting the materials to be burned: "Dry combustibles" are used first: old newspapers, magazines, and leaves. Next all heraldry, medals, and signs of aristocracy are consumed and a shout of joy is given by the "plebeian spectators."

Some people make individual contributions to the fire, but what startles Hawthorne is that some women consider flinging in their clothes in order to "assume the garb, together with the manners, duties, offices, and responsibilities, of the opposite sex" (389). In 1844, when this sketch was written, Hawthorne had some reason to be frightened of the feminist movement going on around him in Concord. (Henry James gives a much more extended ironic picture of some of the creatures involved in this movement in *The Bostonians.*)

After all artillery, cannons, and banners of war are hoisted into the flames and melted, a great parade celebrates the coming era of universal peace. Hopeful that mankind will never return to war, Hawthorne is horrified when an old commander tells him: "'When Cain wished to slay his brother, he was at no loss for a weapon'" (391). Hawthorne protests that "'in this advanced stage of civilization, Reason and Philanthropy combined will constitute just such a tribunal [for settling disputes] as is requisite'" (391). The old warrior replies ironically: "'Ah, I had forgotten that, indeed!'" Certainly the irony of this exchange was pungent in Hawthorne's time—less than a hundred years removed from the American and French Revolutions—but how bitter it seems today as our minds tick off the Civil Wars, World Wars I and II, Korea, Vietnam, and what next?

The bonfire now receives a global complement of all the machinery used to administer death to criminals: headsmen's axes; halters; the guillotine; and, finally, the gallows. The gallows blazes black then red

(Hawthorne's special colors for evil and guilt). Hawthorne and his double, the grave observer, express more and more concern over the enthusiasm for the burning and reforming of everything, as the fire blazes on. Marriage certificates are thrown into the inferno; all monies, paper and coin; and businessmen burn their books as well as their debts. When all written constitutions are burned along with deeds to individual property, the crowd proclaims public and communal ownership.

Then all books are piled on the flames and a modern philosopher (Emerson?) rejoices that "'we shall get rid of the weight of dead men's thought. . . . Now you are enlightening the world, indeed!'" (395). Hawthorne agrees, stating in his most harmless and limpid prose, which barely conceals a scorching irony:

> The truth was, that the human race had now reached a stage of progress, so far beyond what the wisest and wittiest men of former ages had ever dreamed of, that it would have been a manifest absurdity to allow the earth to be any longer encumbered with their poor achievements in the literary line. (395)

Voltaire gives off sparkles; German stories, a scent of brimstone; Milton sends up a powerful blaze; Shakespeare gushes a "flame of such marvelous splendor, that men shaded their eyes" (396), and Hawthorne believes he is still blazing; Shelley emits a pure light, but Byron, black vapor. Hawthorne slyly watches the length of time it takes for the "combustion of American authors," but he will not betray this secret! Hawthorne cannot see his own works but believes they are immediately vaporized. A groaning man, identified by the observer as a bookworm, is consoled by Hawthorne with more irony and Emersonian cheerfulness: "'Is not Nature better than a book—is not the human heart deeper than any system of philosophy?'" (398).

Hawthorne thinks the fire must now be over, but he is warned by the observer that he will be startled at the next discards, which turn out to be all religious articles and emblems from the great cathedrals to the simple pulpit of the New England meetinghouse. When Hawthorne tries to be lighthearted and speaks again of a return to the simplicities of religion, the companion agrees, but questions whether the mob will stop here. So far the Bible has been spared, but now Hawthorne says fiercely:

> The inhabitants of the earth had grown too enlightened to define their faith within a form of words, or to limit the spiritual by any analogy to our material existence. Truths, which the Heavens trembled at, were now but a

fable of the world's infancy. Therefore, as the final sacrifice of human error, what else remained, to be thrown upon the embers of that awful pile, except the Book, which, though a celestial revelation to past ages, was but a voice from a lower sphere, as regarded the present race of man? (400)

In this acidulous irony, Hawthorne comes as close as he ever does to making a statement of his religious faith and belief.

Hawthorne's "brave friend" assures him that in the ashes will be everything really valuable: "'Not a truth is destroyed—nor buried so deep among the ashes, but it will be raked up at last'" (402). Hawthorne is partially reassured when he observes that the Holy Scriptures "only assumed a more dazzling whiteness." He is so pleased at this that he again seeks the observer's reasons why the world will not learn from the bonfire. The grave friend refers him to the Arch-Fiend himself who says the most important item has not yet been put into the fire.

"What, but the *human heart* itself!" said the dark-visaged stranger, with a portentous grin. "And, unless they hit upon some method of purifying that *foul cavern,* forth from it will re-issue all the shapes of wrong and misery . . . which they have taken such a vast deal of trouble to consume to ashes. I have stood by, this live-long night, and laughed in my sleeve at the whole business. Oh, take my word for it, it will be the old world yet!" (403)

Hawthorne concludes this flammable sketch with his own moral and in this case, unlike his evasions in many of the stories and sketches, he could not be more lucid:

How sad a truth. . . . Man's age-long endeavor for perfection had served only to render him the mockery of the Evil Principle, from the fatal circumstance of an error at the very root of the matter! The Heart—the Heart—there was the little, yet boundless sphere, wherein existed the original wrong [certainly a not too ambiguous reference to mankind's shared birthmark—Original Sin] of which the crime and misery of this outward world were merely types. (403–04)

The sketch ends with Hawthorne's imprecation to purify our hearts; unless we go beneath the intellect, he states, "our whole accomplishment will be a dream" (404). In this vision of the earthly bonfire, Hawthorne expresses supremely his sorrowing view of the world and its sinful creatures. His Calvinist view of man's depravity dictates his most effective and withering ironic mode.

*Mosses from an Old Manse* is a festival of vintage Hawthorne. With "The Birthmark," "Young Goodman Brown," "Rappaccinci's Daughter," and "Roger Malvin's Burial" alone, he has written *himself*—his Calvinist-ordained ironic mode—into fame and immortality. He has effectually refuted the earlier Puritan's complaint:

> Alas! what boots it with uncessant care
> To tend the homely slighted shepherd's trade
> And strictly meditate the thankless Muse?[15]

THE SNOW-IMAGE and THE UNCOLLECTED TALES

# *"Promenading Broadway in My Shroud"*

---

I

In *Mosses From an Old Manse* Hawthorne told the public in his opening sketch, "The Old Manse," that this was to be his last collection of short tales inflicted on readers, but he had his mind changed by his publishers after the success of *The Scarlet Letter* and *The House of the Seven Gables*. James T. Fields thought that Hawthorne's name should be kept before the public and Hawthorne rather unwillingly agreed.[1] He did not pay much attention to gathering the stories, but had his sisters and Fields search them out in old *Token* annuals and other early magazines. Four of the fifteen stories were close at hand, having been published between 1849 and 1851: "Main Street," 1849; "Ethan Brand," 1850; "The Great Stone Face," 1850; "The Snow-Image," 1851. The other eleven date from 1832 to 1843. The first edition of *The Snow-Image, and Other Twice-told Tales* was printed December 11, 1851 (dated 1852). It was far less popular than Hawthorne's two earlier collections.

Not many reviews of *The Snow-Image* appeared, but most of the reviewers it had were kind. One of the reviewers, Hawthorne's and Melville's friend, Evert Duyckinck, was fulsome except for "My Kinsman, Major Molineux." He found its ending difficult to understand, calling it "broadly comic" with a "most lame and impotent conclusion!" (393–94).

In addition to the sketches and tales of *The Snow-Image,* the *Centenary* editors (Vol. XI) have included thirteen uncollected tales. Nine of these, published between 1830 and 1844, are undoubtedly Hawthorne's, and the other four have been accepted, on the basis of internal and external evidence, as part of the Hawthorne canon. These tales have a particular interest for readers because they were either undetected by Fields or passed over by Hawthorne.

In the preface to *The Snow-Image,* written in the form of a letter to Horatio Bridge, Hawthorne opens up the vexed "Hawthorne Question" for later critics:

As for egotism, a person, who has been burrowing, to his utmost ability, into the depths of our common nature, for the purposes of psychological romance,—and who pursues his researches in that dusky region, . . . — will smile at incurring such an imputation in virtue of a little preliminary talk about his external habits, his abode, his casual associates, and other matters entirely upon the surface. These things hide the man, instead of displaying him. You must make quite another kind of inquest, and look through the whole range of his fictitious characters, good and evil, in order to detect any of his essential traits. (4)

It is agreeable to speculate about what Hawthorne would think of the hundreds of graduate students and professors, myself among them, who believe they have been given *carte blanche* by Hawthorne to ferret him out in his characters, or about the libraries that bulge grimly with the results of such inquiries. Poor reclusive Hawthorne, you have been made everything from Daffydowndilly to Ethan Brand!

The preface continues with Hawthorne commenting with more feeling than is his wont about his long neglect by the publishers and the public: "I sat down by the wayside of life, like a man under an enchantment, and a shrubbery sprung up around me, and the bushes grew to be saplings, and the saplings became trees, until *no exit* appeared possible, through the entangling depths of my obscurity" (5). Then follows a poignant passage in which the forty-seven-year-old author expresses his fear that he may already be "written out": "In youth, men are apt to write more wisely than they really know or feel; and the remainder of life may be not idly spent in realizing and convincing themselves of the wisdom which they uttered long ago. The truth that was only in the fancy then may have since become a substance in the mind and heart" (6). This seems almost prophetic, because Hawthorne finished only two novels (*The Blithedale Romance* and *The Marble Faun*) after this dedication to Bridge.

For examples of the great Hawthornean themes—the repeated Fall from Eden, the tragic-ironic view, and the isolation and alienation of every person—*The Snow-Image* and the *Uncollected Tales* provide only thin specimens. There are, however, two remarkable exceptions to this: "My Kinsman, Major Molineux" and "Ethan Brand," which will be discussed in detail.

The dream of the unfallen Adam is always with Hawthorne, even though he knows obsessively that age and death destroy beauty, youth—everything. The collection *The Snow-Image* has some brightness, as in the saccharine "The Great Stone Face" and "Little Daffydowndilly," but its two great masterpieces, tales that will survive as long as does the short story, "My Kinsman, Major Molineux" and "Ethan Brand," both end tragically and echo with the diabolic, ironic laughter characteristic of Hawthorne. Robin becomes "shrewd" and Ethan Brand leaps into the great, fiery, demon furnace which crumbles the marble man of the unpardonable sin into caustic lime. Inexplicably, Hawthorne, not his own best critic, passed over "My Kinsman, Major Molineux" twice in his two previous collections. It was written in 1832 and seems to have been included in *The Snow-Image* with some reluctance on Hawthorne's part. "Ethan Brand," subtitled "A Chapter from an Abortive Romance" was written in 1850 after Hawthorne had published *The Scarlet Letter*. He had decided not to write any more short stories, because he found they took a disproportionate amount of time; he could more easily write a novel. Fortunately, Hawthorne did not expand "Ethan Brand" but tried to get it placed by his sister-in-law Elizabeth Peabody for more money than he usually got for a short story. Sophia's sister did not like "Ethan Brand" so Hawthorne had to settle for publication in the *Dollar Magazine* and it is not certain that he received any compensation.

"Graves and Goblins," one of the *Uncollected Tales*, shows much of the influence of Shakespeare and Dante that haunted the mind of the thirty-one-year-old Hawthorne. The tale's interest lies not in its being death-infected, for this is a Hawthorne characteristic, but in its admixture of the Catholic Dante, the catholic Shakespeare, the gloomy reformer Calvin, and the poet Nathaniel Hawthorne.

The sketch is uneven, contradictory, necrophiliac, Brontëan, and ultimately unsatisfying, and yet in it are all of Hawthorne's most intense concerns: his tragic vision of earthly life; his disbelief in human progress; his fear of the journey from which no traveler returns; his death wish and his death fear; his ironic and bitter feeling of isolation and alienation; and his conviction that he is doomed to solitude in this life and, because of his "idle" storytelling, to probable damnation in the next.

## II

Out of the twenty-nine stories and sketches that constitute *The Snow-Image* and the *Uncollected Tales*, only five of *The Snow-Image* collection and one of the *Uncollected Tales* is told in the omniscient third-person narrative voice. The two great tales, "My Kinsman, Major Molineux" and "Ethan Brand," are told in the ironic third-person narrative voice, as are most of the successful tales of the two other collections. The sketches, "Main Street," "The Devil in Manuscript," and "Fragments from the Journal of a Solitary Man," successfully use the "I" persona, but when Hawthorne has problems with point of view and aesthetic distance, it is usually when he uses the "I," and some awkwardness results from the varying distances Hawthorne manages between himself, the reader, and the "I" persona he establishes.

In "Fragments from the Journal of a Solitary Man," Hawthorne skillfully changes the point of view from the narrator, who is a friend of the dead poet, to the contents of the journal of the unfortunate young man. Hawthorne begins by telling us of the quiet death of his poor young friend, "Oberon." Hearing the name by which Hawthorne was known to his Bowdoin classmates alerts us to the fact that there will be many resemblance between the dead poet and Hawthorne. The "I" persona describes Oberon's last request, which is to burn all of his papers; Hawthorne complies, but he cannot resist Oberon's journal, some fragments of which he says he is guiltily publishing as this sketch.

Hawthorne's description of his friend coincides so well with what we know of Hawthorne that the resemblance can hardly be considered accidental. The tone is slightly mocking as Hawthorne speaks of the dead Oberon, but there is also a tinge of regret since Hawthorne would have been in his thirties and not twenty-five, which was the age at which Oberon died. Oberon is characterized as a "solitary man" who comes every three months from his village to the city to visit bookshops and spend a couple of hours with the narrator:

> He was unequivocally the most original person I ever knew. . . . No tales that have ever appeared in our popular journals have been so generally admired as his. *But a sadness was on his spirit; and this, added to the shrinking sensitiveness of his nature, rendered him not misanthropic, but singularly averse to social intercourse.* (313)

When Oberon learns he is going to die, he does not become more melancholy but seems in better spirits: "life never called the dreamer forth; it was Death that whispered him" (313).

Lengthy selections follow from Oberon's journal, with the narrator entering occasionally to comment. In this fictitious journal, Hawthorne is able to indulge in Keatsian romanticism of the most lugubrious and dolorous kind while attributing it to Oberon, who expresses Hawthorne's deep self-pity.

The narrator interrupts to tell of one of Oberon's "morbid fancies": he is walking down Broadway in the bright sunshine, gazing at the coaches and the people with a vague idea that "'it was not my proper place'" (318). He feels cold and by degrees realizes that he is "'the object of universal attention, and, as it seemed, of horror and affright'" (318). People grow pale, laughter is hushed, horses rear, an old beggar woman points to the graveyard of St. Paul's, and three young girls run shrieking away. As he glances into a looking glass he awakens in "'self-terror and self-loathing. No wonder that the affrighted city fled! I had been promenading Broadway in my shroud!'" (318). Written when Hawthorne was in his early thirties and still self-imprisoned in a room in his mother's house, this waking dream of processing in his own shroud emblemizes Hawthorne's bitter yet romantic self-image. He felt himself doomed forever to being a spectator of his own living death; at the same time he wanted the world to take note.

Of the 1835 story, "Alice Doane's Appeal," we can only conclude that Hawthorne was dissatisfied with the incest theme or the handling of the shifting point of view, narrative voice, and aesthetic distance, since he did not include this tale in any of the three collections. Although his handling of voice in "Alice Doane's Appeal" is amateurish and awkward, his novitiate in this story certainly taught him a great deal that we have to be grateful for in his consummate handling of the narrator-participant seventeen years later in *The Blithedale Romance.*

Hawthorne's early tinkerings with voice, point of view, incest, and shroud parades only confirm our view that, with Hawthorne, blacker is better.

### III

Symbolism in *The Snow-Image* and the *Uncollected Tales,* richest in "My Kinsman, Major Molineux" and "Ethan Brand," functions well in some of the other tales and sketches but not in profusion or profundity as in the earlier collections. The weary, hopeless, and ruined pilgrims to the Shaker community of Canterbury ("The Canterbury Pilgrims") come, Hawthorne suggests, just as do the pilgrims of Chaucer's *Canterbury Tales,* to a grave. However, the New England pilgrims come not out of devotion to the memory of the martyred saint or for any favors, but because they "sought a home where all former ties of nature or society would be sundered, and all old distinctions levelled, and a cold and passionless security be substituted for human hope and fear, as in that other refuge of the world's weary outcasts, the grave" (131).

No medieval monk with the death's head on his desk was more conscious of the grave—of the *ars moriendi*—than Hawthorne. The symbolism of death, demonism, and witchcraft crowds "Alice Doane's Appeal" and "Graves and Goblins"; Richard Digby, the "Man of Adamant," through his bigotry and zeal, gradually petrifies and refuses to drink from the fountain of life brought to him by the kindly ghost of Mary Goffe. In "John Inglefield's Thanksgiving," the wayward Prudence, who gladdens the heart of her old father, sister, brother, and erstwhile lover by returning home on Thanksgiving Eve, leaves when it is time for "domestic worship" (184). Her face becomes deformed when her family pleads with her to stay: "Sin and evil passions glowed through its comeliness, and wrought a horrible deformity; a *smile* gleamed in her eyes, as of triumphant mockery at their surprise and grief" (184). Hawthorne turns the end of this tale into a fearsome image of the power of sin, evil, and damnation: "The same dark power that drew Prudence Inglefield from her father's hearth—the same in its nature, though heightened then to a *dread necessity*—would snatch a guilty soul from the gate of Heaven, and make its sin and its punishment alike eternal" (185). Hawthorne's Calvinist sense of the "dread necessity" of sinning is very clear in this image of the sinful soul, snatched easily from the gates of Heaven to the depths of hell.

Although few Eden images appear in these stories, none is more effective and functional than the one that appears in the long sketch "Main Street," which is Hawthorne's panorama of Salem for two centuries. Here Hawthorne states the basis of the first American dream, that of the first Puritan settlers who, though believing in total depravity, paradoxically thought that they could still establish the new Eden, the New Jerusalem. Through the magic of the narrator-showman of "Main Street," we see the history of Salem presented as a puppet show. Here is Roger Conant, "the first settler in Naumkeag," with his wife and children:

> How sweet must it be for those who have an Eden in their hearts, like Roger Conant and his wife, to find a new world to project it into, as they have; instead of dwelling among old haunts of men, where so many household fires have been kindled and burnt out, that the very glow of happiness has something dreary in it! (53)

What they did not reckon with, Hawthorne knows, were the ordained reenactments of the Fall which would occur in the new Eden.

Hawthorne, the turner of the crank for this puppet show, agrees with the audience that the Salem history is all too grim: "but the blame must rest on the sombre spirit of our forefathers, who wove their web of life with hardly a single thread of rose-color or gold, and not on me, who have a tropic love of sunshine, and would gladly gild all the world with it, if I knew where to find so much" (78). Hawthorne says that there is only one scene of jollity that he can record—a funeral feast: "New England must have been a dismal abode for the man of pleasure, when the only boon companion was Death!" (79).

A combination of symbolism, imagery, type, emblem, and allegory, "Main Street" is a remarkable achievement. But Hawthorne's backward look at two hundred years of old Salem leaves him with his familiar dilemma. Obsessed with death, he looks back upon his history and, with all of his showmanship, he cannot burn the puppets that inform his spirit and imagination with his guilt and depravity. Unlike his manuscripts in "The Devil in Manuscript," which set the whole town ablaze, Hawthorne can finally provide no cleansing and purifying fire for his sin-ridden conscience.

## IV

The two great stories in this collection have masterly ironic structures and are treated in detail, "My Kinsman, Major Molineux" in this section and "Ethan Brand" in section VI. Indeed, "My Kinsman, Major Molineux" shows Hawthorne's greatest control of structure; it is packed with complex imagery and informed with ambiguous implications. Why Hawthorne passed over this great story is impossible to understand. It is laden with foreshadowings of Kafka in Robin's nightmare wanderings up and down the half-deserted streets of a strange town, his bizarre encounters with hostile strangers, and his hearing an unknown language from strangely dressed groups. All of this creates a climate of dole and disaster interspersed with maniacal laughter that forms a demonic nimbus around the young alien, Robin.

Dantean imagery enriches this intricate tale. Robin crosses the ferry to Boston harbor conveyed by a surly ferryman resembling Charon and alights upon an unknown shore not knowing where to go. Lacking the guidance of Virgil, the simple country boy sets off all unknowing into the Inferno-wilderness of a dark and hostile city with only his oaken staff, his innocence, and what he considers his "shrewdness" to rely on. These prove disastrously inadequate. For want of a Virgil or a Beatrice, Robin is doomed to remain in the Inferno.

Robin's journey also resembles a quest, for he seeks, in his kinsman, a patron and securer of success in this world. As in all pilgrimages, a number of knotty obstacles have to be overcome. But Robin, who arrives by night, does not know where he is or how to get where he thinks he must go. Like Gawain, he is ready to do battle with his oaken cudgel, but his green knight is a double-faced, half-black and half-red demonic personage, who laughs at him but finally produces his sought-after kinsman—in a cart. Robin's motives are not as pure as Gawain's or as madly idealistic as Don Quixote's, so his quest for security in the form of a kinsman who will protect and promote him becomes the universal search for the kindly father. His real father, remaining hidden in the forest, has sent his son out of the protection and love of the home nest to the unknown and hostile world. Bird-named Robin is like Adam expelled from the security of Eden, lost and bewildered by the evil into which he is initiated.

The excursion from innocence to experience, an initiation rite ordered for all men since Adam's Fall, is a one-way passage. There is no way back to the Eden that Robin dreams of while he sits on the steps of the church. He is almost eighteen, on the outside looking into the church and religious law. He cannot go home again after he has laughed loudest of all at the fallen authority figure of Major Molineux, and for the first time in his young life he feels estrangement, isolation, and alienation from all that he has known and loved. He learns tragically that this is the plight man was born for—it is Robin that he mourns for.

Bound by iron necessity, by Hawthorne's Calvinist certainty, Robin must lose his way as well as the "kind friend" who coldly observes Robin's fall from grace into true "shrewdness." Although majestic and resembling a fallen King, Robin's redeemer (Molineux) is only a man, beaten and trodden upon by the fallen men of the world. He is not Christ, and Robin's savior does not come. Young Goodman Brown and Robin will have to survive in the evil of this world, but unlike Brown, the doomed man, who is victim of his own belief that all are evil but he, Robin will probably live comfortably and shrewdly and rise in the world. It is not possible to say whether one fate is better than the other, since the Calvinist-ordained irony of Hawthorne damns them both.

But now to examine the structure of this superb story. The tale opens with the historical paragraph which we have come to expect. It is not really the history of a country that interests Hawthorne, but the unknowable and perilous cartography of the human heart.

Robin is a name that suggests cheerful, birdlike, pristine innocence; a Robin Hood who lives in the forest and does cheerful good deeds for the poor, stealing from the rich; and Robin Goodfellow, a puckish spirit who interestingly enough is the servant of Oberon (the name Hawthorne was called by his Bowdoin College friends)—all are parts of Hawthorne's Robin. Although Robin is bewildered by and uncomprehending of his mortal fellows' activities in the city, particularly those of the mysterious and grotesque two-faced man, he speculates "upon the species of the *genus homo*" and settles "this point shrewdly, rationally and satisfactorily" (220). But tragically, the puckish Robin has the joke turned on himself.

Robin sets off to seek his kinsman about nine o'clock in the evening, after leaving the demanding ferryman, but he forgets to ask "Charon" where he can find the major. Undaunted, he decides to ask the next person he sees. Here follow seven encounters which provide the structure of the tale, ordained by Robin's quest and the irony of his ignorance.

On the first encounter Robin pulls the coattails of an old man of magisterial appearance, who utters at regular intervals "two successive hems, of a peculiarly solemn and sepulchral intonation" (210). In answer to his question concerning the dwelling of his kinsman, Robin is amazed at the old man's anger and hostility and the scornful laughter of two barbers that have watched the scene through their shop window. The old man fiercely denies knowledge of Major Molineux: "*I know not* the man you speak of" (211), and we sense, through the laughter of the barber's boys and the Simon-Peter-like denial and fury of the old man, that Robin is in for severe difficulties. But Robin, unabashed, "soon thought himself able to account for the *mystery*" (211) and decides, ironically, that the old man is from the country and ill bred. Robin believes himself "shrewd"; in fact, he describes himself in this way seven times in the tale. As we are to find out, Robin's solutions to the "mysteries" are always wrong, but he proceeds to look for his kinsman.

He becomes entangled in the town's infernally crooked and narrow streets, hopelessly lost but still confident that his shrewdness and the oaken cudgel brought with him from the forest will ensure his quest. He next (second encounter) goes into a tavern occupied by seamen and a couple of sheepish country boys like himself. Still, he is attracted *not* to the "brotherhood of these [country] strangers" (213) but to a weird man having whispered conversation with a group. The man's features are totally grotesque—the forehead bulging "into a double prominence, with a vale between" (213). He has an enormous irregular nose with a bridge wider than a finger, deep shaggy eyebrows, and eyes that "glowed beneath them like fire in a cave" (213). While Robin is staring, the innkeeper comes to take his order. Robin is flattered by the innkeeper's courtesy and concludes wrongly that the little man has seen in Robin a family likeness to the major and thus is being particularly ingratiating. Robin confesses his empty packet and asks his persistent question, "Where is the dwelling of my kinsman, Major Molineux?" whereupon everyone stirs (Robin attributes this to all wanting to be his guide) and the innkeeper reads portentously a "wanted" sign for a runaway servant. Robin begins to produce his oaken cudgel, but sensing the general hostility, he leaves hastily, sneered at by the bizarre-looking stranger and followed by the mocking laughter of all the customers of the tavern.

Robin does think it strange that his admission of poverty has outweighed the name of his kinsman and revealingly wishes he had "one of those grinning rascals in the *woods* . . . where I would teach him that my arm is heavy, though my purse is light" (215). But Robin, out of his native milieu of the woods and despite his cudgel and his imagined "shrewdness," is impotent and lost in the evil city.

Robin searches up and down the streets, but upon hearing the "two sepulchral hems," turns down a side street. Here, in this third encounter, he asks his question of a pert young girl in a scarlet petticoat, who assures him that she is the major's housekeeper and that he must come in. As Robin begins to enter her dwelling, however, the night watchman comes drowsily by and tells Robin to go home, or be put in the stocks. In this fourth skirmish Robin yells his question to the disappearing watchman, but gets no reply except laughter and the giggle of this lady of the evening in her scarlet petticoat, who, as no chaste Beatrice, beckons him back. But Robin, "of the household of a New England clergyman, was a good youth, as well as a shrewd one; so he resisted temptation, and fled away" (219), the narrator ironically observes.

Robin's search becomes desperate as he wearies, having walked thirty miles that day and being a five-day's walk from home. He looks around wildly and twice small parties of men pass him, dressed outlandishly, and speaking a language Robin does not understand. When their code language gets no response from Robin, he is cursed by them "in plain English" (219). Robin's painful isolation is heightened terribly by his inability to communicate with the initiate of the city. Finally, he feels the foreigner and outcast that he is.

Robin determines to stop the next person with his oaken staff and he does so and asks his question. Horror overcomes him when the stranger unmuffles his cloak and reveals himself as the grotesque man of the tavern who has undergone an even more gruesome alteration, for one side of his face "blazed of an intense red, while the other was black as midnight" (220). The sight is so horrible that the third-person omniscient narrator describes it "as if two individual devils, a *fiend* of *fire* and a *fiend* of *darkness,* had united themselves to form this infernal visage" (220). The terrible stranger tells Robin to wait an hour and his kinsman will pass by. Robin's response to this grisly encounter is the inane comment: "'Strange things we travelers see!'" (220). This fifth confrontation leaves the reader in terror for Robin, but the tired and vain youth who thinks he is shrewd sits down on the church steps to await the coming of his kinsman.

Robin is tired and sleepy but finally he hears an ominous murmuring in the distance, which he takes to be the combined snore of the sleeping town. To keep himself awake, Robin climbs a window frame and looks into the empty church, where one ray of moonlight rests on the opened Bible. Robin shivers and senses for the first time his very real estrangement: he is even locked out of the church and Christian sanctuary. He remembers his home in the forest, where he imagines the gracious scene of his clergyman-farmer father praying with family and neighbors in the open air, with all of the family supplicating tearfully for "the Absent One." He sees them go in the door of his home and when he is about to follow, the latch closes and he is "excluded from his home" (223). Now thoroughly frightened and partially aware of his essential homelessness— his ostracism from church and family—he wavers between unquiet sleep and waking. He sees a man walking down the street and calls out to him plaintively. "'Halloo, friend! Must I wait here all night for my kinsman, Major Molineux?'" (224)

The sixth meeting is the most significant yet. Many critics interpret this encounter as Robin's finally finding a kind friend who will witness, in a protective way, the totemistic initiation into manhood. But Hawthorne's grim Calvinism does not permit him the luxury of a facile solution to Robin's initiation into the evil of the adult, sinful world. Certainly the gentleman *appears* to be friendly and offers to be of service. But the *reality* is, as Robin himself realizes after the meeting with his kinsman, that this apparently kind friend is more fiendish than all of the other obviously cruel and cunning people he has met in his first five encounters. The gentleman poses as a friend, but immediately begins questioning Robin in a most officious, prying way. He tells Robin that the major's name is "not altogether strange" (224) to him and then queries Robin as to his business with Molineux. Poor weary Robin, thinking he detects a concerned interest in the stranger, tells him at once the story of his life, of how Major Molineux, a cousin of his father's, offered to help Robin and promote his interests in the city, especially, Robin pathetically adds, because "'I have the name of being a shrewd youth'" (225). Robin describes his futile search for his kinsman and confides that he has been told to wait at the church steps for the major. The stranger continues to grill Robin by asking for a description of the man who told him to wait and, in hearing Robin's description of the horrid-looking two-faced man, replies to Robin's question of whether he knows the man: "'Not intimately,' answered the stranger, 'but . . . I believe you may trust his word, and that the Major will very shortly pass through this street.'" (225). The real character of the "kind friend" is revealed to the reader but not immediately to Robin as the stranger adds: "'In the meantime, as I have a *singular curiosity* to witness your meeting, I will sit down here upon the steps and bear you company!'" (225).

The inveterate Hawthorne reader immediately recognizes by the words "singular curiosity" that we now have with Robin not a friend but a clinical observer, someone who, as a violator of the privacy of the human heart, wishes to witness a meeting that he knows can only be destructive and heart-scalding to Robin and his kinsman. The stranger, therefore, is a perpetrator of Hawthorne's "unpardonable sin."

In answer to Robin's query about the gathering uproar, the stranger lies to Robin, saying there may be three or four riotous fellows abroad, but that Robin must accustom himself to the noise of the city. Robin persists and says there were at least "a thousand voices" (226). The answer to this reveals more of the iciness and hard sophistication of the stranger: "'May not one man have several voices, Robin, as well as two complexions?'" (226). Robin, in his ingenuous "shrewdness," expresses the hope that God forbid that a woman should. However, the stranger's question to Robin suggests the terrible ambiguities of the way of the world in which Robin is to be initiated. The easy acceptance of the prolixity of masks and voices is the "shrewdness" of this cold-hearted observer and his brothers in the evil city.

The gathering noise becomes unmistakable; there are shouts and "wild and confused laughter" (226). Robin confides that he has not laughed since he left home and would like to join the fun. The stranger sits Robin down, saying: "*You forget that we must wait here for your kinsman*'" (226). The stranger seems to proclaim the iron necessity that both he and Robin must wait together. The stranger wishes compulsively to witness the bitter, ignominious scene ordained to follow. As the laughter gathers force, Robin steps to the edge of the pavement to see better a tremendous parade of people led by a single horseman with a drawn sword, the double-faced man. Both revealed and concealed by the torches, "his fierce and variegated countenance, appeared like war personified; the red of one cheek was an emblem of fire and sword; the blackness of the other betokened the mourning that attends them" (227). Many of the riotously laughing company are masked, but they obey the command of the leader to halt in front of Robin: "the trumpets vomited a horrid breath, and held their peace; the shouts and laughter of the people died away" (228). In front of Robin there is an uncovered cart and in it he sees Major Molineux, tarred and feathered. The description of the major is that of a fallen king trying to maintain his dignity—or like Christ mocked by his people—with a deadly pale face contracted in agony, eyes red and wild, body shaking with tremors. But then his eyes meet Robin's and the major recognizes him at once. "They stared at each other [Robin's seventh encounter] in silence, and Robin's knees shook, and his hair bristled, with a mixture of pity and terror" (229). Robin thus experiences two of the necessary responses to tragedy, pity and fear. In his raucous laughter there is catharsis. Excited by all he has seen that night, aware that he and his kinsman are the center of ridicule, he hears the laughter of all those "friends" he has encoutered that evening: the man of the two sepulchral hems, the innkeeper, the "lady" of the scarlet petticoat, the watchman, the barbers, the guests at the inn, "and of all who had made sport of him that night. The contagion was spreading among the multitude, when, all at once, it seized upon Robin, and he sent forth a shout of laughter that echoed through the street; every man shook his sides, every man emptied his lungs, but Robin's shout was the loudest there" (230). Robin's evil is this terrible, tragic laughter with which, his voice the loudest, he greets his kinsman.

The procession moves on and Hawthorne closes a bit the aesthetic distance he has set up through the use of a third-person omniscient voice and the one-hundred-year's remove in time by making a severe statement on the dreadful cruelty he has just described: "On they went, like *fiends* that *throng in mockery around* some dead potentate, mighty no more, but majestic still in his agony. On they went, in *counterfeited* pomp, in senseless uproar, in *frenzied merriment, trampling all on an old man's heart*" (230).

After a pause in the narrative, the stranger asks Robin if he is dreaming. Robin, after his initiation into the brotherhood of evil, has paled. He asks to be directed to the ferry, but the stranger, who has had a satisfactory voyeuristic experience, says blandly: "'You have then adopted a new subject of inquiry?'" (230). This is said to Robin with a smile but Robin, the newly initiated, now understands the language of the city and is able to reply "rather dryly," "'Thanks to *you,* and to *my other friends,* I have at last met my kinsman, and he will scarce desire to see my face again. I begin to grow weary of a town life, Sir. Will you show me the way to the ferry?'" (231). Here, without exception, Robin has grouped the "kind friend" clinical observer with all of the other evil people he has encountered in the town. But the curious stranger realizes what Robin does not—that he cannot go home again, nor can he regain his lost innocence. The cold and curious observer is right. Robin has finally become *shrewd,* a word Hawthorne reserves only for the selfish, ravening brotherhood of evil of which Robin is now a full-fledged member.

The encounters which Robin has in the Inferno-city gather structural significance, irony, and horror through the accusations leveled at Robin and the implied evil of his denouncers. In his first encounter with the consequential old man of the *sepulchral* hems (prophetic of the death of Robin's innocence and his fall from grace to the grave of shrewdness), Robin is accused of criminal disrespect and threatened with the stocks. The "courteous" innkeeper of the second encounter pointedly suggests that Robin is a runaway indentured servant. The prostitute of the scarlet petticoats in Robin's third encounter insinuates fornication—a considerable evil to Hawthorne—and the watchman of the fourth meeting assumes that Robin is a frequenter of lewd houses and also threatens him with the stocks. When the horrified Robin finds that the man he stops forcibly to demand the location of Major Molineux's dwelling is the black-and-red-faced man, Hawthorne suggests that Robin is consorting with the devil, although Robin tries to explain this strange sight *shrewdly* to himself. The "kind friend," who is the sixth antagonist, is the most evil of all; he is the violator of every human heart—the cold clinician who curiously watches the approaching agony. The seventh and final meeting has all of the elements of tragedy, combined with the coruscating laughter of catharsis, when Robin looks into the eyes of his barbarously humiliated kinsman and laughs loudest of all. Hawthorne's final circle of evil, like Dante's, is reserved for those who have betrayed their benefactors: like the three-faced Lucifer—black, red, and yellow—those traitorous individuals are wholly covered with ice. At the end of the story, Robin is cold, pallid, weary, and shrewd, but unlike Virgil, who takes Dante out of hell, Robin's "kind friend" only counsels him to become accustomed to the Inferno-city.

The tale is magnificent but the master stroke is the use of laughter to unite all of Robin's encounters. By its tragically inappropriate quality, the laughter makes prodigal Hawthorne's scorching irony which is directed so penetratingly at all of fallen humanity.

## V

The most memorable characters that Hawthorne has created in *The Snow-Image* and the *Uncollected Tales* are Robin and his "kind friend" in "My Kinsman, Major Molineux" and Ethan Brand, Bartram, and little Joe in "Ethan Brand." Robin is the most developed of all of these characters, but the reader is not likely to forget any of them. Ernest in "The Great Stone Face" persists in the memory, but he is so painfully good that many readers would like to forget him.

There are many improbable or unlikely characters in this collection: Sylph Etherege, who fades away, and her demon lover, Hamilton Vaughan, who is a kind of archetypal sadist; Richard Digby, the man of adamant, whose zeal does not eat him up but petrifies him; Prudence Inglefield, who strays back from her evil life to make her wretched family only more miserable on Thanksgiving; the compassionate Mary and Margaret of "The Wives of the Dead," who are but shadows; Little Daffy-downdilly, who belongs (if anywhere) in one of Hawthorne's moralistic children's stories and not in this collection, and Oberon, in "Fragments From the Journal of a Solitary Man," who is Gothic, Keatsian, self-pitying, and unlikable.

Although this collection, Hawthorne's third, contains two of his greatest stories ("My Kinsman, Major Molineux" and "Ethan Brand"), most of the other sketches and tales are much inferior to these masterworks. Many interesting creations move in and out of the stories but no character, except for Ernest of "The Great Stone Face," is ever developed or lingered over.

This simple tale has more sweetness and light than Hawthorne's more natural melancholy and gloom (so much so that it could almost have been written by Sophia). This story lacks the power of blackness so strong in Hawthorne's best works, and would be altogether vapid without the strong and symbolic character of the great good man, Ernest. As literary artists have always known, writing of someone who is saintly and good is far more difficult than writing of ordinary persons with a mixture of good and evil, or of someone truly villainous. What usually results from a tale about an angelic character is either a sickening, saccharine portrait or a story so boring that no one can bear to read it.

I certainly do not intend to argue a case for "The Great Stone Face" as a superior story, but Hawthorne with his skill at *gentle* irony, creates in this tale a believable and almost palpable character out of the humble Ernest, even while Ernest is performing the double function of acting as a symbolic character. The whole story is an elaboration of the biblical aphorism that "a prophet is not without honor except in his own country."

The humility and unpretentiousness of Ernest and his refusal to believe himself a prophet make him both an almost palatable character and a symbol of Hawthorne's unlikely excursion into the goodness of an elected heart. Difficult as it is to believe, the story of the pious Ernest appeared January 24, 1850, just about seven weeks before the hell-fired *Scarlet Letter* (March 16, 1850). That "blue-eyed darling," as D. H. Lawrence calls Hawthorne, achieved in less than two months this marvel of duplicity—an instance of the Hawthorne dilemma that still plagues the critic—the pure-hearted Ernest juxtaposed with the triumvirate of the damned in *The Scarlet Letter.* "The Great Stone Face" shows that without the demons, the regretful tragic vision, and the great power of darkness, Hawthorne would be just another nineteenth-century romantic writer.

## VI

If the collection *The Snow-Image* and the *Uncollected Tales* contained only "My Kinsman, Major Molineux" and "Ethan Brand," it would be a major work because these two finely wrought masterpieces must rank among the world's greatest stories. Hawthorne's Calvinist-dictated awareness of sin and guilt pervades the best of his tales and sketches, requiring the ironic mode. Since "Ethan Brand" is quintessential Hawthorne, we will now subject it to detailed scrutiny.

"Ethan Brand" has all of the Hawthorne hallmarks: the separation of the head and the heart which occasions the unpardonable sin; the completion of a circular journey or quest; the blackness of theme—the unrepentant search for the unpardonable sin—combined with the blackness of night, the faint moonlight, and the horrible glare of the red furnace; the sickening, despairing, inappropriate laughter more tragic than tears; the ritual sacrifice enacted upon a height; an assemblage of onlookers—Hawthorne's protean crowd—that gradually disappears because of fright; the frightful isolation of the guilty; the damnation of Ethan Brand, who has become a fiend; the aura of mystery; and the obligatory ironic mode, dictated by Hawthorne's Calvinism, that shows a presumptuous Ethan searching for the unforgivable sin, the biblical sin against the Holy Ghost, and finding it in himself.

The story is subtitled "A Chapter from an Abortive Romance," but it seems far better that Hawthorne did not expand this tale. In its eighteen pages "Ethan Brand" compresses the dramatic action from shortly after sunset until sunrise and moves swiftly to its soul-affrighting ending. The setting is a limekiln nestled into the Graylock Mountain and surrounded by a dark forest.

The tale begins with Bartram, the limeburner "grimed with charcoal," watching his kiln with his small son, Joe, playing near him. The silence is broken by a roar of laughter. Little Joe, more sensitive than his rough father, is alarmed by the sound which his father assures him is only the laughter of a drunkard from the village tavern below. But Joe protests "'he does not laugh like a man that is glad'" (83). Bartram is momentarily ashamed of his son's cowardice.

Hawthorne now fills in some facts that, as omniscient narrator, he declares "we have seen." We have seen nothing of the kind (as the story has been aborted), but this only sparks our interest in the brief sketch of Ethan Brand, the former limeburner, who tended this very kiln and developed the "idea" of searching for the unpardonable sin from staring into the kiln's fire. Ethan "had thrown his dark thoughts into the intense glow of the furnace, and melted them, as it were, into the one thought that took possession of his life. . . . [The limekiln] resembled nothing so much as the private entrance to the infernal regions, which the shepherds of the Delectable Mountains were accustomed to show to pilgrims" (84). In Hawthorne country, hell's pit is not very far from the Celestial City itself.[2]

Bartram is a man in no danger of succumbing to intellectual musings, but he is "half-infected" by little Joe's timidity and calls out a threat as they hear approaching footsteps. The man who appears, exposed by the light of the furnace that Bartram throws open, seems rather unremarkable, tall, thin, and gloomy. He says, "'I come from my search . . . for, at last it is finished'" (86). The man identifies himself as Ethan Brand; Bartram laughs for the last time and asks him whether he has found, in his eighteen-year search, the unpardonable sin. Ethan Brand admits he has and points to his own heart, "'Here!'" Then Ethan laughs that terrible, mirthless laugh which Hawthorne tells us is from a recognition "of the infinite *absurdity*" (87) of searching for years for what was in his own breast.

Hawthorne then expatiates on the terrifying qualities of Ethan Brand's laughter:

> It was the same slow, heavy laugh, that had almost appalled the lime-burner. . . .
>
> The solitary mountain-side was made dismal by it. *Laughter, when out of place, mistimed, or bursting forth from a disordered state of feeling, may be the most terrible modulation of the human voice.* The laughter of one asleep, even if it be a little child—the madman's laugh—the wild, screaming laugh of a born idiot, are sounds that we sometimes tremble to hear, and would always willingly forget. *Poets have imagined no utterance of fiends or hobgoblins so fearfully appropriate as a laugh.* And even the obtuse limeburner felt his nerves shaken, as this strange man looked inward at his own heart, and burst into laughter that rolled away into the night, and was indistinctly reverberated among the hills. (87–88)

Ethan Brand's realization of the abnormality of his search prompts this terrible laughter and reminds us of twentieth-century writers rather than writers of the nineteenth-century romantic period. The concept of life as absurd that harrows Kafka, Camus, and Sartre and occasions hysterical, inappropriate laughter in the plays of Samuel Beckett much more closely resembles Hawthorne's view of life than that of any other writer of the nineteenth century. But there is a difference. Hawthorne's use of absurdity points to the craven sinner's evil, and barbarous and cruel as his punishment is, there is behind it a glowering Calvinist God that will not be mocked, not the emptiness or nihilism that Hawthorne may have dreaded but would not allow himself to contemplate.

Hawthorne seems to reject nihilism not because he has absolute faith but because all the piteous examples of what he would consider horrible Special Providences have convinced him that they come from a living but uncompromising God. If this uncompromising God becomes biddable *or* absent (as Hawthorne's God does after the years abroad), Hawthorne's tragic vision is dissipated and his creative imagination is rendered impotent.

Bartram sends little Joe to summon the villagers and, now alone with the burning Brand, he regrets Joe's absence and his proximity to the man who "on his own confession, had committed the only crime for which Heaven could afford no mercy" (88). Hester's *A* quivered when she met other sinners:

> The limeburner's own sins rose up within him, and made his memory riotous with a throng of evil shapes that asserted their kindred with the Master Sin, whatever it might be, which it was within the scope of man's corrupted nature to conceive and cherish. They were all of one family; they went to and fro between his breast and Ethan Brand's, and carried dark greeting from one to the other. (88)

This concept of the unforgivable sin must be examined. There is ample scriptural basis for it—Matthew 12:32: "And whosoever speaketh a word against the Son of man, it shall be forgiven him: but whosoever speaketh against the Holy Ghost, it shall not be forgiven him, neither in this world, neither in the world to come." The same is repeated almost exactly in Luke 12:10. Paul elaborates, in the epistle to the Hebrews (6:4–6): "For it is impossible for those who were once enlightened, and have tasted of the heavenly gift, and were made partakers of the Holy Ghost, and have tasted the good word of God, and the powers of the world to come, if they shall fall away, to renew them again into repentance; seeing they crucify to themselves the Son of God afresh, and put him to an open shame." And again in Hebrews 10:26–27: "For if we sin wilfully after that we have received the knowledge of the truth, there remaineth no more sacrifice for sins, but a certain fearful looking for of judgment and fiery indignation, which shall devour the adversaries." There is no way we can prove that Hawthorne knew the commentaries of the Breeches Bible[3] (Geneva Bible), which he mentions, but it is very likely that in his extensive reading of colonial sermons and Calvinist theology, election sermons, and books on Knox, he had become familiar with the Calvinist commentaries. On Matthew 12:32, for example, the Genevan commentators write: "This is, he that striveth against the truthe which he knoweth, and against his owne conscience, can not returne to repentance: for he sinneth against the holie Gost." On Paul to the Hebrews 6:4–6, the Genevan commentary states: "They which are apostats, and sinne against ye Holy Gost, hate Christ, crucifie and mocke him, but to their owne destruction, and therefore fall into desperation, and cannot repent." All of these would make very likely commentaries on Ethan Brand and his desperate, despairing end, but Calvin is even more to the point. Hawthorne, no matter how much he would have liked to close his ears to the grim reformer, echoes him over and over:

> Hence . . . the supernatural hardening of the heart [is] . . . a sign of reprobation. . . . Voluntary apostates . . . mock God, insultingly reject his favour, profane and trample under foot the blood of Christ. . . . Hence it follows, that to no sin is pardon denied save to one, which proceeding from desperate fury cannot be ascribed to infirmity. . . . He sins against the Holy Spirit who, while so constrained by the power of divine truth that he cannot plead ignorance, yet deliberately resists, and that merely for the sake of resisting. . . . The spirit of blasphemy, therefore, is, when a man audaciously, and of set purpose, rushes forth to insult his divine name. . . . [And what he receives] is the dreadful torment which stings and excruciates the wicked in despair. (*Institutes,* Vol. I, pp. 527–30)

In "Ethan Brand" Hawthorne seems to go beyond even his own definition of the unpardonable sin found in the *American Notebooks:*

> The Unpardonable Sin might consist in a want of love and reverence for the Human Soul; in consequence of which, the investigator pried into its dark depths, not with a hope or purpose of making it better, but from a cold philosophical curiosity,—content that it should be wicked in whatever kind or degree, and only desiring to study it out. Would not this, in other words, be the separation of the intellect from the heart? (251)

Hawthorne's view of the unpardonable sin adjusts and modifies Calvin's into more human terms. Hawthorne's apostate blasphemes against the Holy Spirit by violating the soul of another human being and studying it out of cold curiosity. This violation is blasphemous because the investigator has cooly and defiantly assumed the role of the deity. Certainly there is such a separation of head and heart in Ethan Brand, but he goes beyond merely prying coldly into Esther's heart—"perhaps annihilated her soul" (94). He has outdone the Coverdales and "kind friends" to become a Chillingworth who, as fiend, despairs when his victim dies and eludes him. Chillingworth dies shortly after Dimmesdale, but Ethan Brand, who, according to his prideful blasphemy, has surpassed devils and is alone in his triumphant, voluntary, and unrepented guilt has nothing left but to incinerate himself. The unpardonable sin, then, of Ethan Brand corresponds most accurately with the biblical and Calvinistic unforgivable sin, and goes beyond Hawthorne's early description of how he could dramatize the commission of the unpardonable sin.

While little Joe summons the townspeople, Bartram remembers the legends associated with Brand: Brand "had conversed with Satan himself . . . night after night, in order to confer with him about the Unpardonable Sin; the Man and the Fiend each laboring to frame the image of some mode of guilt, which could neither be atoned for, nor forgiven" (89). Brand startles Bartram by opening the furnace, but he assures Bartram that he is not looking for the devil, of whom he now has no need because he has "left him behind me on my track. It is with such half-way sinners as you that he busies himself" (90). Brand claims to have looked into many hearts "seven times hotter with sinful passions than yonder furnace is with fire" (90), without finding the unpardonable sin. In answer to Bartram's question concerning what this sin is, Brand answers with all of the Miltonic grandeur of archangel fallen:

> "It is a sin that grew within my own breast," replied Ethan Brand, standing erect, with the price that distinguishes all enthusiasts of his stamp. "A sin that grew nowhere else! The sin of an intellect that triumphed over the sense of brotherhood with man, and reverence for God, and sacrificed everything to its own mighty claims! The only sin that deserves a recompense of immortal agony! Freely, were it to do again, would I incur the guilt. Unshrinkingly, I accept the retribution! (90)

Bartram thinks Ethan is mad, but now troops in a typical Hawthorne crowd, laughing boisterously. There are four failures who have drunk themselves into decline: a wilted stage agent; a failed lawyer; the drunken village doctor, who still makes calls; and an old man who keeps asking for his daughter. Hawthorne tells us that the daughter was one of Brand's

diabolical experiments and the old man's pathetic questioning assures
Brand that he has found the unpardonable sin. There is also a group of
young people who come to be amused, but soon tired of looking at Brand,
they turn to "an old German Jew" with a diorama on his back. Hawthorne
tells us that the pictures were cracked and abominable, but little Joe put
his head in the box and "the boy's round, rosy visage assumed the strangest imaginable aspect of an immense, Titanic child" who becomes terrified when Brand looks at him through the glass. The dioramist urges
Brand to look inside the box where the view causes him to start. The old
man tells him: "'I find it a heavy matter in my show-box—this Unpardonable Sin!'" (96). Reminiscent of "Fancy's Show Box," we are led by
Hawthorne as omniscient narrator to believe that Brand has at least caught
a glimpse of his monstrous evil, and that the old dioramist carries it
about, along with his pictures of the other wonders of the world.

At this point a friendly old dog inexplicably chases his tail, is ap-
plauded by the crowd, and just as inexplicably stops. But Ethan Brand
"moved . . . by a perception of some remote analogy [the absurd circular
pursuit that led him back to his beginning and his own heart] between his
own case and that of this self-pursuing cur . . . broke into the awful
laugh which, more than any other token expressed the condition of his
inward being" (97). This laugh of recognition (of the devil-cur), like
Robin's, resounds about the mountain and the crowd disperses quickly,
for Brand's diabolic laughter has made them aghast and horrified.

When the crowd has left, Brand orders Bartram and Joe to sleep in
their nearby hut, as he will watch and tend the fire. Alone, again, Brand
contemplates his passage into evil, from a tender, loving man with reverence for his fellowman who prayed he would never find the unpardonable
sin to the stage of "that vast intellectual development . . . which disturbed the counterpoise between his mind and heart" (98–99). But as his
intellect towered, his heart withered, "had contracted—and hardened—
had perished! It had ceased to partake of the universal throb. He had lost
his hold of the magnetic chain of humanity" (99). He did not now have
sympathy for any other hearts: "he was now a *cold observer,* looking on
mankind as the subject of his experiment, and, at length, converting man
and woman to be his puppets, and pulling the wires that moved them to
such degrees of crime as were demanded for his study" (99). Ethan Brand
has become the Anti-Jehovah, the malignant, manipulative, diabolic
serpent-god, or as Hawthorne says: "Ethan Brand had become a fiend. He

began to be so from the moment that his moral nature had ceased to keep the pace of improvement with his intellect" (99). Now the "summit" had been reached: "as the bright and gorgeous flower, and rich, delicious fruit of his life's labor—he had produced the Unpardonable Sin!" (99).

There is wonderful irony in Hawthorne's using the beautiful imagery of Eden's flowers and fruits to describe Brand's diabolic achievement. But Brand is despairingly satisfied with his treasure: "'What more have I to seek? What more to achieve? . . . My task is done, and well done!'" (99). Brand climbs to the top of the furnace, says a pompous farewell to the earth and mankind, "'whose brotherhood I have cast off, and trampled thy great heart beneath my feet. . . . Come, deadly element of Fire—henceforth my familiar friend! Embrace me as I do thee!'" (100).

A horrible peal of laughter is heard that disturbs the uneasy sleep of Bartram and Joe, but they do not rise until sunlight—and it is a perfect and beautiful day, the day after Brand has gone to hell. Bartram irritably climbs to look at the fire, which he believes Brand has let die out, but then he summons Joe. They see in the perfectly snow-white lime the outline of a human skeleton and heart. Bartram crumbles the remains and rejoices that Brand's marble heart and skeleton have burned into especially good lime, "'and taking all the bones together, my kiln is half a bushel the richer for him'" (102).

The consummate Calvinist-ordained irony of this ending is one of Hawthorne's great achievements. The devil to pay and the devil must get his due. All that the damned Ethan Brand reaps from his unpardonable sin and his cosmic rebellion is one-half bushel of lime. After eighteen years Ethan Brand's blasphemous search results in one brief, lurid moment in the lime light.

And so Hawthorne's snow images melt in the crackling, deadly fire sparked and fanned by his black imagination—a fire that refines and purifies this book of tales into half a bushel of riches, "My Kinsman, Maiches, "My Kinsman, Major Molineux" and "Ethan Brand."

THE ENGLISH NOTEBOOKS
1853–1858

# "A Citizen of Somewhere Else"

Very little study has been made of the *English, French, and Italian Notebooks*—especially regarding their reflection of the enormous change in Hawthorne's view of life, a change revealed both overtly and covertly. Hawthorne's seven years abroad deeply affected him, particularly his religious outlook. From an unacknowledged but often terrifyingly orthodox Calvinist habit of mind, Hawthorne gradually slipped from his stance as defensive American "heretic," as he liked to call himself in the *English Notebooks*. Hawthorne was ambivalent about the meagerness of the Anglican church, yet he was shocked at the horrible destruction wreaked by the Reformation and Cromwellian zealots on the churches, abbeys, and cathedrals that he had come to love. He visited Knox's home in Edinburgh, but then refused to visit "Kirkified" cathedrals. He was a wavering and uncertain Puritan when he departed for France and Italy in January 1858. His simultaneous attraction to and revulsion from Catholic France and Italy provide the cloudy religious climate of his last great completed novel, *The Marble Faun.* Finally, Hawthorne's very real confusion of belief, combined with a great intellectual and physical fatigue, made it impossible for him to complete another romance after his return to America.

The European notebooks record the responses of a provincial New Englander to the Old World. Although at first hostile to anything different from America, Hawthorne gradually lost his nationalistic innocence and became a citizen of the world. This sea change and all of the ambiguities associated with it are recorded in the 300,000 words of the *English Notebooks,* which Hawthorne kept out of a sense of duty and which we can now know well since what was lost in the barbarous editing by Sophia has been restored by Randall Stewart.[1] The *French and Italian Notebooks* have also now been published complete, as opposed to Sophia's edited *Passages,* in the ongoing *Centenary Edition* of Hawthorne.[2]

The signal importance of these notebooks and Hawthorne's letters,[3] as opposed to the *American Notebooks,* is that they stand alone. Without accompanying creative works to reveal a Hawthorne undergoing significant philosophical and temperamental changes, the notebooks faithfully record all of his moral, intellectual, and physical equivocations during this time. When all of these equivocations come together in the remarkable but flawed *Marble Faun,* we are able to understand why this novel was the last of Hawthorne's completed works.

Hawthorne was partly aware of the controversial quality of his journals, but only for his revelations about the English. To his publisher William Ticknor he wrote: "I keep a journal of all my travels and adventures . . . but, unluckily, they would be much too good and true to bear publication. It would bring a terrible hornet's nest about my ears."[4] He similarly wrote to Sophia's sister, Elizabeth Peabody, that his journal "is written with so free and truth-telling a pen that I never shall dare to publish it."[5] Although before leaving for the Continent Hawthorne left the English journals in the care of his friend, Harry Bright, with the injunction that they were not to be opened until 1900 unless claimed by himself or his family,[6] Sophia published them with endless decorous revisions and omissions in 1870. What the notebooks reveal about Hawthorne's views of the English and of some individuals in particular is far less fascinating, however, than what they reveal about Hawthorne himself.

Hawthorne's first impressions of England were far from pleasant and he lost no opportunity during his first months there to compare everything and everybody unfavorably with America and Americans. The English are ugly, he said; they wholly despise Americans; they have no manners; they are smug and self-satisfied; what they call a river is only a brook in New England, etc. But after a while, Hawthorne began to lose his critical view of England. In February 1854 the Hawthornes made a visit to the Brights, whose son Henry, an Oxford scholar, had visited Hawthorne in America, and Sophia was disappointed that she could not find anything to criticize: "It is all peace and love and happiness there, and I cannot discover where the *shadow* is. Health, wealth, cultivation, and all the Christian graces and virtues—I cannot see the trail of the *serpent* anywhere in that Paradise." She was, however, able to fault the English for their noses. "The English are unfortunate in noses. Their noses are *unspiritual,* thick at the end; and there is an expression about the mouth of enormous self-complacency."[7] If it were not Sophia writing, we might think gleefully of *Tristram Shandy.*

When Hawthorne visited London, he was disappointed to find that it was not a Garden of Eden. He recorded the family's visit to the zoo in September 1855: "My idea was, that here every living thing was provided for, in the way best suited to its nature and habits, and that the *refinement of civilization had here restored a Garden of Eden,* where all the animal kingdom had regained a happy home. This is not quite the case" (208).

In time Hawthorne began to be ashamed of America, although earlier he had been extremely defensive about his country. He wrote to Ticknor (July 1854): "I find it impossible to read American newspapers (of whatever political party) without being ashamed of my country. No wonder then, if Englishmen hate and despise us, taking their ideas of us and our institutions from such sources."[8] In a letter to Longfellow, he described his profound ambivalence (August 1854): "For my part, I have no love for England or Englishmen, and I do love my own country, but for all that, *the honest truth is, I care little whether I ever set eyes on it again. . . . I have had enough of progress. . . .* A man of individuality and refinement can certainly live far more comfortably here . . . than in New England."[9]

Visiting Boston, England, the Hawthornes went to a hotel for tea and encountered a waiter who reminded Hawthorne of Boston, Massachusetts: "A very grim waiter he is, and apparently a genuine descendant of the old Puritans of Boston, who peopled their daughter-city in New England" (474). By this point (May 1857), Hawthorne was not showing unadulterated enthusiasm for either the old Puritans or their descendants.

He began by 1857 to criticize Americans from an English point of view. The family packed itself into an omnibus at Kenilworth with two ladies, one of whom was an American:

> I began to agree partly with the English, that we are not a people of elegant manners; at all events, there is sometimes a bare, hard, meagre sort of deportment, especially in our women, that has not its parallel elsewhere. . . . But perhaps what sets off this kind [of] behavior . . . is the fact of such uncultivated persons travelling abroad, and going to see sights that would not be interesting except to people of some education and refinement. (568)

Yet by the time the Hawthornes were ready to leave England, the old ambivalence again asserted itself (December 1858): "*I am weary, weary of London, and of England,* and can judge now how the old Loyalists must have felt, condemned to pine out their lives here when the Revolution had robbed them of their native country. And yet there is still a pleasure in being in this dingy, smoky, midmost haunt of men" (618).

Hawthorne's emotional state is something we know little about, from the time of his growing up in the Manning house with his reclusive mother, his two sisters, and a group of unmarried aunts and uncles, to his four years at Bowdoin and the years of seclusion in his own room. From the beginning of the *American Notebooks,* through his marriage and until his departure for England, there seems to be a deliberate holding back, a refusal to say anything that might be construed as personal or revealing. The love letters to Sophia are somewhat more open, particularly those written from Brook Farm, but the overall impression given by the notebooks and letters is of a man who kept his emotions severely under control, unwilling to record whatever soul-searching he was undergoing, and scrupulously avoiding a personal, agonizing cry of the heart: "hints and guesses, / Hints followed by guesses" is about all we have of the hidden Hawthorne during these years.

Despite the fact that the *English Notebooks* seem more like the travelogues of an innocent abroad than intimate disclosures, they, along with letters of the period, reveal by what they say and what they do not say, a Hawthorne now at least partially exposed. The shock of recognition that a receptive sensibility like Hawthorne's encountered in the home of his forefathers, a region dreamed and fantasized about from his early years and everywhere drenched with the resonance of his favorite English writers, evoked in this diffident Salem artist such complex reactions that at last one can find meditations about personal religious beliefs, marriage, children, chastity, and death that never were allowed to surface before.

Hawthorne's constant emotional and physical restlessness is revealed by his observation (November 1857) of the "weariness and desolation" that another trip to the British Museum cost him. He felt that a lifetime would be hardly enough to take in all that this museum offered and in his despair he hastened to the solace of the busy street outside, taking his son Julian with him: "He seems to have my own passion for thronged streets and the intensest bustle of human life" (591). If Hawthorne could not have complete solitude and peace, then the isolation of the crowd would have to suffice.

Gradually recognizing his essential homelessness, this man, who nev-

er stayed in one place more than a few months after leaving his solitary
chamber in Salem, began to believe that England might be his lost home
after all:

> My ancestor left England in 1635. I return in 1853; I sometimes feel
> as if I myself had been absent these 218 years—leaving England just
> emerging from the feudal system, and finding it on the verge of
> Republicanism. It brings the two far separated points of time very closely
> together, to view the matter thus. (92)

But England was no Eden garden. After speaking of the English
upper classes providing themselves with great, comfortable homes enclosed in private parks, and then leaving them to their progeny, he says
rather sadly, "And really the result seems to be good and beautiful—it is a
*home—an institution which we Americans have not*—but then *I doubt whether
anybody is entitled to a home, in so full a sense, in this world*" (104). And yet
Hawthorne worried about the moral effect of homelessness: "The moral
effect of being without a settled abode is very wearisome" (186). Wondering how this nomadic existence would affect the children he said: "I do
not know what sort of character it will form in the children, this *unsettled,
shifting, vagrant life,* with no central home to turn to, except what we *carry
in ourselves*" (425).

Writing to his publisher, Ticknor, he revealed more anxiety:

> Nevertheless, she [Sophia] is homesick; and I believe we should all be
> glad to return to the old house at the Wayside tomorrow. But I fear we
> shall have outgrown that house before we get back, and I shall at least be
> compelled to make some additions to it, if not to build a new one. I
> sometimes doubt whether this European residence will be good for us, in
> the long run. All of us will come back with altered habits, accustomed to
> many things which we shall not find at home; and as for the children,
> (though they imagine that they love America above all the rest of the
> world) they will really belong on this side of the water, rather than on
> that. [10]

This letter is singularly prophetic. The homeless malaise continued, but
Hawthorne dreaded going back to an America now on the verge of war.
He seems to have accepted homelessness as a way of life, as he wrote to
Longfellow:

I feel quite *homeless and astray, and as if I belonged nowhere.* It seems a great while since I left America; but I confess I have no very strong inclination to return, though I sometimes try to flatter myself that I am homesick. But our country looks very disagreeable and uncomfortable, morally, socially, and climatically, from this side of the water; and I have many qualms at the idea of spending the residue of my days there. I *love* America but do not *like* it. Pray don't tell anybody this.[11]

Ashamed of himself for his unwillingness to return to America, he begged Longfellow not to reveal these feelings.

Two years later he still dreaded returning to what was once home, but he had lost his roots: "The fact is, *I do not take root anywhere,* and never shall, unless I could establish myself in some old manor-house like those I see in England."[12] By March 1857, he was convinced that he had indeed become a "citizen of somewhere else"—a "citizen of the world": "I doubt whether you see us on your side of the water in less than two years from this coming summer; and if it were not for the children (who pine for America) I should consider myself a *citizen of the world,* and perhaps never come home."[13]

Hawthorne's dread of returning to America is symptomatic of the extraordinary changes that were going on within this sensitive man. The American dream of the New Jerusalem and Hawthorne's blood knowledge of its failure and corruption more and more convinced him, perhaps unconsciously, that life in "Our Old Home" was less demanding, less duty bound and infinitely more comfortable than life in the narrow, severe, intolerant New England which awaited him. The old dispensation of sophistication, unabashed shrewdness, and absence of remorse for lost innocence had fairly well undermined this Puritan of Puritans.

The memory of one of Hawthorne's heroes, Dr. Samuel Johnson, elicited an unusual gesture from such a circumspect man. Hawthorne made a solitary pilgrimage to Lichfield (149–53), Johnson's birthplace, and then went to Uttoxeter "on a purely sentimental pilgrimage, to see the spot where Johnson performed his penance" (151). Hawthorne, like Johnson, stood in the rain in the market place where he imagined Johnson had stood for his public confession, an act which the Puritan in Hawthorne entirely approved of: "As beautiful and touching an incident as can be cited out of any human life" (152).

Hawthorne's obsession with death and graveyards is apparent, fla-grantly so, throughout the *American Notebooks* and his sketches, tales, and novels. His European residence of seven years did nothing to abate this passion but only intensified it. The *English Notebooks* are crammed with descriptions of deaths and burials—many of indigents and abandoned Americans which he felt obliged to attend. But in the Hawthornes' frantic sight-seeing, sparked by the tireless Sophia and followed by the dutiful Nathaniel, the first place Hawthorne sought was the graveyard. The following description is representative of dozens of accounts and medita-tions on death and the grave:

> And of all the lovely churchyards that I ever beheld, that of Peterborough Cathedral seems to me the most delightful; so quiet it is, so solemnly and nobly cheerful, so verdant, so sweetly shadowed, and so presided over by the noble Minster, and surrounded by quiet, ancient, and comely habita-tions of Christian men. The most delightful place, the most enviable as a residence, in all this world seemed to me that of the Bishop's secretary, standing in the rear of the Cathedral, and bordering on the churchyard; so that you seem to pass *through hallowed precincts in order to come at it, and find it a sort of Paradise, the holier and sweeter for the dead men that sleep so near.* (482–83)

Hawthorne's comments here and elsewhere in the *English Notebooks* show that his fear and trepidation about death have changed almost to a form of acceptance—even to a longing for the peace and serenity of the grave.

In Europe, Sophia proved herself an intrepid, fanatic sightseer. Sophia, whose health was thought so delicate (before her marriage to Hawthorne she was generally regarded as an invalid), and who despite her mother's admonitions, never did a portion of housework, became a Titan in her endless sight-seeing. As a nineteenth-century "child-wife," who was married at the age of thirty-one, Sophia was quite content to be petted and spoiled all of her life and evidently Nathaniel Hawthorne felt responsible for seeing that she was as pampered as possible. However, in England he began to tire of the incessant visiting of ruins, galleries, historical sites, libraries, museums. Although, like Sophia's, his Puritan conscience told him that he *must* take advantage of all the cultural oppor-tunities at his disposal, he became weary in England. In July 1857, when at Edinburgh's Holyrood Palace, he said irritably:

Here we found some fine old portraits . . . amid which I walked wearily, wishing that there were nothing worth looking at, in this whole world. My wife differs altogether from me, in this matter; her body gets tired, but never her mind; whereas I hold out physically better than mentally; but we agreed, on this occasion, in being tired to death. (535)

But they did not stop. They saw several more places before and after tea, and early the next morning were off again, looking and looking.

The distinction that Hawthorne makes between his wife's physical tiredness and his mental weariness provides us with an understanding of the significant differences between them. Sophia looked at everything and sketched everything; Hawthorne tried to take in the meaning and moral of everything he saw and despaired of ever having enough life or energy to record even a portion of this intellectual and spiritual experience.

There is something pathetic about Hawthorne's determination to educate himself about art so that he could appreciate the masterpieces of England and be prepared for the even greater splendors of France and Italy. Hawthorne went again and again to the galleries and although he preferred sculpture to painting, he gazed determinedly at picture after picture, hoping to understand, to be moved, to judge. He vented his Puritan rage at Etty, but the Calvinism is tempered by a genuine irritability that Sophia predictably edited out but Stewart has restored:

The most disagreeable of English painters is Etty, who had a diseased appetite for woman's flesh, and spent his whole life, apparently, in painting them with enormously developed bosoms and buttocks. I do not mind nudity, in a modest and natural way; but Etty's women really thrust their nakedness upon you so with malice aforethought, and especially so enhance their posteriors, that one feels inclined to kick them. *The worst of it is, they are not beautiful.* (556)

The last sentence in the quotation is reassuring; even an uncomfortable Hawthorne has not lost his delight in feminine beauty.

Hawthorne's appreciation of the beauty of women, manifested in the novels and tales, and suggested occasionally in the *American Notebooks,* was not given much range in England. He found most English women ugly and when he repeated this impression in *Our Old Home,* he brought the wrath of English females down on his head. His attack on women for the way they look and the way they write is as passionate as anything Hawthorne ever wrote, causing us to wonder again about the much publicized idyllic marriage to Sophia. In this passage from the notebooks, he got rid of a tremendous amount of hostility toward the women with whom he was always surrounded:

> What chiefly struck me, however, was the lack of beauty in the women, and the horrible ugliness of not a few of them. . . . My experience is, that an English lady of forty or fifty is apt to become the most *hideous animal* that ever pretended to human shape. No caricature could do justice to some of their figures and features; so puffed out, so huge, so without limit, with such hanging dewlaps and all manner of fleshly abomination . . . unconscious of the wrong they are doing to one's idea of womanhood. *They are gross, gross, gross.* Who would not shrink from such a mother! Who would not abhor such a wife? I really pitied the respectable elderly gentlemen whom I saw walking about with such atrocities hanging on their arms— the grim red-faced monsters! Surely, a man would be justified in murdering them—in taking a sharp knife and cutting away their mountainous flesh, until he had brought them into reasonable shape, as a sculptor seeks for the beautiful form of woman in a shapeless block of marble. . . .
>
> I really and truly believe that the entire body of American washerwomen would present more grace than the entire body of English ladies, were both to be shown up together. American women, of all ranks, when past their prime, generally look thin, worn, care-begone, as if they may have led a life of much trouble and few enjoyments; but English women look as if they had fed upon the fat of meat, and made themselves gross and earthy in all sorts of ways. *As a point of taste, I prefer my own country-women; though it is a pity that we must choose between a greasy animal and an anxious skeleton.* (88–89)

One of the many important changes in Hawthorne during his first English stay was his attitude toward social class. In nineteenth-century England the lines were firmly drawn, not only from royalty to aristocracy to wealthy, but from untitled businessmen to working middle class, to working lower class, to a jumbled assortment of the poor, who did not count. When he first came to England, Hawthorne regarded himself as citizen of a classless republic and as a political Democrat to boot, even though nineteenth-century America had its own class structure. The longer the Hawthornes stayed in England, the deeper their class consciousness became. Sophia was openly envious of the rich, but later adjusted her sights upward to jealousy of the aristocratic wealthy. Hawthorne himself was not uninfected by this attitude, although he shows regret for his snobbishness, despite a certain reveling in his distinction as an eminent foreigner—consul general of Liverpool—representative of the most powerful man in American government, President Pierce, and celebrated as one of the masters of American literature (42, 269).

At the age of fifty-one Hawthorne began a profound reassessment of his own system of values. This would have been painful enough at twenty-one, but at his age it was certain to cause a deep upheaval. Hawthorne's keen sense of privacy and his desire for seclusion were constantly violated by his being lionized by the English. In terms alarmingly Kafkaesque, he describes a London dinner in his honor:

> I grew weary of so many people, especially the ladies, who were rather superfluous in their oblations at my shrine,—quite stifling me, indeed, with the incense that they burnt under my nose. So far as I could judge, they had all been invited there to see me. It is ungracious—even hoggish— not to be gratified with the interest they expressed in me; but, then, it is really a bore, and one does not know what to do or say. I felt like a hippopotamus, or, to use a more modest illustration, like some strange bug imprisoned under a tumbler, with a dozen eyes watching whatever I did. (328)

Hawthorne's continuing dreams of failure coupled with his nightmarish sense of being imprisoned by an adoring public signal the divisions within his psyche and reveal a depth of inquietude that is evidenced throughout the European notebooks. Hawthorne noticed his Puritan conscience receding and worried; Sophia had no such qualms.

I have hinted about my suspicions concerning the "idyllic" marriage of Hawthorne and Sophia. Their happiness is expressed elaborately in letters to each other and in the *American Notebooks,* which they wrote together during their honeymoon years at the Old Manse. Julian and Rose, in their memoirs of their mother and father, speak glowingly of Sophia's devotion to her "prince" or "lord" or "king," as she refers to Hawthorne, and of Hawthorne's concern for Sophia's health and comfort. But, perversely, methinks they do protest too much. The basis of my mistrust is partly the sickeningly saccharine prototypes of Sophia in the tales and novels, those characters who dominate the male characters through passive aggression. Particularly I think of Georgianna in "The

Birthmark" who allows herself to be killed by her husband Aylmer; Beatrice of "Rappaccini's Daughter," the beautiful and poisonous girl who dies speaking the words, "was there not, from the first, more poison in thy nature than in mine?"; Phoebe, of *The House of the Seven Gables,* the little country girl who manages the lives of Clifford and Hepzibah, inherits a goodly amount of money, and converts Holgrave to a country gentleman who will depend on her for his money; Priscilla of *The Blithedale Romance* who by shrinking backwards triumphs over Zenobia, Coverdale, and Blithedale and inherits her idea of the earth in Hollingsworth; and as we shall see, Hilda, of *The Marble Faun.* In addition to these pale conquerors, of whose mastery both Hawthorne and Sophia were probably unconscious, Hawthorne's letters and notebooks after his marriage record his increasing restlessness and unease. Surely he expected, like any good inheritor of the Puritan ethos, to marry and be happy ever after, but the fairy tale of Nathaniel and Sophia was not quite so simple. Hawthorne's rigid conscience would never allow him to admit openly that his marriage to Sophia and the arrival of their three children had frustrated his passion for solitude and reclusiveness. Even if Sophia was happy, Hawthorne was still an atrabilious man, often morose, dejected, wretched, and even despairing—if always a gentleman. Sophia's patented cheerfulness, her complacency about her combination of Puritan and transcendentalist ideas, and her conviction that her husband and children were celestial beings (like herself) must have been hard for the sober Hawthorne to bear. If Hawthorne had his revenge in creating priggish, insipid, passively domineering, pale heroines, neither he nor Sophia seemed fully cognizant of it, but some passages about marriage from the *English Notebooks* are more explicit.

In April 1857 the Hawthornes visited Manchester Cathedral, where six couples were married simultaneously:

> They all seemed to be of the lower orders . . . the men in their ordinary . . . laborer's attire; the women with their poor, shabby shawls drawn closely about them . . . nothing fresh, *virginlike,* or hopeful about them; joining themselves to their mates, *with the idea of making their own misery less intolerable by adding another's to it.* . . . *I think it was the saddest thing we have seen since leaving home.* (456)

In June 1857, on the way to Dumfries, Scotland, the Hawthornes passed Gretna Green[14] and Hawthorne called it *"a spot which many people have visited to their woe"* (499). The next month in Edinburgh, Hawthorne and Sophia celebrated their fifteenth wedding anniversary in this way: "As it was our wedding-day, and as our union has turned out to the utmost satisfaction of both parties, after fifteen years trial, I gave her a golden backed and blue bodied Cairngorm beetle" (537). Although the sentiment is pretty, the present of a beetle made of "pebbles" seems less than romantic.

Sophia thought that her children were angelic, precocious, incomparably beautiful, and perfect. Hawthorne had a more earthy view of them and implied often that they were damned nuisances, since they accompanied their parents everywhere in the American, not the European, fashion. Passages inked out in the *American* and *English Notebooks* by Sophia and restored by Randall Stewart refer to some of the annoyances suffered by adults in the constant company of children. When the Hawthornes left for England in July 1853, Una was nine, Julian seven, and Rose barely two, and Hawthorne himself had just turned forty-nine, not an age which guarantees patience with three small children. Describing a visit to the Lake District in July 1855, he commented:

> I do not care about seeing anything more of the English lakes, for at least a year to come. Besides, a man with children in charge cannot enjoy traveling: he must content himself to be happy with them, for they allow him no separate and selfish possibility of being happy. Sophia, however, suffers far less from this impediment [a most Calvinist word] than I do. (184–85)

On a visit to London in September 1855, after spending a day at the zoo with the children, Hawthorne wrote: "This day has not been spent as my own taste would have inclined me; but, when a man has taken upon himself to beget children, he has no longer any right to a life of his own" (210). This certainly sounds like a bitter statement of Calvinist duty.

On first arriving in Britain, going directly to dirty, crowded, mercantile Liverpool, Hawthorne was far from impressed with England. But the longer he stayed and traveled through the English countryside, the more he was seduced by its age and loveliness—the flowers, the beautifully tended lawns, the stately manor houses. Guiltily, he found himself coming to love England and its "ruin": "Oh, that we could have ivy in America: What is there to beautify us, when our time of ruin comes" (82). In August 1856 Hawthorne and his family stayed in the Francis Bennoch home in Blackheath (then a suburb of London) and Hawthorne rejoiced in the garden and the sunshine, but still suffered a Puritan twinge of conscience: "there is a sort of weight or sting in my conscience for not spending this fine weather in making expeditions" (390). But he yielded to desire: "There never was nor can be, in *Eden* itself, more delightful weather than this, to sit still in; and I have spent these days almost wholly in the garden, sitting in the shadow of the shrubbery, and following the shade as it shifts beneath the sunshine" (390). Although he still sought shade and shadow, Hawthorne yielded to the beauty of the Eden of the Old World.

Hawthorne's first impression of Oxford was the normal one—it was a disappointing, busy, commercial, crowded town. But within a few days, overcome with its beauty and history, he revealed an unaccustomed enthusiasm: "The world surely has not another place like Oxford; it is a despair to see such a place and ever have to leave it; for it would take a lifetime, and more than one, to comprehend and enjoy it satisfactorily" (404). On visiting Blenheim Palace, near Oxford, Hawthorne was again moved to a comparison with Eden: "Really the *Garden of Eden* could not be more beautiful than this garden of Blenheim" (409). He even began to think kindly of the Liverpool fogs: "How misty is England! I have spent four years in a grey gloom. And yet it suits me pretty well" (444). After another little tour to Matlock, Hawthorne surrendered completely and remarkably to the charms of England: *"What a wonderful land! It is our forefather's land; our land; for I will not give up such a precious inheritance"* (495).

Throughout the notebooks, Hawthorne's conversational style compels the reader's attention. Intimate revelations of his state of mind and soul are interspersed with lengthy descriptive passages. Although he frequently despairs of having caught the essence of whatever he is attempting to illuminate, this is only his plaguing perfectionism, because the notebooks are a considerable work of art. His memorable perception of the Elgin marbles at the British museum—"Poor maimed veterans, in this hospital of incurables" (52)—is only one example of dozens of penetrating and trenchant insights. The notebooks have received far less attention than they deserve.

The often covert and furtive references to women's virginity and chastity found in the *American Notebooks* and the tales, sketches, and novels become almost obsessive in the European notebooks. In March 1854, Hawthorne observed apparently apropos of nothing:

A woman's chastity consists, like an onion, of a series of coats. You may strip off the outer ones without doing much mischief, perhaps none at all; but you keep taking off one after another, in expectation of coming to the inner nucleus, including the whole *value* of the matter. It proves, however, that there is no such nucleus and that chastity is diffused through the whole series of coats, is lessened with the removal of each, and vanishes with the final one, which you supposed would introduce you to the *hidden pearl.* (52)

This strangely mixed metaphor indicates the great "value" Hawthorne idealistically placed on chastity, along with the curiously bastardized American Puritanism that would deal with woman's virtue as coin and barter. England mellowed Hawthorne's harsh Calvinist judgments of fornication somewhat, but a late entry (November 1857) shows Hawthorne still in the throes of a rather debased Calvinist judgment. He speaks sadly of the bankruptcy of his friend, Bennoch, and his business partners and draws the following strange analogy with the same mix of money, shame, and virtue: "They will be like a woman who has once lost her chastity; no after life of virtue will take out the stain" (605).

We have noted many of the changes in attitude and outlook that occurred during Hawthorne's years in England, but the most significant remains to be examined fully—the gradual lessening of his ambiguous loyalty to New England Calvinist principles. No one can go to England without being overwhelmed by all of the churches: Saxon, Norman, Gothic, Neo-Gothic, Victorian. Hawthorne, who seems to have spent his Sundays in America at home, sometimes peering out the window at the people going to church[15] and never attending the meetinghouse unless it were empty, became, in England, an inveterate church visitor. True, the visits he made were mainly in the role of sightseer, but he came to be a collector of ancient churches and ruined abbeys, as well as a connoisseur of cathedrals.

Hawthorne's new interest in churches reawakened, or permitted to surface, theological questions that formerly he had treated in his creative writing by making them the problems of his invented characters. Or, as in his *American Notebooks,* he was more concerned with sin and with sinners than with personal soul-searching, although religious questions must certainly have been in his mind. During the English and Italian years Hawthorne wrote no imaginative literature in which he could involve characters with ultimate concerns, and so in the European notebooks we are for the first time given *personal* meditations on religious mysteries.

These are, it seems to me, revelations of Hawthorne's ambiguities and uncertainties about metaphysical questions, which only increased while he was abroad. It is also interesting to speculate about whether Hawthorne was aware of the dangers that his aesthetic delight in these religious ruins could pose to his insular New England Calvinism.

Certainly nineteenth-century Anglicanism did not tempt him. He went by invitation to stay at Smithell's Hall, one of the oldest residences in England, now presided over by the wealthy Ainsworths. (Here, from a legend associated with the manor, is where he got the idea for *The Ancestral Footstep*.) He commented sharply on the religious practices of the Ainsworths:

> The Englishman goes from prayer to pleasure, and is a worldly man in all respects till morning prayer-time comes about again. If an American is an infidel, he knows it; but an Englishman is often so without suspecting it—being kept from that knowledge by this formality of family prayer and his other regularities of external worship. They feel nothing, and bring themselves no nearer to God when they pray, than when they play at cards. (198)

A harsh judgment indeed from an American claiming no church affiliations but sounding like a nineteenth-century Calvin admonishing the hypocrites. A lover of ruined abbeys and cathedrals does not have to approve a religious exercise that he deems counterfeit. Of one thing we can be sure: Hawthorne's interest in the churches and religious practices of England forced him to try to come to terms with his own belief or lack of it.

During a visit to a workhouse, Hawthorne saw an infant, diseased and apparently dying. This raised for him some serious theological questions:

> In this room (which was large, containing a good many beds) there was a clear fire burning, as in all the other occupied rooms; and beside it sat a woman holding a baby, which was, beyond all comparison, the most horrible object I ever saw in my life. *It really seems to lie upon the floor of my heart, and pollute my moral being with the recollection of it.* The Governor said to me, apart, that it was the child of a diseased mother. True enough, it must have been. This wretched infant had been begotten by Sin upon Disease— diseased Sin was its father, and sinful Disease its mother—and the off-spring of their hideous embrace looked like a sucking Pestilence, which, if it could live to grow up, would make the world more accursed than ever

heretofore. . . . *Did God make this child? Has it a soul capable of immortality?—of immortal bliss? I am afraid not. At all events, it is quite beyond my conception and understanding.* (276)

Hawthorne baldly states the unadulterated Calvinist doctrine of inherited sin and guilt and the belief in infant damnation, but he does so with infinite sorrow and uncertainty. He is afraid that the child begotten by Sin upon Disease does not have a soul capable of immortal bliss, but he ends his painful questioning of God's providence with the *mystery*—"It is quite beyond my conception and understanding." Hawthorne's submerged Calvinism, which he seemed to take for granted in America, underwent, in Europe, a painful and conscious reevaluation. Everywhere he turned, he seemed to find his passive, unacknowledged, and unexamined beliefs challenged. Hawthorne became desperately weary in his seven years abroad, but the fatigue was more of a moral and spiritual nature than the physical exhaustion caused by working and interminable sight-seeing. To have to confront, between the ages of forty-nine and fifty-six, a painful and unresolved soul-searching of one's deepest being proved to be a death-dealing experience for Hawthorne.

While Sophia was in Lisbon, Hawthorne took a trip to Scotland and visited, as a good Calvinist would, the Edinburgh house of John Knox. Yet his remarks about the old churches of York were not in accord with Calvin's strictures against images or stained-glass windows:

It is a good symbol of religion; the irreligious man sees only the pitiful outside of the painted window, and judges it entirely from that view; but he who stands within the holy precincts, the religious man, is sure of the glories which he beholds. And to push the simile a little farther, it requires light from Heaven to make them visible. If the church were merely illuminated from the inside—that is, by what light a man can get from his own understanding—the picture would be invisible, or wear at best but a miserable aspect. (349)

Even in his delight with such ornamentation, Hawthorne expresses the Calvinist idea of man's illumination necessarily coming from God.

During this period in England (1856), when Hawthorne's theological dubieties were surfacing, Melville came for a visit (November 10–18, 1856), on his way to Europe and the Levant. Hawthorne is strangely unforthcoming in his comments about Melville's visit. However, when the two old friends sat down together in the sand hills for a long talk,

Melville resumed what had probably been a continuing dialogue five years before in Lennox:

> Melville, as he always does, began to reason of Providence and futurity, and of everything that lies beyond human ken, and informed me that he had "pretty much made up his mind to be annihilated"; but still he does not seem to rest in that anticipation; and I think will never rest until he gets hold of a definite belief. It is strange how he persists—and has persisted ever since I knew him, and probably long before—in wandering to-and-fro over these deserts, as dismal and monotonous as the sand hills amid which we were sitting. He can neither believe, nor be comfortable in his unbelief; and he is too honest and courageous not to try to do one or the other. If he were a religious man, he would be one of the most truly religious and reverential; he has a very high and noble nature, and better worth immortality than most of us. (433)

Even for the reclusive Hawthorne and the reserved Melville this was probably not a satisfactory meeting. The conversation on the beach appears to be the most intimate of the visit. Hawthorne's response to Melville's metaphysical questioning of "Providence and futurity and of everything that lies beyond human ken" is strangely embarrassed yet sympathetic. The notebooks indicate that Hawthorne was asking similar questions and the talk may have touched on some sore places in Hawthorne's own psyche. Hawthorne believed in something; Melville did not, although he was not comfortable in his unbelief. Hawthorne, rather abashed at his failure to get Melville any position in the consular service, empathized completely with Melville's need to "take an airing through the world, after so many years of toilsome pen-labor and domestic life" (432), and there seems to be, if anything, a slight envy on Hawthorne's part as Melville went off with only a carpetbag to travel the world. Hawthorne, married to his consular duties, his wife and children, and his Calvinist sense of duty, was restless and equivocal about his beliefs and he may have been happy to see the last of a friend who could so roil his already present doubts of Providence and immortality. Hawthorne's reading of Melville's mind was keen, for when Melville reached Palestine, he recorded in his journal: "Ride over mouldy plain to Dead Sea . . . foam on beach & pebbles like slaver of mad dog—smarting bitter of the water,—carried the bitter in my mouth all day—bitterness of life— thought of all bitter things—Bitter is it to be poor & bitter, to be reviled,

& Oh bitter are these waters of Death, thought I." On seeing Jerusalem, Melville wrote: "Is the desolation of the land the result of the fatal embrace of the Deity? Hapless are the favorites of heaven."[16] Both great writers finally subsided into weariness and despair—the two American Titans who were wont, according to Melville, to say "No! in thunder."[17]

Hawthorne's Puritan contempt of elaborate ritual became almost violent in his reaction to the Easter Day services at the Cathedral of York. The cathedral inspired him to great praise, but not the ceremonies:

> *The spirit of my Puritan ancestors was mighty in me, and I did not wonder at their being out of patience with all this mummery, which seemed to me worse than papistry because it was a corruption of it. . . . The Puritans showed their strength of mind and heart, by preferring a sermon of an hour and a half long, into which the preacher put his whole soul and spirit, and lopping away all these externals, into which religious life had first gushed and flowered, and then petrified.* (451)

Nothing could be more Calvinist than Hawthorne's response to this Easter service—the "mummery," the cold, dry sermon, the distraction of the magnificent cathedral from the sermon "which, to be anything must be all" (451)—the strictly Orthodox Calvinist view of the importance of preaching the Word. Later in the day, Hawthorne recorded some regrets for his morning outrage and blamed, indirectly, the Puritan emphasis on the sermon for his vehement attack, leaving the reader with an acute sense of Hawthorne's own ambiguity regarding his belief:

> This morning, while listening to the tedious chanting and lukewarm sermon, I depreciated the whole affair, Cathedral and all; but now I do more justice at least to the latter. . . . But, after all, it was the Puritans who make the sermon of such importance, in religious worship, as we New Englanders now consider it; and we are absurd in considering this magnificent church and those embroidered ceremonies only in reference to it. (453)

Throughout the notebooks, we see that, as Hawthorne became more enamored of old churches, ruined abbeys, and cathedrals, he also became more hostile towards Cromwell (whose life he read in 1827),[18] the great Puritan hero, and to the Henry Tudor Reformation zealots for the depredations and obscenities they committed on these religious edifices. In May 1857 the Hawthornes visited Lincoln, and Hawthorne went at once to the cathedral. He was again frustrated that he could not adequately describe its beauties. He was, however, sharp in his criticism of the damage done to the cathedral: "The Cathedral is not rich in monuments; for it suffered great outrages and dilapidation both at the Reformation and in Cromwell's time. The soldiers of the latter stabled their steeds in the nave, and hacked and hewed the monkish sculptures at their wicked pleasure" (469). Hawthorne's toughness, which emerges often through the politeness of his writing, is especially evident when he describes the castle of Lincoln and its keep, wherein were buried the bodies of executed criminals who had been hanged on its summit: "There could not be a better position to publish the deed of retribution, both to earth and Heaven" (470). Cromwell himself, just taken to task by Hawthorne for his destructiveness, could not have uttered a harsher Puritan judgment.

At Peterborough Cathedral, Hawthorne again bemoaned the destruction by Cromwell's soldiers, and marveled that, unlike the French, the English did not lose their religion with the shattering of the externals:

> All the carved wood-work . . . is modern. . . . This Cathedral seems to have suffered terribly from Cromwell's soldiers, who hacked and hewed at the old oak, and hammered and pounded upon the marble tombs, till nothing of the first, and very few of the latter, remain. It is wonderful how suddenly the English people lost their sense of the sanctity of all manner of externals in religion, without losing their religion too. The French, in their Revolution, underwent as sudden a change; but they became pagans and atheists, and threw away the substance with the shadow. (481)

During the last few months (May 1857–January 1858) of Hawthorne's first stay in England, he became more and more outraged at the damage wrought by his Puritan ancestors on the churches, abbeys, and cathedrals, particularly those in Scotland. At Peterborough Cathedral he remembered "a recumbent figure of a prelate, whose face had been quite obliterated by *puritanic violence*" (482), and in Edinburgh he refused to describe St. Giles's Cathedral, "it having been *kirkified* into three interior divisions by the Covenanters" (536).

We learn through the *English Notebooks* that after four and a half years in England, Hawthorne had undergone many changes. From a man who was defensively American and who compared every sight, activity, and person in England disparagingly with American sights, activities, and persons, Hawthorne became a man in love with the English countryside, the ruins, the abbeys, the old churches, and cathedrals. He even suffered some embarrassment over American tourists. He made a valiant effort to

understand art—painting and sculpture—and considered this development of taste a duty, unpleasant but necessary. His emotions, which he
had always felt he understood and kept under control, became unpredict-
able and unsettling. Most importantly, his submerged and unanalyzed
Calvinism became progressively less rigorous, undermining his sympathy
for his youthful heroes, John Knox and Oliver Cromwell. Melville's visit
and the stirring up of questions of Providence and immortality which
Hawthorne had always tried to avoid, coupled with his unease about
Puritanism, Anglicanism, and "Popery," left him disturbed and unsettled
in his mind, heart, and spirit. This inner chaos would not leave him nor
could he bury the enigmas, as he seems to have done in America, in his
stories. He found it difficult to understand why he was so attracted to old
churches and cathedrals, but he had no doubts about their poetic beauty.
He found everywhere examples of the depravity of man, especially in the
workhouses and in the children born of sin, but he also found some
kindness in human beings, and pleasures both in the beauties of nature
and in England's great historical endowments.

Hawthorne's haunted mind, filled with thoughts of death and the
grave, did not abate its intensity during his English years and he examined every graveyard he came to, as if he might be able to probe life's
mystery in it. Hawthorne, the unaccommodated man, continued to wres-
tle with the mysteries of life and death; but like Prufrock, he did not ask
aloud, "What is it?" He merely went and made his visit.

THE FRENCH AND ITALIAN NOTEBOOKS
1858–1860

# "This Remorseless Gray, With Its Icy Heart"

---

On a note of weary, exhausted questioning of the reason for existence, Hawthorne prepared to leave England for France and Italy, where he hoped to shake himself out of this enervation. For a record of this two and a half years from January 1858 to May 1860, we now have the restored text of the notebooks (*Centenary Edition,* Vol. XIV, 1980) instead of the bowdlerized version that Sophia edited—she omitted some of the most interesting passages and changed what remained to suit her idealized picture of Hawthorne, substituting inoffensive words for Hawthorne's truth.[1]

The Hawthornes left London in a deep January chill and arrived in France to find it even colder. They broke their rail journey to Paris by stopping overnight at Amiens. Despite the cold the family went out the next morning to see the cathedral. Hawthorne says: "My impression of France will always be, that it is an Arctic region"(6). The love of cathedrals and churches that Hawthorne felt in England underwent a change the moment he arrived in the traditionally Roman Catholic countries of France and Italy. His submerged Calvinism, which had been tempered in the English years but had never been really threatened by the low-church Anglicans who surrounded him there, returned in force when he lighted on the "foreign" shores of France and Italy. Here he did not understand the language and was affronted by the "popery," which Europeans accepted so casually that it reawakened all of his Puritan suspicions of "the whore of Babylon," the true "Anti-Christ."[2] While Hawthorne admired the loftiness of Amiens Cathedral, he was bitterly sarcastic about its good repair:

> I did not see a mutilated shrine, or even a broken-nosed image, in the whole cathedral. But probably the very rage of the English fanatics against idolatrous tokens, and their smashing blows at them, was a symptom of sincerer religious faith than the French were capable of. These last did not

care enough about their Saviour to beat down his crucified image; and they preserved the works of sacred art for the sake only of what beauty there was in them. (10)

Only an uneasy Calvinist would speak so ironically of Catholic worship and of the emptiness of beauty and ornament for its own sake. Hawthorne's reawakened Calvinism extended even to the food eaten the night they arrived half-frozen at their hotel in Paris:

All the dishes were very delicate, and a vast change from the simple English system, with its joints, shoulders, beef-steakes [*sic*], and chops; but I doubt whether English cookery, for the very reason that it is so gross, is not better for man's moral and spiritual nature, than French. In the former case, you know that you are gratifying your coarsest animal needs and propensities, and are duly ashamed of it; but in dealing with these French delicacies, you delude yourself into the idea that you are cultivating your taste while filling your belly. (11)

Hawthorne's hackles were also raised by the pomp and drama of a Catholic funeral that he observed clinically, and he spoke condescendingly of the demise of the church. Not since his 1853 arrival in England had he assumed so thoroughly the role of cold observer and voyeur.

The visit to France and the decision to spend a year in Italy was more Sophia's idea than Hawthorne's, but he had no desire to return to America, either, and it was assumed from the beginning of their European expedition that Rome, for which Sophia yearned, was to be the final cultural glory visited.

France was disappointing for Hawthorne, but Italy seemed better until the family reached Rome. They took a steamer from Marseilles to Genoa and although Hawthorne was not impressed with the city, he found the churches beautiful beyond description. From the Civita Vecchia Hawthorne made arrangements to be driven to Rome in a four-horse carriage. He felt cheated because one of the horses gave out en route and the coach went slowly at night along a road rumored to be the favorite target of the banditti. When they finally reached Rome: "I perpetrated unheard of briberies on the Custom House officers at the gates, and was permitted to pass through and established myself at Spillman's Hotel—where we were half-frozen, and have been so ever since. And this is sunny Italy, and genial Rome!" (52).

Hawthorne's response to Rome was as complex as the man himself. It would be fairly simple if we could say that, at the beginning of the Italian visit, January 20, 1858, Hawthorne despised Rome, gradually lost his antipathy to it, and by the time he left, May 25, 1859, had become fond of it. But this would be far from the truth. During the year and a half that Hawthorne was in Italy, he vacillated between complete disgust and disaffection and a fondness that he finally defined as love, but this love-hate relationship did not develop chronologically. It seems judicious, however, to view Hawthorne's contradictory reactions to Italy in historical sequence and then see what we can make of them.

The first two weeks of the Roman stay were miserable—cold and icy—and Hawthorne compared the Roman ruins unfavorably with the English "gray and ivy-hung antiquity" (58). Also, he was horrified by Rome's filth; delicate always, he confessed: "I hardly know how to express it" (87), but he little expected to find the "gold mines" of Brook Farm in the Roman streets. He tried to find a reason for this state of affairs:

> Perhaps there is something in the mind of the people of these countries that enables them quite to dissever small ugliness from great sublimity and beauty. They spit upon the glorious pavement of St. Peter's and wherever else they like; they place mean-looking wooden confessionals beneath its sublime arches, and ornament them with cheap little colored prints of the crucifixion; they hang tin hearts and other tinsel and trumpery at the gorgeous shrines of the saints. . . . It must be that their sense of the beautiful is stronger than in the Anglo-Saxon mind. (88)

Hawthorne revealed himself curiously concerned with the human detritus of Rome in a passage that Sophia edited severely:

> We entered beneath the colonade of St. Peter's, and immediately became sensible of the evil smell—*the bad odour of our fallen nature*—which there is no escaping in any nook of Rome, or wherever a column, or a wall of a temple, or any sort of a corner, offers its temptation to the necessitous man. Under the Arch of Janus Quadrifons, as I remember, we saw a whole hecatomb of oblation. (135–36)

Soon Hawthorne began to wonder if there were not a curse on Rome. As he wandered through the grounds of the Villa Ludovisi, he suspected "that the Roman atmosphere is never wholesome, always more or less *poisonous*" (148). By the next year he was convinced of Rome's poison during Una's near fatal fever.

Toward the end of May 1858 the Hawthornes decided to leave Rome and go north to Florence for the summer to enjoy the treasures there and escape the malevolent Roman air. Hawthorne was perturbed that after four months Una spoke regretfully of leaving Rome and of her love for it:

> We shall have done the child no good office [Una is fourteen] in bringing her here, if the rest of her life is to be dreams of this "city of the soul," and an unsatisfied yearning to come back. On the other hand, nothing elevating and refining can be really injurious, and so I hope she will always be the better for Rome, even if her life should be spent where there are no pictures, no statues, nothing but the dryness and meagreness of a New England village. (230)

Hawthorne's response to Una's "fervor" is almost prophetic, for Una returned to Europe (1868) with the family four years after Hawthorne's death and died in England in 1877 in an Anglican convent.

When Hawthorne left Rome for Florence, he meditated on his paradoxical response to it:

> On the whole, I was not sorry to see the Gauls still pouring into Rome; but after all, I begin to find that I have a strange affection for Rome. . . . *It is very singular, the sad embrace with which Rome takes possession of the soul.* . . . It may be because the intellect finds a home there, more than in any other spot in the world, and wins the heart to stay with it, in spite of a good many things strewn all about to disgust us. (232–33)

On their return to Rome from Florence, Hawthorne found himself anticipating the journey with ironic pleasure:

> It was a most delightful morning, a genial atmosphere, the more so, I suppose, because this was the Campagna, the region of pestilence and death. I had a quiet, gentle, comfortable pleasure, as if after many wanderings, I was drawing near home; for, now that I have known it once, Rome certainly does draw into itself my heart, as I think even London, or even little Concord itself, or old sleepy Salem, never did and never will. (488)

Hawthorne's parting from Rome shows his ambivalence to it as clearly as his arrival. Early in the morning of their departure from Rome (May 25, 1859), Hawthorne took a farewell look at the Pincian, the Borghese gardens, and St. Peter's:

I looked at everything as if for the last time; nor do I wish ever to see any of these objects again, though no place ever took so strong a hold of my being, as Rome, nor ever seemed so close to me and so strangely familiar. I seem to know it better than my birthplace, and to have known it longer; and though I have been very miserable there, and languid with the effects of the atmosphere, and disgusted with a thousand things in daily life, still I cannot say I hate it—perhaps might fairly own a love for it. But (life being too short for such questionable and troublesome enjoyments) I desire never to set eyes on it again. (524)

Hawthorne could draw no moral from his months in Rome—all remained ambiguous. Certainly, while in Italy the Hawthornes did not associate with Italians to any extent but confined their considerable social activities to their friends in the American colony and to English friends and acquaintances.

Hawthorne continued to suffer from a sense of rootlessness and deprivation. In Italy, he was a man without a country even more than in England, which he came to think of as his "old home." During the stay in Florence, Hawthorne visited the studio of the American sculptor, Hiram Powers. He recognized in Powers what he felt in himself: with "his idea of moral deterioration in America [the corruption of the American Dream], I think it doubtful whether he ever crosses the sea again. Like most twenty-year exiles, he has lost his native country without finding another" (280). Hawthorne was constantly torn over what he imagined as dutiful loyalty to one's own country, not having a country at all, or adopting another country. He seemed to realize that he did not want to go back to America, but his Calvinist conscience could not approve of the "disloyalty" of outright expatriation, especially to a papist country. Shortly before leaving Florence for Rome he and Una went again to the Uffizzi gallery which he preferred to the Pitti Palace: "The splendor of the gilded and frescoed saloons is perhaps another bore; but, after all, my memory will often tread them as long as I live. *What shall we do in America!*" (428). What, indeed? In the few letters written from England before Hawthorne's return to America, he seems to have unconsciously willed his own death. Writing to his publisher, James T. Fields (September 3, 1858) about his feelings on returning to America, Hawthorne commented: "After so long an absence (more than five years already,) which will be six before you see me at the old 'Corner,' it is not altogether delightful to think of returning. Everybody will be changed, and I myself, no doubt, as much as anybody"

(OSU). As Hawthorne remarked in the *English Notebooks,* he would have thought better of himself had he been homesick. Siena, a lovely hill town preserving much of its medieval pageantry and the birthplace of Saint Catherine who in the fourteenth century brought the pope back from Avignon, appealed to him, but he despaired of roots anywhere:

> It is a fine old town, with every promise of health and vigor in its atmosphere; and really, if I could take root anywhere, I know not but it could as well be here as in another place. It would only be a kind of despair, however, that would ever make me dream of finding a home in Italy; a sense that I had lost my country through absence or incongruity, and that earth, at any rate, is not an abiding-place. (463)

Again and again in letters to Fields and William Ticknor, Hawthorne was critical of America and extremely fearful of returning. This to Fields, February 3, 1859:

> I shall come home, I fear, with a heavy heart; not expecting to be very well contented there; for I quite agree with you (at least, I suspect these to be your opinions) that America is a country to boast of, and to get out of, and keep away from, and that England is the only country to live in. If I were but a hundred times richer than I am, how very comfortable I could be! (OSU)

And to Ticknor, from Rome, May 23, 1858: "I shall be delighted to see you all again; but I will fairly own that it is not altogether agreeable to think of coming back, after so long an absence as mine. I am afraid I have lost my country by staying away too long" (OSU). Hawthorne did not solve his problems of homelessness, lack of roots, antipathy towards going home to America, a land he no longer considered his home. Instead, he postponed facing them. His decision to stay another year in England and finish *The Marble Faun* seemed a practical idea since the romance could be published simultaneously in England and America and he would reap financial benefits from two editions. But after the publication of that book there seemed no further excuse to avoid what he considered a "duty" to his children—to give them back their country.

After many months in Rome and Florence, Hawthorne lost his initial hostility to icy Italy and was able to enjoy its natural beauty. He walked with delight through all of the gardens, and he believed Florence to be unlike any other place in the world for there "life is more *delicious* for its own simple sake" (285). Yet Hawthorne continued to look for moral lessons in the beauty that surrounded him and refused to revel with any kind of real abandon.

Hawthorne's preoccupation with virginity, which we noticed in the earlier tales, continues in the notebooks. The fact that Hawthorne is obsessed with virginity does *not* mean that he approves of it; like any good Calvinist, he perfectly agrees with Sophia that nuns and monks lead abnormal lives, but his curiosity about virginity never flags. In Rome they visited Miss Bremer, a foreign lady whom they knew in America. Hawthorne commented: "There is a very pleasant atmosphere of old-maidishness about her; we are sensible of a freshness and smell of the morning, still, in this little withered rose,—its recompense for never having been worn in anybody's bosom, but only smelt at on the stem" (255). Again on the *Venus di Medici* in the Uffizzi: "I am glad to have seen this Venus, and to have found her so tender and *so chaste*. On the wall of the room and to be taken in at the same glance, is a painted *Venus* by Titian, reclining on a couch, *naked and lustful*" (298–99). Then there is the "holiest" of Raphael's Madonnas in the Pitti: "she hangs her eyelids before her like a veil, as it were, and has a primness *of eternal virginity about the mouth*" (377). Hawthorne's fascination with virginity reached its zenith in *The Marble Faun* with the Dove Hilda, who, like Raphael's Madonna, has a primness about her which seriously compromises the reader's sympathy for her.

Until Italy, there was no clear-cut heresy from Calvinism, despite Hawthorne's openness to churches and cathedrals in England, his fury at the Covenanters for destroying the beauty of the great, opulent houses of worship, and his restraint in dealing with Una's infatuation with Anglicanism. His conscience had been easier in England, but now he began to speak of Purgatory as if he believed in it. The admixture of Calvinist and Catholic terminology in the *Italian Notebooks* shows a mind disturbed, at the very least, and certainly confused. In one entry, for example, he calls monks "reprobates," a solid Calvinist judgment, and yet he casually mentions Purgatory, which is unorthodox. The *Italian Notebooks* persuade us that Hawthorne's tacit Calvinism has undergone a vast eruption in his five years abroad and prepare us for the doctrinal confusion of *The Marble Faun,* which he was sketching out at the time. Much as Hawthorne protested that he was not concerned about dogmatic religion, he was unknowingly knee-deep in some muddied sectarian waters.

Whatever heterodoxies Hawthorne may have unwittingly acquired, his pursuit of an understanding of art had all of the earnestness, dogged-ness, dutifulness, and grim determination of a good seventeenth-century Calvinist going about a prescribed but most unpleasant task. Of course, no good seventeenth-century Calvinist would be studying graven images and pictures in Rome,[3] the seat of "the whore of Babylon," but Haw-thorne, a faint nineteenth-century Calvinist, growing fainter the longer he stayed in Europe, did just that, all because he felt that he had to make himself a man of culture and taste. There are innumerable passages in the *French and Italian Notebooks* concerning Hawthorne's wrestling with the endless galleries in Rome and Florence. He was increasingly interested in art; he gradually acquired a measure of discrimination and taste beyond the provincialism that Henry James condescendingly allowed him. He also suffered great weariness because of his compulsive wandering through endless aisles of pictures and sculpture.

It has become a critical cliché (since James) to describe Hawthorne as a rather pitiful, benighted New Englander—a kind of innocent abroad—expressing naïve and simplistic ideas about art and complaining about the prevalent nudity of the statuary. This seems to me to be the most arrant and patronizing snobbery. I am not going to try to make a case for Hawthorne as a Ruskin, Pater, or Berenson; however, he was an earnest, questioning, and avid viewer. Although his natural and intuitive tastes, instructed by hours and days of empathetic viewing and studying, did not turn him into a sophisticated art critic, he did become knowledgeable about and familiar with many great works of art and his appreciation of them was deep, if limited. No one knew his limitations more thoroughly than Hawthorne himself, and if he often became fatigued and sated, he was perhaps more honest in admitting it than average people, who assume a virtue though they have it not.

In his pursuit of culture, Hawthorne did not indulge in rapturous "O Altitudos," as did Sophia, but he had his favorites. Guido's *Beatrice Cenci* moved him beyond words and he despaired of describing her although he visited and revisited the picture. He speaks of the depression that accompanies hours of gallery grinding: "It depresses the spirits to go from picture to picture, leaving a portion of your vital sympathy at every one, so that you come with a kind of half-torpid desperation, to the end" (115). Many patrons of the arts might admit that they had sore feet after a day in the galleries, but few would be able to say with Hawthorne that they had expended a portion of their vital sympathy on each picture.

The *Laocoön* filled Hawthorne with a kind of terror: "There was such a type of human beings struggling with an inextricable trouble, and entangled in a complication which they can never free themselves from by their own efforts, and out of which Heaven will not help them" (138). In addition to being a startling description of that intricate piece of sculpture, this passage provides a remarkable précis of Hawthorne's best tales and novels and it adumbrates the intricacies of *The Marble Faun.*

Hawthorne's Puritanism underwent another jolt when he found himself admiring Veronese's *Rape of Europa:*

> It must have been, in its day, the most brilliant and rejoicing picture, the most voluptuous, the most exuberant, that ever put sunshine to shame. The bull has all Jupiter in him, so tender and gentle, yet so hot and passionate with desire that you feel it indecorous to look at him [nevertheless Hawthorne looks hard]; and Europa, under her thick, rich stuffs and embroideries, is as much a woman as if she were naked. (178)

Thank Heaven Hawthorne sometimes enjoyed himself.

But such enjoyment was short-lived. Titian's *Magdalene* reawakened all his Calvinist rigor:

> The golden hair, indeed, seemed to throw out a glory of its own. This Magdalene is very coarse and sensual, with only an impudent assumption of penitence and religious sentiment. . . . She a penitent! She would shake off all pretence to it, as easily as she would shake aside that clustering hair and offer her nude front to the next comer. Titian must have been a very good-for-nothing old man. (334)

Although Sophia severely edited this comment, it does reveal that Hawthorne was experiencing his customary ambivalence. The *Magdalene* was splendid but unregenerate and Titian was a dirty old man.

The seeds of *The Marble Faun* are scattered throughout the *Italian Notebooks;* here one can trace the gradual evolution of the romance.[4] Hawthorne wrote very little in his notebooks after he and his family moved from the heart of Florence to an enormous suburban villa, which they rented from the impoverished Count Montauto. The extensive quarters and grounds of the run-down house pleased Hawthorne, especially the tower, which became the tower of Donatello in *The Marble Faun.* After a month (September 1, 1858) in these dusty but spacious quarters, Hawthorne recorded: "Few things journalizable have happened during the past month, because Florence and the neighborhood have lost their novelty;

and furthermore, I usually spend the whole day at home, having been engaged in planning and sketching out a Romance" (396).

One of the most significant changes in Hawthorne's attitudes toward Italy, reflected in the notebooks and later in *The Marble Faun*, was his response to the carnival, the eight-day celebration which precedes Ash Wednesday and the penitential season of Lent. Just about three weeks after the Hawthornes' arrival in Rome, on January 20, 1858, the carnival began. Hawthorne was still chilled to the bone, weary from the journey, suffering from a cold, and trying to see all of the sights of Rome at once. His Puritan sensibilities, awakened again by Catholic France and Italy, disposed him to disapprove of the carnival. His descriptions of the first festival were desultory and he ignored it as much as he could while he tore about viewing the compulsory sights of Rome. He described some of the frisking of the carnival: "The sky being blue and the sun bright, the scene was much gayer and brisker than I had before found it, and I can conceive of its being rather agreeable than otherwise, up to the age of twenty" (83).

The next year Hawthorne enjoyed the carnival; he actually reveled in it and devoted six pages of the notebooks to its description:

> As we threaded our way through the Corso, Una kept wishing that she were a boy, and could plunge into the fun and uproar as Julian would; and for my own part, (though I pretended to take no interest in the matter), I could have bandied confetti and nosegays as readily and as riotously as any urchin there. (497)

> But the spectacle is strangely like a dream, in respect to the difficulty of retaining it in the mind and solidifying it into a description. I enjoyed it a good deal, and assisted in so far as to pelt all the people in cylinder hats with handsful of confetti. (501)

> The pervading noise, and uproar of human voices, is one of the most effective points of the matter; but, in fine, the scene is quite indescribable, and its effect not to be conceived, without both witnessing and taking part in it. If you merely look at it, it depresses you; if you take even the slightest share in it, you become aware that it has a fascination, and you no longer wonder, at last, that the young people take such delight in plunging into this mad river of fun, that goes roaring through the heart of solemn old Rome between the narrow limits of the Corso. (503–04)

> All last night, . . . there was a noise of song and late revellers, in the streets; but to-day, we have waked up in the sad and sober season of Lent. (505)

The change in Hawthorne is profound. From a prim Calvinist onlooker, filled with disapproval of the gamboling, rollicking crowd in 1858, Hawthorne, in 1859, has become a delighted participant in the revelry.

Hawthorne's religious and emotional sentiments, tacit and virtually unchallenged in Concord where a latter-day, unacknowledged Calvinist was no special phenomenon, were constantly undergoing assaults and subtle attacks in Europe that were often not overt but furtive. In England, the very countryside was a seduction to a New Englander who prided himself on enduring and surviving bitterly cold and bleak winters and summers in which the sun burned viciously over the parched land. England was green all the time and Hawthorne marveled over its winter greenness, even in the midst of chilly rain and occasional fleeting snow. He rejoiced in the large hearths and the huge, cheerful fires, seemed to thrive on the dampness, and took a deep, sensual pleasure in the mild, sunny days.

But it was not the milder climate alone that undermined Hawthorne's patriotic attachments to America. Most of the English people that Hawthorne encountered were pleasant, admiring of him, hospitable, and unselfconsciously beef-and-aley. When his first defensiveness about America began to fade, because it was so seldom required, he grew more comfortable, and the more he saw of England and the English the better he felt. After several years, he found himself being taken for an Englishman by strangers; rather than resenting this, it seemed to give him covert pleasure. He fell in love with little churches—he who never went into a meetinghouse at home—and became so enamored of the great majestic cathedrals that he began to resent more and more the depredations of the Reformers and Covenanters. He had a strange but overwhelming sense of having come back to his "old home."

All these attractions were great temptations to the thrifty Yankee Calvinist, who arrived in England prepared to despise a country that his ancestors had left in courage and obduracy for the right to worship freely and against which they had fought a bloody and costly revolutionary war. Hawthorne's roots in America were deep on both sides of his family. From his long years in Salem, the stern, inflexible image of his earliest ancestors—the one famed for his persecution of the Quakers and his son, the witchcraft trial magistrate—haunted Hawthorne. He felt their disapproval of him, the "topmost bough" of the family tree, an idler who wrote story books.[5] But because England was now offering him respect, dignity, prestige, and comforts, Hawthorne's defenses against the enemy country were slowly transformed into love and warmth. Beneath his dignified exterior as the American consul general at Liverpool, there were seething, complex, and antipathetic emotions of love and hate, restlessness and quiet, Calvinism and the special English brand of worship—required by custom but ignored in its specific precepts by the general public. For Hawthorne, *going abroad* had its own special significance; there was a broadening of interests beyond the provincial New England preoccupation with pseudo-intellectual ideas of success and progress, of which he had never approved. The leisurely European acceptance of the present, dictated by centuries of tradition, protocol, and sophisticated unconcern with "new truths," simultaneously calmed and disturbed Hawthorne. In Europe, life went on comfortably in the midst of wars and disaffections; activism and reform were only discussed after long, hearty, soothing dinners in a wreath of cigar smoke, among odors of brandy and aged port. For Hawthorne, who had eaten his meals from a tray placed outside his room during his years of solitude in Salem; who had tried to live "off the land" at Brook Farm; who had spent over three years munching apples and rice, often prepared by his own hand, at the Old Manse; and who had fared little better in Salem, Lenox, or at the Wayside before going to England—for this man the bountiful tables of the English inspired such reverence that he often copied full menus into the *English Notebooks*.

But France and Italy, openly Catholic, roused Hawthorne's newly mellowed Calvinism, for he was repelled by what he considered ostentatious liturgy and evil, rapacious clerics. All of Hawthorne's most powerful defenses against and suspicions about the unfamiliar and the foreign surfaced when he arrived on the Continent. Again, as on his arrival in England, his repressed emotions were in a state of confusion. Gradually, as the January cold was replaced by some February sunshine, he learned his way about Rome and his spirits began to rise. But the emotional upheavals in his breast never ceased during the sixteen-month residence in Italy. Consequently, the *Italian Notebooks* reveal many intimate feelings which Hawthorne had kept so carefully hidden in America.

In Florence, where Hawthorne sketched out *The Marble Faun,* he complained of lack of privacy and the constant movement of his family entourage:

The atmosphere, or something else, causes a sort of alacrity in my mind and an affluence of ideas, such as they are; but it does not thereby make me the happier. I feel an impulse to be at work, but am kept idle by the sense of being unsettled, with removals to be gone through, over and over again, before I can shut myself into a quiet room of my own, and turn the key. I need monotony, too—an eventless exterior life—before I can live in the world within. (316)

But monotony and quiet seclusion were never to be Hawthorne's lot, and in Rome he endured visits with American and English friends and the endless sight-seeing that Sophia orchestrated.

In complaining of the size of the mosquitoes in Florence, Hawthorne sounds a bit like John Donne in "The Flea," but, of course, Hawthorne is not writing a seduction poem:

They are bigger than American musquitoes [*sic*], and, if you crush them, after one of their feasts, it makes a terrific blood-spot. It is a sort of suicide—at least, a shedding of one's own blood—to kill them; but it gratifies the old Adam to do it. It shocks me to feel how revengeful I am; but it is impossible not to impute a certain malice and intellectual venom to these diabolical insects. (427)

Hawthorne's shock over his own natural response to the mosquitoes reveals an acute moral awareness of the smallest act he performs, the effect of his still-active Calvinist conscience.

The distinction Hawthorne makes between American and Italian curiosity is provocative, as we are always conscious of Hawthorne's own voyeurism, which is now elevated to the highest degree in his observations and sight-seeing: "Indeed, I never saw an idle curiosity exercised in such a pleasant way, as by the country-people of Italy. It almost deserves to be called a kindly interest and sympathy, instead of a hard and cold curiosity, like that of our own people; and it is displayed with such simplicity that it is evident no offense is intended" (477).

Perhaps the description most revealing of Hawthorne's see-saw emotional state is that of the frescoes in the Church of Santa Croce in Florence. He perhaps has not come as far as the skeptical Melville, who in *Moby-Dick* pictured the tail of the whale to suggest that good and evil differ only in the mind of the beholder,[6] but Hawthorne's comments display an uneasy emotional and moral state that borders on despair:

In several of the chapels, moreover, there were some of those horrible frescoes by Giotto, Cimabue or their compeers, which whenever I see—poor, faded relics, looking as if the Devil had been rubbing and scrubbing them for centuries, in spite against the Saints—my heart sinks and my stomach sickens. There is no other despondency in the world like this; it is a new shade of human misery, akin to the physical disease that comes from dry-rot in a wall. These frescoes are to a church what dreary, old remembrances are to a mind, the drearier because they were once bright; Hope fading into Disappointment, Joy into Grief, and festal splendor passing into funereal duskiness, and saddening you all the more by the grim identity that you find to exist between gay things and sorrowful ones. *Only wait long enough, and they turn out to be the very same.* (344–45)

Hawthorne's months in Italy, far from calming his mind and heart, had the opposite effect. He was constantly challenged in his deepest self regarding his unexamined beliefs and he was not disposed or prepared to come up with any answers. He was alternately confused and despairing, carefree and hopeful; *The Marble Faun* is an index of his emotional and moral confusion at this time and he did not try to resolve this interior chaos but wished only to escape in expatriation and death.

In this chapter, I have tried to appraise amidst all of his descriptions of place, some substantial changes in Hawthorne. I have noted how Hawthorne's ambivalence about Italy differed from his response to England because Italy was more challenging to his Calvinism; his growing sense of homelessness and yet his reluctance to return to America; his continuing pleasure in the beauty of women, especially in the unthreatening statues; his delight in the mild and benign beauties of nature; his continuing obsession with virginity paradoxically linked with a horrified response to the celibacy required of the Catholic clergy; his earnest and tireless attempts to cultivate taste in art; the evolving ideas and impressions, which he later used in *The Marble Faun;* and his struggles with his own ill-defined emotions and amorphous beliefs that were constantly exacerbated by the easy-going morality of the Italians.

It is time now to examine the most important change in Hawthorne—his response to the Catholicism which surrounded him in Italy. Hawthorne had no intimate knowledge of Italians—he had no Italian friends and continued to surround himself with Americans and Englishmen—but was engulfed by the climate of Catholicism in Italy, its exterior forms in the churches, cathedrals, art, and artifacts, and its practitioners, the populace and the clergy. Finally, his constant pre-occupation with death became most acute in the Eternal City—the city of the soul, as Hawthorne (echoing Byron) called it.

As in studying other important selections from the notebooks, the following will be considered chronologically; what is particularly impor-tant about this approach is that it best reveals the *constant ambivalence* in Hawthorne. In the *Italian Notebooks* there is no fairly continuous progres-sion (as in the *English Notebooks*) to a differing point of view toward religion and its adherents. One day Hawthorne saw much to be admired in Catholicism; the next day he was revolted and all of his hidden Calvin-ism surfaced as disgust. This ambivalence is impressive and important.

In the bitter chill of January 1858, the Hawthornes stopped at Genoa on their way to Rome and Hawthorne was almost as rapturous as Sophia at his first sight of Italian churches and the Cathedral of San Lorenzo:

> However, this church was dazzled out of sight by the Cathedral . . . the exterior front of which is covered with alternate slabs of black and white marble, which were brought, either in whole or in part, from Jerusalem. Within, there was an immense richness of precious marbles. . . . I used to try to imagine how splendidly the English Cathedrals must have looked in their primeval glory, before the Reformation, and before the whitewash of Cromwell's time had overlaid their marble pillars; but I never imagined anything at all approaching what my eyes now beheld. . . . At any rate, nobody who has not seen a church like this [probably San Matteo] . . . can imagine what a splendid religion it was that reared it. (47–49)

Hawthorne's early ardors were not evoked by all of the churches of Italy, but in February he was still overwhelmed—now by the Pantheon—and he made a remarkable statement for a New England Puritan: "It is my opinion that a great deal of devout and reverential feeling is kept alive in people's hearts by the Catholic mode of worship" (98). Walking through the streets of Rome on a Sunday, he observed the crowds and reflected: "In however adulterated a guise, the Catholics do get a draught of devotion to slake the thirst of their souls, and methinks it must needs do them good, even if not quite so pure as if it came from better cisterns, or from the original fountain-head" (99). Cloudy and muddied as the cistern may be—and this is certainly the reaction of a Puritan—Hawthorne suspects some good is done by the draught. In becoming physically acclimated to Rome, Hawthorne is also adjusting himself spiritually for his dalliance with the *felix culpa* and the possibility of good coming out of evil.

Hawthorne visited the dungeon where Saints Peter and Paul were confined and drank from a supposedly miraculous spring which Saint Peter had opened and in which he baptized his jailer. Hawthorne found the water hard "and almost brackish, while my wife thought it the sweetest she had tasted in Rome. I suspect Saint Peter still dabbles in this water, and tempers its qualities according to the faith of those who drink it" (105). Some of the initial awe of Rome has left Hawthorne and he is able to be ironic about the brackish water tempered to the faith of the drinker. This is more the Hawthorne we are used to; he is not the "innocent abroad," but the mood of belief and disbelief swings like a pendulum.

On visiting the Jesuit church of the Gesu, Hawthorne was embarrassed to have entered during a sermon: "We made but a very short stay, our New England breeding causing us to feel shy of moving about the church in sermon-time" (113). Not until later did Hawthorne notice, as he did in the Anglican Cathedral of Chester, that here the preaching of the Word was not held in nearly as high esteem as by the Calvinists, for whom the sermon is the be all and end all of religious worship. For the Catholic, of course, it is only a small part of a larger whole, the Eucharistic service.

The Catholic sacrament of penance or confession seemed irresistible to Hawthorne and, in the following description, we see the preparations for Hilda's great scene of confession at St. Peter's:

Saint Peter's offers itself as a place of worship and religious comfort for the whole human race; and in one of the transepts I found a range of confessionals, where the penitent might tell his sins in the tongue of his own country, whether French, German, Polish, English, or what not. If I had had a murder on my conscience or any other great sin, I think I should have been inclined to kneel down there, and pour it into the safe secrecy of the confessional. What an institution that is! *Man needs it so, that it seems as if God must have ordained it.* This popish religion certainly does apply itself most closely and comfortably to human occasions; and I cannot but think that a great many people find their spiritual advantage in it, who would find none at all in our formless mode of worship. . . . In the church of San

Paulo yesterday I saw a young man standing before a shrine, writhing and wringing his hands in an agony of grief and contrition. If he had been a protestant, I think he would have shut all that up within his heart, and let it burn there till it seared him. (59–60)

Hawthorne seems to be speaking from his own experience; he had unhappily discovered the flammability of his own heart and he was not comfortable in the searing heat. Also, Hawthorne's Calvinism has lost ground when we remember Calvin's fierce views on the practice of penance, which made him refuse to retain confession as a sacrament. Hilda's use of the English-speaking confessional becomes a dramatic scene in *The Marble Faun*. Hawthorne, although always characterizing himself as a "heretic," found himself favorably disposed towards the "convenience" of the Catholic church.

Although Hawthorne continued to think of himself as a Puritan, he saw efficacy in the graven images of which Calvin heartily disapproved. For example, in admiring the mosaic copy in St. Peter's of Guido's *Michael Defeating Lucifer,* Hawthorne wrote:

These old painters were wonderful men, and have done great things for the Church of Rome—great things, we may say, for the church of Christ and for the cause of good; for the moral of this picture (the immortal youth and loveliness of virtue, and its irresistible might against evil) is as much directed to a Puritan as to a Catholic. (100)

On May 1, 1858, Hawthorne wandered about Rome "stopping here and there in a church" and he again began to contemplate the custom of confession and to wonder if it did not have some place even in the "purified church":

But, really, to good Catholics, it must be a blessed convenience—this facility of finding a cool, quiet, silent, beautiful place of worship, in even the hottest and most bustling street, into which they may step, leaving the fret and trouble of the world at the threshold, purifying themselves with a touch of holy water as they enter, and kneeling down to hold communion with some saint, their awful friend; or perhaps confessing all their sins to a priest, laying the whole dark burthen at the foot of the cross, and coming forth in the freshness and elasticity of innocence. It is for Protestants to inquire whether some of these inestimable advantages are not compatible with a purified faith, and do not indeed belong to Christianity, making part of the blessings it was meant to bring. It would be a good time to suggest and institute some of them, now that the American public seems to be stirred by a Revival, hitherto unexampled in extent. Protestantism needs a new Apostle to convert it into something positive. (195)

It seems perfectly clear that Hawthorne really had no intention of converting to Catholicism, as some critics have argued, yet he now saw some distinct advantages to what he once thought of as heinous popish practices, particularly confession, which he came to view as a Christian institution and compatible, despite Calvin's teaching, with a *purified* religion. He longed for a new *Protestant* apostle to make the *protest* against Catholicism positive rather than negative; he seemed to envy the ease with which Catholics invoke mediators between themselves and God—the Virgin, the saints, the confessional, the images of Christianity—in short, the *conveniences* of the Roman Church.

In the Sistine Chapel, Hawthorne was impressed with Michelangelo's *Last Judgment,* but disappointed with the darkness of the chapel and disapproving of the portrait of Jesus:

> In the Last Judgment . . . and above sits Jesus, not looking in the least like the Savior of the world, but with uplifted arm denouncing eternal misery on those whom He came to save. I fear I am myself among the wicked, for I found myself inevitably taking their part, and asking for at least a little pity, some few regrets, and not such a stern denunciatory spirit on the part of Him who had thought us worth dying for. . . . It would be a very terrible picture to one who should really see Jesus, the Savior, in that inexorable Judge; but it seems to me very undesirable that he should ever be represented in that aspect, when it is so essential to our religion to believe him infinitely kinder and better towards us than we deserve. At the Last Day, I presume—that is, in all future days when we see ourselves as we are—man's only inexorable Judge will be himself, and the punishment of his sins will be the perception of them. (214–15)

Hawthorne, like Milton, seems here to be inventing his own Puritanism—he does not want Jesus to be an inexorable judge, as Wigglesworth had portrayed him in Calvin's terms in "The Day of Doom," and yet he considered himself among the wicked for taking their part—the Calvinist dogma of reprobation. In wanting Jesus to be portrayed as kinder to us than we deserve, Hawthorne is merely stating Calvin's doctrine of God's sovereignty and man's depravity. But the careful omission of hell and damnation for the reprobate is a bit too kindly for Calvin.

Without a doubt, Rome has proved dangerous to Hawthorne's orthodoxy and even more importantly, to Hawthorne's artistry. It has, in fact undone him, as we will see in looking at *The Marble Faun* and the aborted romances.

Yet a great deal of Calvinist-ordained irony still informs Hawthorne's language, as in his comments on the beggars of Italy:

> No shame is attached to beggary in Italy. In fact, I rather imagine it to be held an honourable profession, inheriting some of the odour of sanctity that used to be attached to a mendicant and idle life in the days of early Christianity, when every Saint lived upon Providence and deemed it meritorious to do nothing for his living. (238–39)

Hawthorne was far too ingrained with the Puritan work ethic ("idleness is the devil's workshop") to approve of even a "saint's" living upon Providence and doing nothing, since he obviously did not believe that begging for the poor or praying for sinners was a proper occupation.

Never a transcendentalist, Hawthorne still was able to see with extreme pleasure the beauty of the mountains and valleys in the approach to Perugia. Hawthorne did not see nature as a mirror image of himself but rather: "When God expressed Himself in this landscape to mankind, He did not intend that it should be translated into any tongue save His own immediate one" (255). Hawthorne did not believe that Emerson had translated God's language correctly, nor did he see nature as deformed by the Fall, as Calvin did, except when it was ugly, as in the workhouses and almshouses of Liverpool, or icy and filthy as it was in his first wintry sight of Rome. If this seems contradictory, as it surely is, we must remember that Hawthorne's religious beliefs were never schematic nor consistent enough to allow him total loyalty to any sect. He, like Bartleby, preferred not to think deeply about his personal convictions or skepticisms, unlike Bartleby's creator, Melville, who continually "troubled deaf Heaven with his bootless cries."

After six months in Italy, Hawthorne began to meditate seriously on the bare-bones structure of New England meetinghouses, without any pictorial adornment, and began to wonder about Calvin's denunciation of images. In June 1858 in Florence, wandering about the Uffizzi gallery and looking at the old masters, Hawthorne felt an emotional response to a picture, a feeling that he had never experienced before:

Occasionally, today, I was sensible to a certain degree of emotion in looking at an old picture; as, for example, by a large, dark, ugly picture of
Christ bearing the cross, and sinking beneath it, where, somehow or other,
a sense of his agony, and the fearful wrong that mankind did to its Redeemer, and the scorn of his enemies and sorrow of those that loved him,
came knocking at my heart, and partly got entrance. Once more, I deem it
a pity that Protestantism should have entirely laid aside this mode of
appealing to the religious sentiment. (294)

When Hawthorne visited the Pitti Palace, he saw Michelangelo's
*Three Fates;* they made such a terrifying impression upon him that he
prayed. He described them:

Michael Angelo's Fates are three very grim and pitiless old women, who
respectively spin, hold, and cut, the thread of human destiny, all in a mood
of sombre gloom, but with no more sympathy than if they had nothing to
do with us. . . . If they were angry, or had the least spite against human-
kind, it would render them more tolerable. They are a great work, containing and representing the very idea that makes a belief in Fate such a cold
torture to the human soul. God give me a sure belief in his Providence!
(306)

Hawthorne's religious beliefs, probably never before articulated but always Calvinist, had undergone a severe assault during his five European
years. But rather than succumbing to Anglicanism or Catholicism,
Hawthorne feared that, like Melville, he might become a skeptic or a
fatalist or even a nihilist. He prayed agonizingly for a *sure* belief in the
Providence of God, aware as always of the icy tendencies of this heart.

At the Academy of Fine Arts in Florence, Hawthorne was much taken
by Fra Angelico's *Last Judgment,* although he usually did not care for this
Tuscan artist:

In one of Fra Angelico's pictures . . . he has tried his saintly hand at
making devils indeed, and showing them busily at work, tormenting the
poor, damned souls in fifty ghastly ways. Above sits Jesus, with the throng
of blessed saints around him, and a glow of tender and powerful love in his
own face, that ought to suffice to redeem all the damned, and convert the
very fiends, and quench the fires of hell by its holier light. (324–25)

Hawthorne certainly read the picture correctly, including Fra Angelico's
Arminianism, or his heterodoxy as Calvinists would call it, in showing a

Savior who died to redeem all of mankind and not just the blessed saints or the elect. This idea, so radically different from Calvin's doctrine of limited atonement (Christ died to save only the elect), must have caused yet another rent in Hawthorne's orthodoxy.

On returning to his Florentine residence from the holiday race for the Feast of St. John, which he did not like, Hawthorne "saw the Teatro Goldoni, which is in our street, lighted up for a representation on this Sunday evening. It shocked my New England prejudices a little" (342). Hawthorne was still capable of being shocked by the Catholic casualness about Sabbath restrictions, but he had come to the point of recognizing this response and calling it prejudice. In the Church of Santa Croce during Mass—"the organ playing . . . and the white-robed priest bowing, gesticulating, and making Latin prayers at the High Altar, where at least a hundred wax tapers were burning in constellations"—the hidden Calvinism again asserted itself as poor Hawthorne was caught in constant, conflicting responses to a religion he had grown up despising:

> Everybody knelt, except ourselves, yet seemed not to be troubled by the echoes of our passing footsteps, nor to require that we should pray along with them. They consider us already damned irrevocably, no doubt, and therefore right enough in taking no heed of their devotions; not but what we take so much heed as to give the smallest possible disturbance. (345)

In a fascinating, unconscious switch, Hawthorne judged himself as he imagined the Catholics must, not realizing that he was ascribing the Calvinist dogma of predestination to Catholics who believe—and this would indeed horrify him—that individuals even at their dying moment can *cooperate freely* with the grace of God and thus be saved.

Despite the disturbances in his religious beliefs, the Calvinist-ordained ironic mode still allowed Hawthorne to describe the church of "Or San Michele" in the old acerbic way. This church, once an open-air market, was transformed "four or five hundred years ago" into a Gothic church "where a man may buy his salvation instead of his dinner. At any rate, the Catholic priests will insure it to him, and take the price" (350–51). However much Hawthorne admired the aesthetic quality of Catholicism and its comfort to believers, his weakening Calvinism did not point him toward the throne of Peter.

In Santa Maria Novella Hawthorne observed a man calling his two little dogs toward him during Mass. He mused and puzzled about this *strange* religion:

> The cool, dusky refreshment of these holy places, affording such a refuge from the hot noon of the streets and piazzas, probably suggests devotional ideas to the people; and it may be, when they are praying, they feel a breath of Paradise fanning them. If we could only see any good effects in their daily life, we might deem it an excellent thing to be able to find incense and a prayer always ascending, to which every individual may join his own. I really wonder that the Catholics are not better men and women. (357)

This comment seems really naïve from the great prober of the foul caverns of the human heart.

The sacrament of confession continued to interest Hawthorne enormously and he even clocked the length of time penitents spent in the confessional, probably using time as an index of the gravity of the offenses: "Yesterday morning, in the Cathedral [of Siena], I watched a woman at confession, being curious to see how long it would take her to tell her sins, the growth of a week perhaps" (458). Hawthorne was truly captivated by the cathedral in Siena, where the Hawthornes visited for twelve days on their return to Rome from Florence. He visited every day and spent long hours there meditating and musing or timing confessions. The cathedral seemed to obsess him and, although he wroted pages about it, he despaired of ever really recording his impression of it. He does say he loved it dearly, which is extravagant language for a man so chary of his affections.

The following excerpt shows his serious consideration of the Catholic church and his conviction that however beautiful its externals may be, it is only a "fossil shell":

> I heartily wish the priests were better men, and that human nature, divinely influenced, could be depended upon for a constant supply and succession of good and pure men; their religion has so many admirable points. And then it is a sad pity that this noble and beautiful Cathedral should be a mere fossil shell, out of which the life has died long ago. . . . Generally, I suspect, when people throw off the faith they were born in, the best soil of their hearts is apt to cling to its roots. (459–60)

Is Hawthorne saying here that his Calvinism has been uprooted, but that the best soil of his heart clings to its roots? And if so, are those roots still in his heart or have they been completely extirpated? Surely, Hawthorne does not know at this point with any certainty what his religious faith is.

Before leaving Siena, Hawthorne confessed again: "This Cathedral has certainly bewitched me to write about it so much, effecting nothing with all my pains" (462). But his pains were not without effect, for we are convinced, as never before, that Hawthorne was undergoing some kind of religious crisis.

After leaving Siena for Rome, the Hawthornes had their passports examined by the papal customhouse officers at Ponte Certino: "I was invited into an office, where sat the Papal Custom-House officer, a thin, subtle-looking, keen-eyed, sallow personage, of aspect very suitable to be the officer of a government of priests" (475). The bewitchment of the Duòmo dell' Assunta, the cathedral of Siena, perhaps had now been translated into what, to Hawthorne, was the black witchcraft of a government of priests.

Back in Rome Hawthorne read over his description of Sodoma's *Christ Bound,* which he had viewed in Siena:

> I see that I have omitted to notice what seems to me one of its most striking characteristics—its loneliness. You feel as if the Saviour was deserted, both in Heaven and earth; the despair is in him, which made him say, 'My God, why hast thou forsaken me!' Even in this extremity, however, he is still divine; and Sodoma *almost* seems to have reconciled the impossibilities of combining an Omnipotent Divinity with a suffering and outraged humanity. (492)

What Sodoma "almost" did Hawthorne was unable to do, and his religious uncertainties remained unresolved and unreconciled. Hawthorne had lived with ambiguity and ambivalence for over fifty-four years and it had been good for his art. Surely he hoped that, in writing *The Marble Faun,* he could do as he had done before, write a purgative ironic novel. But the chasms were too great; his heart had been too deeply invaded by older cultures and religions to allow, even superficially, the old Calvinist defeat for his characters.

In Italy Hawthorne's lifelong preoccupation with death was only intensified. The Eternal City built upon pagan ruins, which, in turn, rested on the ruins of prehistory, was to Hawthorne a constant *memento mori.* He needed no skull on his desk to remind him of the fleeting transitoriness of human life; besides, his own increasing weariness and his dread of returning to America had changed his natural fear of death into a longing for eternal repose.

Hawthorne had anticipated death for many years. When it was truly imminent, his fears of death were far less oppressive to him than the weight of death which he had carried with him for so many years. He had anticipated with joy (unusual for Hawthorne) his return to Rome from Florence, but he had not been back a week before he complained:

> I walked . . . to the Church of St. John Lateran, into which I went, and sat down to rest myself, being languid and weary, and hot with the sun. . . . I do hate the Roman atmosphere . . . —all my homefeeling— has already evaporated, and what now impresses me, as before, is the languor of Rome—its nastiness—its weary pavements—its little life pressed down by a weight of death. (493–94)

As the Hawthornes prepared to leave Florence forever, Hawthorne commented ironically: "There is one comfort in thinking of the last, long journey we shall ever take:—we can carry no luggage along with us. There will be no luggage-car, nor carpet-bags under the seats" (439).

Leaving Rome over a month after they had planned, May 25, 1859, because of the almost fatal illness of Una, the Hawthornes arranged to return to England via Civita Vecchia, Leghorn, Genoa, Marseilles, Avignon (for a week), Lyon, Geneva (visiting the Castle of Chillon), Paris and Havre, Southampton, London (for about a week), then Liverpool and home. When they reached London, Hawthorne found that Fields, who was there with his wife, had arranged an English copyright for the new romance, *The Marble Faun,* which Hawthorne had sketched out in Rome. To secure the English copyright and to postpone going home to America, Hawthorne decided to spend another year in England to rewrite *The Marble Faun* and get from the publishers, Smith and Elder, the £600 which he needed after the expenses of maintaining a large household almost two years on the Continent.

This return journey to England revealed Hawthorne's increasing weariness and restlessness. Una was in fragile health and Sophia sprained her ankle, which mercifully inhibited some of her relentless sight-seeing.

Approaching Lyon from Valence, Hawthorne tells of the beauty of the scenery but more about himself:

> The scenery along this part of the Rhone (as we have found all the way from Marseilles) is very fine and impressive; old villages, rocky cliffs,

castellated steeps, quaint chateaus, and a thousand other objects, that ought really to interest me, if I were not so very weary of being greatly interested. Rest, rest, rest! There is nothing else so desirable; and I sometimes fancy, but only half in earnest, how pleasant it would be to be six feet underground, and let the grass grow over me. (549)

This desire for rest is expressed more emphatically than anything Hawthorne ever said in his notebooks, and the desire for death "only half in earnest" grew more and more pressing after he finished *The Marble Faun* and returned to America.

On the way to Lyon from Geneva weariness again negated whatever pleasure Hawthorne could take from the natural beauty and he gave up trying to describe it:

> The scenery was very striking throughout the journey, but I have come to see the nonsense of attempting to describe fine scenery. There is no such possibility; if scenery could be adequately reproduced in words, there would have been no need of God's making it in reality. It is the one possible expression of the meaning which the Creator intends to convey. . . .
>
> I have no heart any longer, as I have said a dozen times already, for journalizing. Had it been otherwise, there is enough of picturesque and peculiar in Geneva to fill a good many of these pages; but really I lack energy to seek objects of interest, curiosity even so much as to glance at them, heart to enjoy them, intellect to profit by them. I deem it a grace of Providence when I have a decent excuse to my wife, and to my own conscience, for not seeing even the things that have helped to tempt me abroad. It may be disease; it may be age; it may be the effect of the lassitudinous Roman atmosphere; but such is the fact. (551–52)

It may also have been the knowledge that, because of financial pressures, he had to write his novel and at this point he did not know he was to have another year in England. Although he worked extremely hard—six to seven hours a day in England on *The Marble Faun*—he was able to postpone what he dreaded most, the return to America. In fact, Hawthorne summoned up the energy to write the novel and enjoy some of his friends in England, but once back in the States, the absence of "curiosity," "heart," and "intellect" and the inroads of "disease" or "age" or "Rome" were too much for him. He had not been back more than a few weeks before his friends began to notice the slow but persistent decline that continued until his death less than four years after his return.

When the Hawthornes attempted to visit the cathedral in Geneva, they found it locked: "This being a protestant country, the doors were all shut; an inhospitality that made half a Catholic of me" (552). Hawthorne was irritable and weary and there is no evidence to indicate that he was half a Catholic or even one-sixteenth a Catholic, but he had developed a hostility to Calvinism.

After the glorious opulence of Rome, he became disgusted even with the cathedral of Lausanne:

> The interior disappointed us; not but what it was very beautiful; but I think the excellent repair which it was in and the puritanic neatness with which it is kept, does much towards defacing the majesty and mystery which belong to an old church. Every inch of every wall and column, and all the mouldings and tracery, and every scrap of grotesque carving, had been washed with a drab mixture. There were also seats all up and down the nave, made of pine wood, and looking very new and neat; just such seats as I shall see in a hundred meeting-houses (if I ever go into so many) in America. (566–67)

Of one thing we can be sure: Hawthorne was not going to go into a hundred meetinghouses when he got back to America, but he had become so accustomed to the "images" and aesthetic beauty of the old churches of Europe that he could no longer tolerate Calvinist plainness and neatness.

While the Hawthornes were still in Geneva, Hawthorne wrote for passage home to America from Liverpool. They did not return for another year, but at the time he was not aware that a year's reprieve from the Wayside awaited him in England. He wrote prophetically:

> It makes my heart thrill, half pleasantly, half otherwise; so much nearer does this step seem to bring that home whence I have now been absent six years, and which, when I see it again, may turn out not to be my home any longer. I likewise wrote to Bennoch, though I know not his present address; but I should deeply grieve to leave England without seeing him. He and Henry Bright are the only two men in England to whom I shall be much grieved to bid farewell; *but to the island itself I cannot bear to say that word, as a finality. I shall dreamily hope to come back again at some indefinite time;—rather foolishly, perhaps, for it will tend to take the substance out of my life in my own land. But this, I suspect, is apt to be the penalty of those who stray abroad, and stay too long.* (570)

Hawthorne, indeed, had become "a citizen of somewhere else"—a homeless man.

Hawthorne rejoiced when he found he could spend another year in England, but still his shaken Calvinist conscience upbraided him for his lack of loyalty to his country and he felt guilty about it, even though he had the perfect excuse of reworking his book and seeing it through publication in England.

After a mild social whirl in London the Hawthornes moved to Redcar, Yorkshire, on the northeastern seacoast of England. They reached England on June 23, 1859, went to Whitby then on to Redcar on July 22, where Hawthorne began rewriting *The Marble Faun.* They then removed on October 5 to Leamington, his favorite "cosy nook" in England, where he continued to write. *The Marble Faun* was published in England on February 28, 1860, under the title *Transformation,* of which Hawthorne did not approve, but it was published under the title *The Marble Faun* in America on March 7, 1860, by Ticknor and Fields. The return journey to America was begun June 16, 1860, and the Hawthornes arrived in Boston June 28, 1860. The return to America was a religious, emotional, and cultural shock from which Hawthorne never recovered.

THE MARBLE FAUN

# *"Everywhere a Cross—and Nastiness at the Foot of It"*

---

I

Since James T. Fields, Hawthorne's publisher, had arranged a profitable and nearly simultaneous English and American publication of Hawthorne's new romance, the difficult return to America was postponed for another year. Hawthorne was to rewrite his novel in England and secure his publication rights.[1] After a brief social visit in London, Hawthorne went to Whitby; however, after making several visits to St. Hilda's Abbey, he removed his family to Redcar where he could obtain suitable lodgings. On July 26, 1859, he began in earnest to rewrite his book. He got the name of his heroine from the abbey at Whitby and the eighth-century saint who had founded it. Renowned for her wisdom,[2] Hilda, who was probably converted by Saint Paulinus at the age of thirteen, was abbess at Whitby for many years, admitted Caedmon to his vows, and, despite a dreadful fever for the last seven years of her life, performed all of her duties. The cult of Saint Hilda sprang up in the eighth century and continued unabated through the Reformation. Hawthorne's Hilda is not renowned for her wisdom, but her stubbornness may have been modelled on her patron saint.

Hawthorne finished the novel on November 8, 1859, but had difficulty in choosing a title. After discarding several, he decided on *The Romance of Monte Beni,* but on February 28, 1860, the English version came out with the title *Transformation,* subtitled *The Romance of Monte Beni.* Hawthorne was angry about the title but stopped complaining when the English publishers reminded him that it was a title he himself had suggested. The American edition, carrying the title *The Marble Faun* with the same subtitle as the English edition, was published March 7, 1860.

The reviews were respectful but somewhat restrained, echoing many readers' dissatisfactions with the ending of the novel, which left so much of the mystery unresolved. Hawthorne was disgusted with the literal-mindedness of his public, but wrote a Postscript, which appeared in the

English second printing and in a later American printing. Even with the Postscript, which explains little, the reviewers found fault with various aspects of the novel—its tone, plot, theme, characters, and setting. Yet most reviewers faulted and admired different qualities of the novel. The only reviewer to be unreservedly fulsome was James Russell Lowell in *The Atlantic.*

*The Marble Faun,* Hawthorne's longest novel, is nearly twice as long as *The Scarlet Letter* and *The Blithedale Romance* and over one hundred fifty pages longer than *The House of the Seven Gables.* But longer does not mean better. The themes and variations in *The Marble Faun* are multiple, complex, and, as we have come to expect from Hawthorne, ambiguous. But this is ambiguity with a difference. The ironic ambiguity in the endings of *The Scarlet Letter, The House of the Seven Gables, The Blithedale Romance,* and so many of the great tales occurs because Hawthorne, reluctant to push his tragic vision of man to its logical, horrible conclusion, stops short and allows the reader to make the leap from the *apparent* ending, unsatisfactory, equivocal, unconsummated, to the *reality* of the secret, covert, cunning, bitter irony. This is artistic ambiguity of the highest level. But in *The Marble Faun,* although the ending remains circumspect and unsatisfying, closer examination and a search for the *reality* reveals only a Hawthorne confused, unsettled, and deeply disturbed. While the artistic ambiguity of the earlier tales and novels *reveals,* upon careful consideration, a planned, deliberate and stealthy irony that is the Hawthorne trademark and a remarkable literary achievement, the inartistic ambiguity of *The Marble Faun* betrays a confusion that is not a wily literary technique but a serious derangement, a muddle, a chaotic disturbance in the mind of Hawthorne himself. His usual firm control of the material wobbles dangerously here and our unease at the end of *The Marble Faun* is symptomatic of a similar disquiet and agitation in the mind of its author. The equation of Rome with ruin that Hawthorne makes in the *Italian Notebooks* is borne out in *The Marble Faun.* His convulsed Calvinism is not tranquilized by the heterodoxy of an *apparently* rejected *felix culpa.* Indeed, the mere suggestion of good coming from evil sends tremors through Hawthorne's literary cartography—the constantly renewed Fall of Adam-Everyman in a bent world of corruption given over to Satanic morasses, sloughs, impenetrable wildernesses, and quicksand.

Undoubtedly, Hawthorne wanted his readers to be more interested in the fate of his displaced Americans—Hilda and Kenyon—than in the

Italian faun-become-man, Donatello, and the mysterious English-Jewish-Italian, Miriam. But it does not work out this way. The priggish, prim Dove-Hilda and the marble Kenyon, who has disengaged himself from the reader's concern by his soft, fatuous devotion to his self-righteous Dove, go back to Puritan New England to avoid the dangerous challenges to belief that Italy has posed. The reader is happy to know they are leaving. Despite Hawthorne's attempts to capture the sympathy of his readers for Hilda, her self-absorbed denial of Miriam and her prissy fears about the contamination of her innocence force the reader's attention and solicitude away from her. We remain in Rome with the penitent, atoning Miriam and Donatello.

The faun becomes human through a love that requires the murder of the beloved's evil tormentor; when Miriam consents to the deed with her eyes, Donatello hurls the devilish model over the Tarpeian Rock. But after the initial ecstasy of freedom and union, Donatello, who was only the shell of a human being, pays the price of his humanity. Burgeoning, he discovers his Furies, his conscience, which brings along with knowledge and understanding, despair. Forsaking his faun's simple pleasures of devotion to his beloved and sportive dancing, he is hurled into hopelessness when he realizes that he has taken another human life. The education of Donatello begins after his crime and continues throughout more than two-thirds of the novel. The English title *Transformation*, which Hawthorne disliked, is more accurate in epitomizing the theme of the novel than is *The Marble Faun*.

The fact that two of the titles suggested by Hawthorne to his English publishers were *Hilda: A Romance* and *Marble and Life: A Romance* strongly suggests that Hawthorne was unaware of the pallor of the love between Hilda and Kenyon, the two Americans abroad. However, his theme of innocents abroad became a great central thesis in the American novel. Twain quickly exploited all of the possibilities for American swagger and simultaneous embarrassment that this thesis offered and it afforded Henry James material for a lifetime. Fortunately, Hawthorne does not pursue Hilda and Kenyon back to America, to dramatize the changes that Italy made in their lives; it is fortunate because we suspect that they will attempt to obliterate their Italian experience and, sadly, will probably succeed.

The two magnificent themes that Hawthorne initiates in *The Marble Faun*, original and unique in conception—the gradual humanizing through sin of a nature boy into a total human being and the pleasurable yet desperate experiences of two American artists confronting Old World beauty, antiquity and decadence—are not enough to make *The Marble Faun* more than a gravely qualified success, a splendid failure.

Many minor themes that play in and out of the novel are familiar to Hawthorne readers. Hawthorne's suspicion of the *appearance* of human progress is once more enunciated: "It is the iron rule in our days, to require an object and a purpose in life. It makes us all parts of a complicated scheme of progress, which can only result in our arrival at a colder and drearier region than we were born in. . . . We go all wrong, by too strenuous a resolution to go all right" (239). American Franklinian technology was always held suspect by Hawthorne and his years abroad confirmed his belief that a major part of the corruption of the American Dream had been instigated by the promoters of "bigger is better."

Despite his ambivalence about Catholicism, Hawthorne uses the setting of St. Peter's, "the world's cathedral," to enrich and deepen the moral struggles of the characters in *The Marble Faun*. From the Pincian Hill, Hilda and Kenyon acknowledge that "It requires both faith and fancy to enable us to feel . . . that, yonder, in front of the purple outline of hills, is the grandest edifice ever built by man, painted against God's loveliest sky" (106–07). Later in the novel, while Hilda is suffering so acutely because of witnessing the murder, she goes to St. Peter's and makes her confession in one of Hawthorne's great scenes. Here Hilda flouts her Calvinism, which condemns the sacrament of penance, and accepts the "convenience" of the Roman Catholic church.

Hawthorne's obsession with virginity continues unabated in *The Marble Faun*. Most of the virginal imagery centers on Hilda, her person and her tending of the shrine of the Virgin, but Hawthorne's search for the perfect virgin, as recorded in the *Italian Notebooks*, permeates the romance. We know through Hawthorne's not so subtle emphasis that Hilda is a virgin, but Miriam's chastity remains a mystery, although there are many hints that, like Zenobia, she is an "opened rose." The naked sexuality about which Hawthorne is so arch is not concealed in his flower imagery.[3] There is a peculiar suggestion by Hawthorne, the supposedly happily married man, that virginity is perhaps preferable to conjugal satisfaction:

> If we knew what is best for us, or could be content with what is reasonably good, the sculptor might well have been satisfied for a season with this

calm intimacy, which so sweetly kept him a stranger in her heart, and ceremonious guest, and yet allowed him the free enjoyment of all but its deeper recesses. The flowers, that grow outside of those inner sanctities, have a wild, hasty charm, which it is well to prove; there may be sweeter ones within the sacred precinct, but none that will die while you are handling them, and bequeathe you a delicious legacy, as these do, in the perception of their evanescence and unreality. (374)

We begin to wonder if this may be the explanation of the reputed statement that Sophia made to her sister Elizabeth: "Mr. Hawthorne's passions were under his feet."[4] Whether Hawthorne regrets his or Sophia's lost virginity, we may only guess.

Hawthorne's ambivalence about Rome, so pervasive in the notebooks, is only too apparent in this novel. He sees it as "the dead corpse of a giant" (110) over which the present Rome is built, a ruin where there is everywhere "a Cross—and nastiness at the foot of it. . . . Yet how is it possible to say an unkind or irreverential word of Rome?—the City of all time, and of all the world . . . for which Decay has done whatever glory and dominion could not do!" (111). As we know from the notebooks, Hawthorne felt that he would rejoice to leave Rome, and yet was amazed to find that he felt a love for the city that had so touched his very soul.

Since Hawthorne's intention in *The Marble Faun* is equivocal, vacillating, and ultimately confused, we must look closely at a variety of statements that he makes through the narrator and his characters, statements that reveal his disturbed and distressed response to Calvinism versus Roman Catholicism. Counting the number of favorable or unfavorable remarks about either religion would be ridiculous, but his weariness with Calvinism and his wariness of papal Rome reveal a struggle of belief that violently agitated him for the remainder of his life and was a major factor in putting the quietus on subsequent creative efforts.

When the four central characters and a group of artists set out on their moonlight ramble through Rome (that ends so terrifyingly with the murder of the model), they go into the Coliseum. Hawthorne is caught between his customary irony and a grudging admiration for what he sees as a religion of convenience. A black cross marks the spot where the Dying Gladiator fell and "an inscription promises seven years' indulgence—seven years of remission from the pains of Purgatory, and earlier enjoyment of heavenly bliss—for each separate kiss implanted on the black cross. What better use could be made of life (after middle age, when the accumulated sins are many, and the remaining temptations few) than to spend it all in kissing the black cross of the Coliseum!" (154). Lest the reader think Hawthorne is taking indulgences seriously, he comments a few lines later that "in Italy, religion jostles along side by side with business and sport, after a fashion of its own; and people are accustomed to kneel down and pray, or see others praying, between two fits of merriment, or between two sins" (155).

There is no disguising Hawthorne's Calvinist disgust in his description of Donatello's tower-room oratory. And he seems to disapprove of the echoing convent bells of the Italian countryside: "for . . . there is a chain of convent-bells from end to end, and crosswise, and in all possible directions, over *priest-ridden* Italy" (266). Yet a moment later he has the New England Puritan Kenyon argue for the validity of good works in remitting sin—an infamous heresy indeed for a Calvinist: "'if, for any cause, I were bent upon sacrificing every earthly hope as a peace-offering towards Heaven—I would make the wide world my cell, and good deeds to mankind my prayer'" (267). Repelled by the distorted Calvinist spiritual pride that pretends to share in the counsels of Providence, and equally revolted by most Catholic spiritual practices, Hawthorne has argued himself into a dangerous position for a naturally religious man— that of unbelief, a skeptical stance that he so deprecated in Melville, perhaps because he feared it too closely resembled his own.

Kenyon, often Hawthorne's spokesman, further attempts to manage Donatello's life, urging him to stop brooding in the poisonous atmosphere of remorse and do something. This is another untenable argument for the Puritan that Kenyon professes to be—a combination of work ethic and good works, but no mention of faith preceding these: "'Not despondency, not slothful anguish, is what you now require—but *effort!* Has there been an unutterable evil in your young life? Then crowd it out with good, or it will lie corrupting there, forever, and cause your capacity for better things to partake its noisome corruption!'" (273). Poor Donatello is bewildered by Kenyon's speeches—"'You stir up many thoughts . . . but the multitude and the whirl of them makes me dizzy!'" (273)—as well he might be, since Kenyon echoes Hawthorne's own creedal chaos.

As Kenyon and Donatello travel toward Perugia and the meeting with Miriam, Donatello converts the journey into a penitential pilgrimage, stopping and praying at every wayside shrine. Kenyon-Hawthorne seems to join Donatello: "It may be, too, *heretic as he was,* that Kenyon likewise put up a prayer . . . for the peace of his friend's conscience and the pardon of the sin that so oppressed him" (296). Donatello stops at all crosses but prays most earnestly at the shrines of the Virgin. Hawthorne is strongly tempted to be comforted by the Catholic belief in Mary's mediation with Christ for sinful humanity; he speaks longingly of it (297), but the Calvinist denial of any mediation between God and man still nags his conscience. Hawthorne vexes the question and then temporarily solves it by dismissing Catholicism as an out-worn and moribund religion: "Instead of blossoms on the shrub, or freshly gathered, with the dew-drops on their leaves, their worship, now-a-days, is best symbolized by the artificial flower" (298).

Back in Rome Hilda suffers agonizingly (and here we have to accept Hawthorne's word, which does not match our conviction) because of her exposure to evil in witnessing the murder. Before her horrible experience she had planned to spend many happy weeks in Rome "with the Virgin's aid and blessing, (which might be hoped for even by a heretic, who so religiously lit the lamp before her shrine)" (327). But Hilda sorrows over her lost innocence and "if she knelt—if she prayed—if her oppressed heart besought the sympathy of Divine Womanhood, afar in bliss, but not remote, because forever humanized by the memory of mortal griefs—was Hilda to be blamed? *It was not a Catholic, kneeling at an idolatrous shrine,* but a child, lifting its tear-stained face to seek comfort from a Mother" (332). Focusing on her great need and the childlike nature of her devotion, Hawthorne clears Hilda from the taint of Catholicism.

"Altars and Incense" (chapter 38) describes Hilda's final fateful visit to St. Peter's during which she makes her confession. The chapter opens with one of Hawthorne's longest and most complex meditations on Catholicism. Because it reveals starkly his anguish about his diminishing Calvinism and his ambivalence about the omnipresent Catholicism, the passage deserves to be quoted at length:

> Rome has a certain species of consolation readier at hand, for all the necessitous, than any other spot under the sky; and Hilda's despondent state made her peculiarly liable to the peril (if peril it can be justly termed) of seeking, or consenting, to be thus consoled.
>
> Had the Jesuits known the situation of this troubled heart, *her inheritance of New England Puritanism would hardly have protected the poor girl from the pious strategy* of these good Fathers. Knowing, as they do, how to

work each proper engine, it would have been ultimately impossible for Hilda to resist the attractions of a faith, *which so marvellously adapts itself to every human need.* Not, indeed, that it can satisfy the *soul's* cravings, but, at least, it can sometimes help the soul towards a higher satisfaction than the faith contains within itself. It supplies a multitude of external forms, in which the Spiritual may be clothed and manifested; it has many painted windows, as it were, through which the celestial sunshine, else discarded, may make itself gloriously perceptible in visions of beauty and splendour. There is *no one want or weakness of human nature, for which Catholicism will own itself without a remedy; cordials,* certainly, it possesses in abundance, and *sedatives,* in inexhaustible variety, and *what may once have been genuine medicaments though a little the worse for long keeping.*

To do it justice, Catholicism is such a miracle of fitness for its own ends, (many of which might seem to be admirable ones), that it is difficult to imagine it a contrivance of mere man. *Its mighty machinery was forged and put together, not on middle earth, but either above or below.* If there were but angels to work it, (instead of the very different class of engineers who now manage its cranks and safety-valves,) the system would soon vindicate the dignity and holiness of its origin. (344–45)

Despite Hawthorne's scorn for the machinations of the church, his Calvinist ancestors must have heaved in their graves to hear him speak even a bit kindly of their dread Anti-Christ, Catholicism.

Hilda is impressed (as Hawthorne was in his notebooks) by the humility of the sinner who is "too humble to approach the Deity directly" (347) and therefore seeks the mediation of a saint. She sees a young man writhing before a shrine and then kneeling down to weep and pray, and thinks: *"If this youth had been a Protestant, he would have kept all that torture pent up in his heart, and let it burn there till it seared him into indifference"* (347). This indifference is what seems to frighten Hawthorne most. The spell that St. Peter's exerts over Hilda (and Hawthorne, as recorded in the notebooks) is very real, but neither Hilda nor Hawthorne seems sure that the spell is not some form of Catholic-induced magic (350). But Hilda stops short of betraying her Puritan inheritance. She dips her fingers into the holy water font "and had almost signed the cross upon her breast, but forbore, and trembled, while shaking the water from her finger-tips. She felt as if her mother's spirit, somewhere within the Dome, were looking down upon her child, the daughter of Puritan forefathers, and weeping to behold her ensnared by these gaudy superstitions" (351).

Before Hilda perpetrates her own "heresy" against Puritanism by going to confession, Hawthorne attempts to justify her behavior. She sees the endless confessionals in St. Peter's and is "anew impressed with the infinite *convenience* . . . of the Catholic religion to its devout believers" (355). To Hawthorne, the absolution of the sacrament of penance would be the most attractive feature of Catholicism—a return to innocence, the silent reentry into the Garden of Eden. But what he did not know was that even entertaining such a possibility would emasculate his own art, however comforting it might be to his spirit. If one takes away from the moral climate of Hawthorne's fallen landscape, the heart as foul cavern, the threat of damnation for all, and the necessity and yet culpability of continuous sinning, his characteristic dramatic tension is gone. No longer is there guilty mankind going from evil to more serious evil until, rather than being able to return to Eden, only gaping hellfire awaits. Hawthorne is bleaker than Calvin because Calvin does see salvation for the elect; in his best works, Hawthorne sees redemption for no one. Hawthorne was unaware until he returned to America and tried to write more romances that he had lost the omphalos of his creativity. In fiction, Hilda is allowed to confess and yet remain a Puritan and flee back to America, secure in the arms of Kenyon as a worshipped household saint. In life, Hawthorne did not have this luxury, much as he might have wished it.

Hilda rationalizes her own apostasy: "'Do not these inestimable advantages . . . or some of them, at least, belong to Christianity itself? Can the faith, in which I was born and bred, be perfect, if it leave a weak girl like me to wander desolate, with this great trouble crushing me down?'" (355). And so Hilda confesses, ironically refusing absolution on the ground that only "'our Heavenly Father can forgive my sins,'" certainly no "'mortal man'" (359), and demanding the secrecy of the confessional from a New England priest who hears her wailing revelations, not of *her* sin, but of Miriam's and Donatello's. The priest encourages Hilda to convert to Catholicism, but Hilda's answer is as self-righteous as it is contradictory:

> "Father," said Hilda, much moved by his kindly earnestness, (in which, however, genuine as it was, there might still be a leaven of professional craft), "*I dare not come a step farther than Providence shall guide me.* Do not let it grieve you, therefore, if I never return to the Confessional; never dip my fingers in holy-water; never sign my bosom with the cross. *I am a daughter*

*of the Puritans.* But in spite of my heresy . . . you may one day see the poor
girl, to whom you have done this great Christian kindness, coming to
remind you of it, and *thank you for it, in the better land!"* (362)

Smug, self-righteous, confused, and heretically convinced of her own
salvation, the fatuous Hilda has now managed the best of both the worlds
of Calvinism and Catholicism, at least as far as she is concerned, but
Hawthorne was never to be the same.

Even to the end of this muddled novel, Hawthorne's conflicting
responses to the Roman church are apparent as he embraces and then casts
off Catholicism. On one page he asserts his wavering Calvinism and on the
next he shrugs it off as if it were an encumbrance.[5] Although Hawthorne's
characters are in serious moral difficulties, none is in as great a difficulty
as the author, who is caught in a spiritual morass so sticky that, shunning
conversion or a reaffirmation of his old faith, he seems to wish only for
quiet and death. For the sensitive and disturbed Hawthorne, the equation
Rome equals Ruin is only too poignantly apposite.

The Fall of man, reenacted in *The Scarlet Letter, The House of the Seven
Gables,* and *The Blithedale Romance,* occurs twice in *The Marble Faun*—once
with the characters and once again symbolically. In order to understand
Hawthorne's meaning we have to see Donatello as the unfallen Adam and
Miriam as the seductive Eve-Lilith, with the model as the man-serpent-
Satan whose murder results in Donatello's knowledge of good and evil and
Miriam's terrible remorse. The crime of disobedience against God does
not make Miriam or Donatello equal to God, but after a night of ecstatic
union, it banishes them from a temporary crypto-Eden to the postlapsarian ugliness of the miserable fallen world.

Miriam speaks of Donatello in the second chapter ("The Faun") as a
creature who knows no evil:

"Imagine, now, a real being . . . how happy, how genial, how satisfactory
would be his life . . . revelling in the merriment of woods and streams
. . . as mankind did in its innocent childhood, before sin, sorrow, or
mortality itself, had been thought of! . . . For I suppose the Faun had no
conscience, no remorse, no burthen on the heart, no troublesome recollections of any sort; no dark future neither!" (13–14)

The model is seen, after his emergence from the catacombs with
Miriam, as a devil risen out of hell to persecute Miriam forever by his evil
appearance and ubiquity. The night of the murder he is in the Coliseum

ritually performing, like the damned Hester and Dimmesdale, "an en-joined penance, and without the penitence that ought to have given it effectual life" (159). After the symbolic eating of the apple—Donatello's accepting the command of Miriam's eyes to defy God's law and hurl the model over the Tarpeian Rock—Miriam "turned to him—the *guilty, blood-stained, lonely woman*—she turned to *her fellow criminal, the youth, so lately innocent, whom she had drawn into her doom,* . . . with a clinging embrace that brought their two hearts together, till the horrour and agony of each was combined into one emotion, and that, a kind of rapture" (173–74). Adam-Donatello and Eve-Miriam hide their nakedness from God and each other throughout the night, but the next morning, after the sight of the dead serpent-model-monk in the Church of the Capuchins, Adam-Donatello hears, in the Medici Gardens, "the voice of the Lord God walking the Garden in the cool of the day" (Genesis), and the guilt becomes so real that he becomes filled with a "leaden despondency" (197), and Eve-Miriam feels herself "astray in the world" (202).

Hilda, who has witnessed this reenactment of the Fall as the actual fall of the model down the precipice, is portrayed by Hawthorne (with only partial success) as a creature as innocent and unsullied by the world as Donatello. After her initiation into evil by merely observing the crime, she is as agitated and disturbed as Miriam and Donatello. She weeps through the night with scalding tears:

> The pillow was . . . disturbed. . . . She bedewed it with some of those tears . . . which the innocent heart pours forth, at its first actual discovery that sin is in the world. . . . In due time, some mortal, whom they reverence too highly, is commissioned by Providence to teach them this direful lesson; *he perpetrates a sin; and Adam falls anew, and Paradise, hereto-fore in unfaded bloom, is lost again, and closed forever, with the fiery swords gleaming at its gates.* (204)

Here Hawthorne, in his old convincing Calvinist form, has closed the gates of paradise for Donatello, Miriam, and even Hilda, the observer. But this is less than half-way into the novel and these seeming certainties almost immediately begin their pendulum swing as Donatello returns to his tower near Florence where he alternately prays and despairs.

The second Fall, symbolic rather than actual, occurs in Donatello's tower while Kenyon is visiting. Donatello and Kenyon are at the top of the tower when Kenyon is overcome by the natural beauty of the panorama. Looking down on a stony paved roof, Kenyon is amazed to see "a little shrub, with green and glossy leaves" (259). Donatello explains that the bush has always been there, but he is unable to see the moral which Kenyon insists it has: "'It teaches me nothing. . . . But here was a worm that would have killed it; an ugly creature, which I will fling over the battlements'" (259). Flinging the destructive worm over the side of the parapet, Donatello symbolically recapitulates the Fall—and the murder of the model. But now the symbolism becomes muddled and disordered. The first and actual Fall—the murder—has all of the Calvinist implications of inevitability and irrevocability—there is no way back to Eden—but this second metaphorical descent of the worm is not even *confused* Calvinism. Certainly, there is the suggestion that Donatello has done well to rid the ancient thriving plant of a worm that would destroy it—a seeming justification for the first murder of the worm-serpent-model. But Donatello is unaware of anything but his feelings of guilt and remorse over murder. Is Hawthorne implying that Donatello has done well to rid Miriam of her satanic follower? It is unlikely that Hawthorne would condone such an evil means to a desired end, but the implication is made in the second Fall. There is also the suggestion of Christ's parable of the seed falling "upon stony places, where they had not much earth: And when the sun was up, they were scorched; and because they had no root, they withered away" (Matthew 13:5–7). Parabolically, this could explain the second Fall, but not the first. Donatello is the stony place upon which the seeds—God's words—fall; at first he is innocent and happy but in his despair, guilt, and sin he is one of those who "for a while believe[s], and in time of temptation fall[s] away" (Luke 8:13). Donatello cannot abide the suffering, torment, and despair of his new humanity and he rejects it for the time being. But he does feel that the shrub must teach a good lesson and Kenyon concurs, proclaiming that "it has its moral, or it would have perished long ago. And, no doubt, it is for your use and edification, since you have had it before your eyes, all your lifetime, and now are moved to ask what may be its lesson!" But Donatello responds, "'It teaches me nothing'" (259). The religious implications are unmistakable but contradictory. We do not expect a one-to-one relationship in Hawthorne's symbolism any more than we do from any other writer who employs symbol and emblem, but we do expect some consistency. The reading of the second Fall cannot be understood in a Calvinist context, as can the first Fall, but only as the Catholic fortunate fall. Donatello sins and through his suffering and anguish allows the seeds of the Word to grow in his heart and is moved to atonement, penance, and penitence. Through sin he has become truly human; through his agony and remorse he will be able to "work out his *salvation* with diligence," confined in prison, even if it takes the rest of his life: "O inaestimabilis dilectio caritatis: ut servum redimeres, filium tradidisti! O certe necessarium Adae peccatum, quod Christi morte deletum est! *O felix culpa,* quae talem ac tantum meruit habere Redemptorem!"[6]

Throughout the rest of the novel, Hawthorne plunges his characters and himself, as Kenyon's narrator, into a heterodoxy that bewilders and separates his characters—New England Puritans from Old World Catholics—and himself—New England backsliding Calvinist from the "citizen of somewhere else"—so that unlike his countryman and contemporary, Walt Whitman, he makes nearly impossible any "retrievements out of the night." Although Hawthorne continues valiantly with his romance, his ambivalence begins to get in the way of the narrative and his own personal ambiguity befogs the artistic ambiguity of Calvinist-ordained irony with which he had achieved such artistic prodigies earlier.

After observing the symbolic Fall from the tower, Kenyon roves around the immense grounds of Monte Beni, revelling in the beauty of the land, the orchards, and the vineyards:

> The sculptor strayed . . . with somewhat the sensations of an adventurer who should find his way to the site of *ancient Eden,* and behold its loveliness through *the transparency of that gloom which has been brooding over those haunts of innocence, ever since the fall. Adam saw it in a brighter sunshine, but never knew the shade of pensive beauty which Eden won from his expulsion.* (276)

Again, even to the Puritan Kenyon, Hawthorne gives a modified vision of the fortunate fall—a world in which the sunshine is not as bright as Adam's, but with a lovelier and more pensive beauty seen through a *"transparent gloom,"* (or Miltonic "darkness visible") that Eden gained from Adam's expulsion. What a distance there is between Kenyon and the doomed Goodman Brown who, after one night in the forest with the devil-worshippers, could affirm with Calvin that expulsion from Eden not only resulted in a broken world, but doomed all mankind to depravity and perpetual sin.[7]

Hawthorne's psychological unease—occasioned during his European travels by his sensitive response to ancient religious foundations and beauty and art—forced him into a deeper examination of his belief than he had ever permitted himself. Much as he tried to avoid the metaphysical questions that had driven Melville to near madness, he was unable to avoid the implications of his inherited Calvinism; here was the dissolution and corruption of the Puritan American Dream into a Franklinian pragmatism which disgusted him, or an Emersonian fantasy of self-divinity, which appalled his very soul. He began to see his youthful country from a European perspective—with an Old World amused tolerance and cynicism about the American ideal that had lost its high-souled utopian ambitions to become a New Jerusalem and was now wallowing in cut-throat materialism. From this distance, he looked at a land—unhallowed by deep traditions or the gentle decay of ivied ruins—in the clear light of day. Without the moonlight of romance, he saw a people nakedly and unashamedly involved in secularism and commercialism. Europe was no better than America, but then it did not pretend to be. In England Hawthorne began to fear his return to what he now recognized as a blighted land. But no European conversion, political or religious, was forthcoming to replace his instinctive loyalties to a revolutionary colony and a dissenter's belief. Hawthorne's mind, no longer bounded by a nutshell, was disordered by bad dreams: he was cast adrift in a leaky boat with no provisions and "a haul that would not bear examination."

Hawthorne's increasingly urgent need, felt at the end of his English residence, to escape and forget religious doubts and skepticism was only exacerbated in France and Italy. England's complacent Anglicanism was far easier for him to tolerate than Roman Catholicism, which he had hated from a distance in New England and now found confronting him everywhere. If he could have continued to hate it wholeheartedly, he would not have been so challenged and upset, but he kept finding, paradoxically combined with his basic Calvinist repulsion for the "whore of Babylon," a growing tolerance and even affection for the outward forms and "conveniences" of the Catholic church. At the age of fifty-five, he had no energy, no interest, and no heart for trying to do what he had never done before—analyze and sort out his religious beliefs. There was also probably the very real fear that, although he had depended subconsciously or at least unthinkingly upon an inherited Calvinism to give his life its ground of being and his art a necessary tension, a passionless and reasonable examination of his religious convictions might reveal that he had none. He grew to dread nihilism more than death or the realm of quiet for which he now longed.

All of these internal conflicts are reflected in *The Marble Faun*. The concept of the "iron necessity," by which Chillingworth explained to Hester his hell-fired persecution of Dimmesdale, is apparently ascribed to Miriam's mysterious model. After their fateful meeting in the catacombs, the model follows her everywhere and when she pleads with him to keep away from her, he argues that if they parted now, "'our fates would fling us together again, in a desert, on a mountain top, or in whatever spot seemed safest.'" Miriam replies, "'You mistake your own will for an *iron necessity*. . . . Even now, you might bid me pass . . . freely.' 'Never!' said he, 'with *immitigable will!*'" (96). This is predestination with a vengeance.

At first Miriam seems to believe in predestination as much as her model. As she looks at some of Kenyon's sculptures, she meditates: "As these busts in the block of marble, . . . so does our individual fate exist in the limestone of time. *We fancy that we carve it out; but its ultimate shape is prior to all our action*" (116). Hawthorne, in the voice of the narrator, comments on the preordination of events as he describes the apparently aimless wanderings of Kenyon and Donatello: "it will be seen that whatever appears most vagrant, and utterly purposeless, turns out, in the end, to have been *impelled the most surely on a preordained* and unswerving track" (289).

Such Calvinist meditation on man's inability either to control his own destiny or cooperate with God's plan for him continues in some reflections on Providence. Miriam assures Kenyon, who "religiously believes it," that there is "'certainly a Providence on purpose for Hilda'" (180). Kenyon regrets that he has smiled at Donatello's belief that the statue of the pope in Perugia can give an efficacious blessing. Kenyon admits (in his New England Puritan way): "'I did wrong to smile. . . . It is not for me to limit Providence in its operations on man's spirit'" (315). Hilda assures that Catholic priest who has heard her confession, "'Surely, Father, it was the *hand of Providence* that led me hither'" (360).

While these references to the Calvinist concept of Providence, predestination, and iron necessity exist in the novel, they occur less often than in Hawthorne's earlier works. The Calvinist-ordained ironic mode is weak: when irony occurs in *The Marble Faun* it appears to be unconscious. In speaking of Hilda's agony, which is occasioned merely by the sight of Miriam's and Donatello's crime, Hawthorne says: "Indeed, partaking the human nature of those who could perpetrate such deeds, she felt her own spotlessness impugned" (329). The reader is willing to go along with

Hawthorne's fantasy of Donatello as a not-quite-human faun, but rebels when he is expected to believe in Hilda's immaculate conception. The ending of *The Marble Faun* also contains unconscious irony. Throughout the novel Hawthorne has labored to interest us in Hilda and Kenyon more than in Miriam and Donatello. But as *The Scarlet Letter* is the dark and luscious Hester's story, and the most colorful character in *The Blithedale Romance* is the sumptuous Zenobia, so in *The Marble Faun* the readers are kept emotionally in Rome, anxious about the fate of Miriam and her humanized faun, and not really caring about the self-righteous Kenyon and his smug prig of a Dove when they hasten back to New England, where we are content they should disappear into a snow drift.

From being a defensive American, when he first arrived in England, Hawthorne soon became at home in the old dispensation. Going to the Continent aroused all of his old suspicions of things foreign, and the unfamiliar language in France and Italy made him feel, again, like an exile. But he soon found Rome more familiar than Salem. It is not that he ever forgot America—certainly it was always much in his mind—but the distance from it, the years away from it, and the cultural riches of Italy effectively sundered the umbilical cord. The agony was that he could find no new home.

Hawthorne had hoped that his early preference for solitude, his alienation from society, and his homelessness would be cured by his marriage. When this did not happen, his restlessness was somewhat alleviated by the required social years in England, and he looked forward to Italy—one more move among the numerous ones he had made on both sides of the Atlantic. But in many ways Italy only compounded the paradox of his enjoyment of fame and his dread of society. The American and English colony in Rome made him feel alternately comfortable and confined; his emotions continued to fluctuate unquietly between enjoyment of the wonders of Italy and dreadful weariness from the continual sight-seeing imposed upon him by his Puritan conscience (the duty to see what he had gone to Italy to see) and the injunctions of his tireless wife. In *The Marble Faun*, reflections about home, homelessness, and solitude are revelatory of this anxious state of mind (301, 304, 305, 318).

But homeless as Hawthorne felt he must be, he could hardly bear to leave Rome: "we are astonished by the discovery, by-and-by, that our heart-strings have mysteriously attached themselves to the Eternal City, and are drawing us thitherward again, as if it were more familiar, more intimately our home, than even the spot where we were born" (326). At the very end of the novel, in speaking of the return to America to be undertaken by Hilda and Kenyon, Hawthorne meditates on his own exile:

> And, . . . the years, after all, have a kind of emptiness, when we spend too many of them on a foreign shore. We defer the reality of life, in such cases, until a future moment, when we shall again breathe our native air; but, by-and-by, there are no future moments; or if we do return, we find the native air has lost its invigorating quality, and that life has shifted its reality to the spot where we have deemed ourselves only temporary residents. Thus, between two countries, we have none at all, or only that little space of either, in which we finally lay down our discontented bones. (461)

Four months after *The Marble Faun* was published, Hawthorne returned to America and the words in his novel about coming home seem prophetic. Less than four years after his return, Hawthorne died, his "discontented" bones buried in Sleepy Hollow Cemetery, Concord. The last four years of his life in America were restless and miserable; he was disastrously frustrated by not being able to complete any new work, depleted of all energy, debilitated by disease and by the more miserable despair of soul and spirit. There is a Calvinist-ordained irony about Hawthorne's death which he would have appreciated most: he died on a journey to regain his health.

The brotherhood of evil, of which the Calvinist in Hawthorne is so much aware, operates in *The Marble Faun,* spreading from Miriam to Donatello to Hilda. Because he does not witness the murder, Kenyon is somehow exempted from this contagion, unless we judge his arguments for the fortunate fall Calvinistically, in which case he is also infected. But after the murder the confraternity of sinners closes in on Miriam and Donatello. In the initial ecstasy of their crime, they turn into Pompey's Forum, where Miriam explains to Donatello:

> "For there was a great deed done here . . . a deed of blood likes ours! Who knows, but what we may meet the high and ever-sad fraternity of Caesar's murderers, and exchange a salutation?" "Are they our brethren, now?" asked Donatello. "Yes; all of them," said Miriam; "And many another, whom the world little dreams of, has been our brother or our sister, by what we have done within this hour!" (176)

Miriam is thrilled by the thought of the blood-stained fellowship, but Hawthorne allows us to make no mistake about his judgments of evil-doers. Much in the vein of the Calvinist fellowship of evil-doers pictured in "Young Goodman Brown," he remarks: "It is a terrible thought, that an individual wrong-doing melts into the great mass of human crime, and makes us—who dreamed only of our own little separate sin—makes us guilty of the whole. And thus Miriam and her lover were not an insulated pair, but members of an innumerable confraternity of guilty ones, all shuddering at each other" (177).

Hard as Hilda tries to repel Miriam when the guilt-ridden girl comes to visit her, she feels the evil as if it were palpable: "'Ah, now I understand how the sins of generations past have created an atmosphere of sin for those that follow! While there is a single guilty person in the universe, each innocent one must feel his innocence tortured by that guilt. Your deed, Miriam, has darkened the whole sky!'" (212). Hilda, so confident in her own innocence, accuses her dearest friend of cosmic guilt and Hawthorne echoes the indictment: "Every crime destroys more Edens than our own" (212). We are reminded of one of the most Calvinist of Hawthorne's early sketches, "Fancy's Show Box" (1837), in which he proclaims: *"Man must not disclaim his brotherhood, even with the guiltiest, since, though his hand be clean, his heart has surely been polluted by the flitting phantoms of iniquity."*[8] Despite these harsh judgments upon Miriam, Donatello, and even the angelic Hilda, Hawthorne manages to end the novel with a hopeful Hilda and an *apparently* remorseful Miriam and Donatello—all this through the agency of the fortunate fall.

The fortunate fall—that most perilous of human hopes for a Calvinist—is rejected by Hilda with such aversion that Kenyon, who has told her of its beneficent influence on Donatello, recoils from its implications with terror, denies he has ever believed it, and cries pitifully to Hilda to guide him home. But the damage had been done as far as Hawthorne's art is concerned. The suggestion is so alluring, so seductively healing, that it remains attractive no matter how vigorously the Puritan Hilda and Kenyon deny it. In fact, the two pairs of lovers, Calvinist Hilda and Kenyon and Catholic Miriam and Donatello, seem to emblemize Hawthorne's divided conscience. Indeed, as Miriam speculates to Kenyon on the *felix culpa*, we think of Hawthorne's own wandering into that "unfathomable abyss":

> "I tremble at my own thoughts, yet must needs probe them to their depths. Was the crime—in which he and I were wedded—was it a blessing

in that strange disguise? Was it a means of education, bringing a simple and imperfect nature to a point of feeling and intelligence, which it could have reached under no other discipline?" [Kenyon answers,] "You stir up deep and perilous matter, Miriam, . . . I dare not follow you into the unfathomable abysses, whither you are tending." (434)

But Miriam continues to elaborate the concept:

"Yet there is a pleasure in them. I delight to brood on the verge of this great mystery. . . . The story of the Fall of Man! Is it not repeated in our Romance of Monte Beni? And may we follow the analogy yet farther? *Was that very sin—into which Adam precipitated himself and all his race—was it the destined means by which, over a long pathway of toil and sorrow, we are to attain a higher, brighter, and profounder happiness, than our lost birthright gave?* Will not this idea account for the permitted existence of sin, as no other theory can?" (435)

The Puritan voice of Hawthorne, Kenyon, is terrified at this theory and says so: "'It is too dangerous, Miriam! I cannot follow you!'" (435). But the seed has been planted and later, when Kenyon repeats much of Miriam's arguments to Hilda—who recoils in horror—Miriam's exegesis is not obliterated but becomes almost inevitable.

In the last chapter Kenyon and Hilda walk through the Pantheon and Hilda speculates about Donatello. Kenyon is puzzled: "'Here comes my perplexity. . . . Sin has educated Donatello, and elevated him. Is Sin, then—which we deem such a dreadful blackness in the Universe—is it, like Sorrow, merely an element of human education, through which we struggle to a higher and purer state than we could otherwise have attained? *Did Adam fall, that we might ultimately rise to a far loftier Paradise than his?*'" (460).[9] Hilda shrinks in horror at this heresy of the *felix culpa.*

We are now far more concerned with the atoning and repentant Miriam and Donatello than we are with the marble-become-limestone Kenyon and the tiny Hilda, who is revealed throughout as a martinet with a whim of iron. And for Hawthorne, the "perilous" and "dangerous" matters of the fortunate fall that he has proposed, condemn him to a moral vacuum making it impossible for him to finish another novel. Because he has doubted the central, if unconscious, thesis of his art—that once man falls from Eden, there is no return—the dramatic tension is gone from his art and he himself is left a moral cripple, emasculated of his great theme.

II

In *The Marble Faun* Hawthorne's authorial voice lacks the subtlety of that in *The Scarlet Letter,* which moves so inconspicuously from the curious onlooker of the mid-nineteenth century to the judgmental, directive Calvinist of the seventeenth century. It also differs signally from the cosy, cheery, confiding voice of *The House of the Seven Gables.* Nor does Hawthorne conceal himself ironically behind the whine of the narrator-participant as in *The Blithedale Romance.* Hawthorne's uncertainty about where he stands in relationship to his four main characters, to Italy, and to his own belief is reflected in the wavering aesthetic distance he establishes from his characters and in the contradictory voice that one moment avows Calvinist orthodoxy and in the next conducts a half-hearted flirtation with Roman Catholicism. The blanching, Calvinist-ordained dissembling voice is nearly absent from this novel. The irony that does occur at the end of the novel—the flight of Kenyon and Hilda back to New England which allows the reader to concentrate on Miriam and Donatello, who are engaged in atonement and reparation suggesting probable redemption—seems thoroughly haphazard and fortuitous, not sly or devious.

The justly famous preface to *The Marble Faun* sets the tone of humility and diffidence which we have come to expect from Hawthorne's prefaces. But this is a preface with a difference: it is not the leisurely, autobiographical, seminal "Custom House" of *The Scarlet Letter;* it is not the plea for immunity from reality of *The House of the Seven Gables;* nor is it the elaborate disclaimer of *The Blithedale Romance,* which petitions the reader not to identify the fictional characters with the real companions in misery of Hawthorne's Brook Farm days. This preface has a valedictory undercurrent prophetic of its finality; there were to be no more finished romances. Sadly, plaintively, and with a barely concealed despair, Hawthorne addresses that "one congenial friend—more comprehensive of his purposes, more appreciative of his success, more indulgent of his shortcomings, and, in all respects, closer and kinder than a brother—that all-sympathizing critic, in short, whom an author never actually meets, but to whom he implicitly makes his appeal, whenever he is conscious of having done his best" (1). But he does not expect to find this paragon alive since it has been eight years since he wrote a novel: "Therefore, I have *little heart or confidence* . . . to presume upon the existence of that friend of friends." So, he will now stand upon ceremony, make "my most

reverential bow, and *retire behind the curtain"* (2). Hawthorne finally realizes that this "all-sympathizing" friend will never materialize; it is certainly not his wife or any friend he knew. Therefore, he disappears behind
the curtain of his despair, makes his valedictory bow, and, like an unwit-
ting Prospero, breaks his magic wand.

Hawthorne gives the circumstances surrounding the writing of *The
Marble Faun,* explaining that it was sketched in Italy and rewritten in
England, but denies "attempting a portraiture of Italian manners and
character" (3). He is too wise to attempt what other temporary residents
of a foreign country have assayed. What follows is the famous paragraph
that Henry James used and exaggerated in his critical biography of
Hawthorne and appropriated to himself as his reason for residing in
England. As Americans, both Hawthorne and James learned that "Romance and poetry, like ivy, lichens, and wall-flowers, need Ruin to make
them grow" (3).

Hawthorne's knowledge of the chilling pragmatism of the corrupted
American Dream illuminates what has become obvious in his works. The
best of the short stories occur in the historical past ("Young Goodman
Brown," "My Kinsman, Major Molineux," "Roger Malvin's Burial") or in
another land ("Wakefield," "Rappaccini's Daughter"). As for the novels,
*The Scarlet Letter* is set in the seventeenth century; *The House of the Seven
Gables* occurs in a house where time has stood still, but has its action
ordained by a seventeenth-century curse; *The Blithedale Romance,* also in
the historical present, is two removes away by being a romance about a
doomed utopian community. But the Italian setting, romantic as it is,
solves none of Hawthorne's perplexities about his religious belief or unbelief, nor does it assist him in assuming a comfortable aesthetic distance
from his fictional characters, or in establishing a consistent point of view.

Hawthorne waits until eighty-five percent of the novel is over to
inform the reader that he, as an apparently omniscient narrator, got the
material for the romance from Kenyon. He says that his contemplations of
Kenyon's unfinished bust of Donatello "originally interested us in his
history, and impelled us to elicit from Kenyon what he knew of his
friend's adventures" (381). To be told over four-fifths of the way through
a book that the narrative voice is less the author's persona than that of one
of the four major characters is disconcerting, even though Kenyon seems
usually to mouth Hawthorne's views. Chapter 11, "Fragmentary Sentences," provides a more appropriate place to make this declaration of

biased authorial voice, although even this chapter has taken the reader through a fifth of the novel. In this chapter, Hawthorne admits his incomplete knowledge about the story and poses a difficult problem for the reader who has come to believe in the authority of the narrator:

> Owing, it may be, to this moral estrangement— . . . there have come to us but a few vague whisperings of what passed. . . . In weaving these mystic utterances into a continuous scene, we undertake a task resembling, in its perplexity, that of gathering up and piecing together the fragments of a letter, which has been torn and scattered to the winds. Many words of deep significance—many entire sentences, and those possibly the most important ones—have flown too far, on the winged breezes, to be recovered. If we insert our own conjectural amendments, we perhaps give a purport utterly at variance with the true one. Yet, unless we attempt something in this way, there must remain an unsightly gap, and a lack of continuousness and dependence in our narrative; so that it would arrive at certain inevitable catastrophes without due warning of their imminence. (93)

The weakness of this confession's logic is obvious and such a lapse of narrative control reveals Hawthorne's confusion about his own role in the novel. He writes about four pages of mysterious conversation between Miriam and the model and the apparently inscrutable hold he has over her—which is never explained even at the end of the book—and then hedges further by saying: "The wind has blown away whatever else they may have spoken" (97). Thus, as readers, we suspect that Hawthorne is holding a great deal back, a suspicion that is made more acute by the casual announcement late in the novel that Kenyon told Hawthorne the story which he is telling us. In the postscript added to the second edition of *The Marble Faun,* which was meant to answer complaints by critics and readers that too many puzzles were unsolved, nothing is really explained, but then Hawthorne does introduce himself as a character who "cross-examines" Kenyon and Hilda at the top of St. Peter's. What emerges from all this confusion is a display of an uncertain and wavering point of view, a lack of professionalism that we can hardly attribute to Hawthorne. Not since the early "Alice Doane's Appeal" has Hawthorne seemed less sure of his authorial voice than in this powerful novel. But all of the excellences of the novel are compromised by Hawthorne's personal and tenuous velleities. The reader is thus required to deal over and over again with Hawthorne's ambivalent voice.

When Hilda goes to confession, Hawthorne tries to explain her reasons and ends up in a religious tug-of-war that he never resolves: "She went (*and it was a dangerous errand*) to observe how closely and comfortingly the Popish faith applied itself to all human occasions. It was impossible to doubt that multitudes of people found their spiritual advantage in it, who would find none at all in *our own formless* mode of worship, which . . . can be enjoyed only at stated and too infrequent periods" (346). Hawthorne's disapproval of "the Popish faith" is evident, but he is also critical of "our" worship (the relics of Calvinist orthodoxy) which is "formless" and unavailable to needy souls. He goes on to praise the mediation of the saints in a way that would have given mortal offense to his Puritan ancestors and to Hawthorne himself seven years before.

Hawthorne ends his romance with many unsolved puzzles, such as the details of Hilda's mysterious disappearance and reappearance on the balcony overlooking the carnival. In the final chapter he appeals to the "Gentle Reader" addressed in the preface:

> The Gentle Reader, . . . would not thank us for one of those minute elucidations, which are so *tedious,* and, after all, so *unsatisfactory,* in clearing up the *romantic mysteries* of a story. He is too wise to insist upon looking closely at the wrong side of the tapestry, after the right one has been sufficiently displayed to him, woven with the best of the artist's skill, and cunningly arranged with a view to the harmonious exhibition of its colours. . . . For the *sagacity,* by which he is distinguished, will long ago have taught him that any narrative of human action and adventures—whether we call it history or romance—is certain to be a fragile handiwork, more easily rent than mended. The actual experience of even the most ordinary life is full of events that never explain themselves. (455)

But Hawthorne's flattery of his gentle, kindly readers did not have the desired effect and their clamor for him to unweave his tapestry was so insistent that he tacked on the postscript, a postscript which really only compounded the tedious mystery.

Although Hawthorne has not found his own voice in this novel, because at this point in his life he is not precisely certain what his own voice is, his diction remains, as always, apparently lucid. The greatest prose in the novel is reserved for Hawthorne's remarkable paragraph on the paradoxes of Rome:

> When we have once known Rome, and left her where she lies, like a long decaying corpse, retaining a trace of the noble shape it was . . . left her in utter weariness . . . of her narrow, crooked, intricate streets . . . left her tired of the sight of those immense, seven-storied, yellow-washed hovels . . . left her, worn out with shivering at the cheerless and smoky fireside, . . . left her, sick at heart of Italian trickery, which has uprooted whatever faith in man's integrity had endured till now, and sick at stomach of sour bread, sour wine, rancid butter, and bad cookery . . . left her, disgusted with the pretence of Holiness and the reality of Nastiness . . . left her, half-lifeless from the languid atmosphere . . . left her, crushed down in spirit with the desolation of her ruin, and the hopelessness of her future;—left her, in short, hating her with all our might, and adding our individual curse to the Infinite Anathema which her old crimes have unmistakeably brought down;—when we have left Rome in such mood as this, we are astonished . . . that our heart-strings have mysteriously attached themselves to the Eternal City, and are drawing us thitherward again, as if it were more familiar, more intimately our home, than even the spot where we were born! (325–26)

It would be difficult to find a more powerful and poetic passage anywhere in Hawthorne, or in any other writer. Nowhere has he expressed more poignantly or puissantly his equivocal and ambiguous response to the perdurable city of light and darkness.

### III

The intricate and rich symbolism and imagery of *The Marble Faun* often becomes subsumed into multiple, extensive, and detailed descriptions of the art and artifacts of Rome. Some critics, severe about Hawthorne's untrained eye and occasionally provincial artistic judgments, natter endlessly about the novel as if it were a guide book to Italy written by a puerile, callow, and ingenuous oaf. This kind of reading misses a very real theme in the novel—the thunderously complex impact of an ancient, sophisticated, and often decadent culture upon the consciousness of American innocents abroad. The novel is truly an original and, however unschooled Hawthorne might have been in art history, he was by no means an unsympathetic or insensitive observer; his lengthy, painstaking, and scrupulous study of the treasures of Italy should evoke admiration and not condescension in the reader. Certainly, he sometimes gets carried away either by disgust or adulation, but these responses only serve to give the romance a verisimilitude it would otherwise lack.

In addition to the use of art works as symbols (Donatello as *Faun* of Praxiteles, Miriam and Hilda as Guido's *Beatrice Cenci*), Hawthorne employs many of the images and symbols we expect of him. There are frequent images of paradise—fallen and unfallen—in a work which recounts two falls from Eden. The Borghese gardens become a dangerous Eden with the "final charm . . . bestowed by the Malaria. . . . For if you come hither in summer, and stray through these glades in the golden sunset, Fever walks arm in arm with you, and Death awaits you at the end of the dim vista. Thus, the scene is like Eden in its loveliness; like Eden, too, in the fatal spell that removes it beyond the scope of man's actual possessions" (73). The Campagna is also most dangerous when the natural beauties "most resemble Paradise. What the flaming sword was to the first Eden, such is the malaria to these sweet gardens and groves. We may wander through them, of an afternoon, it is true; but they cannot be made a home and a reality, and to sleep among them is death" (327). The pre-Lenten carnival seems Edenic to youth: "No doubt, however, the worn-out festival is still new to the youthful and light-hearted, who make the worn-out world itself as fresh as Adam found it, on his first forenoon in Paradise." But "Age and Care . . . chill the life out of its grotesque and airy riot" (437). With all of its palpable delights, Rome cannot provide one Eden that does not crumble.

Hawthorne's most comprehensive metaphor in *The Marble Faun,* St. Peter's as the world's cathedral, occupies all of chapter 39 and dominates the second half of the romance. The world's cathedral provides temporary solace for Hilda in her confession, but when she is confronted with the full implications of Catholicism in terms of the fortunate fall, she clutches Kenyon and they plan to leave the "evil" city which houses the world's cathedral and hasten back to the simple meetinghouses of New England built for the elect.

The admixture of history and religion that is Rome "seems" to Hilda "like nothing but a heap of broken rubbish" (110). T. S. Eliot must have had this description in mind when he described his vision of the modern world in *The Waste Land:* "What are the roots that clutch, what branches grow / Out of this stony *rubbish?* Son of Man, / You cannot say, or guess, for you know only / A *heap of broken images.*"

Hawthorne's ubiquitous obsession with graves, shrouds, and death is given free rein in *The Marble Faun*. Rome, built upon the detritus and decay of past civilizations, undermined by catacombs whose very air is filled with malaria and death, appealed to Hawthorne's deepest fantasies. Of the numerous images of death, two are particularly striking. One is Donatello's horror when, after the murder, he realizes that he can no longer call the animals to him. None responds but a venomous tarantula. In response to Kenyon's query ("'What has happened to you?'"), Donatello replies: "'Death, death! . . . They know it! . . . All Nature shrinks from me, and shudders at me! I live in the midst of a curse, that hems me round with a circle of fire! No innocent thing can come near me!'" (249). Kenyon tries to comfort him, but Donatello has experienced in a most poignant way his new, culpable and guilt-ridden humanity: his fall from innocence and his initiation into evil bring with it Adam's curse of death.

The other notable instance of death imagery occurs while Kenyon is hastening along the Appian Way to meet Miriam and Donatello. All along the way he passes sepulchre after sepulchre—some pyramids, some mounds, some towers—all in a state of immemorial ruin. The narrator comments:

> For, . . . these mountainous sepulchral edifices have not availed to keep so much as the bare name of an individual or a family name from oblivion. Ambitious of everlasting remembrance, . . . the slumberers might just as well have gone quietly to rest, each in his pigeon-hole of a columbarium, or under his little green hillock, in a graveyard, without a headstone to mark the spot. It is rather satisfactory than otherwise, to think that all these idle pains have turned out so utterly abortive. (420)

Hawthorne, Hamlet-like, muses bitterly about the evanescence of man's works and pomps after death: "die two months ago, and not forgotten yet? Then there's hope a great man's memory may outlive his life half a year. But . . . he must build churches then." There is a tone of weary despondency here that becomes more and more noticeable in Hawthorne's letters from this time on. Hawthorne knew in his heart that he could never extirpate his homelessness in this world; what he did not know was whether a lasting home—either of salvation or reprobation—could truly exist. We recall with compassion his last four years back in America, as he frantically and unsuccessfully tried to finish just one more novel before his mortal remains were buried with the lone word "Hawthorne" on his modest tombstone.

Death and time imagery usually appear together in Hawthorne. As Kenyon walks the streets of Rome searching for the vanished Hilda, Hawthorne meditates on the vanity of human wishes—each one of us demanding a special niche in time:

> How exceedingly absurd! All men, from the date of the earliest obelisk—and of the whole world, moreover, since that far epoch, and before—have made a similar demand, and seldom had their wish. If they had it, what are they the better, now? But, even while you taunt yourself with this sad lesson, your heart cries out obstreperously for its small share of earthly happiness, and will not be appeased by the myriad of dead hopes that lie crushed into the soil of Rome. How wonderful, that this our narrow foothold of the Present should hold its own so constantly, and, while every moment changing should still be like a rock betwixt the encountering tides of the long Past and the infinite To-Come! (410–11)

Although a man cries out unceasingly, like Clifford, for his happiness, Hawthorne sees time only as destroyer, not preserver. What had time to give Hawthorne? If Calvinism could not serve him after his European exile and Catholicism was as repellent to him as transcendentalism, what was there but the gaping nothingness that seemed to have overcome his friend Melville?

The deceptive quality of appearance and reality causes Hawthorne to describe the joyous but faded frescoes on the walls of Donatello's castle with this startling comment:

> For it is thus, that, with only an inconsiderable change, the gladdest objects and existences become the saddest; Hope fading into Disappointment; Joy darkening into Grief; and festal splendour into funereal duskiness; and all evolving, as their moral, a grim identity between gay things and sorrowful ones. *Only give them a little time, and they turn out to be just alike!* (226)

If joy and sorrow soon become indistinguishable, we know that Hawthorne will soon take the next dangerous step for those of faltering beliefs—the step in which, given enough time, good and evil turn out to be the same.

Chapters 48 and 49 are perhaps the most brilliant in the novel. Hawthorne uses the carnival to epitomize the problem of detecting the

masked from the unmasked—the bare-faced from those who "prepare a
face to meet the faces that they meet." For Hawthorne, Roman holidays
reflect all of the ambiguities "of sin and sorrow."

## IV

The structure of *The Marble Faun* is apparently quite simple: four friends
stroll through the capitol in Rome; certain events follow which divide
them; three leave Rome for a time; all reassemble in Rome; the four are
then divided into two couples; the last chapter reveals that the American
couple will return to America and the foreign couple will remain in Italy;
the circular plot is completed and closed. But nothing like this simplicity
constitutes the action of *The Marble Faun*. While the circular structure is
perfectly sound, the unified effect that it should leave with the reader not
occur.

Even so, within the psychological and religious complexities of the
romance occur four great set-piece actions that are as brilliant as anything
Hawthorne has ever written. They compel the interest of the reader as
thoroughly as the three great pillory scenes in *The Scarlet Letter;* the escape
of the two owls, Clifford and Hepzibah, the *The House of the Seven Gables;*
and the great judgment scene of Eliot's pulpit in *The Blithedale Romance*.

Hawthorne's extraordinary psychological prescience and his piercing
knowledge of the contaminated human heart enable him to dramatize
unforgettably the ecstatic union of evil that occurs after Donatello has
murdered, with Miriam's approving glance, the diabolical model. After
rapturously embracing, the guilty pair walk throughout the night united
by their love and their sin:

> Their deed—the crime which Donatello wrought, and Miriam accepted on
> the instant—had wreathed itself . . . like a serpent, in inextricable links
> about both their souls, and drew them into one, by its terrible contractile
> power. It was closer than a marriage bond. So ultimate, in those first
> moments, was the union, that it seemed as if their new sympathy an-
> nihilated all other ties, and that they were released from the chain of
> humanity; a new sphere, a special law, had been created for them alone.
> The world could not come near them; they were safe. (174)

All the sounds and activities of the world about them are obliterated—"So
remote was all that pertained to the past life of these guilty ones, in the
moral seclusion that had suddenly extended itself around them. But how

close, and ever closer, did the breadth of the immeasurable waste, that lay between them and all brotherhood and sisterhood, now press them one within the other!" (174–75). They are momentarily disturbed as they realize that their union is cemented by the blood of the model, but Miriam passionately urges that they cast it all behind them: "'The deed has done its office, and has no existence any more'" (176). This is unlike *The Scarlet Letter* in which Hawthorne says about Hester: "The scarlet letter had *not* done its office" (166). Hawthorne describes the sense of freedom which Miriam and Donatello feel for a short while:

> They flung the past behind them . . . or else distilled from it a fiery intoxication, which sufficed to carry them triumphantly through those first moments of their doom. For, guilt has its rapture, too. The foremost result of a broken law is ever an ecstatic sense of freedom . . . a bliss, or an insanity, which the unhappy pair imagined to be well-worth the sleepy innocence that was forever lost to them. (176)

Miriam tells Donatello that they now belong to the confraternity of criminals: "Where, then, was the seclusion, the remoteness, the strange, lonesome Paradise, into which she and her one companion had been transported by their crime?" (176). In this opulent scene, Hawthorne uses the passions of love, ecstasy, and fire to unite the two lovers through the violence of their crime into the violence of sensual love—made irresistibly attractive because it arises from forbidden fruit. Here is an artistic triumph that any twentieth-century writer, so confident of his post-Freudian insights, might well envy.

The second of the set pieces in the novel does not inflame the pages but represents a different kind of success. After the months of Donatello's remorse, penitence, and growth, Kenyon, the moral arbiter of the relationship between Donatello and Miriam, permits the meeting of the lovers in the great square of Perugia under the felicitous aegis of Pope Julius. Miriam, truly remorseful, awaits the voice of Donatello, for if he does not summon her, she will wander away in total rejection and isolation.

When high noon is struck by the cathedral clock, Miriam appears, as if from nowhere, with her head bowed on her hands. After considerable suspense, Donatello speaks Miriam's name and this one word tells her what she wants to hear:

It told Miriam things of infinite importance, and, first of all, that he still loved her. The sense of their mutual crime had stunned, but not destroyed the vitality of his affection; it was therefore indestructible. That tone, too, bespoke an altered and deepened character; it told of a vivified intellect, and of spiritual instruction that had come through sorrow and remorse; so that—instead of the wild boy, the thing of sportive, animal nature, the sylvan Faun—here was now the man of feeling and intelligence. (319–20)

Miriam and Donatello, unsure of what they should do next, turn to Kenyon. Without any qualms he assumes the God-like role of spiritual director: "'possibly, as a *by-stander,* though a deeply interested one, I may discern somewhat of truth that is hidden from you both'" (321). Assured by Miriam and Donatello that they know him to be upright and just, Kenyon speaks with a religious authority that is a curious blend of belief in the fortunate fall and Calvinist dogma. It seems to be Hawthorne's voice and reflects his own spiritual confusion and crisis of belief. Kenyon says that the bond between Miriam and Donatello, because of its origin in crime, has begun to educate Donatello and that he therefore requires Miriam's utter devotion, "'[The bond] is a true one, and never—except by Heaven's own act should be rent asunder'" (321). But anxious "not to violate the integrity of his own conscience," Kenyon warns that their union is only for "'mutual support . . . for one another's final good; it is for effort, for sacrifice, but not for earthly happiness'" (322). They agree readily to these solemn pronouncements as if Kenyon were the spokesman of both Pope Julius and a Calvinist minister. Kenyon continues as a crypto-Jehovah: "'Not for earthly bliss, therefore, . . . but for mutual elevation and encouragement towards a severe and painful life, you take each other's hands. And if, out of toil, sacrifice, prayer, penitence, and earnest effort towards right things, there comes, at length, *a sombre and thoughtful happiness,* taste it, and thank Heaven'" (322).

The scene is vastly dramatic. Miriam and Donatello stand hand-in-hand in the noonday throng, taking solemn marriage vows required by a curious but interested bystander, Kenyon, who somehow has assumed (like Hollingsworth at Eliot's pulpit) an astounding religious authority. The authority is only temporary, however, because when Kenyon gets back to Rome and has to deal with Hilda, he becomes a whining, bumbling Puritan schoolboy who wants to go home.

Hilda's confession at the "World's Cathedral" is Hawthorne's third great set piece. It needs no further discussion other than considering whether it is artistic or melodramatic. But whether we view the scene as realistic or merely sensational, it has all of the trappings of true theater.

The carnival scene is one of Hawthorne's master strokes, surpassing even the mask scene at Blithedale. The carnival, the Roman Mardi Gras, precedes Ash Wednesday by about a week and ends at midnight on Shrove Tuesday. It is a great imaginative feat for Hawthorne to use the backdrop of the carnival for consummating his most important plot developments. The joyousness, foolishness, and grotesqueness of the carnival and its masked participants contrast stunningly with the worried, desperate Kenyon searching for his lost Dove. As Kenyon is struck by a rosebud thrown by Hilda, who has mysteriously appeared on the appointed balcony, the disguised Miriam and Donatello are apprehended and forever unmasked. Kenyon and Hilda, although not wearing an exterior carnival mask nor the minister's black veil, retain their invisible masks of insensitivity toward Miriam and Donatello and all of the ambiguities of Rome. Kenyon is reunited with his cooing Dove, and Miriam and Donatello begin their long Lent, which probably will last forty years, not forty days.

In the last chapter Kenyon propounds two morals to Hilda to account for the complexities of the romance. "'It seems the moral of his story that human beings, of Donatello's character, compounded especially for happiness, have no longer any business on earth, or elsewhere. Life has grown so sadly serious, that such men must change their nature, or else perish'" (459). Hilda refuses to accept this moral, so Kenyon sets forth his concept of the fortunate fall which so shocks her that Kenyon denies his belief and begs to be guided home. When Hilda finds a priceless Etruscan bracelet in her dovecote, a wedding present from Miriam, she wonders what Miriam's life was to be "And where was Donatello? But Hilda had a hopeful soul, and saw sunlight on the mountain tops" (462). This final sentence is truly ironic but not in the customary Hawthorne style. Since Hilda has effectively damned Miriam and Donatello by refusing even to listen to the concept of the fortunate fall, the last sentence indicates that her hope, evidently unperceived by Hawthorne, is based only upon the fact that she is a moral imbecile.

## V

The archetypal Hawthorne novel is a book concerning quartets of characters: in *The Scarlet Letter,* Hester is at the apex of the triangular *A,* related legally and carnally to Chillingworth, and carnally to Dimmesdale, with

Pearl as the cross-bar constituting a blood connection; in *The House of the Seven Gables* there are Hepzibah, Clifford, and Phoebe, related by blood, and Holgrave-Maule united with all of the Pyncheons through the house and the curse and finally through marriage; in *The Blithedale Romance* there are the half-sisters, Priscilla and Zenobia, both in love with the blacksmith-reformer, Hollingsworth—Coverdale is finally separated from all, but "ballads" to us their ultimate story. *The Marble Faun* also has a quartet: the New England Puritans Hilda and Kenyon are in Rome for their art, which, for Kenyon, turns out to be Hilda, and the Italian faun-Donatello and the mysterious artist Miriam, are united by a crime-shared love. In this final complete novel the lines of separation are drawn distinctly and at the end of the romance the two couples separate forever.

Kenyon, the American sculptor, as we know, has Hawthorne's voice although we learn very late that the narrator has been told the events of the novel by Kenyon. Therefore, Kenyon's character sometimes seems rather inchoate and capricious and his religious beliefs alternate between rigorous Calvinism and confused heterodoxy. At the beginning of the romance Kenyon seems a not very compelling man but pleasant and handsome: "the sculptor had a face which, when time had done a little more for it, would offer a worthy subject for as good an artist as himself; features finely cut, *as if already marble;* an ideal forehead, deeply set eyes, and a mouth much hidden in a light brown beard, but apparently sensitive and delicate" (116). In short, except for the beard, he is a man very like Hawthorne.

We are never quite sure of Kenyon's motives when he follows Donatello, after the murder, to spend the summer at Monte Beni. Apparently he is truly sympathetic with Donatello's agony, but he manifests some of Coverdale's clinical observer qualities in his desire to sculpt Donatello's face as it grows from carefree faun to suffering man. He also relishes the role that the distraught Donatello allows him to play—that of the almost godlike man who is able to *control* the destinies of others. He becomes to Donatello and Miriam the man of moral authority, a role which he assumes gladly after he has an epiphany of sorts on the tower of Donatello's castle. He looks out at the expansive and majestic view and says: "'How it strengthens the poor human spirit in its reliance on His Providence, to ascend but this little way above the common level, and so attain a somewhat wider glimpse of His dealings with mankind! He doeth all things right! His will be done!'" (258). After this pious declaration,

Kenyon begins to "ascend above the common level" and take charge of the destinies of Donatello and Miriam, and although they are certainly in need of help, he never questions his right to control their lives.

Shortly after Kenyon's experience on the tower, which seems to convince him that he will be the Virgil to Donatello's Dante, he preaches a short sermon to Donatello:

> "Believe me . . . you know not what is requisite for your spiritual growth, seeking, as you do, to keep your soul perpetually in the unwholesome region of remorse. It was needful for you to pass through that dark valley, but it is infinitely dangerous to linger there too long; there is poison in the atmosphere, when we sit down and brood in it, instead of girding up our loins to press onward. Not despondency, not slothful anguish, is what you now require—but effort! Has there been an unutterable evil in your young life? Then crowd it out with good, or it will lie corrupting there, forever, and cause your capacity for better things to partake its noisome corruption!" (273)

This little homily is notable, not necessarily for its wisdom, but for its strange combination of creeds. Kenyon, the New England Calvinist, is preaching a doctrine not of faith but of good works,[10] although there is a mixture in his words of both the Calvinist work ethic ("idleness is the devil's workshop") as well as some Franklinian prudential and pragmatic advice to do something—"Diligence overcomes Difficulties, Sloth Makes Them."[11]

Kenyon arranges with Miriam to take Donatello on a journey that will end in the square in Perugia. They visit many churches during their journey and in one hold a strange conversation. Kenyon admires the stained-glass windows and tries to interest Donatello in them:

> "The pictures fill me with emotion, but not such as you seem to experience," said Donatello. "I tremble at those awful Saints, and, most of all, at the figure above them. He glows with Divine wrath!" "My dear friend," exclaimed Kenyon, "how strangely your eyes have transmuted the expression of the figure! It is Divine love, not wrath!" "To my eyes," said Donatello stubbornly, "it is wrath not Love! Each must interpret for himself." (305–06)

This is, indeed, an amazing exchange. Kenyon, the New England Calvinist, who later begs Hilda to guide him home, argues here as a Roman Catholic—God is love and all men's sins have been expiated by the saving blood of the crucified Christ if sinners but cooperate with available grace. Donatello, the devout Roman Catholic, sees a God of Calvinist wrath and argues Calvinistically for individual interpretation of what he sees. Kenyon, as Calvinist, should not even be tolerant of a stained-glass image of God. As spokesman for Hawthorne, Kenyon displays a dangerous heterodoxy, but we know from the notebooks that Hawthorne has developed a love for stained-glass windows and most of the aesthetically appealing images of the "popery" that he once so unhesitatingly denounced. To reclaim his orthodoxy Kenyon certainly needs to return to a plain New England meetinghouse.

Kenyon does another complete reversal after Hilda returns from her mysterious sojourn. After rebuking Hilda for her "Catholic propensities," he propounds to her the Catholic view of the fortunate fall to explain the change in Donatello. She is horrified and shocked "'beyond words,'" so Kenyon immediately denies that he has any faith in this doctrine, although his directives to Miriam and Donatello were based entirely on this belief. So Kenyon, no longer a man of marble, is reduced to modeling clay in Hilda's hands and whimpers for his mother to take him home. Kenyon is an inconsistent and vacillating character, dominating the lives of Miriam and Donatello with a Catholic voice and grovelling to Hilda with a Calvinist voice.

Hilda is the culmination of all of Hawthorne's pale, frail women, who are apparently fragile and weak, but possessed of unyielding wills. Hilda's negative aggression, so artfully concealed, enables her to do exactly as she pleases and dominate Kenyon and the apparently stronger Miriam. Dwelling in her tower, tending the doves, she is known to her friends as "Hilda, the Dove." The letters and notebooks have told us that "Dove" was one of Hawthorne's pet names for Sophia, so the identification of Sophia and Hilda is rather more than speculation. What remains a mystery, and probably always will, is how aware Hawthorne was of the distasteful impression that Hilda (like Phoebe and Priscilla) makes upon the reader. My conjecture is that he was only partially conscious that his cumulative representations of Phoebe, Priscilla, and Hilda were as devastating as they are. Nonetheless, he must have taken some inner delight in getting back at Sophia, whose negative aggression made him her slave in the early days of their marriage. Sophia, despite admonitions from her mother, never cooked nor did any housework. When they were without help, Hawthorne did the cooking and the washing up, while from her sketch pad

Sophia admired "her prince" dignifying the menial chores with his "nobility." She wrote to her mother that "Mr. Hawthorne" (she never referred to him in any other way in her letters to her family) would not permit her to engage in household chores. She adored her husband, she wrote, yet she managed him well enough to prevent his smoking or drinking anything alcoholic in *her* house. There must have been, beneath Hawthorne's beautiful manners, a seething resentment against this little Dove who so effectively clipped *his* wings. Hawthorne expected that his marriage to Sophia would "cure him" of his reclusiveness and his restlessness; after all, she had lured him out of the darkness of the "sordid" chamber in his mother's house. But his restlessness persisted all of his life. It must have been difficult to live with a woman transformed by her marriage from an invalid into a tireless sightseer who wore him out in Europe, one who was always so determinedly cheerful and pleased with her lot, her "beautiful" husband, and her "celestial" children—so difficult that he must have wanted, at times, to unsettle some of that smug righteousness. This he accomplished in his novels—by creating apparently submissive, docile Phoebes, Priscillas, and Hildas, whose immitigable wills were concealed beneath their exterior meekness. And Hawthorne's ironic revenge must have been passing sweet, because never did Sophia see more in these heroines than their external pieties.

In Hilda, Hawthorne outdoes himself in developing a sweet innocent who by her negative aggression reduces the assertive Kenyon, the man of marble, to a heap of whimpering lime dust and who diminishes the warm, loving but independent and forceful Miriam to tearful, heartbroken wretchedness. Hilda's religious beliefs are an eclectic mixture of Calvinist orthodoxy and Catholic convenience—a strange union only compatible with the emotion-dominated mentality of a Hilda or Sophia. We are made conscious of the severity of Hilda's judgment of others by her view of Guido's *Beatrice Cenci,* which she discusses with Miriam: "'it was terrible guilt, an inexpiable crime, and she feels it to be so. Therefore, it is that the forlorn creature so longs to elude our eyes, and forever vanish away into nothingness! Her doom is just!' 'Oh, Hilda, your innocence is like a sharp steel sword,' exclaimed her friend. 'Your judgments are often terribly severe, though you seem all made up of gentleness and mercy'" (66). Hilda, the artist, who uses colors so delicately when she copies the great paintings, can see with her heart only in two colors—black and white. The stringency of her view of Beatrice Cenci adumbrates the harshness of her judgment of Miriam and Donatello; however, she herself, unable to survive what she considers moral evil in others, is ironically quick to seek the solace of the confessional, but only on her own terms. After she cruelly disavows Miriam, most readers have lost whatever concern they may have had for Hilda, because of her smug priggishness. Has Hawthorne achieved a possibly subconscious revenge upon Sophia?

Hawthorne gives us a detailed account of the suffering Hilda experiences in her initiation into evil, even though the evil is not her own. We are meant to feel totally sympathetic with her, although this is not the effect achieved. Even after Hilda is driven to the Roman Catholic confessional to pour out Donatello's and Miriam's guilt, her heart has not been softened and she remains intolerably judgmental and self-righteous. Kenyon tries to explain to her that it is possible that there may be "'a mixture of good in things evil.'"

> "So with Miriam; so with Donatello. . . . Might we not render some such verdict as this?—Worthy of Death, but not unworthy of Love!"
>
> "Never," answered Hilda. . . . *There is . . . only one right and one wrong; and I do not understand* (and may God keep me from ever understanding) *how two things so totally unlike can be mistaken for one another; nor how two mortal foes—as Right or Wrong surely are—can work together in the same deed.* This is my faith; and I should be led astray, if you could persuade me to give it up."
>
> "Alas for poor human nature, then!" said Kenyon sadly. . . . "You need no mercy, and therefore know not how to show any." (383–84)

Puritan Hilda's reply is predictable: "'If there be any such dreadful mixture of good and evil as you affirm (and which appears to me more shocking than pure evil), then the good is turned to poison, not the evil to wholesomeness'" (384). Hilda, because of her distorted view of human nature, more Calvinist even than Calvin since she does not acknowledge her *own depravity* but only judges others, feels everything Kenyon says to her a "moral enigma" (385). In regard to Hilda, Hawthorne maintains the external position of uncritical admiration that he exhibited to his wife.

Julian Hawthorne in his biography, *Hawthorne and His Wife,* is aware of the resemblance of Hilda to Sophia: "Hilda . . . has in her some traits of Mrs. Hawthorne, though the latter, and perhaps Hawthorne himself, were not aware of it." Like Hilda, Sophia could not bear evil: "For though Sophia had the strength of a martyr under the infliction of those wounds which necessarily come to individuals by the providential vicissitudes of life, there was one kind of thing she could not bear, and that was, moral evil." In other words, Sophia could not accept the universe. Concerning Daniel Webster, Sophia was as pitiless in her judgment as Hilda was of Miriam and Donatello: "'It blinds me with tears of profoundest sorrow to see that Ambition could make him stoop. He made the fatal mistake which so many make; *he did evil that good might come of it,—which is an insult to God.'*"[12] Thus, Sophia was of the same mind as Hilda towards the idea of the fortunate fall and just as ruthless in her judgment of others. Rose Hawthorne in her *Memories of Hawthorne* tells how her mother wrote to her family of *The Marble Faun:* "'Mr. Hawthorne had no idea of portraying me in Hilda. Whatever resemblance one sees, is accidental.'"[13] Ironically, Sophia fancied Hilda too wonderful and marvelous to be completely drawn from herself. Far from being horrified at seeing herself portrayed as a smug, complacent prude, Sophia thought she was not quite good enough to be Hilda. But for Hawthorne the revenge on his "celestial" wife must have finally been complete in his creation of Hilda.

Miriam, the exotic dark lady, like Hester and Zenobia, stuns the reader with her warmth, commanding beauty, and mystery. Only accessible to her friends, she keeps others at a distance. No one really knows her origins. The only thing agreed upon by all is that there must be aristocratic and noble blood in her veins. Not even Hilda and Kenyon suspect that their generous, talented artist friend might have some catastrophic evil darkening her past. When the four friends visit the catacombs and Miriam vanishes temporarily, she has just said that there exists "'the possibility of going astray into this labyrinth of darkness'" (26). The labyrinth image immediately reminds us of Hester and her dangerous wanderings in the labyrinth of her own mind. Miriam emerges from the catacombs with the dark specter of her past, but she never reveals what her earlier connection with this persistent menacing model might have been—so the darkly exotic Miriam is surrounded by mysteries.

Hawthorne uses a passage from his *English Notebooks* to describe a "beautiful Jewess" he had met, suggesting comparisons of Miriam with the Old Testament women Rachel and Judith. These not only emphasize her beauty but her strength—for Rachel defied and bargained until God saw fit to give her sons, and Judith enchanted Holofernes with her beauty so she could behead him and preserve Israel. Through these biblical praises of Miriam's beauty, Hawthorne adumbrates not only the suffering that Miriam will undergo, but her fearlessness and final triumph in securing Donatello's devoted love.

When Miriam visits Hilda in her dovecote, Hilda blushingly admits she prays to the Virgin whose shrine she tends. Miriam pleads: "'But, when you pray next, dear friend, remember me!'" (69). This *sovegna vos* of Miriam's is similar to Arnaut Daniel's plea to Dante from Purgatory to remember him when he meets his Beatrice, who will lead him to Paradise. This is only one of several reminiscences of Dante that enrich *The Marble Faun*.[14]

The passionate love that Miriam feels for Donatello after he murders the model becomes a psychological reality for the reader because of Hawthorne's tremendous skill in relating violence and sexual passion. Before Donatello kills her enemy, Miriam thinks of the faun as a somewhat retarded but devoted lover—a lover not to be taken seriously, however; a fit companion for sportive and sylvan dancing but not a real man with any of the passions or jealousies of a mature suitor. When she becomes aware in an instant of the strength of Donatello's love for her—the strength that makes an intelligent, enraged man of him—she finds him irresistible and returns his love passionately. Their clinging together as they walk the streets of Rome all night, unconscious of their surroundings and aware only of their union in blood, is a triumph of Hawthorne's psychological intuition. In the clear light of day Donatello begins to feel the unbearable pangs of remorse and Miriam senses the terrible injury Donatello has done to himself for her; in her pity for him she bids him farewell, reminding him that even his unuttered wish will bring her to him.

After the reunion in Perugia of Miriam and Donatello, Kenyon does not see Miriam until she speaks to him from a splendid carriage in Rome, dressed, not as a penitent, but luxuriously, and wearing upon her breast the great red stone (her scarlet letter) that "seemed an emanation of herself, as if all that was passionate and glowing, in her native disposition, had crystallized upon her breast, and were just now scintillating more brilliantly than ever, in sympathy with some emotion of her heart" (396). Hawthorne makes a nice distinction between the symbolic self of Miriam whose brilliant, mysterious red stone is worn openly on her breast, and Hilda whose delicate virginity is expressed by the single rose she flings down from the balcony above the carnival upon Kenyon.

When Kenyon meets Miriam and Donatello upon the Campagna, he finds them dressed in peasant costume, walking hand in hand, savoring the last days of their freedom before Donatello turns himself over to the police. But Kenyon is too concerned about his lost Dove to sense the valedictory quality of Miriam's and Donatello's fitful happiness. Our last view of Miriam is of her stretching out her arms in the form of a blessing on Kenyon and Hilda as they pledge their troth in the Pantheon.

Unlike Hester, who is damned by Hawthorne for her adulterous love, guilty, penitent Miriam is celebrated by him, although she bears the stains of fatality, which would suggest dooming iron necessity to the younger Hawthorne. Miriam is a creature of the aging Hawthorne's religious perplexities, but she is his most satisfying and loving character. Kenyon is diminished by his love for Hilda; Hilda is more aggressive than ever in her ostensible capitulation to Kenyon. But Miriam is enlarged by love, sacrifice, and sin and becomes a suffering, remorseful, and yet complete woman.

Hawthorne's most difficult task in *The Marble Faun* requires him to make a believable character out of a faun-man, a nature boy, whose ancestry goes back to an Arcadian period, a Golden Age, when man still bore some of the features of the animal and lived in close relationship with the earth. Hawthorne must convince the reader that this sylvan age could exist and that Donatello is some kind of throw-back to this age of unsophistication—an unaccommodated man who grows into manhood and sorrow through the reality of sin. That the character of Donatello is convincing and appealing and that the reader finds him more credible than Kenyon or Hilda is both a tribute to Hawthorne's imagination and a sign of his failure to make sympathetic the characters he undoubltedly wanted the reader to admire. This success and failure only emphasize the conscious/unconscious split in Hawthorne's religious sympathies.

At the beginning of the novel the three artists tolerate the presence of Donatello as an amusement and a delight. Miriam is the first to notice a startling resemblance between Donatello and the *Faun* of Praxiteles. Hilda agrees, but feels that the likeness is "strange." Miriam disagrees about the strangeness, "'for no Faun in Arcadia was ever a greater simpleton than Donatello. He has hardly a man's share of wit, small as that may be'" (7). Hilda accuses Miriam of ingratitude because Donatello worships her, but Miriam's rejoinder foreshadows the coming tragic events: "'Then the greater fool he!'" (8). Donatello obligingly poses next

to the statue and the resemblance is uncanny. Indeed, Hawthorne's description of the famous statue is our picture of Donatello:

> The whole statue—unlike anything else that ever was wrought in that
> severe material of marble—conveys the idea of an amiable and sensual
> creature, easy, mirthful, apt for jollity, yet not incapable of being touched
> by pathos. Perhaps it is the very lack of moral severity, of any high and
> heroic ingredient in the character of the Faun, that makes it so delightful
> an object to the human eye and to the frailty of the human heart. The
> being, here represented, is endowed with no principle of virtue, and would
> be incapable of comprehending such. But he would be true and honest, by
> dint of his simplicity. . . . It is possible, too, that the Faun might be
> educated through the medium of his emotions; so that the coarser, animal
> portion of his nature might eventually be thrown into the back-ground,
> though never utterly expelled. (8–9)

Hawthorne has prepared us for the education of Donatello, but the
emphasis on the possibility of the animal nature subdued but never entirely overcome fits Hawthorne's view of Everyman. Donatello's violent
jealousy of Miriam's model and Miriam's consciousness of her catastrophic
past are temporarily forgotten in the glorious scene in which she and
Donatello dance in beautiful abandon to rustic music in the Borghese
gardens. The lovely pastoral ends when Miriam glimpses the model and
then she begs Donatello to leave her to her doom and not complicate his
happy life by following her. Donatello's answer ensures the horror soon to
come: "'Not follow you! What other path have I?'" (91).

The education of Donatello is slow and painful and Kenyon feels
powerless to help him as he does not speak directly of his crime but:

> From some mysterious source . . . a soul had been inspired into the young
> Count's simplicity. . . . He now showed a far deeper sense, and an in-
> telligence. . . . Every human life, if it ascends to truth or delves down to
> reality, must undergo similar change. . . . How ill-prepared he stood, on
> this old battlefield of the world, to fight with such an inevitable foe as
> mortal Calamity, and Sin for its stronger ally. (262)

What is extraordinary here is that Donatello does make this fight and,
through the efficacy of the *felix culpa,* appears to conquer. Even though
the story ends with Donatello in prison and Miriam wandering about as a
penitential pilgrim, the reader does not sniff damnation for Miriam and
Donatello.

When in Perugia Donatello calls Miriam to him, under the benefi-
cence of Roman Catholic indulgence and even the symbolic papal blessing, Hawthorne has abandoned his Calvinist ironic mode. Despite the
tragic circumstances of Donatello's imprisonment and his separation from
Miriam, the reader senses that somehow, somewhere, in the distant future
there will be a glorious reunion of the couple, with the hellfire notably
absent. What this enormous change in belief cost Hawthorne is suggested
by Kenyon's dreary thoughts as he searches Rome for his lost Hilda: "The
growth of a soul, which the sculptor half imagined that he had witnessed
in his friend, seemed hardly worth the heavy price that it had cost, in the
sacrifice of those simple enjoyments that were gone forever. A creature of
antique healthfulness had vanished from the earth; and, in his stead, there
was only one other morbid and remorseful man, among millions that were
cast in the same indistinguishable mould" (393). This comment is surely
one of the saddest Hawthorne ever made and yet *The Marble Faun* does not
end in damnation. Damnation would have been easier for the older
Hawthorne to accept than the precarious belief in Christ's universal atonement of sin and man's freedom to cooperate with this endless grace.
Donatello has acquired credibility and manhood through his sin and his
remorse, his pearl of great price, but Hawthorne remains in a Dantean
limbo—he can neither utterly believe nor utterly deny.

Hawthorne's interest in art and artists was lifelong and so it is no
surprise to find that three of his four characters are artists: Miriam, the
wildly original painter; Kenyon, the man of marble who eventually betrays his art because he values human affection (Hilda) more than art; and
Hilda, the copyist, a fitting occupation for one who never has an original
idea. Since Hawthorne and his family never ventured outside the American and English colony in Rome to form any associations with Italians, it
is to be expected that these expatriates would constitute the population of
the novel and launch Hawthorne himself as an original artist in portraying
the difficulties and achievements of the American artist abroad. Although
much time is lavished on descriptions of works of art and artists, what
dominates, in Hawthorne's own voice, is his excruciating weariness of
picture galleries and sight-seeing. His view of art is given to Hilda:
"'there is a class of spectators whose sympathy will help them to see the
Perfect, through a mist of imperfection. Nobody . . . ought to read
poetry, or look at pictures or statues, who cannot find a great deal more in
them than the poet or artist has actually expressed. Their highest merit is

suggestiveness'" (379). We recognize the tacit plea by Hawthorne for sympathetic understanding and also, more importantly, his licensing of the critic to read into his work what he could only suggest or dimly perceive.

## VI

Hawthorne's letters reveal that he was pleased to be able to stay in England another year to rewrite *The Marble Faun* and see it through the press. He dreaded the thought of returning to America, as can be seen from this excerpt from a letter to his old friend George Hillard (Redcar, July 23, 1839): "For my own part, I have given up the idea of returning before next spring or summer; and, in truth, after so long an absence, it is not altogether pleasant to think of returning at all. Americans, methinks, are particularly liable to get out of sorts with their native land, by being long away from it" (OSU). Not yet aware that he was incapable of writing another romance, Hawthorne assured his American publisher that his next book would be more "genial": "When I get home, I will try to write a more genial book; but the devil himself always seems to get into my inkstand, and I can only exorcise him by pensful at a time."[15] As we know, this exorcism proved impossible as six unfinished manuscripts bear mute witness.

As the time drew nearer the inevitable return to America, Hawthorne tried to make the best of a prospect that was inwardly distressing him tremendously: "I shall not have been absent seven years till the 5th of July next, and I scorn to touch Yankee soil sooner than that."[16] As it turned out he reached Boston June 28, 1860, a week before he thought he could bear it. He tried to put a better face on the unpleasant subject of his return in a letter to Ticknor: "I shall really be glad to get home, although I do not doubt I shall be tortured with life-long wishes to cross the sea again. I fear I have lost the capacity of living contentedly in any one place."[17] The next letter to Ticknor is even more explicit: "The sweetest thing connected with the foreign residence is, that you have no rights and no duties, and can live your own life without interference of any kind. I shall never again be so free as I have been in England and Italy."[18] In a sense, Hawthorne, along with Donatello, was going home to give himself up, to become imprisoned in the tower he had built on the Wayside. The tower, built as a study (in wooden imitation of the tower of Monte Beni), became less and less a study in which Hawthorne could write peacefully and more a prison in which he voluntarily confined himself, impotently pacing out the four remaining years of his life.

Although in many ways *The Marble Faun* is a great novel, it does signal the destruction of the tension motivating Hawthorne's art. Having once opened the Pandora's box of the *felix culpa,* he could never again close the lid. Despite Hilda's vigorous denial of the fortunate fall, this doctrine does account for the transformation of Donatello. Although Hawthorne wants the reader to focus his attention on Hilda and Kenyon and their flight back to Calvinist New England, the reader's attention and affection remain in Rome with the sorrowing Miriam and the imprisoned, penitent Donatello, the faun-become-man. If there is any Calvinist-ordained irony in the ending of the romance, it devolves upon Hawthorne himself, who is seemingly unaware of his defection from the damnatory orthodoxy that dictated the unity and ordained the tragic endings of his three previous novels.

The confusion and mysteries of the novel that Hawthorne's early readers and critics resented could not be solved by any postscript—the confusion derives from Hawthorne's own problem of belief. In attempting to sort out the ambiguities and ambivalences, we come up against a strange double standard—one standard for Hilda and Kenyon and another for Miriam and Donatello. Hilda and Keynon, we realize, are to be judged by the expected Calvinist orthodoxy. Tempted by the old dispensation of Rome, Hilda is exposed to another's sin, makes use of the "convenience" of the "corrupt" Papists in going to confession, and feels that she is being seduced by the old sophistries of Rome. Kenyon, in giving his friendship to Donatello and watching him work out his penance and penitence, is brought up short by Hilda, in his mouthing of Roman Catholic "pieties" about education through sin—good coming out of evil. In his shock of recognition he turns to Hilda to guide him home—to America and lingering Calvinism that Hilda epitomizes. Hilda and Kenyon, then, are to be judged by the standards of Calvin—they have barely escaped with their lives from the Roman Catholic church, the whore of Babylon, the Anti-Christ.

With Miriam and Donatello there is another standard. The old Hawthorne—the Hawthorne who had not lived for seven years exposed to European venality—would not have hesitated a moment to damn Miriam and Donatello. As sinners, despite their apparent remorse, they had effectually brought down upon themselves the wrath of the Calvinist Jehovah.

But he does no such thing. Try as we may, we cannot make hypocrites or whited sepulchres out of Miriam and Donatello. They are left in desperate sorrow, indeed—Donatello languishing in prison and Miriam making endless penitential rounds of churches and shrines—but there are subtle signs of the possibility of their salvation and resurrection. Although they may never be together in this life, the dungeon in which Donatello suffers may have a tower to which, through Miriam's prayers and his own, he might rise. The arrest of Donatello and Miriam on the last day of the carnival (Shrove Tuesday, the vigil of Ash Wednesday and the forty days of Lent), prefigures those days of fasting and abstinence and remorse and contrition leading to the greatest feast for all Christians—Easter, the Resurrection. Lent for Miriam and Donatello may be endless but the preparations for salvation are being made by these sorrowing pilgrims in "prayer, observance, discipline, thought and action."

If Easter comes, it will not be the deceptive and false resurrection of Dimmesdale who rises up a new man after further adulterous plans with Hester in the forest. If Easter comes for Miriam and Donatello, it will be the true good that comes out of evil—the Arminian, not the Calvinist, belief in Christ's unlimited atonement and forgiveness of all sinners who contritely cooperate with infinite grace. This is the grace that Christ purchased for all mankind through his death on the cross and his triumphant rising from the dead. Nor can this salvation be seen in the Calvinist terms of the regenerate elect endeavoring to work through compunction and humiliation back to irresistible grace; here there is too much of what Calvinists would call the taint of Roman Catholic freedom of choice to cooperate with God's grace, epitomized by Pope Julius' apocalyptic blessing of the self-acknowledged sinners.

Unconsciously, surely, Hawthorne has made his readers focus their emotions on Miriam and Donatello; they do not give a damn about prim little Hilda, who will give up art for hearth and home to be the angel of the house, nor for Kenyon, who will worship at her domestic shrine, safe from the terrors and ambiguities of Rome. If there is a way back to Eden for Miriam and Donatello, even an agonizing, tormenting, and racking one, Hawthorne loses the dramatic tension of the final and fleeting expulsion from Paradise. Having once allowed into his novel what Calvin would call the "hydra" of the fortunate fall, there can be no more central conflict for Hawthorne. If anyone can slip back into Eden by penitence and good works, the collision with damnation is avoided, and the Fall is only temporary, not terrible, terminal, and irrevocable. Consequently, this is Hawthorne's last complete novel.

After Rome, even a submerged Calvinism would no longer exist for Hawthorne, providing the battleground of his romances. And there seemed to be no satisfactory alternative. For him Roman Catholicism was corrupt and worn out; Anglicanism was shallow and imitative; Melville's nihilism was tempting but too destructive of self and family. Even to attempt at the age of fifty-six an assessment of his religious beliefs—a discipline he had avoided all of his life—was too much for Hawthorne. He could not, after *The Marble Faun,* go on saying he was a heretic, since he seems not to know any more what heresy is, or even to care if he did know. He was too weary to sort it all out; his basic if perhaps unconscious assumptions were no longer there. There was nothing left for him but the anguish and frustration of trying to write and failing. Finally, there was nothing left for him but to die of weariness, illness, doubt, and despair.

THE ABORTIVE ROMANCES

# "Love Grows Cold and Dies: Hatred Is Pacified by Annihilation"

I

This chapter will of necessity be sad and melancholy because it treats of Hawthorne's brave but futile attempts to write a new romance during the last four years of his life after he came back to America. Everything was against him: he had returned reluctantly from an England he loved to a country on the brink of a horrible internecine war; his loyalty to his old friend, former president Pierce, put him on the "wrong" side of the war; also there was no peace in his own house because the additions to it—extra rooms and tower—took twice as long to build and were twice as expensive as planned; the expected financial independence from his consular service had not happened, so he again had to write for a living; his repatriation was unheralded—he was not a celebrity as in Europe, but just another returned Concord eccentric; finally, he had lost the moral center of his life and art, and his health, previously robust, was failing miserably.

The manuscripts of *The American Claimant* and *The Elixir of Life* were published posthumously. Hawthorne, the perfectionist, would not have approved of displaying these sad, abortive fragments written during the last four years of his life. But though these broken stories add nothing to Hawthorne's reputation as an artist, they are of particular interest to the literary critic who, respecting no author's desire for privacy or personal preference, can pounce on them as a pathetic witness to Hawthorne's failing creative powers, his confusion, his weariness, and his despair.

The two sets of manuscripts (*The American Claimant* and *The Elixir of Life*) will be considered separately. The editors of the *Centenary Edition* have commendably published the restored fragments in two volumes of carefully edited texts (Volumes XII and XIII). Volume XII contains "The Ancestral Footstep" and the separated fragments of "Dr. Grimshawe's Secret," which were combined ruthlessly and expeditiously by Julian

Hawthorne from two fragments that the editors have designated "Etherege" and "Grimshawe."[1] In these fragmented manuscripts we find evidence of Hawthorne's inability to complete any work in his customary style or with his strong moral tone after he raised the possibility of the fortunate fall in *The Marble Faun.* Even though Hilda is shocked at the thought of the *felix culpa,* and she and her compliant lover Kenyon categorically deny its possibility, Donatello and Miriam remain in Rome to "work out their salvation with diligence." This is in accordance with the ancient Catholic doctrine of the happy fault of Adam's necessary sin, which sent a Redeemer for all of mankind,[2] not just for the "elect," as determined by Calvin's doctrine of limited atonement. Hawthorne probably wanted his readers to be far more interested in the Puritan Hilda and Kenyon, who flee back to the uncompromising moral climate of New England, back to a home and hearth which had not been debased, contaminated or infused with the comfortable Old World sophistries (as Hawthorne viewed them): confession, reparation, forgiveness of sin, and human cooperation with God's grace. But the ploy does not work, because the reader is in the thrall of the flesh and blood characters, Miriam and Donatello, and the subconscious, emotional focus of the novel keeps him imaginatively in Rome and in full empathy with the passionate penitents. The fictive maneuver of sending Hilda and Kenyon back to America to cleanse themselves of the evils of Rome failed for Hawthorne himself when he lived it. Reluctant to go back to his native country, Hawthorne finally returned to give his children the American citizenship and love of country he thought they needed.[3] But Hawthorne, more restless than ever, found himself too changed, too weary, too torn in his patriotic allegiances (especially because of the Civil War) to settle into provincial Concord and continue writing romances whose major theme was the terminal expulsion from Eden after a reenactment of the Fall of Adam.

The three fragments which constitute *The American Claimant* manuscripts provide a mute, moving, and doleful record of a great artist trying to recapture earlier certainties that, ironically, he did not know he had. Apparently, when Hawthorne concocted the sketch of what he thought was to be his English romance (Liverpool, April 1855), he foresaw no great difficulties. While he was thinking of an English romance, friends introduced him to the Ainsworths of Smithells Hall, where there was an intriguing Gothic legend concerning a bloody footstep:

The tradition is that a certain martyr, in Bloody Mary's time, being examined before the then occupant of the Hall, and committed to prison, stamped his foot in earnest protest against the injustice with which he was treated. Blood issued from his foot, which slid along the stone pavement of the hall, leaving a long footmark printed in blood; and there it has remained ever since, in spite of the scrubbings of all after generations. Mrs. Ainsworth spoke of it with much solemnity. . . . The martyr's name was George Marsh; he was a curate and was afterwards burnt.[4]

Hawthorne was impressed enough by the story to accept an invitation from the Ainsworths to visit the hall four months later. Although he declared "it is all a humbug,"[5] the story fascinated him, as did the comforts of life in an English manor house.

Hawthorne was determined to write a story of an American claimant to an English estate, but not, as some critics claim, to demonstrate political differences between England and America or to flout English snobbishness when confronted by American simplicity and candor. Critics who make this type of interpretation concern themselves unduly, I believe, with Hawthorne's politics, especially his alleged resentment of English pretentiousness. It appears to me that Hawthorne was almost entirely apolitical. He did what was necessary, politically, to get his two custom house positions in Boston and Salem, but was enraged at his expulsion from the Salem Custom House because of a change in political parties. Later, he realized that his dismissal was most wholesome for his literary career—after his discharge, he immediately wrote *The Scarlet Letter*—but his hostility against party infighting and patronage remained. When his closest college friend, Franklin Pierce, was nominated for the presidency, Hawthorne reluctantly undertook the writing of a campaign biography,[6] although he was convinced that he was not suited for the task. The reward of the campaign biography, President Pierce's naming him consul general of Liverpool, then thought to be the most lucrative of diplomatic posts, delighted him because it provided him with an opportunity to live abroad and perhaps put away enough money for the future. But he found his position of consul general particularly oppressive and stultifying. He indicates in letters home that he would not have accepted a second term whether Pierce were reelected or not. Except for being lionized by the English as a man of letters, he hated it all: the day-to-day burdens of his position; the onerous and exacting work that involved him with unsavory American sailors and with stranded, impecunious travelers;

the dreary clerical work; the speeches given at mayors' banquets; the trips through workhouses and hospitals; the burials of Americans who inconsiderately died in his jurisdiction; and, especially, the dirt and poverty of Liverpool. He was angry that he could not get preferment for his friends, especially Melville, and his still sturdy Calvinist conscience condemned him to hours of labor that most political appointees cheerfully abrogated. Most of all, he was disappointed that Congress changed enough consular regulations so that the dreamed-of financial freedom, allowing time for writing, never eventuated.

Hawthorne's hostility toward the English was minimal. It must be remembered that he arrived in mid-nineteenth-century England, an England that was a great world power, an empire, with the American Revolution only seventy years in the past. He was treated in the main with courtesy and hospitality, but occasionally he experienced resentment, especially by upper-class English, since he represented a triumphant, rebellious colony whose effrontery in forcibly breaking away from England could only argue a surly, mutinous, uncivilized insurgency for its people. But these unpleasant encounters were rare and the longer Hawthorne lived in England, the less defensive he became about his Americanism, until his only deep desire was to remain in England the rest of his life.

The idea of a romance about an American claimant to a vast English estate was encouraged by the number of Americans Hawthorne met whose baseless claims of their lost inheritance caused him many sorry hours of labor as consul. But Hawthorne himself, probably unconsciously, shared this nearly impossible dream of being the missing heir to a dukedom or earldom which carried with it a vast manor house, acres of beautiful woods, formal gardens, lush green lawns, servants by the score, and an endless supply of English pounds. Shortly after his arrival in England, Hawthorne instituted a genealogical search for his roots, hoping to discover that his stern Puritan ancestors, both Hathornes and Mannings, who had left England for America in the seventeenth century (William Hathorne in 1630 and the Mannings in 1679)[7] were not just middle-class Dissenters but nobility. Surprisingly, the researches turned up nothing, not even disappointing information. But the dream continued, and Hawthorne probably decided that if he were not a missing heir, he could write a romance about one, and with the proceeds buy, if not inherit, a somewhat less grandiose manor house. Although the *English Notebooks* are quite discreet about Hawthorne's wishful thinking, the letters are not. On January 31, 1857, Hawthorne wrote to his American publisher: "The fact is, I do not take root anywhere, and never shall, unless I could establish myself in some old manor-house like those I see in England" (OSU).

Hawthorne's letters continued to be filled with apprehension about returning to America and his desire to remain in England. He wrote to James Fields from Rome on February 3, 1858:

> I shall come home, I fear, with a heavy heart; not expecting to be very well contented there; for I quite agree with you (at least, I suspect these to be your opinions) that America is a country to boast of, and to get out of, and keep away from, and that England is the only country to live in. If I were but a hundred times richer than I am, how very comfortable I could be. (OSU)

After the inevitable return could no longer be postponed, the Hawthornes came back to America on June 28, 1860. After six months back in Concord, Hawthorne wrote to his English friend, Francis Bennoch, on December 17, 1860: "*I lose England without gaining America;* for I have not really begun to feel at home here, though I have been building a tower [the addition to the Wayside], in hope that the burthen of it upon my back will keep me from wishing to wander anywhere" (OSU).

Because the Liverpool consulship had been disappointingly un-lucrative and the stay in Italy far more expensive than Hawthorne had planned, he knew that it was necessary for him to write once again for money. Thus, he took up his sketch of "The Ancestral Footstep," which he had planned in England and worked on briefly in Rome, before he abandoned it to work on *The Marble Faun.* When he began to struggle with this story again (probably between July 1860, and July 1861),[8] he had not yet decided upon the central moral conflict which would give meaning to the whole narrative:

> I have not yet struck the true key-note of this Romance, and until I do, and unless I do, I shall write nothing but tediousness and nonsense. . . . The tragic, and the gentler pathetic, need not be excluded. . . . If I could write one central scene in this vein, all the rest of the Romance would readily arrange itself around that nucleus. (58)

But this is just what Hawthorne could not do. Five times the once masterful storyteller interrupts his story of Middleton, the American inheritor of a vast English estate, to meditate about the plot and ask himself how he can possible resolve it. Twenty pages of the eighty-nine that constitute "The Ancestral Footstep" are given over to recapitulating the plot, planning new characters and new complications, and trying to decide whether Middleton should attempt to wrest the estate from its present occupant, Etherege, who is variously an English gentleman, a half-Italian Catholic, and a sinister character who kills himself trying to kill Middleton. If Etherege is killed or commits suicide, Hawthorne ponders, should Middleton then inherit the estate, or renounce it, and marry Alice (somehow connected with Etherege or the old man in the hospital). Hawthorne could not resist at least contemplating a new Adam and Eve to be subjected to another Fall: "Thus he and his wife become the Adam and Eve of a new epoch, and the fitting missionaries of a new social faith, of which there must be continual hints through the book" (58). Since he thought of ending the book with Middleton and Alice newly together, he would not have to cope with the results of their fall, and resolve the great question of whether it was a fortunate or disastrous one. Hawthorne would never again be able to deal with the enigma of a fall from Eden.

The twenty pages recording Hawthorne's initial struggle with plot, character, tone, voice, and central moral conflict in "The Ancestral Footstep," which were completed in Europe, are pathetic but they are not nearly as hopeless as the two longer versions Hawthorne attempted to write when he was back in Concord. In his second reworking of the plot, he decided that the story should be told to him by the claimant, "he having communicated it to me, in a friendly way, at the Consulate; as many people have communicated quite as wild pretensions to English genealogies" (52). This would seem to settle the question of narrative voice, but even in this short sketch, Hawthorne seems to be identifying with Middleton. He describes the seductiveness of the English country-side with such enthusiasm that Middleton "wandered about the neighbor-hood with *insatiable* interest" (59), so insatiable that "he rather felt as if he were the *original emigrant,* who long resident on a foreign shore, had now returned, with a heart brimful of tenderness, to revisit the scenes of his youth, and renew his tender relations with those who shared his own blood" (60). The aesthetic distance between Hawthorne's created narrator of a story told him by someone with "wild pretensions" to English in-heritance, and his own voice, filled with secret desires to stay in England, comfortably ensconced in a manor house, closes before three-fourths of the sketch is completed. Hawthorne's own frustrated ambivalence about wanting to stay in England and at the same time thinking it cowardly is expressed as Middleton's dilemma: "There is much that is seductive in English life; but . . . it is not upon the higher impulses of our nature that such seductions act" (72). If he resigns his claim to the English estate, Hawthorne says that "Middleton shall not come to the decision to resign it, without having to repress *deep yearnings for that sense of long, long rest in an age-consecrated home,* which he had felt so deeply to be the happy lot of Englishmen" (85). Always tormented by secret guilt, Hawthorne has now added the burden of crypto-expatriate to his heavily forlorn soul.

Concerning the imagery of the bloody footstep, the less said the better. Having heard the grotesque story, Hawthorne was determined to use it in some way, but since his own first impression of the footstep when he saw it at Smithells Hall was that it was all "humbug," he never succeeds in making it seem real. He ran into what seemed to him insuperable difficulties with the plot and the moral conflict, even though he concludes: "The moral, if any moral was to be gathered from these paltry and wretched circumstances, was, *'Let the past alone;* do not seek to renew it; press on to higher things—at all events to other things; and be assured that the right way can never be that which leads you back to the identical shapes that you long ago left behind. Onward, onward, onward!'" (56). This passage occurs only two-thirds of the way through the sketch and Hawthorne was never able to follow his own advice. He kept worrying about the past through thirty-two more pages of "The Ancestral Footstep" and four hundred and eight more pages of *Etherege* and *Grimshawe,* but it did not yield up to him another scarlet letter.

After Hawthorne's first recapitulation of the story, he has Middleton confront Eldredge (later Etherege) concerning his claims to the estate. Eldredge strikes Middleton with the butt of his gun, which injures Middleton's shoulder, but then discharges and kills Eldredge himself. Alice arrives with a possible solution to Hawthorne's plot difficulties, the Calvinist doctrine of predestination: "'It was foreordained that, by digging into that old pit of pestilence, you should set the contagion loose again. You should have left it buried forever. But now what do you mean to do?'" (23). Hawthorne finds the question unanswerable. Calvinist pre-ordination ends the conflict and yet the sketch drags on, with Hawthorne unable, despite his tortured self-questioning, to resolve what was predestined to be merely an "old pit of pestilence." But even more pitiful are his next two attempts to form an English romance out of a "loose contagion" that no longer challenged his weary, doubt-ridden mind.

The next section of *The American Claimant* manuscript, entitled "Etherege," is, at two hundred fifty-two pages, the longest of the three. The actual working time that Hawthorne spent on this and the subsequent sketch, "Grimshawe," is tentatively identified by the Centenary editors as not beginning before July 24, 1860 and ending about a year later (501). The "Etherege" section is only twelve pages shorter than the entire *Scarlet Letter,* but the difference is so profound that it is hard to conceive that the same author wrote both works, except for some occasional flashes of powerful description and the sombre melancholy tone in the later work. Hawthorne never manages here to contrive a satisfactory plot nor can his characters, about whom he is so uncertain, ordain any action because he is unable to ascribe to them any convincing motivation.

Although the tortured questions Hawthorne asks himself in the nine meditative portions (of sixty-nine pages) appear to be painful self-reproaches about the absurdities of the plot, they are really tacit confessions of his total helplessness to continue a tale which has no central intention, no moral center. Gone is the assurance that the wages of inherited sin is death. Hawthorne is now tentative about guilt, the devastation of an ancestral curse and the necessity for the characters to reenact another Fall. These agonizing doubts, which challenge Hawthorne's very existence as an artist and man, demonstrate more eloquently than anything else his weariness, his inability to take a convincing moral stance on the question of good and evil, and his despair. Haunted and half-convinced of the possibility of the fortunate fall, he is able only to manufacture Gothic machinery (bloody footsteps, gigantic spiders, secret dungeons accessible by hidden sliding panels, the body of a centuries-old maiden transformed into golden curls, and poisoned drinks). The farther he goes in the story, the more he realizes that all the elements of his tale are trashy and peripheral.

Hawthorne's questions to himself, written in the margins of his manuscript, grow more anguished, anxious, distressing, bitter, confused, and futile as he tries to continue his hopeless endeavor:

> There is still a want of something, which I can by no means get at, nor even describe what it is. (115)

This old man—what could he possibly be? . . . I can't make it out. . . .
He is an eater of human flesh—a vampire—a ghoul. He finds it necessary
to eat a young child, every year, in order to keep himself alive. . . . pah!
. . . He shall have been to Hell—and I wish the Devil had kept him
there. . . . 'Twon't do. . . . What, what, what! How, how, how!
. . . *The story must not be founded at all on remorse or secret guilt—all that I've
worn out! Alas me!* (198–99)

Shall he be a Quaker—I don't know. . . . 'Twon't do. . . . What shall it
be that has made him and his ancestors anathema for so many ages? Why
don't you have oysters? Don't know; can't tell. . . . 'Twon't do. (200–
201)

I don't in the least see my way. . . . That'll not do. Nothing seems to do.
(202–03)

It is not possible to work this out; the idea does not take to itself representative form. (219)

I can't get hold of it. I will. (220)

*What unimaginable nonsense?* (262)

The life is not yet breathed into this plot, after all my galvanic efforts. Not
a spark of passion as yet. How shall it be attained? (264)

Shall there be an influence in the house which is said to make everybody
wicked who inherits it?—*nonsense*. Remorse it must not be. A Resurrection
Man? What? What? What? (265)

Some damn'd thing is the matter. (266)

All this amounts to just nothing. I don't advance a step. (268)

The old bloody footstep business! No; that won't do. . . . Supposing him
to have once tasted blood, and got an appetite for it—how? *But that is
vulgar*. . . . 'Twon't do. . . . I can't see it. (269)

I don't see the modus operandi. . . . Oh, Heavens! I have not the least idea
how to get on. *I never was in such a sad predicament before*. (286)

Oh, fie! . . . Now here. . . . *It must relate to property; because nothing else
survives in this world. Love grows cold and dies; hatred is pacified by annihilation.*
(287)

Try back! . . . *What shall I do?* . . . *The Devil knows; I don't*. . . . Pshaw!
(325)

I can't possibly make this out, though *it keeps glimmering before me.* . . . The moral of this might be—that if a man could have all the desires of his heart executed, there could be no way so sure of bringing him to hell. . . . Come on! Conceive such a man. . . . What? A crime which is bequeathed to each generation, and of which this servant becomes the instrument. It would do magnificently, *if it were not an absurdity.* (327)

These frantic, frenzied, pitiful questions to himself[9] demonstrate most potently Hawthorne's exhausted, enfeebled, chaotic state of mind which was no longer able to function because he had lost the subtle ambiguities of his damnatory Calvinist inheritance. He kept on trying, hopelessly and helplessly, because he was a genuine artist driven to work, because he felt financial pressures, and because he never could allow himself, diluted as his Calvinist conscience now was, to rest and relax. Ensnared by the work ethic and public and family expectations, Hawthorne paced his Wayside tower, worrying himself to death in an effort to produce another work of art.

The narrative voice of the "Etherege" fragment is first person, but in the longer descriptive sections it seems to shift to a kind of omniscient third-person narrator. The sections in which Hawthorne talks to himself about the fruitlessness of his muddle are probably the most personal of all his comments, more so even than the letters, because here there is no expectation of publication or reader and his total anguish reveals itself.

What pervades the "Etherege" fragment, like the refrain of an inconsolable mourner for a lost love, is the elegiac sense of loss for an England which Hawthorne unexpectedly found to be his old home. Shame at his lack of patriotism, guilt for betraying his independent, militant Puritan ancestors, remorse for the relative peace that England offered his self-lacerating, Calvinist conscience—all these very real regrets could not overcome his grief at having returned to a brash, brawling America which was increasingly pushing for material progress through the ashes of the corrupted American Dream. Over and over again the beauties of the English countryside and the easiness of the English way of life obtrude into the hopelessly jumbled plot, suggesting an idyl of romantic respite from the commonplaceness and barrenness of provincial Concord:

And being here . . . he began to feel the deep yearning which a sensitive American—his mind full of English thoughts, his imagination of English poetry, his heart of English character and feeling—cannot fail to be in-

fluenced by, the yearning of the blood within his veins for that from which
it has been estranged; the half-fanciful regret that he should ever have been
separated from these woods, these fields, these natural features of scenery,
to which his nature was moulded, from these men who are still so like
himself, from these habits of life and thought which (although he may not
have known them for two centuries) he still perceives to have remained, in
some mysterious way, latent in the depths of his character. (147–48)

Hawthorne makes further and rather ambivalent comments on Americans
abroad, a theme which he provided for Mark Twain and Henry James.
But his arguments now falter and quaver; his early pride in his country,
and even in those stern Calvinist magistrates who were his forefathers, has
been eroded by his long stay abroad in the dispensations of the Old
World. He found himself desperately longing for a home. Since he could
not easily return to England, and America had become foreign to him, it
is not surprising that he longed for the grave where he could at least hope
that "all losses are restored, and sorrows end."

Unlike fellow New Englander Robert Frost (born ten years after
Hawthorne's death), who went to England to attain his first fame and
then returned to America as a crotchety, uncrowned American poet laure-
ate proclaiming in "The Death of the Hired Man," "Home is the place
where, when you have to go there, they have to take you in," Hawthorne
was more and more conscious of a sense of loss and *homelessness*. Whether
England ruined Hawthorne for life in America or just eased his nagging
Puritan conscience, it played the Siren during his last four years, increasing to the point of desperation his lifelong restlessness. Hawthorne gives
his character Etherege all of his own dreams of finding home: "He wondered at himself for being so much wrought up by so simple a thing
. . . but it seemed to him like a *coming home,* after an absence of centuries"
(255–56); "it seemed the ideal of home. The thought thrilled his bosom
that this was his *home*" (259); "'Oh, *home, my home, my forefather's home!*'"
(260).

But as we have come to expect in Hawthorne, there are no simple
feelings nor simple answers, so Etherege agonizes over his decision to take
over the English property and title. Since the romance was never concluded, we gather that the problem remained insoluble for Hawthorne.
Etherege never makes a choice because Hawthorne, hopelessly mired in a
labyrinthine plot that he could not untangle, abandons the fragmented
tale and tries to make a new beginning.

There are no consistent symbols and images in a story so unstructured and fractured. A familiar Eden reference occurs in the symbol of England as Paradise (129), but no Fall occurs, either because Hawthorne had not identified his characters enough for them to be considered an Adam and Eve, or, what is more likely, because he had abandoned the idea, which had infused his earlier novels with such power, that a second Fall was irremediable and terminal. The giant spider (like one he had seen in the British Museum) surrounds the old doctor in the beginning of the tale, but Hawthorne is unable to decide whether the spider's cobwebs yield a secret restorative or whether they are diabolic and poisonous.

Enough has been said already about the absence of any ongoing plot in the "Etherege" fragment; the nine interruptions in the story give tacit testimony to Hawthorne's inability to work out the action.

There is no Calvinist-ordained irony in "Etherege," the longest fragment of *The American Claimant Manuscripts,* nor is there in "The Ancestral Footstep," "Grimshawe" or *The Elixir of Life Manuscripts.* Hawthorne's Calvinism was quieted in England and quelled in Italy and thus the corrosive irony that gave him his particular black genius was destroyed. All that is left by the time of this late, tortured fragment is a heart-breaking, ironic self-attack. In the seventh meditative section of "Etherege," as Hawthorne is desperately trying to define the character of the present Lord of Braithwaite Hall, he asks himself a series of hopeless questions: "Something monstrous he must be, yet within nature and Romantic probability—hard conditions. A murderer—'twon't do at all. A Mahometan?—pish. . . . A monkey? . . . A man of straw? . . . He has been poisoned by a Bologna sausage, and is being gnawed away by an atom at a time. . . . This wretched man!—A crossing-sweeper?—a boot-black? . . . He has yielded to some great temptation, which particularly besets the members of his family. *The Unpardonable Sin"* (265–66). Hawthorne's savage disgust at himself and his scornful regard for his earlier mastery of creative difficulties, exemplified by "Ethan Brand," the story of the unpardonable sin, is as great as Melville's similar lamentations at the Dead Sea: "Bitter it is to be poor and bitter, to be reviled . . . nought to eat but bitumen and ashes with dessert of Sodom apples washed down with water of Dead Sea."[10]

The third fragment, "Grimshawe," is forty-two pages longer than "The Ancestral Footstep" and one hundred twenty-four pages shorter than "Etherege." Hawthorne dwells on the old doctor (called Ormskirk, then

Grimshawe), surrounded by his cobwebs and his enormous spider. Hawthorne drops the story, still baffled by the problems of his plot. In his introduction to *Our Old Home,* the collection of essays on England expanded from portions of the *English Notebooks* (September 1863), Hawthorne expresses his disappointment in not writing another romance:

> I once hoped, indeed, that so slight a volume would not be all that I might write. These and other sketches, with which, in a somewhat rougher form than I have given them here, my Journal was copiously filled, were intended for the side-scenes, and backgrounds, and exterior adornment, of a work of fiction, of which the plan had imperfectly developed itself in my mind, and into which I ambitiously proposed to convey more of various modes of truth than I could have grasped by a direct effort. Of course, *I should not mention this abortive project, only that it has been utterly thrown aside, and will never now be accomplished. The Present, the Immediate, the Actual, has proved too potent for me.*[11]

The present, immediate, actual—the Civil War and his own misery—was Hawthorne's excuse for not finishing a work on which he had labored for at least thirteen or fourteen months without success.

Hawthorne's increasing weariness and his ill-concealed bitterness about life seem to surface perhaps unconsciously in some of the sections of the fragmented *American Claimant* manuscript. We have already noted his savage, brutal self-attacks in the meditative, disruptive sections of "Etherege." In "Grimshawe" there is only one such passage, placed just thirty pages before he abandons the story altogether, but in its description of half-fiendish doctor, there is a cynicism not found in any of Hawthorne's earlier writing, a cynicism that seems to be too heart-felt not to reflect his own acidulous view of life back in America. Little Ned asks the doctor to tell him where he has come from and Doctor Grim chooses to reply philosophically:

> "Whence did you come? Whence did any of us come? Out of the darkness and mystery, out of nothingness, out of a kingdom of shadows; out of dust, clay, impure mud, I think, and to return to it again. Out of a former state of being, whence we have brought a good many shadowy recollections, purporting that it was no very pleasant one. Out of a former life, of which this present one is the hell! And why are you come? Faith, Ned, he must be a wiser man than Doctor Grim who can tell why you, or any other mortal come hither; only, one thing I am well aware of, it was not to be happy. To

toil and moil, and hope, and fear, and to love in a shadowy doubtful sort of way, and to hate in bitter earnest—that is what you came for!" (356–57)

Here is a despair almost too deep for utterance. It seems to be as much Hawthorne's as Doctor Grim's because it is immediately followed by the marginal notation: "He answers, as many thoughtful and secret people do, letting out his secret mood to the child, because he knows he will not be understood" (357). We are reminded of Hawthorne's rather embarrassed entry in his *English Notebooks* about Melville's visit to him in Liverpool and their lengthy talk in the sand hills: "Melville, as he always does, began to reason of Providence and futurity, and of everything that lies beyond human ken, and informed me that he had 'pretty much made up his mind to be annihilated' . . . He can neither believe, nor be comfortable in his unbelief."[12] The last four difficult years of Hawthorne's life back in America suggest, through his letters and his abortive romances, a similar loss of faith which he desperately tried to keep himself.

After Doctor Grim dies, Ned returns from school and finds himself alone, with Elsie and the crusty Hannah dispatched. He throws himself on the old man's grave and weeps "as if his heart would break." But Hawthorne adds an equivocal sentence that seems to mock not only his characters but all human feeling: "But the heart never breaks on the first grave; and, after many graves, it gets so obtuse that nothing can break it" (439). These "hints and guesses" reveal a Hawthorne so desperate, hopeless, and despairing that we wonder not that he was unable to finish the six fragments he agonized over, but that he could write anything. In his one short meditative section in "Grimshawe," he writes: "The Doctor is *able to love—able to hate; two great and rare abilities, now-a-days*" (440). As he neared the end of his life, Hawthorne apparently found that his own energy for loving or hating was almost totally depleted.

In this short, aborted fragment Hawthorne at first assumes, as he has in the other two *Claimant* fragments, the first-person narrative voice, but he soon slips into a voice much closer to omniscient. His symbolism and imagery, slight as it is, resembles that of the other fragments. There is the comparison of Eden to England: "such a *Paradise* it [a hedge] was for the birds that built their nests there, in a labyrinth of little boughs and twigs, unseen and inaccessible, while close beside the human race to which they attach themselves, that they must have felt themselves as safe as *when they first sang to Eve*" (442). The irony that Hawthorne does not intend is that he has found a new equation: England equals Eden; the New World equals the failed Eden.

Examination of the three sections of *The American Claimant* manuscript is a depressing exercise for the reader who sees in them Hawthorne's straining and struggling with material that refuses to yield to a once creative imagination that has become bewildered, enfeebled, and inchoate. Without an informing Calvinism to ordain the ironic mode, Hawthorne was an artist contending grimly with human hearts that he could neither understand nor control.

## II

The three *Elixir of Life Manuscripts* have, if possible, a stranger history than *The American Claimant Manuscripts*.[13] After abandoning *The American Claimant* romances sometime about the middle of 1861, Hawthorne turned his attention to another legend that had begun to interest him when he bought his dwelling, the Wayside, in 1852. He mentions in a letter to his friend, George Curtis (July 14, 1852) that "I know nothing of the history of the house; except Thoreau's telling me that it was inhabited a generation or two ago by a man who believed he should never die."[14] The irony of Hawthorne, who longed for death and felt its near approach, writing a romance about a man who wished to live forever, is one that must have given him a distinct, poignant pleasure. The theme was not foreign to him; there are references to it in the *American Notebooks,* and the tale, "Dr. Heidegger's Experiment," shows a mordant greed for life and youth manifested by the unsavory characters that Dr. Heidegger assembles around his table. Moreover, in writing about the obsessive urge for life and youth, Hawthorne is paradoxically able to come to terms with his own approaching death, until he can affirm resolutely "in favor of that poor maligned individual, Death."[15]

In their "Historical Commentary" on *The Elixir of Life,* Simpson and Davidson state:

> The documents developing the Elixir of Life theme consist of two independent sequences, one of which clusters around a young student named Septimius, the other an old apothecary named Dolliver. The Septimius tale exists in two substantial drafts, the first here labeled "Septimius Felton," the second "Septimius Norton," after the predominant form of the protangonist's name in each. Associated with the "Septimius" drafts are eight

Studies—memoranda detailing aspects of plot and character, and probably composed as the "Felton" drafts progressed—together with a Scenario written between the "Felton" and "Norton" drafts. Hawthorne abandoned the "Norton" revision well before the end of the story and thereafter conceived a wholly new approach to the Elixir theme. *The Dolliver Romance,* as he called it, exists only in fragments: three chapter-length segments of narrative plus a handful of memoranda—eleven Studies that offer fitful insight into the story as it might have unfolded had he not become too enfeebled to continue.[16]

I will consider the three incomplete versions of *The Elixir of Life* separately. The first one, "Septimius Felton," was surely abandoned before mid-1863, when Hawthorne was at work on "Dolliver," but no exact date can be fixed from mid-1861, when he probably started "Felton," to the date he abandoned it and began on "Norton."[17] As it appears in the *Centenary Edition,* "Septimius Felton" is a document of one hundred ninety-one pages.

The setting of "Felton" is presumably that of the Wayside, the Hawthorne residence at the edge of Concord and on the Lexington road, and the time is the beginning of the Revolutionary War, not too surprising as Hawthorne was witnessing the gathering of troops for the Civil War. "Felton" is burdened by a most complicated plot, which the younger Hawthorne would probably have disdained, distilling from it a small portion for a short story. As it stands, the story suffers from a lack of ordained structure and central idea; nor is the character of Septimius, who is bent on finding the elixir of life, of sufficient interest or credibility to command the reader's interest.

Hawthorne has left nothing out of the cluttered, tortured plot except a moral center and adequate motivation for all of its Gothic grotesqueries: the bloody footstep, the crimson flower-fungus, the silver key, the claims to an English estate, the foul Indian brew of Aunt Keziah who is half witch and half Christian, the Revolutionary War background, the ancestral coffer of Aunt Keziah opened mysteriously by the English soldier's key, and other diverse improbabilities. The impalpable Sybil, who dies like Georgiana (in "The Birthmark") and Beatrice (in "Rappaccini's Daughter"), is far less believable than they, since it is impossible to understand her love for the self-serving Septimius, who seems to have no redeeming qualities.

Septimius' first conversation with the minister, whò fears that Septimius' studies are less of divinity than alchemy, sets the theme of the romance. Septimius says that "the fall of man, which Scripture tells us of, seems to me to have its operation in this grievous shortening of earthly life; so that our life here at all is grown ridiculous" (12). Hawthorne seems too worn out and too dubious about salvation to make the theme valid, but allows the labyrinthine plot to illustrate the absurdity of human life. The bitterly ironic trick of fleeting life, which Hawthorne might have made into a searing *non serviam* had he the savage indignation to manage it, becomes an occasionally remembered bitterness that only further confuses the many-engined contrivances of the plot. Septimius says in Hawthorne's broken tones: "We are the playthings and fools of Nature, which she amuses herself with, during our lifetime, and then breaks for mere sport, and laughs in our faces as she does so."[18] We have no sympathy for Septimius nor does Hawthorne really seem to expect us to, but we cannot laugh at him either, because Hawthorne's impotent rage, reminiscent of Lear's and Gloucester's, is buried beneath a creaky plot that distracts us. Hawthorne's death wish is submerged and craftily inverted into a silly search for earthly immortality.

The war setting, with the Revolutionary War as a paradigm of the Civil War, deepens the cynical attitude towards an elixir of life, when human life has become so cheap. Although the voice Hawthorne employs here is generally the first person, after a particularly revelatory passage, he cautions himself to "put the above in the third person" (130). He describes Septimius' depression, which results from having no tangible purpose in life:

> I know well what his feeling was! I have had it oftentimes myself, when long brooding and busying myself on some idle tale, and keeping my faith in it by estrangement from all intercourse besides, I have chanced to be drawn out of the precincts enchanted by my poor magic; and the look back upon what I have thought, how faded, how monstrous, how apart from all truth it looks, being now seen apart from its own atmosphere, which is entirely essential to its effect. (129–30)

Far more interesting than poor egotistical Septimius are these tired, despondent revelations by Hawthorne, who sadly identifies with his character's doomed search for the endless life which is, in reality, death.

The account of Septimius' pacing on his hilltop is so close to the descriptions we have from relatives and friends of Hawthorne's pacing on his own hillside, in those hopeless last couple of years of his life, that we immediately sense Hawthorne's personal agony in his fictional account:

> There was Septimius treading a path of his own on the hill-top; . . . there was something in the broodings that urged him to and fro along this path, alien to nature. . . . There was another opinion, too, that an invisible fiend . . . walked side by side with him, and so made the pathway wider than his single footsteps could have made it. But all this was idle; and was indeed only the foolish babble that hovers like a mist about men who withdraw themselves from the throng, and involve themselves in unintelligible pursuits and interests of their own. (44–45)

Hawthorne was still capable, despite his weakness and weariness, of attacking the corrupted American Dream epitomized by the prudential, self-regarding saws in Franklin's *Autobiography* and *Poor Richard's Almanack*. The first document that Septimius is able to decipher contains rules of life which appear pearls of wisdom to him. They explain how to ensure his earthly immortality in a parodic list that would do the inventive Franklin proud:

> Do some decent degree of good and kindness in thy daily life; for the result is a slight, pleasurable sense, that will serve to warm and delectate thee with felicitous self-laudings; and all that brings thy thoughts to thyself tends to invigorate that central principle, by the growth of which thou art to give thyself indefinite life. . . . *Do not any foolishly good act, it may change thy wise habits.* . . . Practise thyself in a certain continual smile.[19] . . . Read not great poets; they stir up thy heart; and the human heart is a soil which, if deeply stirred, is apt to give out noxious vapors. (105–07)

Poor Septimius—Hawthorne has little trouble showing what an ass he is.

The symbolism and imagery of "Septimius Felton" seems parodic, but the reader is not quite sure of Hawthorne's intention. He heaps together all of the Gothicism of *The American Claimant* fragments—the bloody footsteps, the enormous spider and his webs, the demonism of the half-witch, Aunt Keziah, the poisonous flowers growing out of the bloody grave, Septimius' mixed Indian blood—none of which do more than hobble an already faltering plot progression. It is almost as if the weak and hopeless Hawthorne decided to put in everything—all of the grotesque trappings that he could not control and make work for him in *The Amer-*

*ican Claimant* fragments—to see what would happen. Out of the potpourri came a limping plot, halted and unresolved, with characters who are bloodless, uninteresting, and unattractive.

Hawthorne's death obsession, a lifetime preoccupation, becomes even more obvious in *The Elixir Manuscripts* written so close to his death. Even the wispy Septimius has a moment, on his way to Doctor Portsoaken's, when he is aware of the disorder and chaos that nature would endure should the death process be arrested:

> Then mortals, dusty, encrusted with the mud of life, and the perspiration of life's hot summer, could never bathe themselves in the cold river of Death, and wash off all, and begin anew, pure and refreshed, leaving the worthless ill behind them . . . hope; there would be no hope; and of ineffable weariness, men would lie down and die in spite of fate; then the light tenderness of grief would all be gone, and we would hate our dearest, for lack of the possibilities of death; *tenderness would be no more, for it feeds upon the possibilities of bereavement.* (127)

Immediately following this touching but realistic meditation, Hawthorne puts in a note to himself: "bring in religion finally" (127). In the next fragment, "Septimius Norton," Hawthorne stops his story as Septimius is on the way to the doctor's, and so "religion" is not brought in "finally," as Hawthorne has directed himself to do. The truth is that the despairing Hawthorne *had no religion to put in.*

Friable as the character of Septimius is, Hawthorne puts much of himself into the creation. He draws a sad, melancholy, isolated, withdrawn individual in his own image. Septimius is not interested in the Revolutionary War going on in front of him, nor was Hawthorne able or desirous of becoming involved with the Civil War surrounding him—his heart and mind were elsewhere, in his private broodings:

> Septimius . . . sat there, in his study, for some hours, in that unpleasant state of feelings, which a man of brooding thought is apt to experience when the world around him is in a state of intense motion, which he finds it impossible to chord with. . . . He felt himself strangely ajar with the human race, and would have given much, either to be in full accord with it, or to be separated from it forever. "I am dissevered from it. *It is my doom to be only a spectator of life, to look on as one apart from it* [like Wakefield]. Is it not well therefore that sharing none of its pleasures and happiness, I should be free of its fatalities, its brevity? How cold I am now, while the whirlpool of public feeling is eddying around me. It is as if I had not been born of woman!" (22–23)

Certainly Hawthorne was not desirous of a longer life, but his feeling of dissociation from everything around him is as clear here as it is in his letters of the time—clearer even, because, in the guise of a character in a romance, he could speak more honestly, with less fear of upsetting his family. And yet even Rose, who was just thirteen the day after her father died, sensed his calm valedictory feeling:

> Certainly my father did not like to die, though he now wished to do so. My mother, later, often spoke, in consolation for us and for himself, of his dread of hopeless old age; and she tried to be glad that his desire to disappear before decrepitude had been fulfilled. But such wise wishes are not carried out as we might choose. The sudden transformation which took place in my father after his coming to America was like an instant's change in the atmosphere from sunshine to dusky cold.[20]

A broken, disappointed, sick man, with his religious sense severely shattered, was now trying desperately to write, out of his sense of duty and in an effort to provide his family with some financial security. The reality of these last fragments of romances is pathetic.

One of the reasons that Septimius is such an unsympathetic character is that he becomes a clinical observer, removed from the stream of life. Hawthorne, in his own voice, declares that he understands this feeling well: "he had strayed into a region long abandoned to superstition . . . a *Limbo* into which living men sometimes stray" (100). Septimius feels that everything and everyone—Aunt Keziah, the doctor, Rose, Sybil—all are illusions:

> It was a moment, such as I suppose all men feel (*at least, I can answer for one*) when the real scene and picture of life swims, jars, shakes, seems about to be broken up and dispersed, like the picture in a smooth pond, when we disturb its smooth mirror by throwing in a stone; and though the scene soon settles itself, and looks as real as before, a haunting doubt keeps close at hand, as long as we live, asking—*"Is it stable? Am I sure of it? Am I certainly not dreaming? See; it trembles, ready to dissolve."* (101)

Hawthorne and Septimius are both in limbo, both in doubt as to appearance and reality, but it is Hawthorne we respond to with quick sympathy and compassion, not his lifeless creature Septimius.

For a moment it seems that Hawthorne has somewhat revised his ideas about the value of woman, and sees her able, perhaps, to do and be more than just a seamstress like Hester. When Aunt Keziah dies, helped along by the poison flower Septimius puts in her brew, she says: "'how I hate the thought of the dull life that women lead. I'm glad I'm going from it. Thank heaven, I'm done with it'" (122). But it would be a mistake to think that Hawthorne has changed from his earlier opinions of woman's worth. When Septimius and Sybil speak of all of the wonders they will perform after they drink the elixir, Sybil says:

> "And I . . . will find out what is the matter that woman gets so large a share of human misery laid on her *weak* shoulders. . . . And then, if, after all this investigation it turns out—as I suspect—that woman is not capable of being helped, that there is something inherent in herself that makes it hopeless to struggle for her redemption, then, what shall I do? Nay; I know not, unless to preach to the sisterhood that they all kill their female children as fast as they are born. . . . —Woman, so feeble and crazy in body, fair enough sometimes, but full of infirmities, not strong, with nerves bare to every pain, ailing, full of little weaknesses, more contemptible than great ones!" (171)

It is to be hoped that Hawthorne felt better after this outburst, for there was probably no man ever more woman-ridden. From childhood, surrounded by a reclusive, withdrawn mother, two eccentric sisters, maiden aunts, all of the aggressive Peabody women, Margaret Fuller and her noisy following of feminists in Concord, and later by his two female children, the man finally speaks out in Swiftian rhetoric to damn all of them.

Robert Hagburn is the normal foil to the obsessed and driven Septimius. He sums up, in a conversation with Septimius, the rather comforting Calvinist view of faith without the necessity of good works—comforting only in contrast to Septimius' driven desire to change the laws of nature: "'There is no use of life, but just to find out what is fit for us to do, and doing it, it seems to be little matter whether we live or die with it. God does not want our work, but only our willingness to work;—at least, the last seems to answer all his purposes.'" Septimius sneers at Robert "rather contemptuously, and yet enviously" (157). At this point in his life, Hawthorne, like Septimius, seems to envy even a simple Calvinist solution to the mystery of God's purposes for man. What Hawthorne seems to be left with at the end of the fragment and in his own fragmented belief, is a confusion (similar to Melville's) about good and evil. Can one tell them apart? Or are they the same? The heirloom glass in which Septimius places what he believes to be the elixir of life was said "to have been the instrument of the devil's sacrament, in the forest, and of the

Christian, in the village-meeting-house" (186). In this hopelessness, Hawthorne quickly drops the first fragment of his three on the theme of *The Elixir of Life.*

"Septimius Norton," the second draft of *The Elixir of Life Manuscripts,* is published for the first time in the *Centenary Edition,* except for some quotations and summaries used by Julian Hawthorne in an 1890 series of articles for *Lippincott's Magazine.* "Septimius Felton" had been published in 1872 to mixed reviews, with some reviewers acknowledging that only Hawthorne could have written it, and others outraged by the failure of the story and the possible damage it might do to Hawthorne's reputation. Hawthorne undoubtedly wrote the fifteen-scene Scenario ("Ancillary Documents") before he tried to revise "Septimius Felton" into "Septimius Norton," but even though he seems to have had the earlier manuscript before him, he expanded the new version. The physical state of the manuscripts presents the greatest difference—the "Norton" manuscript having tight small handwriting and far more revisions than the earlier draft and more than were characteristic of Hawthorne. This evidence argues general strain and debility.[21]

In Hawthorne's revision, much more is made of Septimius' study for the ministry and of his doubts. Septimius is described as "directing his further studies to that pursuit, which state, as it had been ever since the Pilgrims came, was deemed the highest object of earthly ambition, as well as Christian duty, the ministry" (195). These remarks are preceded by Hawthorne's note to himself, "some short remark as to the influence of puritanism" (195). But Septimius is ravaged by doubts, and not slight ones either, doubts as deep as those of Mr. Prendergast in Evelyn Waugh's *Decline and Fall:* "I couldn't understand why God had made the world at all."[22] Septimius' doubts have led him: "'It is my [Septimius'] belief, that, according to the original scheme of the Creator, each individual man was to inhabit the world until he guessed its riddle; else it is but a mockery to him. . . . The effect of Man's Fall, it seems to me, has been to deprive him of all the benefit of his earthly existence by the shortening of his stay here, so that his coming here at all is made ridiculous'" (196–202). Shocked, the minister advises Septimius to give up his books and go to war. The skepticism expressed by Septimius seems as much Hawthorne's as his.

In his revision and expansion of the earlier manuscript, Hawthorne retains those most revelatory comments made about Septimius' despondency. However, in "Norton" he elaborates on his sympathy for his hero's (now called Hilliard Veren) despair after he has dispatched Aunt Nashoba with her brew, to which he has added the poisonous flowers. This is done just one paragraph before the last, when Hawthorne gave up entirely on the manuscript. Hilliard is experiencing a sense of unreality about his journey to Boston, thinking himself to be nothing but a vapor, when he suddenly feels a shiver of reality:

> *Every man . . . knows something of this despair. . . . Perhaps none are more subject to it than Romance writers;* they make themselves at home among their characters and scenery, and know them better than they know anything actual, and feel a blessed warmth that the air of this world does not supply, and discern a fitness of events that the course of human life has not elsewhere; so that all seems a truer world than that they were born in; but sometimes, if they step beyond the limits of the spell, ah! the sad destruction, disturbance, incongruity, that meets the eye; distortion, impossibility, everything that seemed so true and beautiful in its proper atmosphere, and nicely adjusted relations, *now a hideous absurdity. Thus he that writes the strange story of Hilliard Veren may well sympathize with the emotion of that moment.* (446–47)

It appears, as Hawthorne ends this fragment, that he, like Hilliard, has stepped out of his spell and has been overcome not only with the "hideous absurdity" of his valiant effort to spin a romance out of the unpromising interior life of a dreary hero searching for the elixir of life, but with the "hideous absurdity" of life itself.

This fragment contains a list of physical ailments that is appallingly long and anguished, but too accurate to be invented: rheumatism, weak knees, shortness of breath, inexplicable weeping, laughter and anger, difficulty in sleeping, irresolution, continuous weariness ("that only a church-yard nap can help"), reluctance to think of graves and coffins, inability to get warm, a feeling as if one had a perennial cold, inability to eat but little, aching eyes, the necessity of giving up drink and tobacco so "as not to swamp my brain," money worries and fear of dying in the poor-house, incapacity for grief, loss of hearing, awkwardness of the hands, lack of sense of smell, the forgetting of names, garrulousness, and "a great many nameless aches all over me" (295–99). Hawthorne's struggle against premature aging, exhaustion, and despair, and his dogged resolve to write against the most formidable odds, only increase our admiration for his doomed battle and our compassion for his brave failures.

In this fragment Hawthorne's death obsession vitiates his theme of Septimius' serious, dedicated search for earthly immortality. After Septimius kills the British soldier, he is greatly disturbed by the transfiguration of the boy's face: "It seemed as if a light were gleaming and glowing within him, and making its way through his mortal substance, and etherealizing it in its passage. . . . This expression the likeness of which is seen so often on dead faces, has been *decreed by God's Providence"* (244–45). Septimius refuses to believe it is anything but a cheat. Later Sybil answers Septimius' assurance "that Death is a weakness, the grave a wretched mistake . . . and that we shall finally rise above it" (331) with a long Shakespearean paean of praise for death:

> I will say a word in defense of this *poor slandered skeleton death, this meagre atomy, this ill-fed fellow.* . . . I can see the kindness of a heavenly Father when he made Life so uncertain, and threw Death in among the continual probabilities of our being, and surrounded him with those awful mysteries, into which we vanish. . . . *God gave the whole world to man, but were he left alone with such a great, perilous plaything, it would make a beast of him at last; but to remedy this danger, God gave him the final gift of Death, and it redeems all, while it seems to destroy all and bury all. You put a dead into the grave, and behold a spirit comes from it.* (331–32)

Although she later disclaims her argument, the celebration of death has been achieved. Death was a matter of imminent concern for Hawthorne, so he meditates about it and perhaps convinces himself that it is as sweet as he would like to think it is—that it "seals up all in rest."

This second fragment is more leisurely and expansive than the first but it ends far more abruptly, with nothing resolved. The tone is elegiac and throughout this impotent straining of Hawthorne for just one more complete romance, we hear the nightingale's seductive song urging him "to cease upon the midnight with no pain—to thy high requiem become a sod" before the word *forlorn* brings him back to his sole, suffering self.

After Hawthorne completed the essays for *Our Old Home* in July 1863, which were based on his *English Notebooks* and hence did not require an act of sustained creative imagination such as a new romance would, he turned again to the elixir of life theme. He did not give up on his attempts to complete *The Dolliver Romance* until February 1864, just three months before his death. The irony of a man interrupted by his own death as he is writing a novel about the real possibility of earthly immortality would have offered Hawthorne grim amusement. However, the irony is more apparent than real; *The Elixir of Life Manuscripts* are praises of death, the "strong deliveress," much more than they are serious attempts to divine the secret of endless life.

His publishers Ticknor and Fields were delighted that Hawthorne was going to make another attempt at a complete romance. Quite apart from their interest in having a book that might be a good seller, they were truly concerned about Hawthorne's writing block and were convinced that the sales of *Our Old Home* would be severely diminished because of Hawthorne's glowing, loyal prefatory dedication to the now most unpopular Franklin Pierce. Their agreement was that *The Dolliver Romance* would appear serially in *The Atlantic,* at two hundred dollars per installment, and later be published as a complete book. Fields was still waiting for the book Hawthorne had promised to write upon his return to America. Although a discussion about *The Dolliver Romance* (not then named) with Fields had taken place in August 1863, Hawthorne was still unable to begin in October. From Concord he wrote Fields on October 18, 1863: "I can't tell you when to expect an instalment of the Romance, if ever. There is something preternatural in my reluctance to begin. I linger at the threshold and have a perception of very disagreeable fantasms to be encountered if I enter. I wish God had given me the faculty of writing a sunshiny book" (OSU).

Hawthorne had not made much progress by Thanksgiving, but he delivered the first chapter to Fields in early December, "the first part of a story which he says he shall never finish. J. T. F. [Fields] says it is very fine, yet sad."[23] In the next several weeks he seemed not to have been able to write anything and in a letter to Longfellow in January he spoke prophetically of his death:

> I have been much out of sorts of late, and do not well know what is the matter with me, but am inclined to draw the conclusion that I shall have little more to do with pen and ink. One more book I should like well enough to write and have indeed begun it, but with no assurance of ever bringing it to an end. As is always the case, I have the notion that this last book would be my best; and full of wisdom about matters of life and death—and yet it will be no deadly disappointment if I am compelled to drop it.[24]

Fields visited him January 7, and found that he was "sitting alone gazing into the fire. . . . He said he had done nothing for three weeks."[25] The picture of a prematurely old Hawthorne, weary unto death, wanting nothing more than death and rest (the rest that Goethe promised, "Balde ruhest du auch"), staring into the fire that he had always loved and surrounded by the Furies of his own mind and his family and publishers, is pitiful. Even though the external Harpies were somewhat domesticated, the black caverns of his own unquiet mind and heart were, as always, untamed and terrifying.

Sometime before the end of February, Hawthorne managed to correct the proof of his first chapter and write two additional ones, but on February 25, 1863, he wrote to Fields:

> I hardly know what to say to the Public about this abortive Romance, though I know pretty well what the case will be. I shall never finish it. Yet it is not quite pleasant for an author to announce himself, or to be announced, as finally broken down as to his literary faculty. It is a pity that I let you put this work in your programme for the year for I had always a presentiment that it would fail us at the pinch. Say to the Public what you think best, and as little as possible;—for example—. . . "Mr. Hawthorne's brain is addled at last, and, much to our satisfaction, he tells us that he cannot possibly go on with the Romance announced on the cover of the Jan^Y Magazine. We consider him finally shelved, and shall take early occasion to bury him under a heavy article, carefully summing up his merits (such as they were) and his demerits, what few of them can be touched upon in our limited space." . . . I cannot finish it, unless a great change comes over me; and if I make too great an effort to do so, it will be my death; not that I should care much for that, if I could fight the battle through and win it, thus ending a life of much smoulder and scanty fire in a blaze of glory. But I should smother myself in much of my own making. . . . I am not low-spirited, nor fanciful, nor freakish, but look what seem to be realities in the face, and am ready to take whatever may come. If I could but go to England now, I think that the sea-voyage and the "Old Home" might set me right. This letter is for your own eye, and I wish especially that no echo of it may come back in your notes to me. (OSU)

Certainly, this is one of the most poignant letters ever written. Hawthorne, honest as always, looks only at what he calls the realities of his situation, and considerate as ever, does not want his own household alarmed.

The initial chapter of *The Dolliver Romance* was published in *The*

*Atlantic* in July 1864, two months after his death, with an obituary by Dr. Oliver Wendell Holmes who had seen Hawthorne briefly in Boston as he was setting out with Pierce on his last journey. The pirated first chapter soon appeared in England. The title page reads "PANSIE" by NATHANIEL HAWTHORNE—His last Literary effort—LONDON—JOHN CAMDEN HOTTEN, PICADILLY—Price Sixpence." There is an introduction "by a friend and fellow countryman": unidentified in the English edition, this is the Holmes piece.[26] The other two chapters, existing in rough draft, came later. Chapter 2 was published in *The Atlantic* of January 1865, and chapter 3 was not published until 1867, when all three sections appeared in a volume entitled *The Dolliver Romance and Other Pieces*. When the *Dolliver* fragments appeared there was very little critical comment, but what appeared was kind, sympathetic, and regretful.[27]

On the whole, the forty-eight pages of *The Dolliver Romance* do nothing to enhance Hawthorne's reputation, although Dolliver is certainly a far more agreeable character than Septimius, and the scene of his romping in the graveyard with the small child, Pansie, has a full measure of charm. But Dolliver's "senile predicament" is made terrifying. Psychologist that he was, Hawthorne knew what everyone learns but tries to ignore: we cannot really believe in the reality of our own aging any more than we can believe in the reality of our own death. Hawthorne does not "rage against the dying of the light," nor like Lear cry bitterly: "I confess that I am old; Age is unnecessary." Rather, he is so sweetly reasonable, accepting, and desirous of an endless sleep that he rends the reader's heart in another way.

In "Study 4" of the "Ancillary Documents,"[28] Hawthorne writes that "the shortness &c. of life shows that human action is a humbug," and Septimius is dissatisfied with death because *"it so breaks off and brings to naught all human effort; so as to make man a laughing stock to whoever created him"* (507). This memorandum is the bluntest statement Hawthorne ever made about a creator who is fiendishly amused with his doomed creatures. This is not the Calvinist God of vengeance and justice; he is angry and threatening but is accorded glory and praise even by the reprobate. This is a devil-god who scorns his creature—man—who has brought death upon himself, but is continuously wiled into believing that there is some value in human effort. Nowhere is there a more frightening instance of Hawthorne's state of mind; this is not doubt or depression, but unbelief in the tortured diaspora. When he lost the Calvinist faith he did not even know he had, there was nothing to take its place but a loathsome, static vacuum. It is not surprising that death came quickly to the Hawthorne who equated man's disappearance from life with the "empty skin of an enormous spider" (193).

Hawthorne shored up six fragments against his ruin. Weary, ill, and bewildered with primal doubts about the reality of a creator and the necessity of a doomed, short life for man, Hawthorne shuffled off his moral coil for a consummation that he devoutly wished—to die—to sleep.

EPILOGUE

# "The Hydra Lurks in Every Breast"

This investigation of Hawthorne's life and works stresses the preeminent, conspicuous, and signal importance of his inherited Calvinism, which has been rarely acknowledged by Hawthorne or his critics. His submerged Calvinism stimulated and provoked his creative imagination, elected his manner of living, and compelled him into the coruscating, corrosive, and mordant irony that is both the birthmark and hallmark of this American genius.

Hawthorne's life—his isolation in his sepulchral room; his lifetime longing for seclusion; his immersion in the American Puritan past, of which he was both a proud and ashamed inheritor; his paradoxical desire for anonymity and for fame; his guilt and his exaltation over his vocation as an artist; his ambivalence about his role as husband and father; his enduring restlessness; his equivocal response to seven years abroad as a reluctant Calvinist in the old dispensation; his loss of faith in all his old loyalties, religious, cultural, traditional; his yearning for the terminal deliverance of death—offers mute testimony of the dismal failure of the American Dream to establish another prelapsarian Eden in the vast uncharted wilderness of the New World.

Hawthorne's works, before his European hegira, are prodigies of a Calvinist-ordained ironic mode that conditions his narrative voice, determines the aesthetic distance between himself, his characters, and his readers, prescribes his concept of character, orders his ritualistic structure, controls his murky atmosphere and settings, enjoins his symbolism, and decrees his theme. Most particularly, the Calvinist dogmas of total depravity, predestination, reprobation, and denial of freedom of the will infuse his works. Beneath the deceptive lambency and lucidity of Hawthorne's style boils a brutal, barbarous, dooming underview of man's moral nature. Yet this partially submerged, damnatory Calvinism that betrayed Hawthorne into irony proved the healthiest climate for producing the dramatic tension of his art. It dictated the iron necessity for his characters to reenact the Fall from Eden, which Hawthorne could spy on from his chary nineteenth-century remove, his uneasy survival amidst the mouldering remnants of the American Dream.

Europe destroyed for Hawthorne the Calvinist conviction of an exigent Fall. His experiences there challenged his Puritanism, for if there were a way back into Eden, especially if good could come from evil, and the Fall could be fortunate (the *felix culpa*), then Hawthorne's moral and dramatic center was gone. His art was emasculated of its primal terror and instress; the heart of his mystery had been plucked out. The faltering final attempts at writing a romance, made during the last four years of his life after his return to America, were aborted—a tragic revelation of his impotence.

Hawthorne's four-year decline and fall after his return to discordant Concord in 1860 possesses a Hawthornean irony at its most savage: here he lingered until the end in quiet desperation, cheerful hopelessness, calm despondency, and intense longing for the refuge of the tomb.

In summing up Hawthorne's life and work, Calvin has the appropriate words: "we learn that this life . . . is restless, troubled, in numberless ways wretched, and plainly in no respect happy; that what are estimated its blessings are uncertain, fleeting, vain, and vitiated by a great admixture of evil. . . . If heaven is our country, *what can the earth be but a place of exile?* If departure from the world is entrance into life, *what is the world but a sepulchre, and what is residence in it but immersion in death? . . . let us ardently long for death, and constantly meditate upon it. . . . Let us despise life, and, on account of the bondage of sin, long to renounce it*" (*Institutes,* Vol. II, pp. 26, 28, 29; emphasis mine).

Hawthorne went to his grave feeling as gloomed and doomed as *Old* Goodman Brown. But on Hawthorne the sun also rises. He has secured fame in his masterpiece, *The Scarlet Letter,* and in his great novels, *The House of the Seven Gables, The Blithedale Romance, The Marble Faun,* and in dozens of his tales. Nathaniel—"Gift of God"—is now with the immortals. Undoubtedly, he is still peeping about the Celestial Railroad station wearing his covert, ironic smile.

# Notes

1. Herman Melville, "Hawthorne and His Mosses," *The Literary World,* Aug. 17, 1850, Aug. 24, 1850, pp. 125–27, 145–47.

2. Frederick Crews, "Deconstructing a Discipline," *University Publishing* (Summer 1980), pp. 1–2.

3. These ideas of mine have been expressed in somewhat the same language in the preface to my *Casebook on the Hawthorne Question* (New York: Thos. Y. Crowell, 1963), pp. vii–viii.

4. "When the course of years had made the features of the unobtrusive mourner familiar in the settlement, she [Catherine] became a subject of not deep, but general, interest; a being on whom the otherwise superfluous sympathies of all might be bestowed. Everyone spoke of her with that degree of pity which it is pleasant to experience; everyone was ready to do her the little kindnesses which are not costly, yet manifest good will; and when at last she died, a long train of her once bitter persecuters followed her, with decent sadness and tears that were not painful, to her place by Ilbrahim's green and sunken grave." "The Gentle Boy," *Twice-told Tales,* Vol. IX of *The Centenary Edition of the Works of Nathaniel Hawthorne,* ed. William Charvat et al. (Columbus, Ohio: Ohio State Univ. Press, 1962–80), pp. 104–05.

5. Melville, "Hawthorne and His Mosses."

6. Benjamin Franklin, "Articles of Belief and Acts of Religion," 1728.

7. See Randall Stewart, *Nathaniel Hawthorne: A Biography* (New Haven: Yale Univ. Press, 1948); Arlin Turner, *Nathaniel Hawthorne: A Biography* (New York: Oxford Univ. Press, 1980); James Mellow, *Nathaniel Hawthorne in His Times* (Boston: Houghton Mifflin, 1980); and the rather unreliable Julian Hawthorne.

8. Nathaniel Hawthorne added the "w" to his name.

9. *Our Old Home,* Vol. V of *Centenary Edition,* p. 225.

10. Through the generosity of L. Neal Smith, textual editor of the *Centenary Edition* of Hawthorne, the Ohio State University Press, I was able to read and copy Hawthorne's letters, soon to be published. This letter was written by Hawthorne from Bowdoin to Elizabeth Hawthorne on October 28, 1821.

11. Letter to Hawthorne's mother (in Maine), just before he entered Bowdoin, Salem, March 13, 1821. Julian Hawthorne, *Nathaniel Hawthorne and His Wife,* Riverside Edition, 2 vols. (Boston: Houghton Mifflin, 1884), Vol. I, pp. 107–08. All emphases in the quoted material throughout this chapter are mine.

12. *The American Notebooks,* Vol. VIII of *Centenary Edition,* pp. 415, 420–21, 425.

13. Calvin's epigraph for the pope.

14. *The French and Italian Notebooks,* Vol. XIV of *Centenary Edition,* p. 524.

15. *The French and Italian Notebooks,* pp. 60, 436, 548–49.

16. *The French and Italian Notebooks,* pp. 551–52.

17. In this section I will be dealing only with the Calvinism of Hawthorne. The later chapters will illustrate the way in which this Calvinism ordained the ironic mode.

18. *The Scarlet Letter,* Vol. I of *Centenary Edition,* pp. 9–10.

19. *The Scarlet Letter,* p. 10.

20. *The Scarlet Letter,* p. 10.

21. Calvin always supplies scriptural references to underline his doctrines and often quotes from the church fathers. These will not be included in my quotations from Calvin because they do not affect Hawthorne's use of Calvin.

22. John Calvin, *Institutes of the Christian Religion,* translated by Henry Beveridge (1845; rpt. Grand Rapids, Michigan: Wm. B. Eerdmans Publishing Co., 1966), Vol. II, p. 68. I have used the Beveridge translation, rather than the later translation by Ford Lewis Battles, edited by John T. McNeill, Westminster Press, 1960, because the Beveridge translation, completed in 1845, when Hawthorne was forty-one, has a more nineteenth-century flavor and is therefore more consonant with Hawthorne's thought. Hereafter, references to this work will be cited in parentheses in the text.

23. *Twice-told Tales,* Vol. IX of *Centenary Edition,* p. 226.

24. "The Great Stone Face," *The Snow Image,* Vol. XI of *Centenary Edition,* p. 48.

25. *The Scarlet Letter,* p. 174.

26. Cf. these stanzas on the pleadings of the condemned infants who stand before the throne of Christ in Michael Wigglesworth's "Day of Doom" (1662), the most popular poem of its day in colonial America. This excerpt is from *Colonial American Writing,* ed. Roy Harvey Pearce (New York: Holt, Rinehart and Winston, 1961), pp. 280, 283, 284.

166

| | |
|---|---|
| Compared with Rom. 5:12, 14; 9:11, 13 | Then to the bar, all they drew near<br>who dy'd in Infancy,<br>And never had or good or bad<br>effected pers'nally,<br>But from the womb unto the tomb<br>were straightway carried,<br>(Or at the last ere they transgressed<br>who thus began to plead: |

167

| | |
|---|---|
| Ezek. 18:2 | If for our own transgression,<br>or disobedience,<br>We here did stand at Thy left-hand<br>just were the Recompence:<br>But *Adam's* guilt our soul hath split,<br>his fault is charg'd on us;<br>And that alone hath overthrown,<br>and utterly undone us. |

Christ replies:

176

Matt. 23:30, 31

You think, if we had been as he,
whom God did so betrust,
We to our cost would ne'er have lost
all for a paltry Lust.
Had you been made in *Adam's* stead,
you would like things have wrought,
And so into the self-same wo,
yourselves and yours have brought.

180

Ps. 58:3
Rom. 6:23
Gal. 3:10
Rom. 8:29, 30; 11:17

Rev. 21:27
Luke 12:48

You sinners are, and such a share
as sinners may expect,
Such you shall have; for I do save
none but mine own Elect.
Yet to compare your sin with their,
who lived a longer time,
I do confess yours is much less,
though every sin's a crime.

181

Matt. 11:22
The wicked all
convinced and
put to silence.

Rom. 3:19
Matt: 22:12

A crime it is, therefore in bliss
you may not hope to dwell;
But unto you I shall allow
the easiest room in Hell.
The glorious King thus answering,
they cease, and plead no longer:
Their Consciences must needs confess
His Reasons are the stronger.

27. *The Scarlet Letter,* pp. 191–92.

28. See William Bradford's *Of Plymouth Plantation, 1620–1647,* ed. Samuel Eliot Morrison (New York: Knopf, 1952) for the story of the sailor on the *Mayflower* who abused and cursed the Puritans, yet was himself the first to die.

29. *American Notebooks,* Vol. VIII of *Centenary Edition,* p. 251.

30. The ministers of Calvin's churches were chosen by the Congregation, thus suggesting the "Congregational Way" of American Puritan churches. Membership in the church was denied to those leading obviously flagitious lives. The people had a duty to venerate and obey kings and magistrates, as they were ruling with a divine right. Obedience to the ruler was required as far as his laws were compatible with the Word of God. See Book IV of the *Institutes.*

31. Today in America the Presbyterians—Calvin to Knox—have (except for the Orthodox Presbyterian Church) abandoned, partly in 1925 and completely in 1957, the Westminster Confession based on Calvin. The present-day Congregational Church has forgotten Calvin. Only the Dutch Reformed Church remains true to Calvin and his central thought; yet, even theologians of this church are debating in their Reformed journals questions concerning reprobation and man's knowledge of his own election. However, no American writer, conscious of his country's religious past, is able to ignore his Calvinist inheritance, despise it though he may.

CHAPTER 2

1. Factual information taken from Introduction to *The Scarlet Letter*, Vol. I of *Centenary Edition*, pp. xv–xxiv. All page references are to this edition. All emphases in the quoted material throughout this chapter are mine.

2. "Righteousness is not obtained by few works, but by an indefatigable and inflexible observance of the divine will. . . . The adulterer or the thief is by one act guilty of death, because he offends against the majesty of God." Calvin, *Institutes*, Vol. II, p. 129.

3. See Hyatt H. Waggoner, *Hawthorne: A Critical Study*, revised edition (Cambridge: Belknap Press of Harvard University, 1955, 1963), p. 25.

4. See F. O. Matthiessen, *American Renaissance* (New York: Oxford Univ. Press, 1941), pp. 276–78.

5. Quoted in Introduction to *The Scarlet Letter*, p. xxv.

6. *Institutes*, Vol. I, p. 305.

7. *Institutes*, Vol. I, pp. 66, 129, 470.

8. See Q. D. Leavis, "Hawthorne as Poet—Part II," *Sewanee Review* 59 (Summer 1951), pp. 456–58.

9. Cf. Dante, *The Vision*, translated by Henry Cary (London: Oxford Univ. Press, 1929). See *Inferno*, Canto XV. When the parched spirit of Brunetto Latini greets Dante, he answers, "And are ye here?" (50).

10. See Larzer Ziff, "The Artist and Puritanism," *Hawthorne Centenary Essays* (Columbus: Ohio State Univ. Press, 1964), pp. 262–65.

11. "Mrs. Hutchinson," *Biographical Sketches*, in Vol. XII of *The Complete Works of Nathaniel Hawthorne*, ed. G. P. Lathrop, Riverside Edition (Boston: Houghton Mifflin, 1882), p. 225.

12. "They [Papists] pretend that God is appeased by their *frivolous satisfactions;* in other words, by mere dross. We maintain that the *guilt of sin is too heinous to be so frivolously expiated;* that the offence is too grave to be forgiven to such valueless satisfactions; and, therefore, that forgiveness is the prerogative of Christ's blood alone." *Institutes*, Vol. II, p. 102.

13. "Among the temptations with which Satan assaults believers, none is greater or more perilous, than when disquieting them with doubts as to their own election, he at the same time stimulates them with *a depraved desire of inquiring after it out of the proper way*. By inquiring out of the proper way, I mean *when puny man endeavors to penetrate to the hidden recesses of the divine wisdom,* and goes back even to the remotest eternity, *in order that he may understand what final determination God has made with regard to him*. In this way, he plunges headlong into an *immense abyss,* involves himself in numberless inextricable snares, and buries himself in the thickest darkness, for it is right that *the stupidity of the human mind should be punished with fearful destruction, whenever it attempts to rise in its own strength to the height of divine wisdom*." *Institutes*, Vol. II, p. 243.

14. "Mrs. Hutchinson," p. 225.

15. See note 13.

16. Quoted in Introduction to *The Scarlet Letter*, from a letter to Fields, p. xv.

17. "For when Scripture enjoins us to lay aside private regard to ourselves, it not

only divests our minds of an excessive longing for wealth, or power, or human favour, but eradicates all ambition and thirst for worldly glory, and other more secret pests. The Christian ought, indeed, to be so trained and disposed as to consider, that during his whole life he has to do with God. . . . There is a world of iniquity treasured up in the human soul. Nor can you find any other remedy for this than to deny yourself, renounce your own reason, and direct your whole mind to the pursuit of those things which the Lord requires of you, and which you are to seek only because they are pleasing to him." *Institutes,* Vol. II, pp. 7–8.

18. Hawthorne, in describing the people of Boston, understands fully the Calvinist doctrine of theocracy: "a people amongst whom *religion and law were almost identical*" (50); there is no confusion in Hawthorne's mind about the function of the Calvinist minister, which is preaching and exhorting—"'under whose preaching of the word you [Hester] have been privileged to sit. . . . It behooves you [Dimmesdale] therefore, to exhort her to repentance, and to confession'" (65–66); the Calvinist dogma of reprobation which holds that the reprobate, in their corruption, give glory to God is avowed by Hawthorne when the narrative voice speaks of Dimmesdale's mission to exhort Hester—"bidding him speak, in the hearing of all men, to that mystery of a woman's soul, so sacred even in its pollution" (66–67); when the magistrates and ministers decide that Pearl should be taken from Hester, good Calvinist reasons are adduced—"on the supposition that Pearl . . . was of demon origin, these good people . . . argued that a Christian interest in the mother's soul required them to remove such a stumbling block from her path. If the child . . . were really capable of moral and religious growth, and possessed the elements of ultimate salvation, then, surely, it would enjoy all the fairer prospect of these advantages by being transferred to wiser and better guardianship than Hester Prynne's" (100–101); any good Puritan child such as Hawthorne had been should know the New England Primer and the Westminster Confession. Pearl knows them but is too perverse to recite them— "Pearl . . . so large were the attainments of her three years' lifetime, could have borne a fair examination in the New England Primer, or the first column of the Westminster Catechism" (172); because Pearl will not answer the Reverend Mr. Wilson's questions, the governor decides she is a hopeless reprobate—"'Without question, she is equally in the dark as to her soul, *its present depravity,* and future destiny!'" (112); Hawthorne's crowd interprets the arrival of Chillingworth to tend the ailing minister as a marvelous example of a Special Providence—"Heaven had wrought an absolute miracle, by transporting an eminent Doctor of Physic, from a German university, bodily through the air, and setting him down at the door of Mr. Dimmesdale's study! Individuals of *wiser faiths,* indeed, who knew that Heaven promotes its purposes without aiming at the stage-effect of what is called miraculous interposition, were inclined to see a *providential hand* in Roger Chillingworth's so opportune arrival" (121); the diabolic Chillingworth uses Calvinist arguments for public confession that are calculated to impress and intimidate Dimmesdale—"'if they seek to glorify God, let them not lift heavenward their unclean hands! If they would serve their fellow-men, let them do it by making manifest the power and reality of conscience, in constraining them to penitential self-abasement!'" (133); the Puritans interpreted all unusual heavenly phenomena as the Special Providences of an immanent God, and thus the meteor of the scarlet *A* was considered a portent of the election to Angel of the newly

deceased Governor Winthrop—"A scroll so wide might not be deemed too expansive for Providence to write a people's doom upon . . . as betokening that their infant commonwealth was under a celestial guardianship of peculiar intimacy and strictness" (155); Dimmesdale declares his Calvinism to Hester when he rejects her doctrine of good works as salvific and says: "'What can a ruined soul, like mine, effect toward the redemption of other souls?—or a polluted soul, towards their purification?'" (191); Dimmesdale abandons his Calvinism long enough to *judge* Chillingworth's sin worse than his and Hester's— "'We are not, Hester, the worst sinners in the world!'" (195), but caught in the devil's mesh, when he confesses to the crowd he proudly proclaims himself "'the one sinner of the world!'" (254); when Dimmesdale returns from the forest where he has planned his adulterous escape with Hester, he huddles himself in his "Geneva cloak" and although he has made a pact with the devil, he still recognizes the inerrancy of Scripture when he returns to his room and his Bible—"There was the Bible, in its rich old Hebrew, with Moses and the prophets speaking to him, and God's voice through all!" (223); finally Hawthorne admits openly that he still has with him the blackness of Puritanism—"Their immediate posterity, the generation next to the early emigrants, *wore the blackest shade of Puritanism, and so darkened the national visage with it, that all the subsequent years have not sufficed to clear it up*" (232).

19. Austin Warren, *"The Scarlet Letter:* A Literary Exercise in Moral Theology," *Southern Review,* New Series 1 (1965), pp. 22–45.

20. Philip Larkin, "As Bad as a Mile," *The Whitsun Weddings* (New York: Random House, 1964), p. 32.

## CHAPTER 3

1. Factual material and letters from Introduction to *The House of the Seven Gables,* Vol. II of *Centenary Edition.* Page references are to this edition. All emphases in quoted materials are mine.

2. For example, the limestone pit of "Ethan Brand"; the circular forest to clearing to forest of "Young Goodman Brown"; the prison and the grave in *The Scarlet Letter;* the rooms of Coverdale in *The Blithedale Romance;* the public building in Rome in *The Marble Faun.*

3. Like Dorcas in "Roger Malvin's Burial"; Georgiana in "The Birthmark"; Priscilla in *The Blithedale Romance;* Hilda in *The Marble Faun,* and many others.

## CHAPTER 4

1. Factual material taken from Introduction to *The Blithedale Romance,* Vol. III of *Centenary Edition.* Page references are to this edition. All emphases in quotations are mine.

2. *Autobiography of Brook Farm,* ed. Henry W. Sams (Englewood Cliffs, New Jersey: Prentice-Hall, 1958), Letter of Hawthorne to Sophia, April 1841, p. 13; Letter of Hawthorne to Sophia, June 1841, p. 21.

3. *Autobiography of Brook Farm,* Letter of Hawthorne to Sophia, April 1841, p. 12.

4. *The American Notebooks,* p. 251.

5. Henry James, *Hawthorne* (London: Macmillan, 1879).

6. See *The Scarlet Letter,* chapter 1, "The Prison Door."

7. Quoted by Mark Van Doren, *Nathaniel Hawthorne* (New York: Viking Press, 1949), p. 51.

8. Letters at the Ohio State University.

9. *Institutes,* Vol. I, p. 353, Vol. II, p. 79.


CHAPTER 5

1. *Hawthorne's Lost Notebook 1835–1841,* Transcript by Barbara S. Mouffe (University Park and London: Pennsylvania State Univ. Press, 1978), p. 25.

2. All factual material taken from "Historical Commentary" to *Twice-told Tales,* Vol. IX of *Centenary Edition.* Page references are to this edition. All emphases in the quotations are mine.

3. In a letter to Horatio Bridge, from Bridge's *Personal Recollections of Nathaniel Hawthorne* (New York, 1893), p. 68, quoted in "Historical Commentary," *Centenary Edition,* p. 486.

4. *The Scarlet Letter,* pp. 200–201.

5. T. S. Eliot, *Four Quartets* (New York: Harcourt, Brace & Co., 1943), p. 16.

6. Hubert H. Hoeltje, *Inward Sky: The Mind and Heart of Nathaniel Hawthorne* (Durham, N.C.: Duke Univ. Press, 1962); Edward Wagenknecht, *Nathaniel Hawthorne: Man and Writer* (New York: Oxford Univ. Press, 1961).

7. This analysis appears in lengthier form in my *Casebook on the Hawthorne Question,* as "'The Fruit of That Forbidden Tree': A Reading of 'The Gentle Boy,'" pp. 159–70.

8. "And Paul . . . immediately enjoins us to put on armour equal to so great and perilous a contest (Eph. vi.12). . . . Being forewarned of the constant presence of an enemy the most daring, the most powerful, the most crafty, the most indefatigable, the most expert in the science of war, let us not allow ourselves to be overtaken by sloth or cowardice, but, on the contrary, with minds aroused and ever on the alert, let us stand ready to resist; and knowing that this warfare is terminated only by death, let us study to persevere." *Institutes,* Vol. I, p. 151.

9. Hawthorne's use of this equivocal, neutral word is enormously suggestive.

10. "[All men] are involved in original sin, and polluted by its stain. Hence, even infants bringing their condemnation with them from their mother's womb, suffer not for another's, but for their own defect. For although they have not yet produced the fruits of their own unrighteousness, they have the seed implanted in them. Nay, their whole nature is, as it were, a seed-bed of sin, and therefore cannot but be odious and abominable to God. Hence it follows, that it is properly deemed sinful in the sight of God; for there could be no condemnation without guilt." *Institutes,* Vol. I, pp. 218–19.

11. "As in *The Europeans,* there is always in Hawthorne's best writings the sense of a deeply significant public drama being enacted behind the deceptively simple apparent story." Q. D. Leavis, "Hawthorne as Poet—Part II," *Sewanee Review* 59 (Summer 1951), pp. 456–58.

12. Cf. the devil's staff in "Young Goodman Brown."

13. Cf. Robin in "My Kinsman, Major Molineux," who finally becomes shrewd *after* his initiation into evil.

14. *Institutes,* Vol. I, p. 251.

15. The prime example is the chapter, "Governor Pyncheon," in *The House of the Seven Gables,* which annoys the reader.

16. Chillingworth—the "iron necessity"; Coverdale's "fatality" which makes him witness the tragic events; Rappaccini's and Aylmer's compulsion to be gods; Reuben Bourne's return to the rock gravestone of Roger Malvin "by the strength of many a hidden motive"; Ethan Brand's ordained pursuit of the unforgivable sin.

17. Cf. the problems of former President Jimmy Carter after he confessed that he had "lusted in [his] heart."

## CHAPTER 6

1. All factual information taken from Introduction to *Mosses from an Old Manse,* Vol. X of *Centenary Edition.* All page references are to this edition. All emphases in quoted texts are mine.

2. Hawthorne's procession undoubtedly influenced Flannery O'Connor's powerful and forceful short story "Revelation." O'Connor admits freely and happily that Hawthorne is the writer she admires most in American literature. Both Hawthorne and O'Connor deal in their own way with what she describes as "my subject in fiction [which] is the action of grace in territory largely held by the devil." Flannery O'Connor, *Mystery and Manners* (New York: Farrar, Strauss & Giroux, 1961), p. 118. In "Revelation" Mrs. Turpin, who smugly thanked Jesus every day for making her herself, not white trash, nor black or ugly, is given a personal message by an angry, repulsive, and epileptic Wellesley girl: "Go back to Hell where you came from, you old wart hog." Infuriated because a message like that should have gone to white trash, not to her, respectable and hardworking, she goes to the pig parlor, confronts the hogs, and then shrieks to heaven "'Go on,' she yelled, 'call me a hog . . . from hell. Call me a wart hog from hell. . . . Who do you think you are?'" Then the soul-splitting epiphany comes when she sees a procession:

> There were whole companies of white-trash, clean for the first time in their lives, and bands of black niggers in white robes, and battalions of freaks and lunatics shouting and clapping and leaping like frogs. And bringing up the end of the procession was a tribe of people whom she recognized at once as those who, like herself and Claude, had always had a little of everything. . . . She leaned forward to observe them closer. They were marching behind the others with great dignity, accountable as they had always been for good order and common sense and respectable behavior. . . . Yet she could see by their shocked and altered faces that even their virtues were being burned away.

Mrs. Turpin's revelation flaws and fleers her fury, squelches her self-righteousness, and she comes to see herself in a pig's eye, "her eyes small but fixed unblinkingly on what lay ahead." Flannery O'Connor, "Revelation," in *Everything that Rises Must Converge* (New York: Farrar, Strauss & Giroux, 1966), pp. 217–18. In both Hawthorne and O'Connor there is the same contempt for priggish complacency and a terrible showing to the readers of truths that most of us wish to ignore or deny. For a further comparison of Hawthorne and O'Connor see my article, "The Numinous Vision of Flannery O'Connor," *The Critic,* 34 (Spring 1976), pp. 32–42.

3. T. S. Eliot, *Four Quartets* (New York: Harcourt, Brace and Co., 1943), pp. 13–14.

4. Melville, "Hawthorne and His Mosses," p. 126.

5. "But such is the character given to Satan in . . . Genesis, where he is seen seducing man from his allegiance to God, that he may both deprive God of his due honor, and plunge man headlong in destruction. . . . Hence it is evident that his whole nature is depraved, mischievous, and malignant. . . . God, therefore, does not allow Satan to have dominion over the souls of *believers,* but only gives over to his sway the impious and unbelieving [like Giovanni, Rappaccini, and Baglioni], whom he deigns not to number among his flock. For the devil is said to have undisputed possession of this world. . . . In like manner, he is said to blind all who do not believe the Gospel, and to do his own work in the children of disobedience. And justly; for all the wicked are vessels of wrath, and accordingly to whom should they be subjected but to the minister of divine vengeance? In fine, they are said to be of their father, the devil." *Institutes,* Vol. I, pp. 152, 154, 155.

6. "Wherever this living faith exists, it must have the hope of eternal life as its inseparable companion, or rather must of itself beget and manifest itself; where it is wanting, however clearly and elegantly we may discourse of faith, *it is certain we have it not.*" *Institutes,* Vol. I, p. 506.

7. This analysis is considerably shorter than the original which appeared in my "'From Whose Bourn No Traveler Returns': A Reading of 'Roger Malvin's Burial,'" *Nineteenth-Century Fiction,* 18 (June 1963), pp. 1–19.

8. In his article, "Hawthorne and the Sense of the Past, or, the Immortality of Major Molineux," *ELH,* 21 (December 1954), pp. 327–49, Roy Harvey Pearce mentions "Roger Malvin's Burial" as one of the variations of the Molineux theme but maintains that the focus of the story is blurred:

> The least compelling of these is "Roger Malvin's Burial," in which the protagonist is made accidentally to kill his own son at the very place where he had long ago left a wounded companion to die alone. With the killing of his son, the protagonist's "sin" is said to be expiated, and he is free to pray and enter fully into the company of men. "Roger Malvin's Burial" is blurred in focus, however. On the one hand there is the sense of his own past which deadens the protagonist's life until he expiates the sin which made it; on the other hand there is the act of expiation and the events leading immediately up to it. In effect, Hawthorne cannot make up his mind which he is primarily interested in. At any rate, the tale itself is not of sufficient compass to let his interest in both, had he been able to develop it equally, achieve adequate expression. (335)

9. Note the opening of "My Kinsman, Major Molineux," "The Gray Champion," "The Maypole of Merrymount," and "The Gentle Boy."

10. This spying on Roger is a violation of the human heart—a profanation which concerned Hawthorne especially as he felt the artist-writer did much the same thing.

11. Yvor Winters, "Maule's Curse or Hawthorne and the Problem of Allegory," in *In Defense of Reason* (New York: Swallow Press & William Morrow, 1947), p. 157.

12. Cf. Herman Melville, *Moby-Dick,* Norton Critical Edition, ed. Harrison Hayford and Hershel Parker (New York: William D. Norton & Co., New York, 1967), p. 317: "So in dreams have I seen majestic Satan thrusting forth his tormented colossal claw from the flame Baltic in Hell. But in gazing at such scenes, it is all in all what mood you are in; if in the Dantean, the devils will occur to you; if in that of Isaiah, the archangels."

13. Herman Melville, "After the Pleasure Party," in *Collected Poems of Herman Melville* (Chicago: Packard & Company, 1947), p. 219.

14. T. S. Eliot, "American Literature and the American Language," in *To Criticize the Critic* (New York: Farrar, Strauss & Giroux, 1965), p. 52.

15. John Milton, "Lycidas," ll. 64–66.

CHAPTER 7

1. All factual material taken from "Historical Commentary" to *The Snow-Image and Uncollected Tales,* Vol. XI of *Centenary Edition.* Page references are to this edition. All emphases in quotations are mine.

2. The description is so like Melville's "Tryworks" chapter in *Moby-Dick* (*Moby-Dick* begun early in 1850 and published late summer 1851, "Ethan Brand" published January 3, 1850) that one wonders whether Melville read Hawthorne's story. This was the time that he and Hawthorne were very close—the Lenox period. Note Melville's end to the chapter (p. 355): "Give not thyself up, then, to fire lest it invert thee, deaden thee. . . . There is a wisdom that is woe; but there is a woe that is madness."

3. Hawthorne saw a copy of the famous Breeches Bible at the house of Dr. Burroughs. *American Notebooks,* p. 270. The term "Breeches Bible," for Calvin's Geneva Bible (1560), is taken from the rendering of Genesis 3:7. The Geneva Bible has Adam and Eve making "themselves breeches" to cover their nakedness. *American Notebooks,* "Explanatory Notes," p. 622.

CHAPTER 8

1. "I have really made it a matter of conscience to keep a tolerably full record of my travels." *The English Notebooks by Nathaniel Hawthorne,* ed. Randall Stewart (1941; reissued New York: Russell & Russell, 1962), p. 456 (April 1857). Emphases in quoted material are mine.

2. *The English Notebooks* are scheduled for publication by the *Centenary* editors in the 1980s. *The French and Italian Notebooks,* restored, are in Vol. XIV of *Centenary Edition.*

3. Hawthorne's letters are scheduled for publication by the *Centenary* editors in the 1980s. Through the kindness of L. Neal Smith, textual editor, the Ohio State University, I was able to read and study these letters and make copies of them. Hereafter cited as OSU in notes and in the text.

4. Introduction to *The English Notebooks,* p. ix. Stewart's quotations from Hawthorne's letters to Ticknor (May 1856) are taken from *Letters of Hawthorne to William D. Ticknor, 1851–1864* (Newark: Carteret Book Club, 1910), p. ix.

5. Rose Hawthorne Lathrop, *Memories of Hawthorne* (Boston: Houghton Mifflin, 1897), p. 336.

6. Introduction to *The English Notebooks*, p. x. *The English Notebooks* will hereafter be cited in parentheses in the text.

7. Lathrop, p. 233 (Sophia's letter to her family at home, July 1854), p. 242 (Sophia's letter to her father, August 1853).

8. Hawthorne to Ticknor, July 7, 1854, OSU.

9. Hawthorne to Longfellow, August 30, 1854, OSU.

10. Letter from Liverpool, Hawthorne to Ticknor, November 9, 1855, OSU.

11. Letter from Liverpool, Hawthorne to Longfellow, November 22, 1855, OSU.

12. Letter from Liverpool, Hawthorne to Ticknor, January 31, 1857, OSU.

13. Letter from Liverpool, Hawthorne to Ticknor, March 13, 1857, OSU.

14. Gretna Green—where English couples often went to marry in a hurry because of the easiness of marriage laws in Scotland.

15. See "Sunday at Home," *Twice-told Tales*, p. 19.

16. Herman Melville, *Journal of a Visit to Europe and the Levant, October 11, 1856– May 6, 1857,* ed. Howard C. Horsford (Princeton, N.J.: Princeton Univ. Press, 1955), pp. 136, 154. Melville arrived back at Liverpool on May 4, 1857 at noon and sailed the following day. On May 4, he records only "Saw Hawthorne," pp. 261–62. Hawthorne says nothing of Melville in his notebook.

17. Letter from Pittsfield, Mass., Melville to Hawthorne, April 1851, in *The Portable Melville,* ed. Jay Leyda (New York: Viking Press, 1952), p. 428.

18. *Hawthorne's Reading, 1828–1850,* comp. Marion Kesselring (New York: New York Public Library, 1949), p. 52, entry 207.

## CHAPTER 9

1. Page references for quotations from *The French and Italian Notebooks* are from Vol. XIV of *Centenary Edition* and will be placed in the text after the entry. All emphases in quotations are mine.

2. Calvin's characteristic descriptions of the popes.

3. "This . . . I maintain, that when we teach that all human attempts to give a visible shape to God are vanity and lies, we do nothing more than state *verbatim* what the prophets taught." *Institutes,* Vol. I, p. 95. (Emphasis is Calvin's.)

4. See *The French and Italian Notebooks,* Vol. XIV of *Centenary Edition,* pp. 993– 1008 for cross references with *The Marble Faun.*

5. See "The Custom House" in *The Scarlet Letter,* pp. 9–10.

6. Melville, *Moby-Dick,* chap. 86, "The Tail."

## CHAPTER 10

1. Factual material and letters taken from Introduction to *The Marble Faun,* Vol. IV of *Centenary Edition.* Page references are to this edition. All emphases in quoted materials are mine.

2. All knowledge of St. Hilda derived from Venerable Bede.

3. See *The Marble Faun,* p. 373.

4. Quoted by Edward Wagenknecht, *Nathaniel Hawthorne: Man and Writer* (New York: Oxford Univ. Press, 1961), p. 163.

5. See *The Marble Faun,* pp. 368, 375, 411–13, 416, 458.

6. "Exultet." From Roman Catholic liturgy for Holy Saturday, Station at St. John Lateran. (O inestimable affection of charity: That Thou mightest redeem a slave, Thou didst deliver up Thy Son! O truly needful sin of Adam, which was blotted out by the death of Christ! *O happy fault,* which deserved to possess such and so great a Redeemer!). Dom Gaspar Lefebvre, O.S.B., *Daily Missal* (St. Paul, Minn,: E. M. Lohman, 1930), p. 831.

7. See *Institutes,* Vol. I, p. 291.

8. *Twice-told Tales,* p. 226.

9. Kenyon's "perplexity" is no mean one. He asks the question that the unorthodox Puritan Milton has Adam raise in *Paradise Lost,* Book XII, 473–78:

> . . . "Full of doubt I stand,
> Whether I should repent me now of sin
> By mee done and occasion'd, or rejoice
> Much more, that much more good thereof shall spring.
> To God more glory, more good will to Men
> From God, and over wrath grace shall abound."

No doubt Hawthorne, the great lover of Milton, has these difficult lines resounding in his ears. The concept is far from Calvin's and contains a fair suggestion of Antinomianism. See A. O. Lovejoy, "Milton and the Paradox of the Fortunate Fall," *ELH,* 4 (1937), 161–79.

10. Cf. Hester's ministerial directive to Dimmesdale in the forest after their roles have been exchanged: "'Preach! Write! Act! Do any thing save to lie down and die.'" *The Scarlet Letter,* p. 198.

11. Ben Franklin, *Poor Richard's Almanack.*

12. Julian Hawthorne, *Nathaniel Hawthorne and His Wife,* Vol. II, p. 225, Vol. I, pp. 248, 479.

13. Lathrop, p. 348.

14. See also *The Marble Faun,* p. 305.

15. Letter from Bath, Hawthorne to Fields. Fields is in England and returns to America with the Hawthornes (April 26, 1860), OSU.

16. Letter from Leamington, Hawthorne to Fields, December 30, 1859, OSU.

17. Letter from Leamington, Hawthorne to Ticknor, January 26, 1860, OSU.

18. Letter from Leamington, Hawthorne to Ticknor, February 10, 1860, OSU.

## CHAPTER 11

1. *The American Claimant Manuscripts,* Vol. XII of *Centenary Edition.* All page references are to this edition. All emphases in quoted materials are mine. The meager facts of the quarrel concerning the manuscripts between Julian and Rose Hawthorne Lathrop and her husband, George Lathrop, are outlined carefully in the "Historical Commentary" of Vol. XII by Edward Davidson and Claude Simpson, pp. 491–521.

2. See "Exultet," chapter 10, note 6.

3. The move to America did not seem to have the desired effect on the Hawthorne children. Four years after Hawthorne's death, Sophia took the three children back to Europe, believing that they could live there more frugally. Sophia died in London in 1871; Una died in 1877 in an Anglican convent in Clewer, England; Julian and Rose returned to America and lived long lives, Rose as Mother Alphonsa, O.S.D. (after the death of her husband, George Lathrop) and Julian as a would-be writer.

4. *English Notebooks,* p. 106.

5. *English Notebooks,* p. 194.

6. *Life of Franklin Pierce,* Vol. XII of *Complete Works of Nathaniel Hawthorne,* pp. 347–436.

7. Randall Stewart, *Nathaniel Hawthorne,* pp. 1, 3.

8. *American Claimant,* p. 501.

9. I have quoted only a few of the many questions.

10. Melville, *Journal of a Visit to Europe and the Levant,* p. 136.

11. *Our Old Home,* Vol. V of *Centenary Edition,* pp. 3–4.

12. *English Notebooks,* ed. Randall Stewart, pp. 432–33.

13. All firm data taken from "Historical Commentary" by Claude Simpson and Edward Davidson, *Elixir of Life Manuscripts,* Vol. XIII of *Centenary Edition,* pp. 557–90. The speculations are my own. All emphases in quoted materials are mine. Page references are to this volume.

14. Quoted in "Historical Commentary," *Elixir of Life Manuscripts,* p. 557.

15. "Ancillary Documents," *Elixir of Life Manuscripts,* p. 545.

16. "Historical Commentary," *Elixir of Life Manuscripts,* pp. 559–60.

17. "Historical Commentary," *Elixir of Life Manuscripts,* pp. 583–84.

18. Cf. *King Lear,* Act IV, Scene i, 36–37: "As flies to wanton boys, are we to th' Gods; They kill us for their sport."

19. Hawthorne is certainly thinking of Emerson here. See Lathrop's *Memories of Hawthorne,* p. 413: "Yet I caviled at his self-consciousness, *his perpetual smile.*"

20. Lathrop, p. 478.

21. "Historical Commentary," *Elixir of Life Manuscripts,* pp. 568–70, 585–87.

22. Evelyn Waugh, *Decline and Fall* (Boston: Little, Brown & Co., 1946), p. 38.

23. Diary entry of Mrs. Fields, "Historical Commentary," p. 575.

24. "Historical Commentary," pp. 576–77.

25. "Historical Commentary," pp. 576–77.

26. Listed in Bodleian Library: *Pansie: A Fragment 250.* K. 17 (10). It is included in a collection labeled *Miscellaneous Literature PAMPHLETS.*

27. "Historical Commentary," pp. 582–90.

28. "Ancillary Documents," pp. 498–553.

# Texts and Sources

Because this study depends more on Hawthorne's works, notebooks, and letters than it does on any argument with critics, I list only sources.

*The Centenary Edition of the Works of Nathaniel Hawthorne.* Edited by William Charvat, Roy Harvey Pearce, Claude M. Simpson, Thomas Woodson, Fredson Bowers, L. Neal Smith, and James Rubino. 14 vols. Columbus, Ohio: Ohio State Univ. Press, 1962–80.

*The Complete Works of Nathaniel Hawthorne.* Edited by G. P. Lathrop. Riverside Edition. Boston: Houghton Mifflin, 1882.

Hawthorne, Julian. *Hawthorne and His Circle.* New York: Harper & Brothers, 1903.

————. *Nathaniel Hawthorne and His Wife.* Riverside Edition, 2 vols. Boston: Houghton Mifflin, 1884.

Lathrop, Rose Hawthorne. *Memories of Hawthorne.* Boston: Houghton Mifflin, 1897.

*The English Notebooks by Nathaniel Hawthorne.* Edited by Randall Stewart. 1941; reissued New York: Russell & Russell, 1941.

The Letters of Hawthorne at the Ohio State University.

## BIOGRAPHIES

Mellow, James. *Nathaniel Hawthorne in His Times.* Boston: Houghton Mifflin, 1980.

Stewart, Randall. *Nathaniel Hawthorne: A Biography.* New Haven: Yale Univ. Press, 1948.

Turner, Arlin. *Hawthorne: A Biography.* New York: Oxford Univ. Press, 1980.

In 1963 when I edited *A Casebook on the Hawthorne Question* (New York: Thos. Y. Crowell), I used some "classical" Hawthorne criticism. I would like to repeat the names of those classical critics and add some to this list: Edgar Allan Poe, Herman Melville, Henry James, D. H. Lawrence, Yvor Winters, Mrs. Q. D. Leavis, F. O. Matthiessen, *and* Richard Harter Fogle, Roy Male, Randall Stewart, H. H. Waggoner, and the late Arlin Turner and Lionel Trilling. My debt to all these writers is so profound that it would be impossible to enunciate it.

# Index

Agnes McNeill Donohue is Professor of English and American literature at Loyola University in Chicago. She has edited a casebook on Hawthorne as well as on Steinbeck, and her articles cover a wide range of literary topics.